Jazz and Postwar French Identity

Jazz and Postwar French Identity

Improvising the Nation

Elizabeth Vihlen McGregor

LEXINGTON BOOKS
Lanham • Boulder • New York • London

Published by Lexington Books
An imprint of The Rowman & Littlefield Publishing Group, Inc.
4501 Forbes Boulevard, Suite 200, Lanham, Maryland 20706
www.rowman.com

Unit A, Whitacre Mews, 26-34 Stannary Street, London SE11 4AB

Copyright © 2016 by Lexington Books

All rights reserved. No part of this book may be reproduced in any form or by any electronic or mechanical means, including information storage and retrieval systems, without written permission from the publisher, except by a reviewer who may quote passages in a review.

British Library Cataloguing in Publication Information Available

Library of Congress Cataloging-in-Publication Data

Names: McGregor, Elizabeth Vihlen.
Title: Jazz and postwar French identity : improvising the nation / Elizabeth Vihlen McGregor.
Description: Lanham : Lexington Books, [2016] | Includes bibliographical references and index.
Identifiers: LCCN 2016020999 (print) | LCCN 2016021165 (ebook) | ISBN 9781498528764 (cloth : alk. paper) | ISBN 9781498528771 (Electronic)
Subjects: LCSH: Jazz--Social aspects--France--History--20th century.
Classification: LCC ML3917.F8 M34 2016 (print) | LCC ML3917.F8 (ebook) | DDC 781.650944/09045--dc23
LC record available at https://lccn.loc.gov/2016020999

∞™ The paper used in this publication meets the minimum requirements of American National Standard for Information Sciences Permanence of Paper for Printed Library Materials, ANSI/NISO Z39.48-1992.

Printed in the United States of America

Table of Contents

Acknowledgments — vii

Introduction — xi

1. *Le Monde du jazz* — 1
2. The Gendered Jazz Public — 43
3. The Question and Politics of Race — 77
4. More than an American Music — 125
5. Red, White, and Blue Notes: French Jazz — 161
6. And What of Empire? — 199

Conclusion: Improvising the Nation — 235

Bibliography — 245

Index — 259

About the Author — 267

Acknowledgments

I am humbled by the many people over the years who contributed in ways both large and small to the completion of this project. This book started as my doctoral dissertation at Stony Brook University so I would first like to acknowledge those professors I encountered in graduate school who exposed me to their own scholarship and criticisms and also provided a welcoming sense of community: Fred Weinstein, Joel Rosenthal, Helen Lemay, Gary Marker, Barbara Weinstein, Ruth Cowan, Bill Miller, Kathleen Wilson, Matthew Jacobson, and Nikhil Singh. As members of my dissertation committee, Tyler Stovall, Judith Wishnia, and Richard Kuisel offered me indispensable advice and guidance and I owe them my deepest thanks for that. As my dissertation advisor, Gene Lebovics often saw the heart of my argument before I did, and was there to help me work through the problems and inconsistencies of my work. In addition, I would like to thank Jane Brickman of the United States Merchant Marine Academy for reminding me, through her own excellence, how rewarding and important teaching can be. During my time at Anna Maria College I appreciated the support given to me by the Center for Teaching Excellence and the ever kind and professional Christine Holmes. Alice Baron tirelessly found obscure sources for me through Interlibrary Loan. I was especially grateful for Jim Bidwell and Barbara Driscoll de Alvarado who were not only fabulous colleagues but also encouraged me to return to this project and to remain with it until the end. I'd like to extend thanks to individuals with whom I have had the pleasure of collaborating at the Society for French Historical Studies and the Western Society for French History conferences: Jeffrey Jackson, Ludovic Tournès, Rachel Anne Gillet, Sandrine Sanos, and Valerie Deacon. I would like to give special recognition to Eric Reed who gave me advice when I was starting to ponder publishing my manuscript and Jonathyne Briggs for sharing his discerning insights and advice on the manuscript while it was still a work in progress.

At Lexington Books, my editor Lindsey Parambo has been instrumental in guiding this process along with her knowledge and insightful suggestions. I am thankful for her professional support, kindness, and willingness to see this project through. I appreciate Nick Johns and his keen eye for improving the manuscript's quality. The thoughtful and detailed analysis of the anonymous reader was indispensible in showing me strengths and weaknesses in the manuscript, and led me to think more cogently about my work. I am grateful for the generous long-distance support of Claude Gueroult de Flamesnil, a member of the French jazz band Les Barbecues, who provided the cover photo for this book.

I would like to thank Seth Armus, Chip Blake, and Hilary Aquino for being a part of my Stony Brook experience and for remaining in my support network still. As an academic, Amy Bass has inspired and informed my research and writing, and she is even more important to me as a friend. I am thankful for individuals from beyond the academic fold who have encouraged my work as well: Betsy Styron, Bob Fulton, Rick and Rose Marie Puncke, Patty Raffa McKenna, Jennifer Meadows Dunn, Sébastien Berger, Sharon Connolly, and Jena Bauman Adams. I would also like to thank Nancy Rojas and Mark Forbes for becoming part of my family every summer; I hope that you will continue to do so for many more years to come.

I am ever grateful for the extensive support of my family. Members of the McGregor/Maresca/Ryan side have given me years of good cheer and encouragement: George Arthur, Eileen, George Kevin, Susan, Kate, Will, Finn, Beth Anne, Kevin, Andrew, Luke, Ian, Megan, Jeannine, Patrick, Emma, Molly, and Clare. The Vihlens continue to make my world a better and happier place: Eric, Jr., Christopher, Adrienne, Abner, and Ellis. My father, Eric Vihlen, Sr., is a shining example of professional and grandfatherly devotion and I am thankful for the many opportunities as well as loving support he has always given me. In thanking my mother Sally Vihlen I do not even know where to begin. Long ago, she taught me the value of knowledge and gave me the courage to seek it far from home. I am privileged to call her both my parent and my friend, and I will always admire the passion and dedication she brings to her many endeavors.

Finally, I would like to thank the most significant people in my life: Tom McGregor, who has given me his unconditional love and encouragement in all things, and who remains my source of inspiration and my anchor; and Nathan, Jack, and Ava McGregor who have brought unimaginable happiness into my life with their energy, curiosity, honesty, and love. I cannot imagine my world without the four of you. Thank you for being your own distinct individual selves, and for reminding me on a daily basis what the most important things are in life.

Portions of this book appeared in a different form in "Jammin' on the Champs Elysées: Jazz, France, and the 1950s," *"Here, There and Everywhere": The Foreign Politics of American Popular Culture*, edited by Reinhold Wagnleitner and Elaine Tyler May (2000) and are used here with the permission of the University Press of New England.

Introduction

In 1986, the French jazz critic Jean Wagner wrote the following words in his book, *Le Guide du Jazz*:

> This splendid garden which is the music of jazz: this is not a French garden but a fertile jungle which overflows with vivid colors. At first, it is not friendly: its undergrowth is forbidding. It does not open itself up to those who scoff at it. But it is good to plunge into it with abandon: at each vine's detour, a surprise awaits you, a surprise without end. . . . [The] itinerary of an artist is always a journey to the end of the night.[1]

In addition to his allusion to Louis-Ferdinand Céline, Wagner nicely illustrated that the story of jazz in France was a journey filled with detours and neverending surprises: "a journey to the end of the night." From his vantage point of 1986, he was in a fine position to reflect on jazz's history. By the time he wrote these lines, the music had been in existence for close to ninety years and had been in France for nearly seventy of those years. During that span, jazz had evolved into a multiplicity of genres that included the traditional as well as the avant-garde, and was played by musicians from the United States and many other parts of the world. Wagner was born in 1928, so that the bulk of his lifetime's interactions with jazz happened after World War II. In this book, I examine how French critics like Wagner, as well as fans, musicians, and journalists, not only understood and appreciated jazz in the twenty-five years following the war, but also how they addressed subjects of vital importance to the French nation.

By 1945, French jazz culture was well established because of the efforts and interests of critics and musicians within the hexagon who had begun their love affair with jazz in the 1920s and 1930s. Jazz had been born around the turn of the twentieth century in New Orleans and arrived in France as the

Great War came to an end, so that French audiences were exposed to jazz while it was still a rather nascent music. As is well-known, jazz originated in the hands of African-American artists who blended together a variety of African, American, and European musics and thereby created a new form of cultural expression that allowed them to build identities and meanings for themselves in an atmosphere that otherwise denied them the ability to do so. Early on, French audiences were aware of the crucial importance of African-American musicians to the birth of jazz and to its continued musical evolution: without African-American culture there would have been no jazz. Jazz dramatically evolved in the years between its 1918 arrival in France and the end of the 1960s when my study comes to an end. This means that the fans who listened to jazz changed as did the music itself as time went on, even if certain conceptions about jazz's connection to African Americans and the United States remained constant. The postwar French jazz culture inherited many elements from the interwar era, including musical forms, professional and popular connections, and a fan base.[2]

The most vocal members of the postwar French jazz public were professional critics, many of whom had become enamored with the music in the interwar period or during World War II. With the exception of the writer Hugues Panassié and his cohort, many of these critics wrote prolifically on a wide range of subjects, often had academic backgrounds in the humanities, and had political leanings that fell to the left. They contributed to jazz periodicals and the mainstream press, and also wrote their own books. In these writings, they addressed subjects that were pressing to them and that were often about much more than the music alone: they reflected their conceptions about French society. The opinions and ideas of average jazz fans were never expressed as frequently as those of this professional group, but their thoughts showed up in polls, concert attendance, and in letters written to the editors of popular jazz magazines. This book is about how French jazz devotees—who could be from different regions and generations, as well as supporters of widely varying musical styles—addressed and worked through the postwar changes in France. How did their ideas reflect both valid observations and inconsistencies in French thought about gender, race, the United States, the colonial empire, and the nation itself?

In the twenty-five years after World War II, jazz professionals and fans spent a good deal of energy arguing over definitions of the music, jockeying for positions on the field of jazz.[3] As the stakes increased with improved and more profitable radio programming, television time, magazine coverage, concert promotions, and record deals, those without a place in these mediums continued to raise their voices, struggling, however futilely, to maintain their standing within the jazz media and promotional network. Simultaneously, this fractured group also had to create room for jazz within France, working to make an American, and more specifically African-American, music part of the aesthetic landscape without threatening to compromise French conceptions of national culture. This was achieved by listeners who used the music to address domestic cultural issues, such as the threat of Americanization and commercialism, while simultaneously dealing with the growing obsolescence of French folkloric and high culture. In addition to these efforts that played out on the national stage, critics and musicians also had to win the respect of those from across the Atlantic, competing with the American creators and commentators of this music who had won the a priori approval of audiences around the world. Therefore the story of jazz in postwar France was defined by a threefold struggle for position within the French jazz community, the national cultural patrimony, and the international world of jazz.

Within the complex scenario that evolved in the decades after the war, jazz was used in France as a means of negotiating an array of multifaceted issues that troubled statesmen and average citizens alike. In 1945, France faced an uncertain future in a much-changing world and people expressed the cultural malaise that characterized the early postwar years in numerous ways. In the immediate aftermath of the war, the shames of defeat and occupation and the coexisting realities of collaboration and resistance shaped French ideas about their country. The immediate economic situation was dire and individuals faced the long-term prospects of rebuilding the country's infrastructure as well as providing consumers with the goods and services they so craved after the many years of deprivation caused by economic depression and then war. French jazz culture reflected the desire among many to maintain not only French international relevance in the face of these hardships, but French distinctiveness and strength. Despite the reality that jazz was fundamentally linked to the multicultural and to the global, critics, musicians, and fans harnessed the music to navigate matters of French concern.

After the war, women at last had the vote and started playing new roles that in time came to complicate and to alter the persistent divide between the private and the public spheres.[4] Within jazz culture though, traditional gender expectations remained the norm. French audiences understood jazz to be part of early postwar youth culture and adopted the sexual stereotypes that had originated out of the music's earliest moments in the United States. In doing so they bolstered their connections to a masculine identity that denied women equal footing as musicians, critics, and fans. French women were expected to buy products that supported their families and that improved standards of living, not jazz records or concert tickets, which remained the purview of male teenagers and young adults.[5] That the French jazz culture was equated in the minds of many with whiskey and late nights in Parisian *caves*, meant that middle class parents did not find jazz an acceptable interest for their teenage daughters, further cementing the music's connection to male culture. Of course, French jazzwomen and female fans did exist, but they worked and appreciated jazz within a framework that assumed the dominance of male creativity and musical understanding. Despite women's changing political and social place in the first decades that followed the war, the most active French citizen (in terms of voting and holding office) remained male, as did the most active jazz fans (in terms of buying records, attending concerts, writing about jazz, or playing it). The gendered jazz culture reflected what was happening in the nation at large.

During World War II, the United States had for the second time in the twentieth century joined France and the Allies to defeat a German enemy, and now the young nation across the Atlantic began to rest atop the geopolitical world as a superpower. French dissatisfaction with this new status quo was often communicated through strident anti-American sentiment as many resented the loss of French economic, military, and cultural might to the United States. It was common in the 1950s and 1960s for French audiences to criticize American consumer products and forms of cultural expression, ranging from Coca-Cola and food to Hollywood.[6] Through the postwar story of jazz, we can see some among the French contending with their national identity as it related to the United States. The rise of the new American hegemon of course happened simultaneously with the decreasing global might of France, so that French commentators and politicians often strove to elevate their country's stature in relation to the United States by finding fault with such things as American culture and society, especially forms of American popular culture and race relations. Jazz was a categorically American music and yet it was never censured as other American cultural products were in the postwar period. Instead, jazz audiences used this music to condemn American racism and to support the American civil rights movement. Fans endorsed an American music while directly criticizing the United States, attenuating French support for the United States, and showing that corroboration with the American liberator and postwar superpower coexisted with strong reservations about the American way of life.

French jazz enthusiasts often asserted that artistic creativity should neither be defined nor controlled by marketplace values and censured American and Americanized companies who seemed to value profit making over artistic merit, communicating a distrust of the American economic model. However, these same jazz fans also supported the global paragon of capitalism, the American government, when they saw it acting in the interest of jazz. When the United States government began sponsoring jazz tours in Africa, Asia, Latin America, and Eastern Europe as part of an effort at Cold War cultural diplomacy, members of the French jazz public offered their general approval even if none of these Goodwill Ambassador tours ever traveled to France. Despite criticisms of the political aims behind the American government's use of jazz, French jazz fans welcomed the fact that both in the United States and abroad this music was being better-appreciated and receiving state endorsement. French jazz musicians played behind the Iron Curtain, sometimes before American musicians were able to do so and simultaneously advanced their own careers and jazz's reputation in Eastern bloc countries by aligning their actions with American State Department goals. When the French critics, musicians, and fans passed judgment on American government initiatives, they reflected important tensions within the French-American relationship during the Cold War and practiced a jazz appreciation that fused the aesthetic with their own national interests.

By the mid-1960s, France's stature and strength on the world stage was diminished by more than American dominance, as the vast number of French colonies had become newly independent nations in Africa and Asia. The Algerian War left lasting scars on France not only because of its brutality but because it created varying amounts of distrust, resentment, and animosity among Algerians, French mainlanders, and former *colons*.[7] As all of these events unfolded, jazz played on. During the Algerian War, *colons* used jazz to bolster a sense of a French-Algerian identity that denied Arabs and Berbers equality with Europeans and largely rendered them invisible. The French had introduced jazz into the colonies so that after independence, native populations worked to disassociate jazz from white European culture and to associate it back to African-American culture and even to a pan-African identity. In the metropole during the postwar decades, traditional notions of national identity were complicated as increasing numbers of immigrant populations from Africa, Asia, and the Caribbean came to France to fulfill the labor shortages caused by the *trente glorieuses*, and the country began to have for the first time a sizeable population with familial roots outside of Europe and who were also practicing Muslims. French citizens often showed their insecurity about these changing French demographics by refusing to see immigrant groups, especially those of Arab descent, as legitimate members of the nation. According to many, these new residents and citizens did not belong to "true" France.[8] Yet immigration only grew as the years went by and some portions of the white population—especially among the lower middle class, the working class, and the former Algerian *colons*—simultaneously saw their economic opportunities stagnate and their vision of what France ought to be being slowly erased. Because of these trends, rising xenophobia has been an unfortunate but defining reality of postwar France as well as of contemporary France, reflected today by the growing electoral might of the Front National in local and national elections.[9] Members of the jazz public, because of their heightened sense of race relations in the United States and their advocacy of an originally African-American music, analyzed the insidious appearance of postwar racism in France. For many, being a jazz fan meant advocating antiracist politics at a time when France itself was becoming increasingly ethnically, religiously, and racially diverse. Nonetheless, ideas about inherent "black" characteristics shaped the perceptions of French jazz listeners who almost always understood the music of black musicians to be superior to that of white musicians, exposing contradictions inherent in French social thought regarding race and cultural difference. Despite their willingness to discuss problems of racism and cultural fundamentalism within France, French jazz writers and fans too often fell into the trope of casting the United States as racist and France as comparatively color-blind, revealing discrepancies in French thought as well as an abiding desire to promote France at the expense of the United States.

In the last fifteen years, much has been written about jazz in France. Ludovic Tournès' pathbreaking *New Orleans sur Seine: Histoire du jazz en France* was the first to provide a detailed narrative about those who listened to, played, and promoted jazz, opening up a new field of inquiry for historians, musicologists, and academics in French cultural studies. For some, the question of exactly *when* jazz became fully assimilated into French culture has been of fundamental importance. The historian Jeffrey Jackson has documented jazz's integration into French culture in the interwar years in his seminal *Making Jazz French: Music and Modern Life in Interwar Paris*, while Matthew F. Jordan has illustrated with great precision in *Le Jazz: Jazz and French Cultural Modernity* the negotiated process through which jazz came to be largely accepted among the French only at the end of World War II, highlighting the very strident criticisms many made of jazz for decades after its arrival in France. Jeremy F. Lane and Andy Fry have both argued for a messier vision of cultural assimilation that shows that the French did not progressively embrace jazz according to a neat timeline. In his *Jazz and Machine-Age Imperialism: Music, "Race," and Intellectuals in France, 1918–1945*, Lane has demonstrated that the work of professional critics in the interwar period as well as during World War II continued to reveal unresolved tensions over identity, race, the United States, and modern technology. Fry has written in his *Paris Blues: African American music and French Popular Culture, 1920–1960* that he preferred "to think of the reception of African American music and musicians as always encompassing multiple contradictory positions."[10]

Unlike the work of these academics, my book is anchored in the postwar period and I am able to illustrate that jazz fulfilled the divergent needs and visions of French audiences who often harnessed the music's understood meanings to express and accomplish different agendas. These agendas reflected the anxieties and desires existent in the complex reality of these audiences' contemporary world and often centered on France's changing status in an era defined by Cold War allegiances, colonial independence, and evolving social realities that were altering France's demographic makeup. Despite the varying conclusions of Jackson, Jordan, Lane, and Fry, all of their works have offered informative insights into French identity and the varied meanings jazz created for its French listeners. In the end, Jordon has presented convincing evidence that jazz was well contested until the time of the Liberation, pushing the date of the music's widespread acceptance back a bit from Jackson's late interwar period, and Lane has illustrated the nuanced meanings as well as the contradictions and conflicts among jazz intellectuals that defy a simple periodization of jazz's acceptance in France, even if he only has focused on an intellectual elite and not on popular audiences. Unlike Jackson and Jordan, Fry has stressed that the story of jazz in France continued after World War II to be fraught with ambivalence and instability and he saw no moment of general acceptedness. Nevertheless, all of these works have proven something crucial to *this* study: that by the time World War II came to a close, French listeners had been exposed to the sounds of jazz for several long decades and that the music was no longer widely characterized as dangerous or foreign, even if it continued to represent varied or conflicting meanings for its listeners. In the decades following World War II, jazz fans and critics might have disagreed among themselves about musical style but few in French society vocally or publicly questioned jazz's place in French culture anymore. I agree with Fry on the fact that assimilation can have pernicious effects and that sometimes those who embraced jazz were motivated to do so by their need not only to absorb but also to diffuse the power of the music. To my mind, by making jazz "French," members of the postwar jazz public harnessed the influence and cultural power of an originally foreign music and used it for their own purposes.

Beyond the work of these academics, Colin Nettelbeck in *Dancing with De Beauvoir: Jazz and the French* and Tom Perchard in *After Django: Making Jazz in Postwar France* have examined jazz in the decades following World War II. Nettelbeck has attested to the music's important location in postwar French culture through an analysis of modernism, literature, philosophy, and cinema through the lens of jazz. As a musicologist, Perchard has delved deeply into the work of French musicians and critics. While examining French responses (especially on a musical level) to American artists like Thelonius Monk and Miles Davis, he has moved his study well beyond the 1960s and therefore into decades beyond the scope of this book. Like him, I am interested in matters of identity and art in the postwar period, but he has examined the music itself in great detail while my aim is to use the rhetoric and cultural practices surrounding jazz as a means of better understanding different facets of postwar French society. We are in complete agreement that jazz reflected the interplay between the local, the national, and the global, and that jazz was always at its core an international music.[11] Nettelbeck and I both believe that jazz can be used to explore crucial aspects of French society, but while he has primarily focused on the various expressions of French culture mentioned above like modernism and cinema, I am more interested in how jazz audiences negotiated subjects crucial to postwar French identity: the evolving youth culture and gendered norms; the relationship between France and the United States and the process of Americanization; the problematic subject of racism and the importance of ensuring political rights for minority populations; the protection of French identity; and the loss of the colonial empire.

Throughout the course of this book, I strive to answer questions that are pertinent for not only understanding jazz in postwar France but for shedding light on a multiplicity of ideas that inform conceptions about present-day France. I began studying jazz in France well over a decade ago because I found that it illuminated aspects of French society that I wanted to examine, the most important of which were the cultural connections between the United States and France, and the subjects of racial, ethnic, and national identity. I was also interested in the gendered expectations and experiences of jazz musicians, critics, and fans, and whether jazz could still be considered a form of popular culture in the postwar period. These areas of interest have shaped many of the questions I seek to answer: In what ways did French individuals work to maintain a distinct national identity in an increasingly multicultural Europe? Why was jazz a predominantly male music? Did jazz culture become more elitist in France as time went on and what was its relationship to youth culture? Why was jazz, a music with stated and essential African-American roots, embraced almost without contestation by French listeners in this period that also witnessed growing anti-Americanism and discrimination against French minority groups? How did race *and* culture work with and against each other in French notions of difference and in forms of discrimination practiced on French soil? Was *jazz français* a legitimate subgenre and what was jazz's place in the former French Empire? These questions inform the crux of my inquiry and have guided my work from the get-go. In attempting to answer these questions, this book is organized into six thematic chapters that focus on the first twenty-five years of the postwar period. I have chosen to stop my study at the end of the 1960s for a variety of reasons. A younger generation of French critics and musicians was by then becoming more influential and the avant-garde music they endorsed and created eschewed widespread popularity and commercial success, placing jazz appreciation in an increasingly constricted elite subculture. At the same time, rock and roll and yé-yé were displacing the position of jazz in French culture, most visibly in youth culture, and the demographic makeup of the country and race relations were evolving in new ways because of continuing extra-European immigration. Due to these multiple trends, in the 1970s the story of jazz in France began to adopt new trajectories that are beyond the scope of this book. Focusing on a twenty-five year span allowed me to hone in on the themes that I found most relevant and telling. When the timeline reached the end of the 1960s, the shadow of the war and its aftermath was fading; understandings and anxieties began to be framed in reference to other concerns and events, such as those of 1968 and postcolonialism. For the bulk of the 1950s and 60s, the most prominent critics remained the same and their work has defined much of this project. As vocal members of a cultural elite, critics communicated important ideas not only about jazz to their readers, but also ideas that reflected their concerns as citizens. Because jazz had American roots as well as a global reach, it forced those French listeners paying attention to look beyond the parochial and placed their nation and their culture into this new global age, whether they liked it or not.

In "Chapter One: *Le Monde du jazz*," my goal is to orient the reader to the earlier history of jazz in France and then to explore the partnerships and the rifts existent in the jazz community between 1945 and the end of the 1960s; in this chapter I also examine the various mediums through which knowledge about jazz and the music itself were disseminated. The remaining chapters are arranged thematically so that the subjects to which I have already alluded can be fully investigated. "Chapter Two: The Gendered Jazz Public" examines jazz's connection both to a postwar youth culture that took male participation to be the norm and to a masculine identity that had its roots in the United States and excluded women from full participation in the jazz public. "Chapter Three: The Question and Politics of Race" investigates the persistent and racialized discourse that existed among the jazz cognoscenti of the 1950s and 1960s, closely examining ideas about intrinsic "black" characteristics as well as the unmitigated support given to the American Civil Rights Movement and the forceful condemnation of American racism (but not necessarily French racism). "Chapter Four: More than an American Music" studies the relationship between the United States and France as it played out through jazz by looking at French criticisms of American economic practices, but also jazz fans' support of the American State Department's Goodwill Ambassador Tours and the celebrity status granted to the American expatriate Sidney Bechet. "Chapter Five: Red, White, and Blue Notes: French Jazz" considers how the French jazz public viewed artists from their own country (especially the Roma guitarist Django Reinhardt), and how these musicians in turn envisioned their participation in creating *jazz français*. "Chapter Six: And What of Empire?" examines the French jazz community's involvement in overseas departments and territories, as well as in former colonial holdings during the 1960s. With the end of colonization and a growing pride in African culture, jazz enthusiasts in what had formerly been French-controlled territories *and* French jazzmen had to reenvision their relationship to jazz and to the music's audiences.

Jazz's continued integration into French culture in the 1950s and 1960s happened at the same time that the country was negotiating the legacies of World War II, including the loss of its colonies and the threat of American power. National issues such as these made their way into the appreciation of jazz, linking the cultural with the political, and reinforcing *French* ties to the music. Jazz fans welcomed an aesthetic that could be labeled foreign, minority, and American at a time when each of these words triggered different degrees of cultural protectionism. Instead of turning away from jazz, critics, musicians, and fans embraced this increasingly complicated and perpetually inventive music, attempting to link themselves with its both its creativity and innovation. Members of the jazz public worked to make France a global capital of jazz. In doing so, they not only expanded a European market for an American music, they grappled with what it meant to be French.

NOTES

1. Jean Wagner, *Le Guide du Jazz* (Paris: Syros, 1986), 8.
2. Numerous contributions have been made by academics studying jazz in France, especially when it comes to the interwar period and the World War II era. I will discuss these works at greater length later in the Introduction: Ludovic Tournès, *New Orleans sur Seine: Histoire du jazz en France* (Paris: Fayard, 1999); Jeffrey H. Jackson, *Making Jazz French: Music and Modern Life in Interwar Paris* (Durham, NC: Duke University Press, 2003); Colin Nettelbeck, *Dancing with DeBeauvoir: Jazz and the French* (Carlton, Victoria: Melbourne University Press, 2004); Matthew F. Jordan, *Le Jazz: Jazz and French Cultural Identity* (Urbana: University of Illinois Press, 2010); Jeremy F. Lane, *Jazz and Machine-Age Imperialism: Music, "Race," and Intellectuals in France, 1918–1945* (Ann Arbor: University of Michigan Press, 2013); Andy Fry, *Paris Blues: African American Music and French Popular Culture, 1920–1960* (Chicago: University of Chicago Press, 2014); and Tom Perchard, *After Django: Making Jazz in Postwar France* (Ann Arbor: University of Michigan Press, 2015).
3. Sociologist Pierre Bourdieu's concept of the *field* is helpful in examining the struggles this group of fans, critics, and musicians faced. Bourdieu's field, like an athletic field, is a system of relations between objectively-defined positions. The "occupants, agents or institutions" on the field work within a structurally bound space with its own distribution of power. These agents then struggle for possession of this power, which will allow them to profit from whatever is at stake in the field, or improve their position within it. In his own words, Bourdieu describes a field as "a network, or a configuration, of objective relations between positions. These positions are objectively defined, in their existence and in the determinations they impose upon their occupants, agents or institutions, by their present and potential situation (*situs*) in the structure of the distribution of species of power (or capital) whose possession commands access to the specific profits that are at stake in the field, as well as by their objective relation to other positions (domination, subordination homology, etc.)." See Pierre Bourdieu and Loïc J. D. Wacquant, *An Invitation to Reflexive Sociology* (Chicago: University of Chicago Press, 1992), 97.
4. Rebecca J. Pulju, *Women and Mass Consumer Society in Postwar France* (New York: Cambridge University Press, 2011); Susan K. Foley, *Women in France Since 1789* (New York: Palgrave MacMillan, 2004); and Claire Duchen, *Women's Rights and Women's Lives in France 1944–1968* (New York: Routledge, 1994).
5. Richard Ivan Jobs, *Riding the New Wave: Youth and the Rejuvenation of France After the Second World War* (Stanford: Stanford University Press, 2007) and Susan Weiner, *Enfantes terribles: Youth and Femininity in the Mass Media in France, 1945–1968* (Baltimore: Johns Hopkins University Press, 2001) have guided my thinking on French youth culture.
6. For more on the subjects of Anti-Americanism and Americanization, see Richard Kuisel's *The French Way: How France Embraced and Rejected American Values and Power* (Princeton, NJ: Princeton University Press, 2012); *Seducing the French: the Dilemma of Americanization* (Berkeley: University of California Press, 1993); Victoria de Grazia, *Irresistible Empire: America's Advance through 20th-Century Europe* (Cambridge, MA: Belknap Press of Harvard University Press, 2005); Mary Nolan, *The Transatlantic Century: Europe and America, 1890–2010* (New York: Cambridge University Press, 2012); Denis Lacorne, Jacques Rupnik, and Marie-France Toinet, eds. *The Rise and Fall of Anti-Americanism: A Century of French Perceptions*, trans. Gerry Turner (New York: St. Martin's Press, 1990); Irwin M. Wall,

The United States and the Making of Postwar France, 1945–1954 (New York: Cambridge University Press, 2002); Seth D. Armus, *French Anti-Americanism (1930–1948): Critical Moments in a Complex History* (Lanham, MD: Lexington Books, 2010); Brian Angus McKenzie, *Remaking France: Americanization, Public Diplomacy, and the Marshall Plan* (New York: Berghahn Books, 2008); Sophie Meunier, "Anti-Americanism in France," *French Politics, Culture and Society* 23 (2005), 126–41; Frank Castigliola, *France and the United States: The Cold Alliance since World War II* (New York: Twayne, 1992); Rob Kroes, R. W. Rydell, D. F. J. Bosscher, eds. *Cultural Transmissions and Receptions: American Mass Culture in Europe* (Amsterdam: VU University Press, 1993); and Rob Kroes, *If You've Seen One, You've Seen the Mall: Europeans and American Mass Culture* (Urbana: University of Illinois Press, 1996).

7. Alistair Horne, *A Savage War of Peace: Algeria 1954–1962* (New York: New York Review Books, 2006); Irwin M. Wall, *France, the United States, and the Algerian War* (Berkeley: University of California Press, 2001); Martin Thomas, *The French North African Crisis: Colonial Breakdown and Anglo-French Relations, 1945–62* (New York: St. Martin's Press, 2000); and *Crises of Empire: Decolonization and Europe's Imperial States, 1918–1975*, eds. Martin Thomas, Bob Moore, and L. J. Butler (London: Hodder Education, 2008).

8. I am employing Herman Lebovic's idea here, as used in his *True France: The Wars over Cultural Identity, 1900–1945* (Ithaca: Cornell University Press, 1994).

9. Contributions on the subject of racism and ethnic divisions in France can be found in numerous places but I have especially drawn on the following works to shape my thoughts: Dominic Thomas, *Africa and France: Postcolonial Cultures, Migration, and Racism* (Bloomington: Indiana University Press, 2013); *Frenchness and the African Diaspora*, eds. Charles Tshimanga, Didier Gondola, and Peter J. Bloom (Bloomington: Indiana University Press, 2009); Alec G. Hargreaves, *Multi-Ethnic France: Immigration, Politics, Culture and Society*, 2nd ed. (New York: Routledge, 2007); Herman Lebovics, *Bringing the Empire Back Home: France in the Global Age* (Durham, NC: Duke University Press, 2004); Miriam Feldblum, "Paradoxes of Ethnic Politics: the Case of Franco-Maghrebis in France," *Ethnic and Racial Studies*, vol. 16, no. 1 (January 1993), 52–74; Catherine Wihtol de Wenden, "From Migrants to Citizens: Muslims in France," *Politics and Religion in France and the United States*, eds. Alec G. Hargreaves, John Kelsay, and Sumner B. Twiss (Lanham, MD: Lexington Books, 2007), 139–153; Azouz Begag, *Ethnicity and Equality: France in the Balance* (Lincoln: University of Nebraska Press, 2007); Verene Stolke, "Talking Culture: New Boundaries, New Rhetorics of Exclusion in Europe," *Current Anthropology*, vol. 36, no. 1 (February 1995), 1–23; Maxim Silverman, *Deconstructing the Nation: Immigration, Racism and Citizenship in Modern France* (London: Routledge, 1992); Michèle Lamont, "The Rhetoric of Racism and Anti-Racism in France and the United States" (1996 manuscript); David Beriss, *Black Skins, French Voices: Caribbean Ethnicity and Activism in Urban France* (Boulder, CO: Westview Press, 2004); and Donald L. Horowitz, "Immigration and Group Relations in France and America," *Immigrants in Two Democracies: French and American Experience*, eds. Donald L. Horowitz and Gérard Norièl (New York: New York University Press, 1992).

10. Fry, *Paris Blues: African American Music and French Popular Culture, 1920–1960* (Chicago: University of Chicago Press, 2014), 17.

11. Tom Perchard, *After Django: Making Jazz in Postwar France* (Ann Arbor: University of Michigan Press, 2015).

Chapter One

Le Monde du jazz

Jazz's cultural location in France after the Second World War depended on a variety of factors that dated back to the interwar period. By 1945, the music's reach was well established, so that in the early postwar period, jazz already had myriad cultural affiliations as well an infrastructure to sustain it. Spanning from the end of the First World War, supporters and detractors alike had created meanings for the music that then informed later understandings in the 1940s, 1950s, 1960s, and beyond. In some cases, jazz—as is often the case with art forms whose popularity covers the course of many years—changed dramatically as time went on. New musicians and musical genres arrived on the scene. Beginning in the 1940s, bebop and other forward-looking manifestations of jazz brought the music far away from the dance sounds of the 1920s and 1930s, and sometimes this meant lessening the music's popular appeal. Postwar jazz essentially moved away from the large and well-attended dance halls of the interwar years into smaller and more intimate *caves*, where jazzmen more often played modern, cerebral, and intentionally un-danceable music. However, certain postwar musicians were able to reach the mass market with songs linked to traditional New Orleans jazz that were anything but avant-garde and that had been enjoyed by fans during the 1920s and 1930s too. Sometimes, American musicians performed and lived in France during both the interwar and postwar periods, and several of the most influential postwar French critics got their start in the 1930s, as did a number of French jazz musicians. So while many new jazz artists and enthusiasts appeared only after the Liberation, there were also those who remained the same, creating important continuities between the eras on either side of World War II. Importantly, the postwar jazz scene was also riven with debate as critics, musicians, and fans argued over the validity of new jazz genres, revealing their divergent visions of art, African-American music, and jazz.

SOUNDS OF FREEDOM IN INTERWAR FRANCE

In a story that has now been well told, jazz initially found a sizeable audience in France as the Great War was coming to a close and African-American bandleaders and their ensembles toured the country for the first time. Music and dance styles connected to black America had enjoyed periods of popularity as far back as 1902, when the musical review *Les Heureux nègres* (*The Happy Negroes*) introduced the cakewalk to Parisian audiences and started a dance craze among adolescents and young adults in the city.[1] Over the following decades, the French public was exposed from time to time to other forms of entertainment—such as ragtime and minstrelsy—that were linked in the popular mind to black American culture as well.[2] When the first jazz bands set foot in France at war's end, they exposed conventional listeners to a valid African-American musical genre that had not been widely appreciated before their arrival. Eventually, a broad range of French men and women were drawn to jazz and some of them were inspired to care passionately about its novel sounds and the American culture that had brought it to life.

The Harlem Hellfighters, a military band attached to the 369th United States Army Infantry Regiment, was the earliest of the African-American jazz ensembles to secure French acclaim, but others such as Mitchell's Jazz Kings and Will Marion Cook's Southern Syncopated Orchestra soon followed. Jazz's approval spread beyond the realm of popular culture so that in the twenties, Parisian modernists such as Jean Cocteau, Darius Milhaud, Igor Stravinsky, and Erik Satie also began studying the music and integrating its innovative sounds into their own works. In this early interwar period, French cultural actors and consumers were fascinated by black culture and were making an effort to study the works of poets, artists, writers, and musicians coming from both Africa and the Americas, reflecting what contemporaries called "Negrophilia."[3]

But not everyone in interwar France welcomed jazz. Some critics equated its noise and rhythms, which for them were the aesthetic opposite of conventional French musics, with a cultural malaise. They hoped to rid the country of cultural practices like jazz so that people would return to their long-established musical tastes and customary ways of life. Observers cautioned against following fashion over tradition and losing self-control through musical abandonment. Following the whims of current styles and trends was connected to cultural instability and change—suspicious qualities for critics who embraced conservative and unbending conceptions of culture. Women who went out dancing were thought to be in violation of traditional gender roles and some doctors even expressed a concern that dancing to the rhythms of jazz could cause physical harm to males and females alike and lead to such things as impotency or neurological damage.[4] In the 1922 novel *La Garçonne* by Victor Margueritte, the heroine attending a nightclub with her female lover to dance to the sounds of jazz overlaps with her deviance from social norms as she engages in sexually promiscuous behavior as well as opium use.[5]

A fear of internationalism permeated anti-jazz discussions as critics worried about losing intrinsic aspects of French civilization through an embrace of both the foreign and the physical as represented by jazz and its African-American creators. Leaders of the Catholic Church in France connected jazz to decaying morality, arguing that jazz dancing brought both bodily and psychological harm to individuals, actually even more harm than war. The secular nature of jazz was painted as being diametrically opposed to the spirituality endorsed by the church. In the early 1920s, the Church prohibited Catholics from dancing to jazz.[6]

With the arrival of the Great Depression, the jazz scene in France lost its strong reliance on American musicians and initially much of its vibrancy as well. American tourists and expatriates returned to the United States, and bands and musicians made fewer international tours. But despite these stark changes that lasted through the 1930s, French jazz enthusiasts continued to sustain the music and actually began building an infrastructure that would impact the jazz public going forward well into the postwar years. French jazzmen achieved previously unknown levels of fame: Grégor, Ray Ventura, André Ekyan, and Alix Combelle all made names for themselves and Grégor even created the first French jazz periodical, *La Revue du jazz*, which ran from the summer of 1929 until the early months of 1930. Another magazine, *Jazz-Tango*, hit the presses in October of 1930 with the aim of informing readers about French dance bands and musicians as well as general musical developments.[7]

In 1932, *Jazz-Tango* announced the establishment of the Hot Club de France, an organization whose stated intent was to support the "hot" sounds of jazz and whose existence brought an important new leader into the forefront of the French jazz scene: Hugues Panassié. The club's beginnings had come several years earlier when two Parisian university students, Edwin Dirats and Jacques Auxenfans, founded the Jazz-Club Universitaire.[8] These men soon asked Panassié to help them with their association, as he was becoming rather well known in the nascent jazz community as a critic through his contributions to *La Revue du jazz*, *Jazz-Tango*, and other periodicals like *Grand'Route*.

Panassié had discovered jazz in 1926 as a fourteen-year-old boy recovering from polio and then went on to become one of the most influential forces in the French world of jazz. His father had made a fortune in manganese mining so that Panassié never had to worry about earning an income and could devote his life from late adolescence forward to jazz, amassing a considerable (and expensive) collection of records and earning an important measure of respect for his knowledge and opinions about the music. His politics were unusual for a jazz aficionado: a vocal critic of the Third Republic before World War II, he was also a monarchist and an early supporter of the anti-republican and Catholic nationalist Charles Maurras.[9] He wrote jazz articles for the right-wing journal *L'Insurgé* before the war and then for the extreme right-wing publications *Itinéraires* and *La Casserole* in the postwar period. Well into the 1970s, he expressed his disproval of modern technology, democracy, and universal suffrage. Despite his idiosyncrasies and rightist politics, the name of the enigmatic Panassié became synonymous with the Hot Club between the wars and he went on to write a number of books on jazz, the first of which was the 1934 *Le jazz hot*, which was translated into English two years later and became a classic in Europe and the United States.[10] Panassié also founded the magazine *Jazz Hot* in 1935, which remained an important fixture in the jazz community for decades to come and remains the preeminent jazz publication in France today.

In the Hot Club, the influence of Dirats and Auxenfans soon waned and within a few years of the club's 1932 formation, their job of organizing club activities passed to one of Panassié's colleagues, Pierre Nourry. By the mid-1930s, Charles Delaunay, the son of painter Robert Delaunay and artist Sonia Delaunay, also became intricately involved with the leadership of the association. He took over as the editor of *Jazz Hot*, and wrote the 1936 book *Hot Discography*, which listed jazz records for readers. Panassié's wealth eventually allowed him to sit out World War II at his family's estate away from Paris and the day-to-day realities of the Occupation, while Delaunay joined the Resistance. Not surprisingly, their professional collaboration did not continue after the war, although the public basis for their postwar disagreements was music, not politics.

From its inception, the Hot Club de France defended "true," "hot," and "black" jazz against "white," "commercial" imitations, and the organization hosted concerts and lectures to educate members about this "real" jazz.[11] In using the word "hot," club founders and participants meant something very specific, and they wanted to emphasize the fundamental worth of improvisation, emotion, and energy in jazz. They did not consider orchestral jazz—like the music played by the white American musician Paul Whiteman—to be authentic. Importantly, Hot Club leaders linked hot sounds to the African-American musicians who had first played jazz. These men were especially supportive of the New Orleans style, particularly the music played by Louis Armstrong, whom Panassié made the club's honorary president. The defenders of "hot" insisted that black jazzmen were superior to white musicians because they were the original creators of jazz, and Panassié ended up holding onto this line of argument throughout his postwar career (as long as the musicians played the music he considered true to the original sounds of New Orleans jazz). Early on, he and others acknowledged that white players could, and should, aspire to playing jazz in the same way as the black inventors, and in the 1930s, the Hot Club promoted the work of both black and white American musicians as well as white French jazzmen, as long as they played "hot." Jeremy Lane has illustrated that Panassié's interwar analysis of jazz relied on binary oppositions between European music and jazz, the modern and the primitive, the written word and the voice, reason and emotion, predetermined and spontaneous musical expressions, commercial forms of entertainment and authentic art, white and black jazz.[12] Importantly, this binary view of jazz production and appreciation informed Panassié's professional worldview throughout his career, which spanned decades into the postwar era and lasted until his death in 1974.

The Hot Club did not have much initial success in expanding its membership before World War II broke out, but it did organize seventy-six concerts of greater or lesser importance across France between 1933 and 1939. Arguably the Hot Club's most notable contribution in this period was its creation of the Quintette du Hot Club de France in 1934. Two French musicians, the Roma guitarist Django Reinhardt and the violinist Stéphane Grappelli, led this ensemble and, of course, played in the "hot" style. The Quintette earned national and international acclaim for its jazz compositions in the years leading up to World War II. The Hot Club's leadership continued to diversify its activities beyond the efforts of club formation, concert organizing, and promoting the famous Quintette. Foreshadowing the extensive pursuits of postwar French jazz professionals, in 1937, the Hot Club's Charles Delaunay and Hugues Panassié created a new record label—Swing—that was the first in the world to focus exclusively on jazz. Working under this new brand name, Delaunay and Panassié held seventy-one recording sessions and published close to ninety record sides before the end of 1939.[13]

The story of jazz in France, no matter when on the timeline of the twentieth century, illustrates the assimilation of a foreign cultural product into mainstream French art and entertainment. Many of the interwar musicians who expanded the jazz public in France were American, and the majority of them were African American. The Frenchmen who launched the Hot Club de France in the 1930s were insistent in their support of music played by these black American artists. Nonetheless, it is important to remember that despite this enthusiastic welcome on the part of French jazz fans, not all French listeners enjoyed or approved of jazz and, in many ways, the culture of the 1930s was increasingly closed to foreign influences. But jazz, with its origins firmly planted in African-American culture, *was* an undeniably important component of interwar French entertainment, and its advocates showed a countertendency to cultural protectionism. During the 1930s, French jazz artists adopted and integrated a musical tradition from well beyond Europe's borders into their own forms of expression. Even if as individuals they neither deliberately embraced cosmopolitanism nor welcomed foreign musicians in a time of increased job scarcity, as Frenchmen they did bring their own interpretations of the music to their countrymen at the same time as they maintained strong international connections. Clearly, there was a strong ambivalence already in play over the French and the foreign in interwar France.[14] Because of economic depression, American musicians were not often seen on French stages, but French musicians built and sustained careers on this music that, for themselves and for their audiences, had permanent links to the United States and to a foreign racial minority.

The impact of interwar jazz culture continued to be felt well into the future. The rhetoric and understandings perpetuated by these early jazz devotees as well as the avenues of appreciating the music that they created persisted in the world of postwar jazz. Sometimes the musicians, the critics, and the actual fans stayed the same, and Django Reinhardt, Louis Armstrong, Hugues Panassié, and Charles Delaunay remained important actors following World War II, as did the musician Sidney Bechet whom I will discuss at length in chapter 5. To be certain, the music, and often personal tastes, evolved but the interwar attraction to jazz nourished a support for this music that ended up being both long-lived and resolute.

Jazz brought to interwar France persuasive connections to a variety of characteristics defining the modern world. It represented not only the modern, the new, the African, and the American, but also an evolving urban culture that embraced not only electricity, automobiles, and music halls, but mass consumption, popular entertainment, energy, movement, and innovation as well.[15] The interwar period saw an audience and interpretation of jazz come into existence that far outlived the music's artistic notoriety among modernist musicians and that continued to lie beneath the surface of the music's popularity after the end of World War II.

LES ZAZOUS AND OCCUPIED FRANCE

All through World War II, French listeners remained disconnected from American jazz artists and their music. During the Occupation, right-wing periodicals and propaganda criticized the "mixed-race" cultural influence of jazz, but authorities never prohibited the music. Ludovic Tournès has posited that this might have been due to the fact that before the war French critics like Charles Delaunay successfully depoliticized the music, and that the Germans wanted to create a positive image for themselves as occupiers, letting the French population believe that life would pretty much continue on the same trajectory after defeat as it had before.[16] French jazz musicians were generally left alone by German authorities in Occupied France. Michael Kater has suggested that this was because Berlin wanted these artists to continue providing entertainment for "scores of fun-starved German soldiers."[17] Of course, music by Jewish composers was forbidden as was all American music once the United States entered the war in 1941, and both Jews and blacks were not allowed inside public performance spaces.[18] This led to an almost singular focus on the music of *French* jazzmen. The professional lives of these native musicians flourished, unlike in the 1920s when they had been constantly forced to compete head-on with Americans who were seen as the bona fide inventors of jazz. French artists like Django Reinhardt reached the pinnacle of their careers during the war, as concerts, tours, and recordings of French musicians continued largely unabated. In occupied Paris, between 1940 and 1944, there were actually *more* jazz concerts per month than there had been in the thirties.[19] Jazz was played on the radio throughout the war on the German controlled *Radio-Paris* and on Vichy's *Radiodiffusion nationale*.[20]

This did not mean that an American influence ceased to exist. To be sure, American songs were still popular, but to evade official notice, French artists, club owners, and radio stations changed the names of U.S. singles to French ones. Before performances, lists of songs were given to the German Propaganda Detachment (the Propaganda Staeffel) in Paris for approval so that *In the Mood* became *Dans l'ambiance*, *Two Left Feet* changed into *Deux pieds gauches*, and *Lady Be Good* morphed into *Les Bigoudis*.[21] American jazz numbers were given new names and performed by French musicians and orchestras to avoid legal entanglements, but the music itself remained essentially the same and continued to provide a means of cultural escape for fans. And, for the politically engaged, it created a potential means of criticizing the Occupation.

The word "jazz" was a label for different forms of music during the war. Professional critics like Delaunay decried the general population using the word to describe trendy dance or variety songs that were considered beyond the realm of "true" jazz. This elite group asserted that "jazz" only referred to a music that held up to analytical evaluations that ensured the genre's legitimacy. But despite this insistence on the part of critics, there were multiple meanings for jazz in this tumultuous period that existed well beyond the strict definitions of music professionals. French men and women used the term *jazz* to identify at least three types of cultural expression: purely popular forms of in-vogue entertainment like swing music; certain musics and behaviors that were linked with political protest; and music that did indeed have the jazz critics' official stamp of approval for meeting required aesthetic standards. After the fall of France, all forms of "jazz" appreciation could be used to convey a listener's disapproval of the societal and governmental status quo. By listening to jazz records, dancing to swing music, and wearing clothes connected to the swing subculture, individuals could publicly and visibly express views that ran counter to the official Nazi and Vichy views on both jazz and Frenchness. For some, jazz became synonymous with the resistance to the German invader, and Pétain's government outlawed dances because authorities believed they could be places for black market exchanges, immoral behavior, or sexual impropriety.[22]

While not gaining much respect from the professional jazz cadre, Zazous were a visibly identifiable group of Parisian teenagers and young adults who shaped the French population's perceptions of jazz. Zazous were reported to have taken their name from a 1938 Johnny Hess song entitled "Je suis swing" that ended with the lines "Je suis swing, je suis swing. / Za zou za zou, c'est gentil comme tout" ("I am swing, I am swing. / Za zou za zou, it's nice as can be").[23] The Zazou men characteristically wore long oiled hair that hung over their collars, oversized checked suit jackets, rolled-up pants, and a neckerchief or tie, while the women donned short pleated skirts paired with large and boxy suit jackets of their own, wore their hair in a bun on the front of their heads, and used dark red lipstick and nail polish. Male and female Zazous were portrayed in illustrations of the day wearing sunglasses and carrying umbrellas (regardless of time of day or weather), and smoking, showing that through their fashion and behavior they challenged the cultural mainstream.[24] For the Zazous, their clothes mirrored the way jazz musicians from Harlem dressed and by donning certain styles, these young French people publicly emphasized their fascination with African-American culture. By supporting "swing" and having an open affinity for both a music and a way of dressing that defied conventional notions of Frenchness, they strove to upend the values of the National Revolution, its xenophobic beliefs, and its quest for racial and cultural purity.[25] Zazous made themselves a noticeable alternative to the Vichy conception of youth, by meeting and dancing in halls, cafes, and cabarets, and donning their creative and eccentric outfits. They listened to American swing musicians like Cab Calloway and Benny Goodman, as well as to French jazz artists like Boris Vian or Django Reinhardt.[26] In doing so, they succeeding in generating an image for themselves that refuted the one embraced by the fascist *Jeunesse Populaires Françaises* or the French Scouts.[27]

Despite their notoriety and public rejection of Vichy, Gérard Régnier has cautioned against falsely elevating the status of the Zazous, arguing that the political beliefs and actions of these youths must not be exaggerated. Jazz appreciation did not automatically indicate a person's disapproval of the National Revolution, and both Jeremy Lane and Andy Fry have stressed that passionate fans of the music could be found among French collaborators and supporters of Vichy, as well as among occupying German soldiers.[28] The lines separating collaboration from resistance were not easily drawn in wartime France and jazz appreciation existed within this culturally and politically complex situation.

Of course, jazz did not *have to* reflect partisan meanings at all, and many of those who appreciated the music were simply enjoying an energetic and modern musical sound. But even if jazz remained apolitical in the minds of some of its listeners, for most it never lost its connection to black culture, to the United States, or to a nebulous sense of freedom. For these listeners, jazz made day-to-day life more endurable and pleasurable and the music was decisively outside the bounds of strict Nazi censorship.[29] Beginning in 1941, Charles Delaunay worked directly for the Resistance as part of a network organized out of the Parisian Hot Club de France headquarters.[30] Delaunay's participation in the Resistance, as well as that of lesser-known Hot Club members, contributed to a postwar association between jazz and a political defiance of the Occupation.[31] Because of the activities undertaken by the Zazous and a certain and select few in the professional jazz community, by the time of the Liberation, jazz came to be more associated with the Resistance than with collaboration. Andy Fry has strongly cautioned against accepting the link between jazz and the Resistance, saying that the early postwar tendency to do so was an effort in mythmaking indicative of what Henry Rousso has termed the Vichy syndrome. According to Rousso's convincing argument, after the war the reality of collaboration was ignored so that the French could envision their nation as one of resisters.[32] Fry has argued that jazz, like the rest of wartime life and culture, did not fall easily into supporting collaboration or resistance. For him, politics in Occupied France (and the appreciation or disproval of jazz) were not illustrated or practiced in black and white, but in "multicolored hues" that illustrated the ambiguity of an era in which French jazz recordings and concerts increased in numbers, French jazzmen like Django Reinhardt reached their height of fame, and some German occupiers and sympathizers were known to support jazz. For Fry, the majority of regular French people (and by extension, jazz fans) did not actively collaborate or resist. Instead they lived lives of "accommodation," going about their day-to-day lives without wanting to get involved in the painful and complicated politics of wartime France.[33]

I agree with Fry that the reality of wartime jazz was messy, but we still must acknowledge the power of the myth that told people in early postwar France that jazz was a music of resistance, not one of collaboration. Historians, after all, did not start refuting this myth until the 1990s, so that the musicians, critics, and audiences I am concerned with in this book either participated in founding and perpetuating the myth or accepted it as undeniable fact. This myth altered the image and meaning of the music for listeners in incontrovertible ways. From the earliest moments following the war, the music retained a number of crucial connotations—connected to antifascism, American culture, and youth culture—that would persist in impacting its popularity. Going forward, public voices rarely raised themselves to seriously question this *judeo-nègre-américain* musical hybrid and its place within France.[34] Certainly no one wanted to discuss who had or had not been listening to jazz under the Occupation. Acknowledging that Zazous, members of the Resistance, German officers, and Vichy sympathizers all did their part to support jazz during the war would have been too painful for the majority of French citizens who did not want to think about France's wartime record or their own. After Allied troops entered Paris in 1944, for the second time jazz was associated with *libération*, cementing a connection between the music, the United States, and freedom. Because of the power of mythmaking, jazz fans entered the postwar era with a sense of legitimacy, which required them to ignore certain portions of jazz's wartime story as well as the fact that the majority of Frenchmen still did not embrace the music.

THE NEW "BATTLE OF HERNANI"

In the early 1940s in the United States, a group of young musicians led by the alto saxophonist Charlie Parker—and including trumpeter Dizzy Gillespie, drummer Kenny Clarke, and pianist Thelonius Monk—created a new jazz style—bebop—which drastically pulled the music in new directions with its unpredictable accents, spliced chords, and improvisations, creating a modern, avant-garde music.[35] Through late-night jam sessions in New York at places like the now-famous Minton's Playhouse, these musicians conceptualized and played jazz in previously unknown ways. They created new songs and recrafted standards like "I Got Rhythm," all while using ever faster tempos and techniques that left their fellow musicians incredulous.[36] The jazz scene in the United States and in Europe would never be the same once the work of these young, revolutionary players reached listeners' ears.

French audiences did not hear the innovative sounds of bebop until the end of World War II and the first concert in France did not happen until February 1948, when Dizzy Gillespie performed on three separate nights at the Salle Pleyel, physically marking bebop's arrival in France.[37] By that time, critic Hugues Panassié had already made his views on the music clear: bebop was not jazz.[38] He still felt that the music of New Orleans musicians like Louis Armstrong represented the "true" music of American blacks. For him, bebop betrayed jazz's roots by becoming too cerebral and by moving its rhythms decisively away from dance music. Panassié was a crucial supporter of revivalism in France, a movement that claimed the sounds of New Orleans were aesthetically pure and represented the authentic spirit and intent of the music, as opposed to, at first, the crass commercial interests of swing and then the progressive sounds of bebop.[39] Charles Delaunay, Panassié's close colleague from before the war, did not agree. He supported jazz's evolution and this meant endorsing bebop, which many at the time simply called "modern jazz." In 1947, Panassié was the acting president of the Hot Club de France and he expelled Delaunay from the organization precisely because of the latter's approval of bebop. Delaunay retaliated, taking the offensive through his newly founded Hot Club de Paris and the magazine *Jazz Hot* which he, not Panassié, continued to direct after the fissure. Because Delaunay and others like him refused to obey Panassié, "modern jazz" found influential promoters in France, and lines were drawn for an extended and bitter confrontation between those who supported bebop and those who did not. With well-connected and experienced advocates on both sides disagreeing about the intrinsic nature of the music, a "jazz war" played out among the jazz cognoscenti in the late 1940s as well as into the next decade.[40]

Contemporaries referred to the dispute as the new "Battle of Hernani" in order to point out the similarities between this cultural rift and a well-known nineteenth-century one. In 1830, a conflict had erupted between the advocates of "classical" theatre on the one side and the supporters of "Romantic" theatre on the other. The Romantics supported Victor Hugo's innovative new play *Hernani*, and on the night of the play's first Parisian performance, the crowd was divided into two combative sections whose members scuffled and exchanged insults and boos with one another. Members of the postwar French jazz community, as well as outside observers from the popular press, could not resist comparing the fight over jazz with this much earlier cultural clash over artistic taste and propriety.

The rupture among jazz professionals had important ramifications because Panassié was the oldest and most internationally-recognized leader of the French jazz public. In addition to creating an infrastructure in the 1930s through which younger generations of jazz fans were exposed to the music, Panassié's Hot Club had continued to expand during the war. Between 1940 and 1945, the organization had created fifty new sections across France and in 1947, there were close to seventy branches in all.[41] In 1945, on the Hot Club de France's thirteenth anniversary, its leaders claimed that the group had organized "over one-hundred concerts with the greatest French and foreign jazz musicians, innumerable conferences and radio programs."[42] Hot Clubs also spread to other European countries so that by 1950, twenty Hot Clubs existed in West Germany and several clubs even existed in the German Democratic Republic.[43] Close to fifty years after Panassié began promoting jazz, a writer for a music journal wrote that between the wars, Panassié was "the French 'Mister Jazz.'"[44] Long after his influence had waned, the international jazz community continued to respect him because his efforts had brought jazz out of obscurity in France. Many of the men who in the 1950s became leaders of the postwar French jazz community—through their positions as writers, as members of jazz magazine editorial boards, and as executives at radio stations and record companies—were involved in Panassié's Hot Club at one time or another: Frank Ténot, André Clergeat, Henri Renaud, Boris Vian, Jean Louis Mialy, Lucien Malson, Daniel Filipacchi, Jean Robert Masson.[45] The majority of these men split with Panassié in the late 1940s but their numbers alone reflected the Hot Club's early influence in establishing a cohesive cadre of jazz specialists in France.

In the years following World War II, Panassié verbally attacked critics who did not agree with his assessments of the music, and in doing so he created an irreparable break between himself and other jazz experts. In 1947, Panassié wrote that Frank Ténot made consistent errors of musical identification and he denounced André Hodeir who became the chief editor of *Jazz Hot* after the schism. His targets did not hesitate to turn around and censure him in return, and this conflict went on for years. In 1952, the critic Lucien Malson condemned Panassié for thinking that he was the only genuine jazz critic in France, asserting that Panassié was "the Father and the Big Shot taken for god among those he appoints because they believe, on his incitement, that jazz critics can be counted on one finger."[46] Another critic, Jacques Hess, wrote that Panassié was perhaps a "folklorist" or an "archeologist" but that he certainly was not a "critic." To be a critic meant to be aware of "the existence of the dialectical movement by which the new and the old reciprocally illuminate each other for the greatest benefit of the observer." This Hegelian proceeded to call Panassié an "old man" who was suffering from "senile schlorosis."[47]

Hostilities were not always kept on the pages of magazines and books, and involved fans as well as professional critics. During the 1948 Dizzy Gillespie concert that brought bebop to France, a group of Panassié supporters whistled in disapproval of Gillespie's music. Gillespie himself did not seem affected and continued his performance, but some in the audience reacted. One spectator reportedly disparaged the whistlers by calling them the "Luter Brigade," named after the French musician Claude Luter who played the traditional New Orleans jazz that Panassié supported. Because of this association, Luter was maligned along with Panassié for being out-of-date. *France-Soir* testified that "the public, needless to say, composed mostly of young bobby soxers, reacted very violently against the 'Brigade of the Purists.' But it did not come to blows. The 'Battle of Hernani 1948' had been more calm than the first."[48] The young fans at this 1948 concert had either already absorbed the intensity of the debates over bebop from the professional critics whose articles they read, or they were simply put off by the new sounds they heard. Regardless, some among them disparaged their fellow fans for appreciating different forms of the music.

Rancorous encounters between Panassié's supporters and opponents occurred at other times as well. A pro-Panassié writer, Jacques Pescheux, claimed that the more traditional musician Bill Doggett had been chased from a concert stage after less than three songs with cries like "Give us our money back" and "We want jazz" because his music was not modern enough. However, the same crowd reportedly listened to the musician Miles Davis without incident. According to this writer, "The jazz fans had suffered [through Davis' music] without flinching. These are the progressives who show intolerance, this time fanaticism. Brain-washing has born its worthy fruit."[49] Pescheux clearly blamed "progressive" critics for creating this negative and judgmental atmosphere that would not tolerate older expressions of the music, and regretted any dismissal of New Orleans jazz. Ironically, writers like him actively denigrated bebop and other modern varieties of jazz and were just as responsible for the poisoned atmosphere as the critics on the other side of the jazz divide. And over the ensuing decades, New Orleans jazz would remain the most popular music among young fans, not the avant-garde sounds of modern jazz. There is little evidence that musicians like Doggett were habitually belittled or denied access to a French fan base.

Both groups in this dispute continued to be rather vicious in their verbal and written attacks on one another, prolonging a rift in the French jazz public that did nothing to promote the music's popularity. In the United States, the jazz community experienced two factional wars in the 1940s: the first between supporters of swing and advocates of New Orleans jazz; and the second between traditional jazz (especially the sounds of New Orleans) and bebop. But by the end of 1948, the sectarian differences in the American jazz milieu had disappeared. The "moldy fig" press in the United States that had endorsed New Orleans jazz at the expense of bebop, admitted that traditional jazz was not the "only" jazz.[50] In France, the situation evolved in a different way, so that throughout the 1950s and into the 1960s, jazz was tainted by sectarianism and disputes that disrupted the cohesiveness that Panassié's leadership had helped to create in the 1930s. In writing about his recollections of the period from the vantage point of the 1980s, Frank Ténot indicated the overinflated importance he and his cohort placed on defeating Panassié in the years following the war and how, despite their passion, their actions were not in fact crucial to the evolution of jazz itself. He wrote, "At *Jazz Hot* we busied ourselves like mad to help Delaunay win his fight against Panassié. In fact, the true battle was working itself out in the United States, there where musicians created. In Paris, as too frequently, we had the impression of being at the center of the world."[51]

As the 1950s wore on, Panassié's realm of influence did increasingly diminish.[52] His one consistent means of communication was through his publication *Le Bulletin du Hot Club de France*, while his opposition was able to publish through a variety of mediums. *Jazz Hot* remained an important mouthpiece for his detractors and in 1955, two of his rivals, Daniel Filipacchi and Frank Ténot, created *Jazz Magazine*. There were other periodicals as well—*Les Cahiers du Jazz*, *La Revue du Jazz*, *La Gazette du Jazz*, *Jazz Revue*, *Jazz News*, *Jazz Hip*—that were created by Panassié objectors, but *Jazz Hot* and *Jazz Magazine* retained the most readership. *Jazz Magazine* printed roughly 25,000 copies of each issue during the academic year (because so many of its readers were students) and 16,000 or 17,000 copies during the summer; its competitor *Jazz Hot* published 18,000 copies each month while the *Bulletin du Hot Club de France* printed only about 4,000 monthly issues. Panassié could not maintain his dominant influence in the face of these numbers, and his prestige and control therefore dissipated. In 1960, the critic Claude Léon wrote, "For twelve years, the role of the Hot Clubs, hereafter without any purpose, has become negligible in the actual activities of jazz in France."[53]

Even with Panassié's lessening authority, he kept the jazz scene severed in France. In 1962, the critic Aris Destombes called out to fans to look beyond this fissure and "open your ears to sixty years of jazz, one and indivisible."[54] Despite the fact that both sides could become rather heated and polemical in their debates, the faction led by Delaunay, Hodeir, Malson, and others never denied the important place New Orleans jazz held in the history of jazz. Critics working for *Jazz Hot* and *Jazz Magazine* continued to write pieces on Louis Armstrong and other central figures of the New Orleans style. Sidney Bechet, who moved to France in the 1950s, was perhaps the most popular jazz musician in France and he played nothing but the "old style" of music; importantly, Charles Delaunay was his agent. These facts calls in to question the accuracy of the accounts written by Panassié supporters (like Jacques Pescheux) who claimed that those who appreciated modern jazz did not tolerate more traditional expressions of the music. The new leaders of the French jazz public did not disparage the sounds of New Orleans—they just endorsed and promoted the new sounds as well. This was something that Panassié, for whatever reasons, could not bring himself to do. He and his associates tended to blame the opposition for only listening to certain select musicians, for treating other artists with disapproval, and for not accepting different forms of jazz. All while Panassié's faction engaged in precisely these kinds of behaviors to advance its own outlook and agenda.

LE MAFIA DU JAZZ: THE PRESS, CRITICS, AND JAZZ ASSOCIATIONS

Despite the infighting and fractured nature of the postwar jazz community, professional critics worked to expose fans to the music's history and artists. Jazz periodicals were the most important vehicle for spreading opinions and knowledge about jazz to a broad readership. The foremost publications were *Jazz Hot* and *Jazz Magazine* mentioned above, both of which followed a very similar format that included features like record reviews, news, profiles of musicians, interviews with critics and musicians, analytical and historical articles, and photographic essays. Other magazines existed during the period as well: *Jazz News* (founded by Eddie Barclay), which was only published for one year between 1949 and 1950; *Jazz Informations*, which lasted for less than a year in 1949; the critic Michel Dorigné's *La Gazette du jazz*, which ran from 1949 until 1951; *La Revue du jazz*, which was founded by Hugue

Panassié in 1949 and continued until 1951 when he created the monthly *Bulletin du Hot Club de France* with the musician Alix Combelle; the Marseille-based *Jazz Hip*, which also ran under the name *Jazz*, and operated between 1957 and 1966; and Filippachi and Ténot's quarterly journal *Les Cahiers du Jazz* whose editions appeared from 1959 until the late 1960s.[55] As already noted, *Jazz Magazine* and *Jazz Hot* maintained the highest circulation in this period while smaller publications like Panassié's *Bulletin du Hot Club de France* and *Jazz [Hip]* only reached an audience of about 3,000 to 4,000 each month.[56]

Jazz enthusiasts could also learn about the music outside of the specialized press. For instance, in 1952, the review *Le Point* devoted an entire issue to jazz with the collaboration of Panassié's Hot Club de France.[57] Other more popular periodicals also began incorporating articles on jazz into their pages during the 1950s and 1960s as well. Beginning in 1955, the weekly *Arts* started putting a jazz section in each of its issues and by 1960—when Lucien Malson regularly contributed to this periodical—editors promoted it to "Friends of jazz" as "the only weekly that serves jazz."[58] By the 1960s, a reader of mainstream magazines and newspapers could explore jazz through a variety of written sources: the critic Michel-Claude Jalard reviewed ten albums in each issue of the music magazine *Diaspason* in a column entitled "Jazz Club";[59] Jacques André wrote a regular column for *Combat*, "Les Lundis du jazz"; and both the cartoonist Siné (who wrote for *Jazz Hot* and *Jazz Magazine* in this period) and the critic Jean Wagner wrote pieces on jazz for the men's magazine *Lui*. Daniel Filipacchi (who had co-founded *Jazz Magazine*) was on this last periodical's editorial board as well.[60] The inclusion of articles and regular columns on jazz in a wide assortment of print media augmented not only jazz fans' knowledge of the music but the general population's awareness of it as well.

Professional critics, with the exception of Panassié's faction, remained remarkably cohesive throughout the early postwar decades. This was largely due to the fact that these men had met through France's tightly knit jazz network before, during, or immediately following the war. In recounting their early involvement in the music, these jazz experts often referred to their early collaboration with one another. In 1961, André Hodeir wrote, "I began to write in student journals during the Occupation and it was during the Occupation that I wrote my first book which was published immediately after the war in 1945. Then, I wrote my first articles for *Jazz Hot*. . . . In 1947, Delaunay asked me to accept the position of Editor in Chief for the review which I continued to fill until 1950."[61] The American musician Kenny Clarke, who spent the greater part of his life after World War II in France, attested to the group's continuity in a 1982 interview where he discussed meeting Charles Delaunay and André Hodeir immediately following the Liberation in 1944 and working with Boris Vian in 1948.[62] In the first several years after the war, the *mafia du jazz* built its foundations on the leadership of men like Delaunay and Hodeir who continued to maintain a decisive presence in French jazz circles for decades.

Only in the late 1960s and early 1970s did a new cohort of younger critics arrive on the jazz scene. This new generation, which included Yves Buin, Michel Le Bris, Guy Kopelowicz, Philippe Carles, and Jean-Louis Comolli, oriented itself almost exclusively around the experimental and avant-garde sounds of free jazz. Perhaps because their aesthetic and political tastes gravitated away from mainstream French society, these younger jazz professionals did not permanently supplant the old guard of critics. Free jazz never enjoyed broad appeal in the United States or in France because of its breakdown of form and rhythmic structure, and the most vocal French supporters of free jazz placed themselves on the far left of the political spectrum, especially in the years following 1968.[63]

The majority of critics were born in the fifteen years between 1925 and 1940 and most had university degrees in classical music or the liberal arts.[64] André Hodeir graduated from the Conservatory in Paris after winning first prize in violin, piano, and harmony; Jean Wagner received his degree in English; Michel Dorigné studied music and in the 1960s was a professor of music history at the Conservatoire National de Romans; and Lucien Malson had studied philosophy as well as the work of cultural anthropologists Ruth Benedict and Margaret Mead.[65] The academic Jedediah Sklower has pointed out that when this "generation of philosophers" took power, with Malson at the head, critics began using a *jazzologie* that linked their work to the intellectual frameworks of the humanities and social sciences interested in cultural and social worlds.[66] Panassié supporter Daniel Janissier wrote an article in 1969 entitled "How to become a jazz critic" where he sarcastically argued, "First of all, it is good to have a degree. One in sociology is appreciated. A doctorate is not indispensable but it is not bad to say that you have one." Because of their educations, many of these critics raised their discussions of jazz above the popular level, incorporating rather highbrow discussions into their articles and books. Janissier saw this as a drawback and he wrote that in order to become a jazz critic, one had to "finally, and this is the most important, get rid of all your sensitivity so that your only filter be cerebral. Smother emotional developments. Be dignified, severe, ironic, cold. And keep your gaze fixed on the blue line, not of the Vosges mountains, but of the cybernetic art to come."[67] For Panassié's allies, this intellectual atmosphere was undesirable; the music they loved best, New Orleans jazz, did not need any academic explanations because listeners automatically felt its energy and rhythms when they heard it played. These supporters of traditional jazz stressed the primacy of emotions and insisted that jazzmen make danceable music. So instead of embracing new innovations in the postwar era, this faction felt threatened by them. As jazz moved further into the avant-garde,

Panassié's relevance and importance to the jazz community steadily disappeared, while this more progressive group of critics gained an unshakable foothold as the music's champion in France.

In writing about postwar France, the historian Philippe Roger has asserted that jazz remained an intellectual music much more than a popular music.[68] The individuals who wrote about jazz and who were the music's most vocal and influential advocates used language and methodologies that some readers from the overall population would certainly find unattractive. Through their work, these jazz writers created an atmosphere for jazz in France that was quite distinct from the one in interwar Paris that had been based on well-attended music halls, cabarets, and dancing. But the same could be said for jazz in the United States as musicians in the decades after the war intentionally guided the music away from general audiences and hummable tunes. French critics were well equipped to comprehend the intentions of these musicians and the trajectory of the music, and were able to cogently explain their understandings of jazz to French readers.

Panassié and his disciples did have some cause to feel threatened by the dominant jazz critics: their influence reached beyond specialized jazz magazines and the mainstream press to government-subsidized positions, especially ones with Radiodiffusion-Télévision Française (RTF). In response to these critics' dominance, the anarchist magazine *Le Monde libertaire* (that had no affiliation with Panassié) published two articles on the *mafia du jazz* in 1964. The writer Jean Claude claimed that "the diffusion of jazz in France has always been circumscribed by a dozen of interchangeable people, four or five of which have quasi-absolute powers. Today, thanks to multiplying means of expression, one finds these individuals everywhere."[69] Claude asserted that these men edited the specialized reviews, wrote the articles on jazz in the conventional press, hosted or produced the radio and television programs, edited record collections, and organized concerts. Certainly the interconnections between these men and their numerous ties to various means of cultural dissemination made them a tightly woven, dominant group within the French jazz community.

A brief description of the professional activities of some of the more prominent members of the *mafia*—Frank Ténot, Daniel Filipacchi, Lucien Malson, Phillipe Adler, Michel Netter, Philippe Koechlin, and Jacques Hess—illustrates their near monopoly on the subject of jazz in the media. Frank Ténot worked for *Jazz Hot* from 1947 until he left to found *Jazz Magazine* with Daniel Filipacchi in 1955. Ténot and Filipacchi's partnership reached beyond the pages of *Jazz Magazine* as they also hosted a jazz program on the radio station Europe numéro 1, and in the 1960s directed the quarterly *Cahiers du Jazz*. In addition, they hosted the radio program *Salut les copains* on Europe numéro 1, which focused on popular yé-yé music for a teenage audience. The critic Lucien Malson began writing for *Jazz Hot* in

1947 and became a member of the magazine's editorial board in 1951. He introduced jazz into the *Que sais-je* series with his 1952 book *Les maîtres du jazz* and published his *Histoire du jazz* with La Table Ronde in 1961. In 1961, he also became the president of the Bureau du Jazz at the RTF where he hosted three weekly programs; in the mid-1960s, he was the editor-in-chief of *Cahiers du Jazz* as well. The critic Philipe Adler hosted a daily show on Radio-Luxembourg with Michel Netter from *Jazz Magazine*; he wrote for over a dozen periodicals, including *L'Express* and *Le Journal musical français*, too. Michel Netter was the jazz specialist for the weekly periodical *Arts* in the mid-1960s, and additionally did work for the RTF and Radio-Luxembourg. Philippe Koechlin worked as the editor in chief of *Jazz Hot* in the mid-1960s while hosting two weekly RTF shows and writing for other periodicals like *Musica* and *Informations et Documents*. Jacques Hess wrote for both *Jazz Hot* (where he had a monthly column in the 1960s and periodicals like *Arts*.[70]

The alliance among these critics was bolstered by their common work for the specialized jazz press as well as their partnerships on outside books and projects. In the early 1960s, for instance, Daniel Filipacchi, Frank Ténot, and Jean Wagner published a book together—*Mais oui, vous comprenez le jazz*—for which Jean-Louis Ginibre wrote the preface.[71] These critics also organized concerts and were therefore responsible in many ways for jazz's exposure in France; their opinions commonly influenced fans, affecting what music they chose to listen to, what records they bought, and what concerts they attended. This was precisely the reason *Le Monde libertaire* published the Jean Claude articles. The editors wanted fans, most of whom were adolescents, to have a chance to decide freely about their aesthetic opinions and thought musicians should have the ability to succeed without the *mafia*'s backing. Claude wrote,

> Under these conditions, how can the jazz musician play his preferred music? How can the simple fan even have access to jazz without passing by them? If you are not a member of the mafia, try to publish an article in *Jazz Hot* or in *Jazz Magazine*. Then try to place a proposal for a show anywhere near the RTF or peripheral stations. Ask the young in a club or at the doors of a concert hall, they will say to you: "Jazz? It's Ténot and Filipacchi." The initiated will be more precise: "It's also Malson" or "In addition, it's Adler."[72]

This situation did not change with time. Instead, these critics became entrenched in their positions of leadership, and some among them retained their influence well into the 1990s. When the journal *Cahiers du jazz* began publishing its second series in 1994, Lucien Malson served as its director, André Clergeat was its secretary, Frank Ténot participated on its three-member editorial board, and Jacques Hess, André Hodeir, Jean-Robert Masson, Jean-Christophe Averty, and Michel-Claude Jalard were members of its twenty-one-member education and lecture committee.[73]

This closely knit unit took the initiative in creating jazz clubs outside of the Hot Club de France that individuals could join regardless of their support for New Orleans, bebop, or other contemporary manifestations of the music like cool or free jazz. Sometimes, these associations were affiliated with the prominent *Jazz Hot* and *Jazz Magazine*. In 1955, the latter founded a new association—the Amis du Jazz (ADJ)—whose goals were "to draw together the ties between sincere fans and musicians. To win to our cause lots of young people wanting to know this music better." Its founders took direct aim at Panassié's Hot Club de France when they asserted, "Too many controversies have clouded the relationships between jazz fans so that for a long time we have not dreamed of an association where all would have the right to prefer any musicians or any style without facing ridicule or exclusion."[74] The rewards of membership with this club were not all that extensive; members received reduced prices at concerts and free entry to the Rose Rouge and 20 percent off of drinks there.[75] Yet by 1960, the ADJ had close to seventy affiliated chapters across France and in overseas departments, and it continued establishing new ones.[76] The group also associated itself with independent clubs in the provinces such as the Jazz Union de Normandie (which included the areas of Rouen, Bayeux, Louviers, and Le Havre) and the Jazz Club du Sud-Est (which included Marseilles, Avignon, Aix, and Montpellier).[77] Each of these smaller organizations arranged a variety of events for its members that included: scheduling concerts, conferences, and dances; providing auditions and rehearsal space for musicians; and showing films. These were all activities that the ADJ endorsed and promoted as well.

Unlike during the 1930s when there was basically only the Hot Club de France, postwar jazz organizations had to contend with multiple competitors. In 1957, *Jazz Magazine* told a reader inquiring about clubs in Paris, "There are several jazz fan associations in Paris: the Hot Club de France, the Hot Club de Paris, the Amis du Jazz, the International Jazz Club, the Jazz Club Français. . . . You see, you have the choice."[78] In addition to these groups, government-sponsored entities like the Jeunesses Musicales also sponsored concerts in Paris and across the rest of the country, while members of the jazz community continued to spread their influence.[79] Supporters established clubs in the provinces, where branches of the Hot Club de France had existed since well before the war and the ADJ continued making its presence felt. In 1963, a group in Toulouse founded another independent organization—the Association Culturelle de Musique du Jazz—which hosted a two-and-a-half-hour gathering every Wednesday where listeners could come and hear jazz as well as discuss the music with critics and club members.[80] The Jazz Club de France was yet another conglomeration of jazz supporters from across the country; its headquarters were in Villiers-le-Bel under the direction of its president Raymond Fonseque but it had just over one hundred affiliated clubs in 1967. In addition to organizing concerts and conferences, and offering professional opportunities for musicians, the Jazz Club de France also established a book and record library for its members.[81]

Champions of French jazz initiated alliances that focused on promoting the music of their own countrymen. In 1960, Roger Guérin started Inter-Jazz which was a "cultural association of French jazz musicians" and, by 1962, its members included a wide range of domestic artists like Claude Luter, Claude Bolling, Guy Lafitte, Michel Hausser, Martial Solal, Michel de Villers, Alix Combelle, and Maxim Saury who played musics extending from New Orleans jazz to the avant-garde. Its principal goal was "to make known French jazz soloists and bands" and in 1962, under the sponsorship of the RTF, Inter-Jazz put together a bimonthly concert series of French musicians at the Théâtre de l'Alliance Française.[82] Inter-Jazz and the RTF worked together beyond this endeavor to promote each other's initiatives, in an effort to broaden the listening audience for the RTF and the general participation in Inter-Jazz.[83]

In 1968, club owner and writer Jean-Claude Albert-Weil set up an organization—the Association pour la Transculture—whose objective was to help French musicians find professional opportunities. It differentiated itself from its predecessors by striving to give prospective club owners advice and guidance about forming jazz nightclubs. Albert-Weil also had goals that included setting up both a *cave* in the Marais quarter where musicians could rehearse and a vacation stage in the small village of Hérault where he hoped to host a summer French jazz festival. The musician Maxim Saury was one of the vice presidents of the Association pour la Transculture and a vocal supporter of its agenda.[84]

Furthermore, critics, musicians, and fans participated in Europe-wide jazz clubs, which gave them increased exposure as members of the international jazz community as well as additional means to promote the music. In May of 1956, the International Jazz Club established a French branch (the IJC-France) to promote an "amicable union" between jazz fans and Hot Clubs in France. The IJC's leaders stated that their goal was "to spread as much as possible the best jazz music, but also to remediate the near-complete isolation in which the majority of provincial clubs find themselves. The Bureau of the IJC-France has decided to help, by all means possible, the Clubs which will support the activities of the association." For an annual fee of 500 francs, each member of the IJC-France gained access to a variety of venues: a forum where jazz fans could establish relationships and exchange information with one another; concerts at the provincial clubs; and a record exchange. Members also received a 10 percent reduction on the subscription rate for the *Bulletin de l'IJC*.[85] To increase their exposure, the IJC-France named the French musician Claude Bolling their honorary president that same year.[86]

At the outset, the group's creators asserted that "the French section of the IJC is . . . a movement completely distinct from the idiotic and inauspicious quarrels about jazz, imposed for too long on its fans. The members of IJC-France, who have the freedom to belong to any other association, will not be subject to any 'doctrine.'"[87] In response to this openness and to the IJC's recognition of Dizzy Gillespie and Stan Kenton as jazz musicians, its communications with *Jazz Hot*, and its sending of "injurious letters and circulars" to Hugues Panassié and his colleagues, the Hot Club de France prohibited any of its clubs to affiliate with the IJC.[88] In the mid-1950s, the "jazz wars" between Panassié's group and the rest of the jazz community were far from over. For Panassié, belonging to any group besides the HCF or reading a French jazz magazine besides the *Bulletin du Hot Club de France* justified exclusion from his organization. The leaders of the IJC-France were not members of the *mafia du jazz* proper but were individuals concerned with propagating jazz's influence in the provinces and moving fans beyond the infighting that had overshadowed much of the French jazz community since the late 1940s.

Over a decade later, in 1967, another international jazz group came into existence: the Fédération Européenne de Jazz (known under its English acronym EJF). Unlike the IJC-France, its program was less focused on national issues, and made a concerted effort to unify the agendas of jazz supporters across Europe. The organization held its first meeting in Warsaw under the auspices of the 10th Polish Jazz Festival in October of 1967. Discussions followed the next week in Czechoslovakia where close to thirty-five delegates from both Eastern and Western Europe participated. In March of that year, twenty representatives had gone to Vienna to form a preparatory committee for the Fédération; this committee had participants from Austria, Belguim, Finland, Great Britain, Hungary, East and West Germany, Yugoslavia, Italy, and Poland. The EJF hoped to bring together festivals, agencies, musicians, and other organizations from across Europe to foster cooperation between them as well as facilitate "the exchange of experience, bands, musicians, groups, critics and organizers, research, records, etc." In addition, it worked on several other agendas: counseling record companies on ways to better expose audiences to jazz; advising radio and television stations in their choice of programming; defending copyright laws; and establishing the EJF Library Center in Brussels to centralize the keeping of records, tapes, films, books, reviews, and photographs from around the world.[89] In May of 1969, Charles Delaunay, Jean-Louis Ginibre, and Simone Ginibre represented France at the group's meeting in Venice. Other delegates also came from countries not represented in 1967: Czechoslovakia, Finland, Denmark, Norway, and Switzerland. At this 1969 meeting, the Austrian Johan Fritz was elected the secretary general, making Vienna the official seat of the EJF, and Charles Delaunay was elected as one of the organization's four vice presidents.[90] The Fédération also created a new quarterly—*Jazz Forum*—that was published in English and included record reviews, news, photographs, and drawings about jazz in Europe. The EJF only printed 3,000 copies of its first issue in 1967 but by 1969 it was printing 15,000 of them.[91] Because of Delaunay's close involvement with the EJF, his magazine *Jazz Hot* became an important link between French readers and the group, and French fans were encouraged to write into the review to express their musical tastes as well as to contribute information about personal record collections to be used by the EJF in assimilating its own collection.[92] Reflecting his intellectual continuity, Delaunay and his colleagues persisted in embracing all forms of jazz, whether traditional, bebop, hard bop, West Coast, modal, Third Stream, free, or fusion. When the music moved into new aesthetic territory, the members of the *mafia du jazz* moved to understand and to promote it.

THE POWER OF THE RADIO

The majority of French jazz lovers first heard the music through sound recordings and in the decades following World War II the radio became an ever more valuable medium for jazz's dissemination in France. In 1945, the French government created Radiodiffusion-Télévision Française (RTF), which held a monopoly over the airwaves in France until 1981. After 1964, this organization went by a new name—the Office de Radiodiffusion-Télévision Française (ORTF)—but its leadership and agenda remained consistent, and no other licensed French radio stations existed to compete with it.[93] From 1945 until 1981, the French government controlled all of the country's radio broadcasts through its state-owned stations. In 1980, there were still only seven of these legal stations, meaning that proportionally France had roughly twenty-five times fewer stations than the United States did.[94] Despite this limited access to the airwaves, radio was the preeminent form of mass media in France in the first decades following World War II. By the mid-1950s there were almost ten million radios in the country and there were also French-language stations outside of France that listeners could tune in to in order to find programs unaffiliated with the French state. By the end of the 1950s, stations in places like Luxembourg, Monaco, the German Saarland, and Andorra all served as important competition for the RTF monopoly, and their programs often incorporated American-style popular music and a nod to the importance of youth culture.[95]

This was especially the case in the early 1960s when technological change—namely, the use of the battery-operated portable transistor radio—made it not only possible, but also less expensive, for more people to listen to the radio stations of their choice.[96] Transistors were imported from the United States in the early 1950s, and by 1960, 70 percent of the radios sold in

France were this type. In 1966, almost half of fifteen- to twenty-year-olds in France had a transistor, while 42 percent owned a record player.[97] Teenage listeners found the portability of these radios especially appealing at a time when the burgeoning youth culture depended on both independence from parental control and the ability to move around freely and autonomously. Adolescents could bring their transistors to both public spaces and private ones—to parks, beaches, restaurants, and cafés as well as into each other's homes.[98] These radios allowed young fans to move their own dials when periodicals like *Jazz Magazine* told them about accessible jazz programs from stations in Algiers, Morocco, Brussels, Monte Carlo, Andorra, Copenhagen, Stockholm, Munich, Luxembourg, Frankfort, Salzburg, and Hamburg, as well as programs on the BBC Service Français and the BBC Service Allemand.[99] Despite the state monopoly on radio in France, listeners did have the option of tuning into shows coming from outside of the nation's borders.

The American government sponsored radio stations across Europe, an effort that began in 1942 with the creation of the Armed Forces Radio Service (AFRS) that after the war continued to send out broadcasts from American bases. This exposed French radio audiences to American programs like *Downbeat*, which spotlighted jazz and to which they otherwise would not have had access. Similarly, the Voice of America (VOA), which dated from 1942 as well, retained a presence in France throughout the postwar era.[100] The British-born Leonard Feather hosted *Jazz Club U.S.A.* in 1952 for the VOA, and then in 1954, the VOA introduced into its lineup a show entitled *Music U.S.A*, which the American Willis Conover began hosting a year later, devoting an hour and a half every day to dance music and jazz.[101] Conover continued to host this VOA program for more than three decades, bringing jazz into people's lives not only in France and other parts of Western Europe but behind the Iron Curtain as well as in Asia, Africa, and the Middle East.[102] Every night at nine o'clock, French listeners could tune into Conover's show.

The success of *Music U.S.A* moved the Voice of America to create an hour-long show—*Panorama U.S.A.*—to air in an earlier time slot. This program presented its audience with short features about American life, people, music, and culture, reinforcing the radio station's use of popular culture to sell "America" abroad.[103] Throughout the 1950s and 1960s, the American government sponsored other jazz programs as well to perpetuate a positive view of the United States; in France the government funded the show *Le jazz en liberté*, which focused on American jazz and aired for over two and a half hours on Saturday afternoons in the mid-1950s.[104] Radio programs were one of the more direct ways French jazz fans were touched by the actions of the American government, improving their opportunities to hear the music.

Beyond these American shows, one of the programs to hit the airwaves after the war was *Pour ceux qui aiment le jazz*, hosted by Daniel Filipacchi and Frank Ténot. Beginning in 1955, these two influential jazz critics hosted this daily broadcast on the commercial station Europe numéro 1 (which was not part of the RTF system and actually began as a pirate station in the Saarland in 1955). The show was inaugurated after Charlie Parker's death on March 12, 1955, when the station editor Maurice Siégal wanted someone to produce a segment on the musician. He asked his friend, twenty-six-year-old Daniel Filipacchi, who was at that time a photographer for *Paris-Match*, to do so. Due to the large amount of fan mail that flowed into the station after the initial broadcast, Europe numéro 1 decided to create a jazz program but hesitated to let the young, little-known Filipacchi be its only host. So the twenty-nine-year-old critic Frank Ténot, who had already been a regular contributor to jazz periodicals by this time, became his partner.[105] Despite what eventually became their lifelong collaboration on the radio, in jazz periodicals, and in books, Filipacchi and Ténot approached both music and life very differently, adding an important degree of comfortable opposition to their show. In 1962, Ténot told an interviewer, "Daniel . . . loves sports cars, movies, skiing, America, and me, I love the bourgeois life, comfort, and staying at home." On the program, they spoke like two "pals" (*copains*), each trying to make the other understand his musical preferences. As the writer for *L'Express* Madeleine Chapsal asserted, "In this way Ténot convinced Filipacchi to listen to Coltrane, who he did not like, while [Ténot] was turned off by 'rock,' Filipacchi's passion." Every night between ten thirty and ten fifty-five the show addressed different subjects: news coming from the United States, works done by musicians passing through Paris, public concerts, contemporary rhythms, European jazz, big bands, New Orleans jazz, and the like. In 1965, Ténot and Filipacchi's fellow members of the jazz cognoscenti, Philippe Adler and Michel Netter (who had their own jazz show, *Place au Jazz*, on Radio-Luxembourg) agreed that the hosts of *Pour ceux qui aiment le jazz* "had certainly succeeded in bringing an immense public to jazz" through their show.

Filipacchi and Ténot went on to host another music program, *Salut les copains*, on Europe numéro 1 that turned its attention to commercialized popular music. The show ran from 1959 until 1969, and during its heyday in the early and mid-1960s reached a much larger audience of teenagers than *Pour ceux qui aiment le jazz* ever did. *Salut les copains* moved away from a concentration on jazz to a focus on yé-yé, a popular genre of music among teenage devotees that was based on the sounds of American rock and roll. The show's success was indicated by the large amount of fan mail it received in its early years: 40,000 letters a week.[106] In 1962, the producers of Filipacchi and Ténot's program introduced a magazine (also called *Salut les copains*) that was dedicated to covering popular music and aimed solely at an adolescent audience. The culture surrounding *Salut les copains* fueled the growth of record sales, concerts, and a sense of teenage identity. The magazine's publishers printed 100,000 copies of the first issue, but for the fourth they printed 600,000.[107] These numbers illustrated the different trajectories that jazz and yé-yé followed in the 1960s. Both music genres counted on young fans as their most numerous and active audience members because teenagers and young adults remained the most likely to buy records and to attend concerts and music festivals. But in the years after World War II, jazz never reached the same widespread general audience or the level of commercial success as rock and roll or yé-yé. Jazz periodicals sold by the tens of thousands while the magazine *Salut les copains* sold by the hundreds of thousands. Fans of *Salut les copains* could buy merchandise (including postcards, cups, and key chains) emblazoned with the show's mascot Chouchou, who wore jeans, a checkered t-shirt, and a shaggy, over-the-eyes Beatles haircut.[108] There was no equivalent to Chouchou for the jazz public, and most jazz professionals and fans would have shunned such open expressions of commercialism, even if they envied yé-yé's general mass appeal.[109]

By the late 1960s, jazz's location within youth culture was displaced by rock and roll and yé-yé as the music's position in French society itself had changed. Eric Drott has observed that this evolution was influenced by several factors. Critics played a crucial role because they had worked to raise jazz's profile among French audiences, and the music came to no longer hold a central position in youth culture but moved from being a popular form of entertainment to being part of an elite subculture.[110] Ever since the advent of bebop, new jazz forms moved further away from having broad-based appeal, as avant-garde music was not a form of popular or mass culture but something that appealed only to a select and privileged few, both in the United States and abroad. The French cohort of critics participated in jazz's evolution in France by giving such avid support to new forms of the music, but their efforts were not all that different from the ones taken by their American counterparts. As the 1960s came to a close, jazz had entered a new phase of development that prized musical innovation above widespread popularity and commercial success.

Within this context, it is perhaps surprising that more funding, not less, went to support jazz programs on French radio as time went on. Despite the competition from shows like *Pour ceux qui aiment le jazz* and the well-loved Filipacchi and Ténot, the RTF maintained a significant and irreplaceable presence on the French airwaves in the postwar period. Going back to the early years following in the war, in 1946, the Services Centraux de la Radiodiffusion Française created four official Divisions: Artistic Programs; Information and News; Technical Services; and Administrative and Financial Services. Music fell under the control of the Artistic Programs Division, which produced the few radio shows sending jazz out over the nation's frequencies in the first decade and a half following the war.[111] During this time, the RTF remained one of the most significant promoters of *all* kinds of music within France, not just jazz. According to one RTF official, André Astoux, by 1965, this organization supported "four national orchestras (279 musicians), three choral societies (120 singers), two choir schools (50 young girls and children), three provincial symphonic orchestras (177 musicians)." In addition, the RTF organized close to four hundred concerts in France each year and more than fifty abroad while also diffusing 14,250 hours of music on the radio each year by the mid-1960s.[112] Yet supporters of jazz had no institutional means by which to lobby to have this music broadcast on a more regular basis until 1961 when the Bureau du Jazz was created within the RTF's Artistic Programs Division. On October 1, 1961, director of artistic services Paul Gilson gave Lucien Malson the job of coordinating all RTF jazz programs.[113] According to Malson in 1962, "To be effective, the jazz policy on the radio must benefit from a certain centralization, that is to say from a service that one can join throughout the day, from a secretary's office capable of responding to mail, of eventually giving information over the telephone to fans, information on concerts and programs."[114] As the magazine *Jazz Hip* asserted, the Bureau du Jazz was created "with the threefold concern of unifying programs, establishing contact with the listener and promoting business policy."[115] For Malson and other members of the RTF system, the Bureau du Jazz's creation was a notable step in centralizing jazz's dissemination within the hexagon as well as a vital means of promoting the music there.

Even in the years before the creation of the Bureau du Jazz, RTF programmers made jazz a consistent facet of postwar radio. In 1950, out of twenty-five weekly music shows, two focused explicitly on jazz: Hugues Panassié's *Jazz Panorama* (which aired every Sunday from six o'clock until six twenty-five in the evening) and Charles Delaunay's *Jazz d'hier et d'aujourdhui* (which was broadcast every Friday night from ten thirty until eleven).[116] By 1954, the RTF-sponsored station Paris-Inter included five jazz programs among its twenty popular or "variety" music shows: André Francis' *Magazine du jazz*, Sim Copans' *Panorama du jazz américain* and *Jazz en liberté*, Gédovius' *Au rendez-vous des jazzmen*, and Jack Diéval's *Jazz aux Champs Elysées*.[117] In 1955, *Jazz Magazine* commended the RTF for the high quality of its jazz programs, writing "if Radiodiffusion Française does not give enough time to jazz programs, it satisfies numerous fans by the quality of its programs."[118] Although the RTF consistently included jazz shows in its postwar lineup, the programs themselves frequently changed. In 1958, Jack Dieval and Sim Copans continued to host their shows *Jazz aux Champs-Elysées* and *Jazz en liberté* but André Francis' show had been changed to *Fortune du jazz* and Sim Copans hosted another show, *Regards sur la musique américaine*, which did not focus on jazz explicitly but rather on American music in general; in 1958, only three of Paris-Inter's programs focused solely on jazz, a significant reduction from 1954.[119] In 1959, André Francis added another show to his radio lineup on Paris Inter-France I: *Soirées de jazz* where he, Michel Netter, and Jean-Louis Ginibre transmitted "important jazz concerts of the year" to their listeners. In 1959, these concerts included ones by Kid Ory, Dizzy Gillespie, the Modern Jazz Quartet, the Jazz Messengers, Duke Ellington, and the Jazz at the Philharmonic (JATP), totaling sixteen in all.[120]

Other RTF stations also produced jazz shows in this period. Beginning in 1954, André Francis hosted *Rendez-vous avec le jazz* with the assistance of André Clergeat and Henri Hubert on France IV (also known as la Modulation de Fréquence or MF) every Saturday evening where they presented a diverse assortment of jazz from around the globe.[121] In 1959, Hugues Panassié was still hosting *Jazz Panorama* on France II every Tuesday as well.[122] Regional stations also took a hand in promoting jazz in their broadcasts. Beginning in the late 1950s, the Jazz-Club du Sud-Est produced *Fenêtre sur le jazz* out of the Marseille-Provence station every Friday evening and by the mid-1960s, twelve regional stations hosted at least one weekly jazz program.[123]

Not all shows with the word "jazz" in their titles focused exclusively on this music. *Jazz aux Champs-Elysées*, created by Jack Dieval and Louis Rey, hosted a public concert of jazz and variety music each month in a different European city like Paris, Helsinki, Geneva, Lugano, Stockholm, Badenbaden, Brussels, or Munich, which was then transmitted throughout Europe on different national and local radio stations.[124] Jazz was part of these concerts but other types of popular music also made their way into *Jazz aux Champs-Elysées* shows. The same went for Hugues Panassié's *Jazz Panorama*, which often focused on blues artists as well as jazz musicians. Other shows like Sim Copans' *Negro Spirituals et Gospel Songs* of the mid-1960s were hosted by jazz critics, listened to by jazz fans, and endorsed by French jazz periodicals but focused on other forms of African-American music. Significantly, radio stations did not always draw a clear line between jazz and other American, especially African-American, music.

Lucien Malson's involvement with RTF programming began in the late 1950s when he started hosting his own shows. By 1960, he had been the host of two shows on France I: *La Jeunesse et le jazz* and *Visages du jazz*, the latter of which the RTF's Comité des Variétés gave a "favorable opinion" in 1960.[125] After the RTF placed him at the head of its Bureau du Jazz, the music received more state-sponsored air time, expanding *Jazz dans la nuit* from a show without a regular spot on the daily schedule (it had appeared periodically at ten fifty at night) into a daily program on France I, and reorganizing France IV's afternoon shows under the general title *Le Club du Jazz*. The RTF also divided France IV's program *Jazz pour tous* into daily shows with different hosts, the same way it had organized *Jazz dans la nuit* from the beginning, adding to the variety and scope of the series.[126]

Malson's leadership at the Bureau du Jazz resulted in the brief cancellation of Hugues Panassié's sixteen-year-old show *Jazz Panorama* in 1963 and 1964.[127] Panassié had owned a certain influence within the RTF until the early 1960s. In 1957, he had been the only jazz representative asked to be a member of the RTF Commission that made decisions on musical programming; *Jazz Hot* directly protested this nomination and in the ensuing years Panassié saw his influence within the RTF structure wane.[128] The Minister of Information, Alain Peyrefitte, wrote Panassié a letter in October of 1963 explaining why his show had been removed from the RTF's lineup after such a long tenure, claiming that "variety music, that which the public at large and the press wrongly calls 'jazz,' did not have a place on the RTF-Haute Fidélité station. The true jazz programs will therefore be continued on RTF-Haute Fidélité." Unlike Panassié, Peyrefitte classified "true jazz" as the music played by Duke Ellington *and* Miles Davis and he excluded Panassié from French radio for denying this.[129] Yet due to Pannassié's protests, the show was reintroduced on France-Inter six months later (on May 6, 1964) as part of the *Jazz dans la nuit* series and featured in its lineup musicians like Willie "the Lion" Smith, Louis Armstrong, Duke Ellington, Sonny Boy Williamson, and Chuck Berry, some of whom—like Williamson and Berry—were better characterized as bluesmen.[130]

As the 1960s evolved, so did the RTF's jazz programming. The *Jazz dans la nuit* series continued basically unchanged while other new shows were introduced. By 1964, France IV (RTF–Haute Fidélité) had replaced *Le Club du Jazz* with *Jazz, sixième continent musical*, which included a Sunday show by Malson himself. Malson also continued to host the Saturday show of *Jazz dans la nuit* and cohosted another France IV program on Tuesdays with André Francis, *Les mardis de l'académie du jazz*.[131] In 1965, he hosted France-Musique's *Les Classiques du Jazz* with André Francis and the station's *Visages du jazz*, as well as France-Culture's *Connaitre le jazz*.[132] By 1965, the national RTF stations (including France-Musique, France-Inter, and France-Culture) produced twelve different jazz programs of which one, André Francis' *Les nouveautés du jazz*, aired each weekday.[133]

The RTF not only took a large part in sending jazz out to the nation's radio listeners, but the organization also participated in organizing concerts which it then broadcast over its stations. To promote jazz across France and encourage nonprofessional involvement in the music, in 1960, the RTF organized a nationwide *Grand Tournoi* open to all amateur jazz bands. The final concert was transmitted on the program *Jazz dans la nuit* and five awards were given to the best of these amateurs: the best band received 1,000 NF, the runner up 500 NF, and third place 250 NF, while the three best soloists also received 250 NF each.[134] Ventures like this one continued throughout the 1960s, often conflating with initiatives sponsored by the Jeunesses Musicales de France, which also promoted tours and competitions for young amateur jazzmen to encourage their involvement in the music.

Jazz concerts remained a central fixture of the Bureau de Jazz's activities in the 1960s. In 1962, the RTF gave Lucien Malson a budget of 20,000 NF (out of a total budget of 41,675 NF) to promote four jazz concerts as part of the second Paris Biennial. The event lasted for thirty-eight days between September 28 and November 5 and also included poetry, *musique légère*, and contemporary music on its agenda. Paris-Inter recorded the jazz concerts and broadcast them to audiences across France.[135] The Bureau du Jazz remained committed to putting such concerts on the air and for a 1961 issue of the magazine *Arts*, Lucien Malson wrote, "France has reserved, on Sunday afternoons, an hour each week where French and foreign recitals, largely open to the public, will be retransmitted. It goes without saying that for ten years, since the théâtre Edouard-VII's *Jazz Parades*, a far-reaching venture of this sort has not been tried."[136] Two years later, he claimed that the RTF had become "the principal organizer of jazz concerts and close to the only organization that works in the moral favor of French musicians."[137] Beginning in 1960, the Jazz Club Français and its regional affiliate the Hot Club Normand had sponsored a Festival International de Jazz in Rouen. By the third such Festival in 1962, the RTF took a sizeable role in promoting the occasion by sending the critic André Francis as correspondent and recording and broadcasting the Festival's events through both radio and television.[138] In 1962 alone, the RTF "organized, supported, or retransmitted 20 concerts by French musicians and 26 concerts by American musicians that sometimes also included French participation."[139] Throughout the decade, the RTF sponsored an array of concerts, including ones by Americans such as Louis Armstrong, Ray Charles, Count Basie, and Errol Garner that were in addition to those by French artists Guy Lafitte, Jean-Luc Ponty, Martial Solal, Daniel Humair, Jef Gilson, and the band the Double Six.[140]

Beginning with Malson's tenure as head of the Bureau de Jazz, the RTF also took a role in supporting the Festival d'Antibes which took place every summer in the small Mediterranean town of Antibes-Juan-les-Pins. The festival was inaugurated in 1960 largely out of tribute to the town's famous seasonal African-American resident of the 1950s, Sidney Bechet, who helped make Antibes famous for jazz before his death in 1959.[141] By the second Festival d'Antibes in 1961, the RTF sent André Francis as its own correspondent to the event and agreed to broadcast its concerts by both radio and television for a fee of 50,000 NF.[142] The following year, the RTF increased its involvement in the festival and became coorganizer of the event with the town of Antibes. Instead of requesting a broadcasting fee, the RTF actually *spent* money promoting the concerts, even paying the airfare for the almost forty musicians coming from the United States. In return, these musicians were also asked to give concerts outside of the Festival d'Antibes format in Paris, Marseille, Bordeaux, and Raule, whose music was then sent out over RTF airwaves.[143]

MAKING THE MUSIC HEARD

The efforts and actions of the RTF exposed important numbers of French fans to jazz but other actors also took part in making the music heard. Corporate involvement in promoting recorded music cannot be discounted in this context. Record companies—both American and French ones—made jazz records available in France and also largely determined which artists became well known through their publishing decisions and marketing promotions, although no jazz records sold on the same scale as variety or yé-yé music. It took close to five years after the end of the war for jazz records to appear in consequential amounts in France. The magazine *Jazz Informations* noted that "even in 1947, only 75 jazz records were published, of which 30 hardly showed any 'jazz' value." But by 1949, the magazine could report that "certain American labels" had recently begun publishing their records in France, that "new specialized French labels" had been created, and that the number of jazz records sold each year had continued to increase.[144] By 1960, more than three hundred jazz records appeared annually in France and one hundred different American labels and close to twenty French ones published these releases.[145] That year, Lucien Malson asked the twelve largest publishers of jazz records in France the percentage of "jazz" they sold in relation to their overall sales. The numbers these companies gave Malson were significantly inflated by the fact that they included rock and roll in the same category as jazz. Nonetheless, on average, they reported that "jazz" records constituted 20 percent of their sales. Malson noted that a single song could expand a company's business, observing that Sidney Bechet's "Petite Fleur" sold 400,000 copies in one year, impressively enlarging Vogue's "jazz" sales.[146] Two years later, in 1962, Malson returned to the question of record sales, reporting that "evolutionary jazz, folkloric jazz, and popular jazz—good or bad—the three of them represent 35% of sales [for record companies]."[147]

The greater availability of jazz records was encouraging news for fans who depended so heavily on them to fill their musical needs. Unfortunately for these listeners, the delay between American and European releases of the same record could be considerable. As a result, businesses sought new ways to shorten this amount of time and to increase European record sales. Early in 1960, the American Jack Lewanke created a production and distribution company called Interdisc whose goal was "to sell in Europe the best American jazz records the same week they appeared in the United States."[148] Throughout the 1950s and 1960s, record companies promoted jazz songs and artists in France by emphasizing their popularity in the United States. For instance, in 1959, Versailles promoted an Ahmad Jamal record as "actually the best selling jazz record in the United States."[149] Consequently, the closer a record company could publish an LP to its American debut, the better it sold.

Within five years of the end of the war, observers were already defining the jazz fan through his record collection. In 1949, one commentator asked, not without humor,

> Do you know what we call a HOT-FAN? It is ordinarily a young, nice person, all the same filled with good qualities, but who possesses an incurable vice: collecting jazz records. All his resources are used for this one goal. It is there that he finds his only reason for living. All of his money (and that of his family) goes to the record store. Some smoke opium, others drink; him, he buys records, not some, but all (all the good ones).[150]

Clearly, recorded music was an essential means by which French listeners explored jazz; the more records that were made available to them, the greater their exposure to the music, and the larger the recording industry's profits.

Jazz devotees relied on the record both to augment their knowledge of jazz and to hear the music played. Yet, especially in Paris, these fans did have the opportunity to listen to live music as well. Dating from Dizzy Gillespie's 1948 initial Parisian performance, jazz artists made regular appearances on the concert stage in France. Americans and Frenchmen alike played regularly in places like the Salle Pleyel, the Olympia, and the Théâtre des Champs-Élysées and American concert promoters brought jazz to Europe beginning in the early 1950s.[151] Norman Granz's Jazz at the Philharmonic (JATP) series was a constant fixture of the jazz scene each year from 1952 until 1967.[152] Moreover, American artists participated in French festivals like the one held annually in Antibes-Juan-les-Pins or in the performances promoted by Radiodiffusion Télévision Française, which took place not only in Paris but also in the provinces.[153] Other events brought live music to French audiences, such as the Salon du Jazz which took place three times between 1950 and 1954, showcasing American artists like Sidney Bechet and Louis Armstrong but also French ones including Django Reinhardt, Alix Combelle, and Hubert Rostaing.[154] Furthermore, French fans had the chance to hear live jazz not only in these organized concert settings but also in the smaller more intimate environments of the Parisian *caves*.

In the first five years following the war, *caves*, which included jazz in their entertainment repertoires, began springing up in Paris, especially in the Latin Quarter. According to the critic Henri Renaud, "Immediately after the Second World War, the most visible jazz clubs were all situated in two arrondissements: the fifth and the sixth. And all were *caves*."[155] In 1950, Boris Vian wrote in his *Manuel de Saint-Germain-des-Près* that the area had "become the principal French production center [of jazz]."[156] One of the most famous places where jazz could be heard, the Club Saint-Germain-des-Près, opened in 1948 and continued to be fashionable among the existentialist crowd as well as jazz lovers far into the 1960s. By 1950, Paris was similarly home to the Tabou (which had opened before the Club Saint-Germain-des-Près in 1947), the short-lived Mephisto, and the Vieux Colombier (which opened in 1948).[157] According to Vian, listeners at the Tabou could hear "black American musicians" who were in Paris like Charlie Parker, Max Roach, Kenny Clarke, and Coleman Hawkins; the Mephisto promoted jazz as well as other musics—like tangos and rumbas—in its lineup; and the Vieux Columbier largely depended on the New Orleans sound of the French clarinetist Claude Luter. Vian went so far as to call Luter "the backbone" of this last club, but the managers of the Vieux Columbier also presented the bands of musicians like the Americans Don Byas and Inez Cavanaugh, who had moved to France in 1946.[158] In 1952, the Métro-Jazz opened on the rue Saint-Julien-le-Pauvre, devoting its musical lineup exclusively to jazz.[159] By 1957, *Jazz Magazine* acknowledged several other Parisian locations where jazz fans could find their music played—the Bidule, the Riverside, the Chat qui pêche, the Caméléon, the Caveau de la Huchette, the Trois Mailletz, and the Kentucky—all of which were in the Latin Quarter. The cost of going to see jazz musicians perform at these places differed widely from club to club. The least costly, the Bidule, had no door charge and the cost of drinks started at 80 francs; the most expensive, the Club Saint-Germain-des-Près, required a membership card costing 500 francs for two people for three months and sold drinks from 400 francs at the bar and 600 francs at the tables. The rest of these *caves* charged somewhere in between the Bidule and the Club Saint-Germain-des-Près: the Riverside and the Chat qui pêche both charged no entry fee and drinks cost 250 francs and higher.[160] Some of these places were known to cater to specific jazz styles. In 1957, Lucien Malson claimed that "modern jazz has its temple at the Club Saint-Germain; traditional jazz, at the Vieux Colombier," while listeners found "very phlegmatic coolmen at the Caméléon."[161] The Huchette depended on the music of the French clarinetist Maxim Saury who performed at this club for twelve years between 1954 and 1966.[162] Overall, New Orleans jazz was more popular than modern forms of jazz at these clubs, a situation that ended up limiting the professional opportunities of some musicians.[163]

The patrons who went to these clubs were often associated with the postwar existentialist crowd, the most famous of whom were Jean-Paul Sartre and Simone de Beauvoir. These intellectuals connected the racism existent in the United Sates and in francophone Africa to the existentialist ideas of spiritual alienation and isolation.[164] Some of the singers—like Juliet Gréco or Boris Vian—injected politics and elements of contemporary philosophy into their work. Popular songs heard in these Left Bank venues, whether they belonged to the genre of jazz or not, were often therefore infused with an aura of intellectual respectability.[165] With close to a dozen *caves* where listeners could go to hear both American and French musicians perform on a regular basis, the Parisian jazz scene thrived during these postwar years, giving enthusiasts with pocket money to spare the opportunity to hear a wide assortment of sounds, or perhaps even to be exposed to some of the latest philosophical ideas and antiracist politics. A few among them might have even rubbed shoulders with well-known intellectuals and musicians.

Despite the intractable differences within the professional jazz community over the "true" form of the music, jazz became an important and well-supported component of French postwar culture. New fan-based organizations, largely modeled on the format developed by the Hot Club de France in the 1930s, continued to appear on the scene, and gave young fans a place where they could listen to jazz, become better educated about the music, meet like-minded people, and find out about live performances. Technology allowed for jazz's further dissemination, and enthusiasts increasingly relied on transistor radios to tune into an array of jazz programs broadcast by French state-owned radio and even by stations beyond French national borders. Though tightly controlled by a professional circle of well-educated and well-connected critics, information about jazz and opportunities to hear the music were abundant. To learn more about jazz and jazz musicians, readers had numerous specialized periodicals from which to choose, and articles and columns about jazz appeared regularly in the popular press. To hear the music live, fans could attend concerts and festivals whether they were in the provinces or in the capital, and if they were in Paris, and were able to afford the expense, could hear the music live at the *caves* that dotted Saint-Germain-des-Près. This rather entrenched infrastructure that defined and provided organization to the jazz community ensured that the music retained its presence in French life following the Second World War.

NOTES

1. Bernard Gendron, *Between Montmartre and the Mudd Club: Popular Music and the Avant-Garde* (Chicago: University of Chicago Press, 2002), 104.

2. Forms of minstrelsy originated in nineteenth-century America and evoked negative stereotypes about blackness more often than they reflected any type of authentic music cultivated by African-American artists, but minstrelsy nonetheless reached a general audience in the United States as well as in Europe well into the twentieth century. For a thorough examination of the racialized ideology historically characteristic of blackface minstrelsy in the United States see Eric Lott, *Love and Theft: Blackface Minstrelsy and the American Working Class* (New York: Oxford University Press, 1993). Minstrelsy was a more popular form in entertainment in Great Britain than in France, but French audiences were certainly aware of minstrel songs.

3. The international black cultural movement known as *négritude* had a significant place in France as well, positively influencing French views of "black" cultures in Europe, Africa, and the Americas. See Dominic Thomas, *Black France: Colonialism, Immigration, and Transnationalism* (Bloomington: Indiana University Press, 2007); Brent Hayes Edwards, *The Practice*

of Diaspora: Literature, Translation, and the Rise of Black Internationalism (Cambridge, MA: Harvard University Press, 2003); and Lilyan Kesteloot, *Black Writers in French: a Literary History of Negritude*, trans. Ellen Conroy Kennedy (Philadelphia: Temple University Press, 1974). Jean-Paul Sartre communicated his own support of *négritude* after World War II in "Black Orpheus," *"What is Literature?" and Other Essays*, trans. John MarCombie (Cambridge: 1988), 291–330 and in "Présence noire," *Présence Africain* 1 (1947), 44–46. African Americans had a notable presence in France from World War I forward, further influencing French perceptions of them while simultaneously impacting French culture. See Tyler Stovall, *Paris Noire: African Americans in the City of Light* (New York: Houghton Mifflin Company, 1996); Michel Fabre, *From Harlem to Paris: Black American Writers in France, 1940–1980* (Urbana: University of Illinois Press, 1991); Ursula Broschke, *Paris without Regret: James Baldwin, Kenny Clarke, Chester Hines, and Donald Byrd* (Iowa City: University of Iowa Press, 1986); Bill Moody, *The Jazz Exiles: American Musicians Abroad* (Reno: University of Nevada Press, 1993); and James Campbell, *Exiled in Paris: Richard Wright, James Baldwin, Samuel Becket, and Others on the Left Bank* (Berkeley: University of California Press, 2003).

4. Matthew F. Jordan, *Le Jazz: Jazz and French Cultural Identity* (Urbana: University of Illinois Press, 2010), 45–67. Charles Rearick also refers to negative connotations associated with "*les dancings*" in *The French in Love and War: Popular Culture in the Era of the World Wars* (New Haven, CT: Yale University Press, 1997), 91.

5. Jeremy F. Lane, *Jazz and Machine-Age Imperialism: Music, "Race," and Intellectuals in France, 1918–1945* (Ann Arbor: University of Michigan Press, 2013), 54.

6. Jordon, 54.

7. Jeffrey H. Jackson, *Making Jazz French: Music and Modern Life in Interwar Paris* (Durham, NC: Duke University Press, 2003), 123–29.

8. Dirats' first name is sometimes spelled "Elwyn" and other times "Edwin." See Tournès 1999, 40; and Jackson, 160–61.

9. Ludovic Tournès, *New Orleans sur Seine: Histoire du jazz en France* (Paris: Fayard, 1999), 35–36.

10. Lane, 90–91; and Hugues Panassié, *Monsieur Jazz: Entretiens avec Pierre Casalta* (Paris: Stock, 1975), 130–31.

11. Ludovic Tournès, "Les hot clubs: des sociétés savantes au service de la diffusion du jazz," *Cahier du GRHIS* 6 (1997), 105–120; and Michel Dorigné, *Jazz 2* (Paris: L'Ecole des loisirs, 1970), 176.

12. Lane, 100, 102.

13. Tournès, 50–51.

14. Jackson, 135.

15. Ibid., 4–6.

16. Tournès, 83.

17. Michael H. Kater, *Different Drummers: Jazz in the Culture of Nazi Germany* (New York: Oxford University Press, 1992), 178.

18. Jordan, 191.

19. Tournès, 60–63.

20. Gérard Régnier, *Jazz et société sous l'Occupation* (Paris: L'Harmattan, 2009).

21. Tournès, 82. The Propaganda Staeffel was under the control of Goebbels in Berlin. See Jordan, 190. For more on how American names of songs and musicians were changed so that they could be played in Occupied France, see Jean-Claude Loiseau, *Les Zazous* (Paris: Sagittaire, 1977); and Jacques Chesnel, *Le Jazz en quarantine (1940–1946)* (Cherbourg: Éditions Isoète, 1994).

22. Jordan, 185–91; Jean-Dominique Brierre, *Le jazz français de 1900 à aujourd'hui* (Paris: Éditions Hors Collection, 2000), 56; and Sophie B. Roberts, "A Case for Dissidence in Occupied Paris: The Zazous, Youth Dissidence and the Yellow Star Campaign in Occupied Paris (1942)," *French History*, vol. 24, no. 1 (22 January 2010), 88.

23. Jordan, 189. Hess claimed that the "Za zou za zou" line was inspired by Cab Calloway's "Zah Zuh Zaz" song from 1934.

24. Jon Savage, *Teenage: The Creation of Youth Culture* (New York: Viking, 2007), 386–87. Jordan also includes a number of contemporary cartoons of Zazous. See pages 196–230.

25. Larry Portis has discussed how the Zazous' rejection of the National Revolution put them in danger. In the summer of 1942, in response to the ordinance requiring Jews to wear yellow stars, some of the Zazous publicly wore these stars with the words "Swing," "Zazou," or "Swing 42" written on them. By participating in the yellow star campaign, Zazous drew the further attention of the authorities. Going forward, the French police raided Parisian cafés, publically shaved Zazous' heads, and sent some of them into the countryside to work or even to Drancy. After the *Service du Travail Obligatoire* was created in 1943, Zazous risked being picked up in public places and sent to labor camps. Larry Portis, *French Frenzies: A Social History of Popular Music in France* (College Station, TX: Virtualbookworm.com Publishing, 2004), 100–105.

26. Roberts, 91.

27. The *Jeunesse Populaire Français* was the youth arm of the fascist *Parti Populaire Français* founded by Jacques Doriot and the French Scouts was a protomilitary youth group. The *JPF*'s official slogan was "Work, strength, joy" and the organization was meant to represent *true* French youth. The writer Yves Ranc described "swing" as being the opposite of the Vichy slogan "Work—Family—Fatherland" (*Travail—Famille—Patrie*). See Yves Ranc, "Swing ou pas swing," *L'Oeuvre* (March 4, 1942), 4. For more on this, see Jordan, 204–9. In Germany during the war, listening to jazz "symbolized a courageous distance from Nazi ideology and any 'German' values that were used and distorted by National Socialism. In postwar Germany, jazz took on an important meaning as it symbolized liberation from the Nazi regime." See Ursel Schlicht, "'Better a Jazz Album than Lipstick' (*Lieber Jazzplatte als Lippenstift*): The 1956 *Jazz Podium* Series Reveals Images of Jazz in Gender in Postwar Germany," *Big Ears: Listening for Gender in Jazz Studies*, eds. Nichole T. Rustin and Sherrie Tucker (Durham, NC: Duke University Press, 2008), 293.

28. Lane, 129; and Andy Fry, *Paris Blues: African American Music and French Popular Culture, 1920–1960* (Chicago: University of Chicago Press, 2014), 199–200.

29. Tournès, 87.

30. The network was code-named "Cart" in reference to the jazzman Benny Carter. See Anne Legrand, *Charles Delaunay et le jazz en France dans les années 30 et 40* (Paris: Éditions du Layeur, 2009), 136–46. For more on Delaunay's actions in the Resistance see Lane, 128; and Charles Delaunay, *Delaunay's Dilemma: De la peinture au jazz* (Mâcon: Éditions W., 1985), 154.

31. Tournès, 73. Other Hot Club members in the Resistance were Jacques Bureau and the sisters Germaine and Annette Tambour. All three, as well as Delaunay, were arrested in 1943. The sisters died after being deported and Bureau remained in prison until the Liberation. Delaunay successfully established an alibi and was released after only a month in prison, but did not feel safe in Paris and left the city in early 1944, not returning until the Germans were defeated.

32. Henry Rousso, *The Vichy Syndrome: History and Memory in France*, trans. Arthur Goldhammer (Cambridge, MA: Harvard University Press, 1994).

33. See Fry, "Chapter 4: 'That Gypsy in France:' Django Reinhart's Occupation Blouze," 172–219. Philippe Burrin coined this term *accommodation* in his book *Living with Defeat: France under the German Occupation, 1940–1944)*, trans. Janet Lloyd (London: Arnold, 1996).

34. Jordan uses this term *judeo-nègre-américain* hybrid to describe conceptions of jazz in this era.

35. John Fordham, *Jazz* (New York: Dorling Kindersley, 1993), 30.

36. Ted Gioia, *The History of Jazz*, 2nd ed. (New York: Oxford University Press, 2011), 198.

37. Claude Baro: "Le jazz et la société française," *Review internationale de musique française* 8 (June 1982), 79.

38. 1947 seems to be the year that Panassié made his pronouncements of bebop yet in 1948 he wrote an article for *Paris-Presse* where he asserted that "saxophonist Charlie Parker, trum-

pet player Howard McGhee, pianist Bud Powell have often known how to make jazz of first quality in this new framework." Hugues Panassié, "Le Jazz symphonique: une trahison le Bebop: un art en enfance," *Paris-Press* (22–23 February 1948), 2. Although Panassié did not seem to be a great advocate of bebop here, he respected it and its defenders. For another description of this schism see Michel Perrin, "Le jazz," *Les Nouvelles Litteraires* (1 April 1965), 12.

39. For more on the New Orleans revival in the United States and France, see Bruce Boyd Raeburn, *New Orleans Style and the Writing of American Jazz History* (Ann Arbor: University of Michigan Press, 2009) and Matthew F. Jordan, "The French Connection: Mythologies of *La Nouvelle Orléans* in French Discourse on Jazz," *European Journal of Cultural Studies* 14 (October 2011), 507–525.

40. Michel Dorigné, *Jazz 2* (Paris: L'Ecole des loisirs, 1970), no. 184. A fight between supporters of "traditional" New Orleans jazz and fans of swing happened in the late 1930s and early 1940s in the United States. In the American context, this debate "established jazz historiography as an oppositional discourse that valued authenticity over mainstream commercial appeal; the so-called moldy-figs asserted that New Orleans jazz was the only 'real' jazz." Lara Pellegrinelli, "Separated at 'Birth': Singing and the History of Jazz," *Big Ears: Listening for Gender in Jazz Studies*, eds. Nichole T. Rustin and Sherrie Tucker (Durham, NC: Duke University Press, 2008), 41.

41. Tournès, "Les hot clubs," 107–17.

42. "Éditorial," *Le Bulletin du Hot Club de France* 1 (1945), 1.

43. Ursel Schlicht, "'Better a Jazz Album than Lipstick' (*Lieber Jazzplatte als Lippenstift*): The 1956 *Jazz Podium* Series Reveals Images of Jazz and Gender in Postwar Germany," *Big Ears: Listening for Gender in Jazz Studies*, eds. Nichole T. Tustin and Sherrie Tucker (Durham, NC: Duke University Press, 2008), 294–5. Also see Robert von Zahn's edited work, *Jazz in Nordrhein-Westfalen seit 1946* (Köln, Germany: Emmons, 1999).

44. Claude Baro, "Le jazz et la société française," *Review internationale de musique française* 8 (June 1982), 72.

45. Tournès, "Les hot clubs," 111.

46. Lucien Malson, "Panassié méglomane," *La Revue du jazz*, 2nd series, no. 1 (July 1952), 5–6.

47. Jacques B. Hess, "Panassié: archéologue où vieillard?" *La Revue du jazz*, 2nd series, no. 1 (July 1952), 7.

48. Willy Schiller, "La guerre des jazz gagne la France," *France Soir* (22–23 February 1948), 1. See Claude Baro, "Le jazz et la société française," *Review internationale de musique française*, no. 8 (June 1982), 75.

49. Jacques Pescheux, "Un scandale," *Bulletin du Hot Club de France* no. 130 (September 1963), 25.

50. Bernard Gendron, *Between Montmartre and the Mudd Club: Popular Music and the Avant-Garde* (Chicago: University of Chicago Press, 2002), 121–55.

51. Frank Ténot, *Jazz* (Paris: Armand et Georges Israël, 1983), 19.

52. A small group of critics did remain loyal to him. In 1963, these "loyalists" still filled the executive positions at the HCF: Jacques Morgantini (vice-president), Pierre Artis (secretary), Madeleine Gautier (treasurer), Jackline Martin (assistant treasurer), André Doutart and Jean-Marie Masse (advisors). Panassié, of course, remained the president of this organization. See "Le HCF communique," *Bulletin du Hot Club de France* no. 124 (January 1963), 40.

53. "Le jazz en France," *L'Express* (21 May 1959), 36; Jacques Lahitte, "Jazz-News: Situation de la presse spécialisée," *Arts* no. 502 (9–15 February 1955), 4; "Avis," *Jazz [Hip]* no. 22 (rentrée 1960), 4; and Claude Léon, "La critique (est aisée)," *Jazz Hot* no. 152 (March 1960), 27.

54. Aris Destombes, "Un manifeste d'Aris," *Jazz Hot* no. 179 (September 1962), 10.

55. Michel Dorigné, *Jazz, culture et société* (Paris: Éditions Ouvrières, 1967), 281.

56. "Le jazz en France," *L'Express* (21 May 1959), 36; Jacques Lahitte, "Jazz-News"; and "Avis," *Jazz [Hip]* 22 (rentrée 1960), 4.

57. "Le Jazz," *Le Point* no. XL (January 1952).

58. *Arts* (July 1960).

59. Lahitte, and see the first issue where this column was included, Michel-Claude Jalard, "Le Jazz," *Diaspason* no. 53 (November 1960), 27.

60. See for example *Lui* no. 13 (January 1965) and *Lui* no. 23 (November 1965). On Filipacchi's involvement see "Le prix de l'humair lui," *Lui* no. 16 (April 1965), 23.

61. André Hodeir, "Je n'appartiens pas 'troisième courant,'" *Jazz Hot* no. 162 (February 1961), 13.

62. Michael Haggerty, *A Flower for Kenny* (unpublished manuscript, 1985), 8–10.

63. Eric Drott, *Music and the Elusive Revolution: Cultural Politics and Political Culture in France, 1968–1981* (Berkeley: University of California Press, 2011), 119.

64. Frank Ténot was born in 1925, Lucien Malson in 1926, Philippe Koechlin in 1938, and Philippe Adler in 1937.

65. See Jean Wagner, *Le Guide du jazz* (Paris: Syros, 1986); Michel Dorigné, *Jazz 2* (Paris: L'Ecole des loisirs, 1970); Tournès, *New Orleans sur Seine: Histoire du jazz en France* (Paris: Fayard, 1999), 114–15; and Jeremy F. Lane, *Jazz and Machine-Age Imperialism: Music, "Race," and Intellectuals in France, 1918–1945* (Ann Arbor: University of Michigan Press, 2013), 183.

66. Jedediah Sklower, *Free Jazz, la catastrophe féconde: Une histoire du monde éclaté du jazz en France (1960–1982)* (Paris: L'Harmattan, 2006), 20.

67. Daniel Janissier, "Comment devenir critique de jazz," *Bulletin du Hot Club de France* 184 (January 1969), 8.

68. Philippe Roger, *Rêves et cauchemare américains: les Etats-Unis au miroir de l'opinion publique française (1945–1953)* (Villeneuve d'Ascq: Presses Universitaires du Septentrion, 1996), 220.

69. Jean Claude, "Les maffias," *Le Monde libertaire* no. 103 (July 1964).

70. See "Jazz," *Informations et Documents* 230 (1 August 1966), 15, 17, 27; and Jean Claude, "Les maffias," *Le Monde libertaire* 103 (July 1964). These critics of course wrote for other magazines and journals as well. For instance, in 1958, Frank Ténot contributed several articles on jazz to the medical journal *Aesculape* (see its May 1958 issue); and beginning in the late 1950s, Ténot and Filipacchi put together a page on jazz every week for the daily paper *Paris Journal*.

71. Jean Wagner, Frank Ténot, and Daniel Filipacchi, *Mais oui, vous comprenez le jazz* (Bruxelles: Éditions du jour, 1964). For another example of this type of collaboration, also see Raymond Mouly, *Sidney Bechet, notre ami* (Paris: La Table Ronde, 1959) that is dedicated to Daniel Filipacchi and Frank Ténot.

72. Jean Claude, "Les maffias," *Le Monde libertaire* 103 (July 1964). Also see Jean Claude, "Pour en finir avec la mafia du jazz," *Le Monde libertaire* 105 (October 1964), 11.

73. *Les Cahiers du jazz* 1 (September 1994).

74. "Les Amis du Jazz," *Jazz Magazine* 3 (February 1955).

75. "Club des Amis du Jazz," *Jazz Magazine* 6 (May 1955), 6.

76. In 1960, the ADJ announced that its principal clubs were in Auboué, Bergerac, Bourg-en-Bresse, Chalon-sur-Saône, Chantilly, Châteauneut-sur-Charente, Draguignan, Epinal, Gien, Gérardmer, Guise, Hyères, Limoges, Nice, Nîmes, Nord-Est de Paris (Le Bourget, Drancy, La Courneuve, Blanc Mesnil, Aulnay-sous-Bois, etc.), Saint-Maur, Saint-Quentin, Thonon-les-Bains, Toulon, Tours, Le Raincy-Villemonble, Paris, Yaoundé, Alger, Annecy, Besançon, Bénodet, Blois, Caen, Cauderan, Charleville, Cherbourg, Dole, Douai, Dunkerque, Etretat, Ouest de Paris (La Garenne-Colombes, Bois-Colombes, Courbevoie, etc.), Louviers, Longwy, Mâcon, Mauléon, Monteau-les-Mines, Oléron, Orthez, Mourenz-Lacq, Meudon, Monélimar, Neufmoutiers-en-Brie, Oran, Orléans, Philippeville, Pierrefitte, Reims, Saint-Dié, Saint-Pièrre-lès-Elbeuf, Saint-Brieuc, Saint-Quay-Portrieux, Binie, Tunis, Valence, Verdun, Villefranche-de-Rouergue, Châtelberault, Lille, Antony, Nantes, Mulhouse. Later that year, the ADJ announced new chapters in Perpignon, Strasbourg, Antony, Ornans, Lamballe, Le Tréport, Pierrefitte, Brive, and Cherbourg. "Cher Frère Jazz," *Jazz Magazine* 56 (February 1960), 9; "Cher Frère Jazz," *Jazz Magazine* 64 (November 1960), 7; and "Cher Frère Jazz," *Jazz Magazine* 66 (January 1961), 7.

77. "Cher Frère Jazz," *Jazz Magazine* 64 (November 1960), 7.

78. "Questions et réponses," *Jazz Magazine* 32 (November 1957), 42.

79. On the Jeunesses Musicales see "Incroyable . . . mais vrai!" *Bulletin du Hot Club de France* 97 (April 1960), 45.

80. "Cher Frère Jazz," *Jazz Magazine* 101 (December 1963), 11.

81. "Jazz Club de France," *Jazz Magazine* 148 (November 1967), 51–52. Branches of the Jazz Club de France in 1967 included: Saint-Quentin, Montluçon (2), Nice (2), Sedan, Lézignan, Narbonne, Arles, Marseilles (2), Saon, Caen, Bourges (2), Dijon (2), Bergerac, Périgueux, Evreux, Nimes, Toulouse, Bourdeaux (2), Montpellier (2), Rennes, Châteauroux, Deols, Tours, St-Pierre-des-Corps, St-Hilaire-du-Touvet, Grenoble (2), Chazelle-sur-Lyon, Le Puy, Nantes, cahors, Saint-Lô, Reims, Nancy (2), Metz, Lille, Roubaix-Tourcoing, Valenciennes, Wasquehal, Compiègne, Arras, Avion, Hénin-Liétard, St-Omer, Bayonne, Gan (Pau), Mulhouse, Lyon (3), Le Mans (2), Chambéry, Paris (6), Le Havre, Chatou, Fontenay-le-Fleury, Mantes, Amiens (2), Albi, Montauban, Hieres, Poitiers, Limoges, Epinal, Auxerre (2), Sens, Athis-Mons, Evry, Montrouge, Neuilly, Plessis-Robinson, Sceaux, Suresnes, Antony, Pavillon-sous-Bois, Chevilly-Larue, Fresnes, Saint-Maur, Nogent, Vincennes, Vitry, Deuil-la-Barre, Enghien, Saint-Leu-la-Fôret, and Villiers-le-Bel.

82. Howard McGhee, "Interjazz," *Jazz Hot* 173 (February 1962), 5. Also see Philippe Koechlin, "Inter Jazz: à suivre, " *Jazz Hot* 176 (May 1962), 21. Also see letter from the Administrateur des Services Artistiques to the Directeur des Services Artistiques, 2 February 1962, ORTF collection, Le Centre des archives contemporaines, année 1982, box 299.

83. Letter from Lucien Malson to M. Dellard, 26 January 1962, ORTF collection, Le Centre des archives contemporaines, année 1982, box 299.

84. Pierre Cressant, "Jean-Claude Albert-Weil et la 'transculture,'" *Jazz Hot* 239 (March 1968), 25–28; and Maxim Saury, "Pour un club des createurs de clubs . . . " *Jazz Hot* 239 (March 1968), 28. Jean-Claude Albert-Weil was also the author of a novel *Jazzmosphère*.

85. Letter from the Bureau de l'IJC-France, May 1956. Taken from an unmarked box at the Institute of Jazz Studies, Rutgers University-Newark.

86. *Bulletin de l'International Jazz Club* 6 (October 1956), 1.

87. Letter from the Bureau de l'IJC-France, May 1956. The Domité Directeur of the IJC-France was as follows: Christian de Barberie (president; responsible for the Radio and the organization of lectures); Jacques Maupoint (vice president); Lionel Ergis (general secretary; responsible for pulbic relations); Michel Gorsd (treasurer); Gérard Szanto (councillor; responsible for the exchange [bourse] of records).

88. Bernard Niquet, "A propos de L'International Jazz Club," *Bulletin du Hot Club de France* 59 (July–August 1956), 34–35.

89. Charles Delaunay, "Naissance d'une Fédération Europpéenne de Jazz," *Jazz Hot* 241 (May–June–July 1968), 8.

90. J. M., "Les Fédérés d'Europe," *Jazz Magazine* 168 (July–August 1969), 16–17. "La fédération européenne du jazz," *Jazz Hot* 252 (July–August 1969), 9. Other elected officials of the group were M. Lance Tschannen from Switzerland (president); M. Byrczek from Poland (vice president); Lubomir Doruzka from Czechoslovakia (vice president); and Wolfram Röhrig from West Germany (vice president).

91. Advertisement for *Jazz Forum* in *Actuel: jazz, pop musique, musique contemporaine* 5 (April 1969), 28.

92. "La fédération européenne du jazz," *Jazz Hot* 252 (July–August 1969), 10.

93. On June 27, 1964, a law changed the RTF to the ORTF. "Les grandes dates de la Radiodiffusion-Télévision française," dated June 1995, Archives de la Direction de la Radiodiffusion française 1925–1964, Le Centre des archives contemporaines, versement numéro 950218. For simplicity's sake I will refer to this organization only as the RTF.

94. Richard L. Derderian, "Broadcasting from the Margins: Minority Ethnic Radio in Contemporary France," *Post-Colonial Cultures in France*, ed. Alec G. Hargreaves and Mark McKinney (New York: Routledge, 1997), 100. Derderian goes onto show how minority groups within France capitalized on the openning radio market after 1981. For more on state radio also see especially Michel Rossinelli, *La Liberté de la radio-télévision en droit comparé* (Paris: Publisud, 1991); François Cazenave, *Les radios libres* (Paris: Presses universitaires de France, 1984); and Raymond Kuhn, *The Media in France* (New York: Routledge, 1995).

95. Geoff Hare, "Popular music on French radio and television," *Popular Music in France from Chanson to Techno: Culture, Identity and Society*, eds. Hugh Dauncey and Steve Cannon (Burlington, VT: Ashgate, 2003), 60.

96. Michael Kelly, Tony Jones, and Jill Forbes, "Modernization and Avant-gardes (1945–1967)," *French Cultural Studies: An Introduction*, eds. Jill Forbes and Michael Kelly (New York: Oxford University Press, 1995), 145.

97. Susan K. Foley, *Women in France since 1789* (New York: Palgrave Macmillan, 2004), 251.

98. Susan Weiner, *Enfants Terribles: Youth and Femininity in the Mass Media in France, 1945–1968* (Baltimore: Johns Hopkins University Press, 2001), 144.

99. Jacques Gourdon, "Radio," *Jazz Magazine* 3 (February 1955), 28. For the following year, see "Jazz Radio," *Jazz Hot* 106 (January 1956), 6.

100. Robert William Pirsein, *The Voice of America: A History of the International Broadcasting Activities of the United States Government, 1940–1962* (New York: Arno Press, 1979), 53, 92, 125–6.

101. Martin Block preceded Conover as the Voice of America's first international disc jockey. John O'Reilly, "Disc Jockey of 'Voice' Winning Good Will for U.S. World Over," *New York Herald Tribune* (27 October 1949), 1.

102. For more on the Voice of America and other U.S. State Department programs that used jazz as part of Cold War foreign policy, see Penny M. Von Eschen, *Satchmo Blows up the World: Jazz Ambassadors Play the Cold War* (Cambridge, MA: Harvard University Press, 2004).

103. Pirsein, 347, 354; and Reinhold Wagnleitner, *Coca-Colonization and the Cold War: the Cultural Mission of the United States in Austria after the Second World War*, trans. Diana M. Wolf (Chapel Hill: University of North Carolina Press, 1994), 211.

104. National Archives, Record group 84, entry 2462, box 7. Schedule of 1954 radio programs written by the Department of State Foreign Service.

105. Madeleine Chapsal, "Réportage: Frank Ténot et Daniel Filipacchi," *L'Express* (1 March 1962), 23. Ténot recounts the creation of "Pour ceux qui aiment le jazz" in his book *Jazz* (Paris: Armand et Georges Israël, 1983), 25. Also see "Le boom de 'Salut les Copains,'" *Candide* (8 November 1962), 4. For a poll of *Salut les Copains*' listeners, see Daniel Filipacchi, "4.300 jeunes ont écrit à Daniel Filipacchi: nos parents ne nous comprennent pas!" *Marie Claire* 85 (November 1961), 16–17, 19, 27.

106. Sébastien Le Pajolec, "Le cinema et les yéyés: un rendez-vous manqué?" *Jeunesse Oblige: Histoire des jeunes en France XIXe-XXIe siècle*, eds. Ludivine Bantigny and Ivan Jablonka (Paris: Presses Universitaires de France, 2009), 185.

107. Madeleine Chapsal, "Réportage: Frank Ténot et Daniel Filipacchi," *L'Express* (1 March 1962), 23–24; Jacques Gourdon, "Radio," *Jazz Magazine* 6 (May 1955), 26; Philippe Koechlin, "Adler et Netter: Place au jazz!" *Jazz Hot* 209 (May 1965), 25; Michael Kelly, Tony Jones, and Jill Forbes, "Modernization and Avant-gardes (1945–1967)," *French Cultural Studies: An Introduction*, eds. Jill Forbes and Michael Kelly (New York: Oxford University Press, 1995), 146; and "Le boom de 'Salut les Copains,'" *Candide* (8 November 1962), 4.

108. Weiner, 147.

109. For more on rock and roll and youth culture in France, see Florence Tamagne, "'C'mon everybody' Rock'n'roll et identités juvéniles en France (1956–1966)," *Jeunesse oblige: Histoires des jeunes en France XIXe-XXe siècle*, eds. Ludivine Bantigny and Ivan Jablonka (Paris: Presses Universitaires de France, 2009), 199–212.

110. Drott, 130.

111. "Organisation des services," Le Centre des archives contemporaines, versement numéro 950218, carton numéro 10.

112. Claude Fachard, "L'ORTF et la musique," *Le Pélerin du 20e siècle,* 4322 (12 September 1965), 55.

113. Memo from Paul Gilson, 4 November 1961, ORTF collection, Le Centre des archives contemporaines, année 1982, box 299.

114. Jean Tronchot, "Lucien Malson, où en est le jazz à la R.T.F.?" *Jazz Hot* 181 (November 1962), 16.

115. "RTF: De l'ordre dans la maison," *Jazz Hip* 32 (Easter 1963), 40.
116. "Emissions presentées," 1950, ORTF collection, Le Centre des archives contemporaines, année 1988, box 125.
117. "RTF: Direction des services artistiques: Rapport annuel," 1954, tome 1, ORTF collection, Le Centre des archives contemporaines, année 1988, box 125.
118. "Jazz et radio," *Jazz Magazine* 6 (May 1955), 3.
119. "RTF: L'Activité des Services Artistiques: rapport annuel 1958," tome 1, ORTF collection, Le Centre des archives contemporaines, année 1988, box 125.
120. "Rapport d'Activité de Paris Inter France I," 1959, ORTF collection, Le Centre des archives contemporaines, année 1971, box 419.
121. "La page de la RTF," *Jazz [Hip]* 18 (Noël 1959), 25.
122. "Du nouveau sur les ondes," *Jazz Magazine* 53 (November 1959), 11.
123. "La page de la RTF," *Jazz [Hip]* 18 (Noël 1959), 25; and "Autour des micros," *Jazz Magazine* 106 (May 1964), 13. These regional stations included Bordeaux, Clermont-Ferond, Grenoble, Lille, Limoges, Lyon, Marseille, Montpellier, Nancy, Rennes, Strasbourg, and Toulouse.
124. "La sesationnelle émission internationale: 'Jazz aux Champs-Elysées,'" *Cannes* (26 January 1958), 4.
125. "Malson sur France I," *Jazz Magazine* 54 (December 1959), 14; and verbal account of Comité de Varietés 3 May 1960 meeting, ORTF collection, Le Centre des archives contemporaines, versement 900214, numéro 26, dossier 1. Other participants in this *Jazz dans la nuit* series were Michel de Villers who hosted *Le jazz français* and Michel Netter and Jean-Louis Ginibre's *Gros Plans*. See "Rapport d'Activité de Paris Inter France I," 1959, ORTF collection, Le Centre des archives contemporaines, année 1971, box 419.
126. "Du nouveau à la R.T.F.," *Jazz Magazine* 76 (November 1961), 15. *Jazz dans la nuit*'s schedule was as follows: Monday: *Jazz Actualités* by Michel Netter and Jean-Louis Ginibre; Tuesday: *Ici New York* by Michel Godard; Wednesday: *Jazz aux Champs-Elysées* by Jack Diéval; Thursday: *Jazz à la carte* by André Francis; Friday: *Jazz sans frontière* by Michel de Villers; Saturday: *Visages du jazz* by Lucien Malson; and Sunday: *Courrier du jazz* by Jean-Robert Masson. *Jazz pour tous*'s schedule was: Monday: *La bourse du jazz*; Tuesday: *Plein jazz* by Philippe Koechlin; Wednesday: *Le jazz moderne* by Lucien Malson; Thursday: *Jazzmen service* by Raymond Mouly; Friday: *Swing a song, l'art vocal du jazz* by André Clergeat; and Saturday: *Rencontre avec le jazz français* by André Francis.
127. "La Radio," *Bulletin du Hot Club de France* 131 (October 1963), 24.
128. "Danger!" *Jazz Hot* 119 (March 1957), 7.
129. The entire letter from Alain Peyrefitte to Hugues Panassié, dated 29 October 1963, is included in *Jazz Hot* 193 (December 1963), 21.
130. "La Radio," *Bulletin du Hot Club de France* 137 (April 1964), 26–7. For Panassié's reactions to his show's dismissal, see Jacques André, "Le scandale du jazz à la RTF," *Combat* (2 December 1963), 8; "Le scandale du JAZZ à la Radio," *Bulletin du Hot Club de France* 132 (November 1963), 9–10; "Directives dictatorialees du Chef du Bureau du Jazz à la R.T.F.," *Bulletin du Hot Club de France* 133 (December 1963), 9–10; "Le chef du 'Bureau de Jazz' de la R.T.F. contre le 'hot-club de france,'" and "Qui supprimé l'émission du h.c.f.?" *Bulletin du Hot Club de France* 134 (January 1964), 6–7; "Nouvelle manoeuvre du Chef de Bureau du Jazz à la R.T.F.," *Bulletin du Hot Club de France* 134 (January 1964), 30–32; "Le Chef de Bureau du Jazz à la R.T.F. partisan de l'émission d'un homme inculte et bouffon," *Bulletin du Hot Club de France* 135 (February 1964), 9–11; and "Le scandale du Jazz à la Radio," *Le Bulletin du Hot Club de France* 136 (March 1964), 8–10. *Combat*'s jazz critic Jacques André (who wrote the "Les Lundis du jazz" column in the 1960s) was a Panassié supporter. Also see his article "Le 'jazz' des statistiques," *Combat* (9 September 1963), 8. When Panassié's program was dismissed, André lined up with him, agreeing that the RTF did not devote enough airtime to *vrai jazz*. For more on this debate, see "Le jazz à la radio," *Jazz Magazine* 103 (February 1964), 5–7; and "Le jazz à la radio," *Jazz Magazine* 104 (March 1964), 5–7.
131. "Autour des micros," *Jazz Magazine* 106 (May 1964), 13. The format remained largely the same with different hosts and programs each day: Monday: *Les meilleurs combos* by André Francis; Tuesday: *Clavier, guitare et vibraphone* by Raymond Mouly; Wednesday: *Recherches*

de l'avant-garde by Philippe Koechlin; Thursday: *Jazz hors frontière* by André Clergeat; Friday: *Les saxophonistes* by Henri Hubert; Saturday: *Compositeurs et arrangeurs* by André Clergeat; and Sunday: *Connaissance du jazz* by Lucien Malson.

132. "Radio," *Jazz Hot* 214 (November 1965), 16–17. For more specific attention on Malson's France-Culture show, see Henri Barraud, "L'air du jazz," *Les Cahiers du jazz* 14 (third trimester 1966), 94–5.

133. "Radio," *Jazz Hot* 214 (November 1965), 16–17. *Jazz dans la nuit* of course continued to air different daily shows like André Francis' *Jazz en stéréo* and *Jazz sur scène*, Sim Copan's *Jazz en liberté*, and Hugues Panassié's *Jazz Panorama*. These statistics remained the same in 1966. See "Radio," *Jazz Hot* 220 (May 1966), 27.

134. "Jazz à la carte," *Jazz Hot* 151 (February 1960), 31.

135. Letter from M. Lebrun to M. le Directeur des services artistiques, dated 26 September 1961, ORTF collection, Le Centre des archives contemporaines, année 1982, box 296. This letter set the budget for the Paris Biennale, which took place the following fall.

136. Lucien Malson, "Le jazz: la R.T.F. bouge," *Arts* (27 September–3 October 1961), 12.

137. Lucien Malson, "RTF: de l'ordre dans la maison," *Jazz Hip* 32 (Easter 1963), 41–42.

138. "La Radio et la Télévision à Rouen pour le IIIème Festival International de Jazz," *Paris-Normandie* (8 November 1962). In 1962, the radio and television branches of the RTF remained separate, so Malson himself had no direct role in what jazz coverage appeared on television. Jean-Christophe Averty was responsible for any jazz programs appearing on the small screen. See Jean Tronchot, "Lucien Malson, où en est le jazz à la R.T.F.?" *Jazz Hot* 181 (November 1962), 17; and Jean Tronchot, "Jazz actualités," *Jazz Hot* 191 (October 1963), 6–7.

139. Lucien Malson, "RTF: de l'ordre dans la maison," *Jazz Hip* 32 (Easter 1963), 42.

140. Letter to M.Gilson, 20 February 1962, ORTF collection, Le Centre des archives contemporaines, année 1982, box 296; Lucien Malson, "Le jazz: la R.T.F. bouge," *Arts* (27 September–3 October 1961), 12; Jean Robert Masson, "Jazz: Basie et le Blues," *Les Lettres Française* (10–16 October 1963), 10; Letter to M. Gilson from M. Dellard, 26 March 1962, ORTF collection, Le Centre des archives contemporaines, année 1982, box 296; and Michel Delorme, "Jazz à l'O.R.T.F." *Jazz Hot* 216 (January 1966), 11.

141. Michel de Villers, "Courrier des lecteurs," *Jazz Hot* 202 (October 1964), 4.

142. Letter from M. Dellard to Madame Mella, Directrice de France I—Paris Inter, 30 June 1961, ORTF collection, Le Centre des archives contemporaines, année 1982, box 296; and Letter from M. Dellard to M. Philippe Hebey, 17 April 1961, ORTF collection, Le Centre des archives contemporaines, année 1982, box 296.

143. "La page R.T.F. Festival," *Jazz Hip* 29 (Summer 1962), 27; and Letter to M. Gilson from M. Dellard, 20 February 1962, ORTF collection, Le Centre des archives contemporaines, année 1982, box 296.

144. POP, "Pauvres Hot-Fans," *Jazz Informations* (May 1949), 3.

145. "La discothèque idéale de l'amateur de jazz," *Arts* (23–9 March 1960), 16; and "Le disque," *Jazz Hot* 152 (March 1960).

146. Lucien Malson, "Le jazz ne doit plus rester une maladie de l'adolescence," *Arts* (July 1960), 13. The companies which provided statistics to Malson and their percentage of jazz record sales in comparison to total sales were as follows: Atlantic (20 percent); Barclay (20 percent); Brunswick (25 percent); Ducretet (30 percent); Fontana (10 percent); Pathe-Marconi (14 percent); Philips (10 percent); Odeon (25 percent); R.C.A. (25 percent); VEGA (12 percent); Vogue (30 percent); Versailles (25 percent).

147. Lucien Malson, "Qui aime le jazz?" *Arts* (7–13 February 1962), 1.

148. "Offensive américaine sur le marché européen," *Jazz Magazine* 58 (April 1960), 13.

149. *Jazz Magazine* 49 (June 1959), 3.

150. POP, "Pauvres Hot-Fans," *Jazz Informations* (May 1949), 3.

151. See for example, Lucien Malson, "John Coltrane à Pleyel," *Le Monde* (3 November 1963), 15; Philidor, "Le Modern Jazz Quartet au Théâtre des Champs-Élysées," *Le Monde* (13–14 December 1959), 15; Philidor, "Le Modern Jazz Quartet à la Salle Pleyel," *Le Monde* (6 November 1956), 12; and P.D. "À l'Olympia: Lionel Hampton . . . et Philippe Clay," *Le Monde* (30 November 1954).

152. L.F., "La fin du J.A.T.P.?" *Jazz Magazine* 145 (August 1967), 15.

153. A.G., "Aujourd'hui à Antibes. . ." *L'Humanité* (6 July 1960), 2; "Du 7 au 14 juillet festival Européen de jazz à Antibes-Jaun-les-Pins," *Le Monde* (2 July 1960), 13; Frank Tenot, "Le Festival d'Antibes," *L'Express* (14 July 1960), 34; Bernard Tournois, "Premier Festival européen de Jazz à Antibes," *Combat* (11 July 1960), 2; and "Jazz à la carte," *Jazz Hot* 152 (March 1960), 48.

154. "Avec son premier Salon le jazz fête son jubilé," *Paris-Presse* 1854 (2 December 1950), 4; "Le premier Salon du Jazz a pris un bon départ," *Paris-Presse* 1855 (3–4 December 1950), 7; "Le premier Salon du Jazz," *Le Monde* (2 December 1950), 12; "Le IIIe Salon du Jazz ouvre ses protes à la salle Pleyel," *Le Monde* (1 June 1954); "Du 1er au 7 juin a eu lieu Salle Pleyel la Semaine du Jazz," *Arts* (9–15 June 1954), 3; and Jacques André, "Quand le bon public acclame les nouveaux prêtres du jazz," *Combat* (3 June 1954), 10.

155. Henri Renaud, "La période du Tabou," *Les Cahiers du jazz*, 2nd series, no. 5 (October 1995), 21.

156. Boris Vian, *Le Manuel de Saint Germain-des-Près*, Noël Arnaud, ed. (Paris: Éditions du Chêne, 1974), 138–42. Vian wrote this book in 1950 and it was posthumously published by Éditions du Chêne. The Club Saint-Germain-des-Près was started by a group coming from the Tabou: Juliette Gréco, Boris Vian, Claude Léon, Léon Doddy, Chauvelot, Lavigne, and others. See Pierre Cressant, "De l'Existentialisme 1948 au Hard-Bop 1959 le Club Saint-Germain-des-Pres est toujours à l'avant-garde," *Jazz Hot* 140 (February 1959), 32.

157. Another well-known club existed for a short time between April 1946 and December 1948—the Lorientais on the rue des Carmes—where Claude Luter played his New Orleans jazz in these early postwar years. When it closed its doors it 1948, those involved in running the Lorientais moved to the Vieux-Columbier and the Tabou, including Luter. See Henri Renaud, "La période du Tabou," *Les Cahiers du jazz*, 2nd series, no. 5 (October 1995), 21.

158. Boris Vian, *Le Manuel de Saint Germain-des-Près*, Noël Arnaud, ed. (Paris: Éditions du Chêne, 1974), 138–142.

159. Pierre Drouin, "'Peanuts' Holland et sa trompette sous les arceaux gothiques du 'Métro-Jazz,'" *Le Monde* (2 December 1952), 9.

160. "Géographie Parisienne de jazz," *Jazz Magazine* 23 (January 1957), 21.

161. Lucien Malson, "Une grande enquête souteraine de Lucien Malson: proménade musicale sur la rive gauche," *Jazz Magazine* 23 (January 1957), 22. Also see M. Romano, "Paris by night," *Jazz Magazine*, 43 (December 1958), 12.

162. Michel Dunoyer, "Maxim quitte la Huchette," *Jazz Hot* 218 (March 1966), 8.

163. Éric Dussault, "Le milieu du jazz à Saint-Germain-des-Près de 1945 à 1960: Mythes et réalité," *French Cultural Studies*, vol. 23, no. 1 (February 2012), 30–48.

164. Stephen Lehman, "I Love You With An Asterisk: African-American Experimental Music and the French Jazz Press, 1970–1980," *Critical Studies in Improvisation*, Vol. 1, No., 2 (2005), 42.

165. Jonathyne Briggs, "Chapter 2: Sounds Traditional: The *Chanson* as a Site of Globalization," *Sounds French: Globalization, Cultural Communities, and Pop Music in France, 1958–1980* (New York: Oxford University Press, 2015), 44–77.

Chapter Two

The Gendered Jazz Public

In postwar France, young men were the most likely to buy jazz records, attend concerts, go to the Parisian *caves*, and join jazz clubs. In the 1950s and 1960s, as in earlier eras, teenagers and young adults were the segment of the general population most drawn to this music. Certainly, the cakewalk as well as the earlier jazz played in cabarets, cafés, and music halls, had been especially loved by a young set of Parisians at the turn of the twentieth century and then in the 1920s and 1930s. But the postwar period was different from these earlier stages because for the first time a distinct youth culture was becoming a permanent fixture of the nation's cultural life. In the years following World War II, teenagers began to overtly distinguish themselves from both older and much younger members of French society through up-to-the-minute forms of cultural identification that separated them from the rest of the population. In postwar France, jazz audiences were made up of two primary groups: those from a generation who had listened to jazz since before the war and who appreciated the music from a well-informed standpoint and who by this time had a well-proven allegiance to the music; and those of a younger generation who embraced jazz because it was closely connected to American culture and to new ways of dancing, dressing, and defining French culture.[1] Because of this second group of fans, the music was identified as part of postwar youth culture, even if jazz eventually ended up playing a less significant role than other imported forms of American culture like rock and roll, Hollywood movies, and blue jeans, which increasingly defined the entertainment and fashion choices of French teenagers.

THE JAZZ FAN AND YOUTH CULTURE

Postwar youth culture began to flourish at a time when French demographics were drastically affected by an increased fertility rate that had begun in the interwar period and that continued to make France a nation with an abundant supply of children and adolescents. As part of the postwar *bébé-boom*, in the years between 1944 and 1958, more than 11 million new French citizens were born. There were just under 616,000 births in France in 1939. In 1950, that number had risen to over 862,000, and then 800,000 babies were born each year for the next twenty years. Because of this high postwar birthrate, the French population rose from 40 million in 1946 to 44.5 million in 1958, and to 49.8 million by 1968.[2] According to the newspaper *Candide*, the expanding youthful population resulted in the fact that ten million young Frenchmen went to school in 1962, representing close to one quarter of the entire population. A writer for the *New York Times* observed in 1965, "France is slowly, steadily getting younger every day. Half the population is now under the age of 33."[3] In 1968, there were close to 8 million people between the ages of sixteen and twenty-four.[4] As these demographic trends made the French younger, not only were social, political, and economic infrastructures affected, but so, too, was culture. By the end of the 1950s, almost one third of the French population was younger than twenty years old, ensuring that there were a considerable number of well-off teenagers to buy transistor radios, record players, records, and music magazines.[5] With the introduction of "pocket money," these young consumers had substantial spending power, estimated at 5 billion francs in 1966.[6]

There was an increasing divide in the cultural life of the nation that depended on age alone and it determined the clothes people wore, the books and magazines they read, the food they ate, the movies they saw, the radio (and eventually television) programs they followed, and the music to which they listened. The generation that came of age during the 1960s had been born after the war and directly benefited from the social mobility and economic prosperity that helped to set the postwar period apart. As teenagers and young adults, members of this age group also challenged the values and traditions of French society, expressing disaffection with the world in which they lived. This trend had started in the 1950s when adolescents were already using the lifestyle surrounding jazz to challenge prewar notions of cultural propriety.[7]

Young people used youth culture to establish an identity that was separate from that of their parents. The commercial-cultural sphere gave teenagers a diverse array of products and practices to choose from in their quest to be generationally different. Not only could they wear blue jeans and listen to jazz or rock and roll, but some also dated and lived through new types of premarital relationships with the legalization of the pill in the second half of the 1960s.[8] At its core, youth culture was heterogeneous and offered multiple choices for young people so that they could live out their lives in ways that distinguished them from their elders. Despite the diverse options and practices contained within youth culture, by the late 1950s, a mass culture was coming into shape that was defined by the young's taste in music, fashion, hairstyles, and even political views. But no matter how rebellious components of youth culture became, teenagers and young adults remained connected to larger French society through their families, the media, employment networks, and the educational system. And it was precisely because of these connections that youth culture of the postwar era contributed so strongly to societal and cultural transformations.[9]

With youth culture, forms of leisure, entertainment, and dress became a means of identifying with a particular generation, not, as in the past, with a particular social class, national group, gender, or region. With this new French youth culture also came a frequent emphasis on popular culture over high culture, and the cosmopolitan over the local. Some of the most ubiquitous elements of youth culture came from the United States, were embraced globally, and were certainly equated with popular culture and the young. Jazz did not fit easily into this same cultural location despite its strong association with adolescence and young adulthood. Jazz occupied a place between high and popular culture due to the fact that even though musicians and critics embraced modern jazz's cerebral and avant-garde nature after the war, fans still turned out in large numbers to hear the sounds of New Orleans jazz that had undeniable appeal for mass audiences. Jazz also convoluted the differences between traditional local musics and cosmopolitan ones because despite jazz's origins in the United States, too many French musicians played the music and too many French fans embraced it for jazz to be labeled as explicitly foreign. The music had been played and enjoyed in France for more than several decades by the end of the Second World War, a length of time it would take rock and roll decades more to emulate. Because young fans were the most visible supporters of jazz at concerts and at record shops, its sounds were linked in the minds of many to youth culture, despite the fact that it defied easy cultural categorization and never drew the mass audiences that other forms of postwar adolescent entertainment did.

For the general French population, jazz could be connected to youth in a suspect way. The 1958 film *Les Tricheurs* (*The Cheaters*), directed by Marcel Carné, associated jazz with the immoral behavior of its young protagonists, two of whom become friends after shoplifting a jazz record. Over the course of the movie, the four main characters (two men and two women) live a life that hinges largely on drinking whisky, listening to jazz, and engaging in casual sex. The year it was released, *Les Tricheurs* won the Grand Prix du Cinéma and was the highest grossing film in France, ensuring that its depiction of postwar youth reached large numbers of viewers. Carné's intent was to startle audiences with visions of youthful debauchery and one publicity poster read, "A film that all youth are going to see and that will become obligatory for parents!"[10] Carné saw the actions of these fictional characters as emblematic of youth behavior, and asserted, "I would like this film to be seen as the testimony of an era."[11] Contributing to this line of thought, *L'Express* also indicated that this problematic and immoral cadre of young people existed beyond the cinematic world, and ran a picture of a young woman and the question, "Who are the Tricheurs?" on a 1958 cover of the magazine.[12]

Beyond the big screen, the public exploits of young French celebrities added to the sense that jazz was a component of youthful rebellion in France. Françoise Sagan, who won the Prix des Critiques for her novel *Bonjour Tristesse* in 1954 when she was only nineteen years old, was known for frequenting Parisian nightclubs. And, like the main characters in *Les Tricheurs*, Sagan too had an alleged fondness for whiskey and jazz, which added to the aura of nonconformism that characterized her public persona. In 1956, Sagan intentionally linked herself to jazz when she told an interviewer for the *Paris Review*, "For me writing is a question of finding a certain rhythm. I compare it to the rhythms of jazz."[13] The "existential adolescents" like Sagan who went to the clubs and *caves* of Saint-Germain-des-Prés were thought not only to appreciate jazz and alcohol, but also to have cavalier attitudes about sex. The seventeen-year-old main character in Sagan's *Bonjour Tristesse* intentionally manipulated the adults in her life and was sexually active. This character's father, who was himself a libertine and admired youthful energy and vivacity, told her, "You must teach me the bebop sometime."[14]

Other famous young women had been connected to jazz in France before Sagan. The seeming epitome of the Saint-Germain lifestyle in the early postwar era was the singer Juliette Gréco, who arrived in Paris from Montpellier in 1943 when she was only fifteen years old, and then went on to have a long career performing in the French *chanson* tradition. In the 1940s and 1950s, photographers from the popular press often showed her dressed in the au courant all-black attire of her cohort that represented a certain cynicism and nihilism and that embraced the life of the Saint-Germain jazz club. By the time she was twenty-one, Gréco had enhanced her notoriety on the French jazz scene by touring across the country with the jazzman Claude Luter and his band.[15] She also met Miles Davis in 1949 at the first Paris Jazz Festival and the two of them began an intermittent romantic relationship that lasted well into the 1950s. In 1957, it was Gréco who introduced Davis to the filmmaker Louis Malle, which led to Davis writing the musical score for the 1958 *Ascenseur pour échafaud*.[16]

By following the early exploits of young jazz fans like Gréco and Sagan and then being subsequently exposed to movies whose soundtracks relied on jazz, such as *Les Tricheurs*, *Ascenseur pour échafaud*, or the 1960 *A Bout de souffle*, general audiences came to associate jazz with a conjured image of intensity that also recalled the smoky clubs of Saint-Germain-des-Près and young French girls stepping outside the bounds of conventional propriety. The narrator of the 1956 television documentary "Les Jeunes et le jazz" indicated these adverse connections to jazz and youth culture when he rhetorically asked, "Isn't it because youth is anxious and worried that they like jazz?"[17] Seemingly, healthy and well-adjusted young people would not be attracted to this music.

Despite the awareness and attention given to jazz, the jazz public remained close to the same size in the decades following the war, and compared to the eventual audience for rock and roll, it was in actuality rather small. Despite new numbers of young fans continuously becoming attracted to the music and jazz being given increased prominence on state radio as well as through other venues, the critic Jean-Louis Ginibre claimed in 1965 that the jazz audience in France did not include more than 15,000 fans.[18] The limited size of this group was due in part to the fact that large numbers of jazz fans remained perpetually young. As men and women moved out of the early stages of adulthood, many of them ceased being the most vocal and noticeable advocates of jazz. Some observers noted that record buying and concertgoing jazz fans seemed to rarely age, and jazz's appeal remained strongest among younger demographic groups.[19] In 1962, Lucien Malson, taking information from listener polls, claimed that "youths between 16 and 18 years old sympathize in proportions of 71% [with jazz], those between 18 and 24 years old in the order of 62%. The passion for jazz disappears progressively as one rises in the pyramid of age, so that 1% of [radio] listeners over 75 years old request more jazz on the airwaves."[20]

At a 1961 Jazz Messengers concert, the jazz writer Daniel Humair also noted "the public's youth," stating that nearly all of the attendees were "young men from 16 to 20 years old." For Humair, this was something to applaud and he went on to say, "If Art Blakey and the Jazz Messengers have succeeded in supplanting in the spirit of today's youth the Elvis Presleys and other fools, then bravo Art and thank you, because, thanks to you, in several years modern jazz will be more 'public' in France and maybe we will be able to dance to the sounds of an orchestra playing 'Blue Monk' or 'Oleo.'"[21] In hindsight, we can see that his hope for jazz to supplant rock and roll was unrealistic, but Humair's celebration of teenage fans is still worth noting as it reflects the desire among jazz professionals for the music to reach and to energize a large popular base of listeners. Despite Humair's disdain for Presley and other "fools" who played music specifically for the young, he admired the impact these artists had and would have been pleased to see jazz artists draw the same sizeable audience.

Not all observers were as optimistic as Humair and some lamented the fickle and unsophisticated nature of young fans. As early as 1948, Boris Vian criticized the French youth's lack of permanent dedication and a tendency to applaud music regardless of artistic merit. At the time, Vian noticed that the older style of New Orleans jazz was attracting large numbers of vocal teenage enthusiasts who at the same time were rejecting more modern variations of the music. Like many of his fellow critics, Vian spurned a close-minded approach to jazz and he thought young listeners tended to reject more complicated rhythms and harmonies for the simpler "hot" sounds of traditional jazz. In an unusual take on youth culture, Vian thought that these fans listened to *old* music too much and did not give enough respect to *new* music. In discussing the current rage for out-of-date styles among teenagers, Vian wrote,

> A young man of sixteen would believe himself dishonored if he appreciated a music younger than himself. For a year especially, a tribe of bawling children has invaded the *caves* on the rue des Carmes, slowly chasing the serious Lorientais old guard away; they ignore all jazz and are sworn to nothing but the banjo and the tuba. Now then, it is this faction who goes to concerts, not to listen to a music that they love, because they cry so loudly that they hear nothing, but to boo those who they decide not to like.[22]

Vian was not critical of New Orleans or other traditional styles per se, because the Lorientais club to which he refers was famous for playing them. What he regretted was the loss of the "serious" old guard who understood and appreciated the history and the nuances of the music, and the simultaneous rise of a vocal and injudicious faction of young fans.

Others besides Vian also bemoaned the connection between jazz and youth because it frequently led only to a fleeting interest in the music. In 1956, the American Fred Appel detected this propensity on the part of fans to outgrow jazz, stating, "In France, I am certain that the majority of regulars at the Club Saint Germain are young men who, when their studies end, will be disinterested in jazz." Three years later, Henri Renaud echoed this very same sentiment when he wrote, "And I find that that is the misfortune in France: a minority of young men who love jazz when they are between sixteen and twenty and who, when their studies end, forget it completely." In 1960, Lucien Malson wrote an article for *Arts* entitled "Jazz must not remain a malady of adolescence" in which he claimed that "since 1933, its public has renewed itself five times: musicians want fans to grow old with them." Malson went on to observe that the people at jazz concerts did not grow old and asked, "Where are the *zazous* from the war, the audience of ten years ago?"[23]

Writers often remarked that the contemporary Zazous tended to fit specific profiles. In addition to being young male students, they could also represent both traditional and countercultural trends within youth culture. At a 1954 Coleman Hawkins, Illinois Jacquet, and Sarah Vaughan concert at the Salle Pleyel, an *Arts* correspondent noted that there were two types of people in attendance: "An 'athletic *normalien*" type (fine face, fine musculature, finely rimmed glasses). A type coming out of the parties of the Resistance (moccasins, mustache and technicolor waistcoat). Thirty years on average."[24] This reading of the crowd seemed to use a stereotype about the average student from the prestigious École Normal Supérieure, with everything about him, including his face, body, and dress, being very "fine" in order to add legitimacy and respect to the jazz concert taking place. The writer did not approach the Resistance-type with the same sort of awe or respect, but rather with an air of dismissal. Ironically, and much to the chagrin of some as the postwar era advanced, this countercultural image would contribute to definitions and conceptions of youth culture more than the staid and highly esteemed *normalien*.

In the mid-1950s, the average male jazz fan was neither part of a significant countercultural trend nor overly dismissive of authority, but was likely a middle-class student doing his best to listen to the music and to see it performed live. In 1956, *Jazz Magazine* published a profile of one of its readers, claiming that this young man was "the most typical" jazz fan. "His name is Jean-Jacques Renaudin, is 19 years old and lives in Concarneau where he pursues his studies. His collection shows 20 records (8 thirty cm., 4 twenty-five cm. and 8 forty-fives). The only musician whom he had ever heard live was Sidney Bechet when the latter was touring in England."[25] Like many of his fellow fans, he lived in the provinces, was a student, bought records when he was able to afford them, travelled a bit, rarely went to concerts, and was drawn to the traditional and popular New Orleans jazz of Sidney Bechet. Provincial Zazous could find going to concerts difficult because most shows were in Paris and the high cost of tickets was beyond the reach of the average student budget. Nonetheless, young fans remained the most well-recognized patrons of jazz, even if they lacked substantial purchasing power of their own and professional critics disparaged them for their transitory appreciation of the music as well as for their attraction to older, more traditional jazz genres.

Professional jazz writers were constantly interested in this fan because he made up their primary reading audience and as a result they went to great lengths to find out more about *him*. In 1959, *Jazz Magazine* published a long thirty-two-question poll to find out who the "typical" fan was, and well over two thousand readers responded. More than half of these respondents were between the ages of fifteen and twenty and 99 percent of them were under forty. Their youth accounted for the fact that 72 percent of them had liked jazz for less than the past six years, bringing the magazine to conclude that "it is around a person's fourteenth year that he feels—generally—the impact" of jazz. Out of these respondents, 40 percent were students and the remaining

60 percent were made up of people working in commerce (15 percent), or as engineers/technicians (12 percent), teachers (9 percent), military personnel (8 percent), doctors/dentists (7 percent), or industrial workers (5 percent). The magazine was "pleasantly surprised . . . by an important group of fans belonging to the class that is usually designated under the term proletariat." *Jazz Magazine* editors did not want jazz to be the "domain of the bourgeoisie" and, according to them, the poll appeared to indicate that the music was penetrating "into workshops and laboratories."[26] This was an idealistic proclamation on the part of jazz professionals who were middle-class arbiters of what had become by the late 1950s a complex musical culture. The music often attracted young individuals pursuing a higher education, something that differentiated it from rock and roll because the latter music did indeed appeal to the majority of French youths regardless of educational level or social status. In the end, jazz culture was not overly inviting to members of the working class, despite the intentions of jazz critics to expand the music's allure to new audiences and groups of people and to not exclude potential fans because of reasons linked to class.

BECOMING A JAZZ FAN

Postwar leaders of the jazz public were interested in better understanding why a jazz fan was attracted to the music in the first place. The 1959 *Jazz Magazine* poll mentioned above offered insight into the fairly wide range of jazz musics and musicians that initially drew fans to jazz. The New Orleans style was by far the most popular: 64 percent of the poll's respondents claimed to have first been drawn to the music by either New Orleans jazz in general, Sidney Bechet, or Louis Armstrong. Following New Orleans jazz in initial popularity were middle jazz (10 percent), modern jazz (8 percent), Django Reinhardt (6 percent), Duke Ellington (5 percent), and commercial jazz (4 percent). In addition, 66 percent of those taking the poll were classical music fans and they most frequently cited Bach, Chopin, Mozart, and Beethoven as their favorites. The majority (55 percent) did not appreciate "variety" music even though individuals did acknowledge liking the following popular artists: Gloria Lasso, Dalida, Aznavour, les Frères Jacques, Yves Montand, Georges Brassens, Juliette Gréco, Gilbert Bécaud, Frank Sinatra, Henri Salvador, Jacques Brel, Léo Ferré, and Charles Trénet. One of these fans wrote, "I like popular music whose rhythm is close to jazz."[27]

In 1958, *Sondages: revue française de l'opinion publique* published a study that addressed the French population's opinions of American music. Out of the 12,088 people polled between 1952 and 1957, 16 percent responded that they were either "very" or "moderately" interested in American music; half of these (8 percent of all participants) were most interested in jazz. Still, the majority of French men and women did not like jazz. When asked "Personally, does American jazz please or displease you? Very much or only moderately?" the breakdown was as follows: pleases very much (4 percent); moderately pleases (17 percent); moderately displeases (16 percent); displeases very much (44 percent); and did not say (19 percent).[28]

Sondages also reported that "the taste for jazz diminishes with age, but it increases with the level of instruction. The young deem more frequently that it has a good influence, but the old university students are very divided on this subject." The journal used poll answers to illustrate this. For those who were between 21 and 29 years old, their feelings about jazz were recorded in the following manner: pleases very much (12 percent); moderately pleases (29 percent); moderately displeases (18 percent); and displeases very much (28 percent). In comparison, for those respondents over age 65, their sentiments were expressed this way: pleases very much (none); moderately pleases (4 percent); moderately displeases (6 percent); and displeases very much (55 percent). When it came to education, jazz appreciation was very much tied to a person's age and level of studies. For those with only a primary education, reactions to jazz were: pleases very much (3 percent); moderately pleases (15 percent); moderately displeases (16 percent); and displeases very much (44 percent). For respondents with higher education, impressions about jazz were: pleases very much (13 percent); moderately pleases (26 percent); moderately displeases (9 percent); and displeases very much (39 percent).[29]

According to this study then, 41 percent of all respondents between 21 and 29 years of age liked jazz "very much" or "moderately," while 39 percent of the poll participants with a higher education fit into this category, either liking jazz "very much" or "moderately." For those polled over the age of 65, 61 percent communicated some sort of displeasure with jazz as did 60 percent of those with only a primary education.

Because educational level determined to a certain degree who became a devotee of the music, a discussion of class was unavoidable among jazz professionals. The critic Mick Bouchard, who thought that a "typical" jazz fan did not exist, nonetheless pointed to the importance of class, writing

> Is there a jazz type? Surely not. I have known bourgeois fans, rebellious fans, lethargic fans, treacherous fans. There is André Hodeir and there is Hugues Panassié!! If personality type does not play a role, we nevertheless observe that the environment already has an effect. Consequently, fans who are workers are rare. A certain measure of comfort is found in a nearly constant fashion among the fan's parents; maybe simply because it is necessary to have time and money to love something, and after eight hours in chains at the factory, one has the right to prefer to relax with *Jolie fleur de papillon* or the *Java Vache*.[30]

In 1962, André Hodeir claimed that bebop had played a considerable role in making jazz a music with a limited audience. He asserted, "Jazz became an art of specialists; in cutting itself off from its popular origins, it voluntarily limited itself to an audience of connoisseurs."[31] Hodeir's observations pertained to both the American and French jazz communities, yet in France, jazz critics and artists had intellectualized the music since Jean Cocteau and other modernists became attracted to its new sounds in the twenties. In the postwar period this trend continued as observers noted that the best-educated segments of the French population were the most likely to appreciate jazz. And the least musically complicated form of jazz—traditional New Orleans jazz—was what drew the largest audiences at concerts, sold the most records, and initiated the most jazz fans. This reality reinforced the divide between professional critics who devoted their careers to studying and furthering the cause of *all* forms of jazz and the visible young fans who tended to age out of jazz as they grew older. But despite the difference between these two groups, they did tend to have their social backgrounds and college degrees in common. In 1962, Lucien Malson pointed to the importance of education, asking

> Is it only age [that determines the jazz fan]? It seems that intellectual formation plays an equal role. "Studies" enlarge tastes, open individuals to foreign cultures, make way for a better welcoming of exotic realities, work in favor of a universal understanding of man. Among individuals who have not had anything but a primary education and who left school at 12, only 30% are interested in jazz; among those who have had a technical education, 48.6% tolerate or appreciate jazz; among those who have been able to prolong their reflection through a higher education, 50.7% accept or are devoted to jazz radio programs.[32]

Malson concluded that "when all is said and done, the love of jazz depends on two factors: age (a community sensitive to syncopated music makes jazz fans) and intellectual level (a well-educated social sector produces 'hot fans')."[33]

Still another study—this time one conducted by Pierre Bourdieu and Jean-Claude Passeron in 1964—highlighted the important relationship between educational level and artistic appreciation among jazz fans. In *Les Héritiers: les étudiants et la culture*, these two sociologists wrote, "In any cultural domain where one measures them, theater, music, painting, jazz or film, students have richer and more extensive knowledge when their level of social origin is more elevated."[34] They went on to conclude that

> Knowledge of cinema and jazz vary in direct proportion with familiarity with traditional arts. It is therefore natural that the groups the most integrated into the scholarly universe and at the highest level get the best results in jazz and in cinema as in the others: for example . . . 73% of students from the École

polytechnique show a minimal knowledge of jazz as opposed to only 49% of students with a bachelor's degree.[35]

In Bourdieu and Passeron's accompanying study done in collaboration with Michel Eliard, *Les Étudiants et leurs études*, they asked 739 students from across France the following question: "Among the musicians cited below, which have you heard on record, on the radio, on television, in concert: Cannonball Adderley, Louis Armstrong, Count Basie, Ray Charles, John Coltrane, Miles Davis, Duke Ellington, Dizzy Gillespie, Jimmy Guiffre, Harry James, Thelonious Monk?" The students' answers were compiled into a graph, entitled "Knowledge of Jazz," which included telling information about geographic location and jazz exposure. In comparing students in towns of populations below 100,000 to students in Paris, students in the smaller towns had been to fewer concerts and had listened to fewer records. Bourdieu, Passeron, and Eliard concluded that those students growing up in Paris and as members of the middle and upper middle class had more opportunities for cultural enrichment; in comparison, those growing up in villages in families of modest means were at a significant disadvantage.[36]

In writing about this study, Lucien Malson summarized another aspect of Bourdieu and Passeron's conclusion, observing that they had taken "a position against what they consider the illusion of a 'mass media' education: true culture, unequal—and unfortunate in this way—is always transmitted, according to them, by its traditional agents: parents and teachers."[37] Observers ranging from Hodeir to Bourdieu to Malson all agreed that social class played a large role in determining which young people became jazz fans: adolescents from the middle and upper middle class with well-educated parents and discretionary incomes were the most likely to appreciate the music. Ironically, even though the majority of French jazz critics were on the left of the political spectrum, they noted that workers did not tend to join the ranks of the Zazous, and jazz professionals did not succeed in bringing this music to people outside of well-educated bourgeois circles. In the postwar era, the jazz public largely remained the domain of an elite cadre of jazz professionals and of middle class male youths.

Adolescent jazz aficionados tuned into a cultural trajectory that predated their own lives by decades, the roots of which had been planted during the cakewalk craze of the early twentieth century. Jazz had made itself at home in France during the interwar period as modernist artists embraced the music's novelty, and popular audiences flocked to music halls and cabarets to listen and dance to its rhythms. Because of the advent of bebop and then other avant-garde jazz forms, the music of the postwar era was more varied than that of the 1920s and 1930s. Yet young fans of this later era were dependably drawn to the sounds of traditional New Orleans jazz that were popular with mass audiences, and they offered rather flat support to the experimental and innovative modern jazzes. After the Second World War, the young French fans who were so strongly linked by the popular press, academics, and professional critics to jazz, were participants in a new youth culture. They helped to define the cultural tastes, practices, and expectations of their generation, and lived differently enough from their parents and grandparents to create a cultural fissure in France based on nothing but age. Few of these young enthusiasts remained devoted, lifelong fans of jazz, as the vast majority of them publicly embraced the music while they were students and then moved on to other life interests as they aged. This does not minimize the fact that through their actions and visible engagement as jazz fans, they created an enduring connection between jazz and postwar French youths.

A MALE DOMAIN

The editors of *Jazz Magazine* were well aware of the male culture surrounding jazz appreciation, and the 1959 poll mentioned earlier documented that only 14 percent of the questionnaire's respondents were women. Even though this low female participation belied the public notoriety surrounding Sagan and Gréco, for critics it was not unexpected, and observers had already "noted that at concerts male attendees clearly dominate." Too often French society tended to envision youths as masculine, often assuming the category of "youth" itself to be male.[38] Making this point in 1961, Geneviève Dormann wrote in the periodical *Arts*, "Why, certain people ask, when the word 'youth' is said, do we cite more easily the examples of boys than of girls? Why do the 'crises,' the problems, the revolts, the books, and the 'follies' in general seem to be the exclusive right of adolescent boys and not of girls? In short, where are the girls and what are they doing?"[39]

A number of factors well beyond the world of jazz impacted the fact that female fans were not more numerous. Being a jazz fan meant becoming an actor in the public sphere, something French society after World War II was slowly coming to terms with when it came to women. After all, women only got the vote in France in 1944, and even then their rights as citizens remained distinct from those of men.[40] It is important to keep in mind that young women attended universities in fewer numbers than their male counterparts, had less freedom to independently pursue their own cultural interests, and had less money to spend at their own discretion.[41] Parents had higher educational aspirations for their sons, and educators also harbored similar prejudices. In 1952, a director general of primary education stated that a male teacher was obliged to form "the man and the citizen" while the female teachers was obliged to form "the housewife and mothers." So while the number of college students tripled between 1945 and 1967, and the female share of that population rose to an encouraging 44 percent, societal expectations for young women changed only slowly.[42] Reflecting the unhurried pace of change, until 1965, husbands had the legal right to stop their wives from working or pursuing an education, while also controlling their families' property. Contraception only became legal in 1967, and abortion in 1975.[43]

In the early postwar period, there was an expectation that the public roles of women and girls should reflect their domestic responsibilities. As "citizen consumers," not as consumers of entertainment or of leisure-time activities, women could fulfill the dual duties of marrying and buying to support their families and to help the economy grow.[44] Families needed to purchase consumer goods so that both physical needs and new standards of comfort and wealth could be met. Those with the means to do so started installing appliances, central heating, and indoor plumbing in their homes, which meant that they had to actively buy products. After the war, the reality of economic reconstruction interplayed with the simultaneous advent of mass consumer society, creating a situation in which women were valued as consumers of household and family necessities, as well as of luxury items. This, at a time when French families remained without many modern household conveniences, especially in the 1950s when even in urban areas 76 percent of households had no running hot water, 90 percent had no washing machine, and 91 percent had no refrigerator.[45] For women, their roles as domestic consumers and managers gave them a way to raise their social positions while simultaneously maintaining their responsibilities as wives and mothers.[46] As buyers, they were not supposed to challenge long-established mores regarding women's behavior, and were expected to spend money on products that would improve the lives, comfort, and perhaps status of their families. This did not include buying jazz records or tickets to concerts.

Families and educators alike continued to think that young French women should remain within the boundaries of traditional female forms of recreation, and not venture out into a cultural world that embraced nightlife, dancing, independence, and maybe even premarital sexual encounters. The well-known young women who did, like Sagan and Gréco, exhibited behavior that most middle-class parents would not condone. That Sagan and Gréco defied the expectations and practices of their peers made them seem all the more rebellious. These young women were understood to be *enfants terribles* because of their defiance of female societal norms. Adolescent girls were given the same message repeatedly: that they must act as "good girls" and not defy the societal norms of heterosexuality, marriage, and family life.[47] This did not mean there was no push back on the part of French women or purveyors of popular culture who acted to challenge and to change these conceptions. The most visible examples in 1950s French cinema were the characters Juliette (Brigitte Bardot) in *Et dieu créa la femme* and Véronique (Yori Bertin) in *Ascenseur port l'échafaud*, who either openly expressed sexuality or defied the law. Women like Sagan, Gréco, Bardot, and Bertin opened new avenues for female expression out of a culture that still embraced the traditional.

With the advent of yé-yé and rock and roll culture in the 1960s, girls began to publically take part in a type of youth culture in ways that were similar to those of their male peers. By this time, youth culture began to override distinctions based on class and sex, and on the pages of magazines like *Salut les Copains*, articles and advertisements were addressed to this broad and inclusive audience of young people. The aim was to draw in working-class apprentices as well as middle-class students, boys as well as girls.[48] However, in the case of jazz, male and female enthusiasts—whether they were fans, musicians, critics, or consumers—were not envisioned as equals. And this remained the case, even as some of the new technological products that teens strove to own (like scooters, cars, transistor radios, and, in time, televisions) permanently changed the place that these adolescents occupied in both family and public life.[49] In 1956, André Hodeir highlighted the gender differences among jazz fans. He wrote that the young have a "fresh, still unsatisfied sensibility" and that this explained why "young people of both sexes—but particularly boys rather than girls—have in a way made jazz their own."[50]

Despite the fact that the French jazz public remained mired in its male culture, by the middle of the 1960s, much was changing for women in France, indicated by a number of important milestones that signaled the growing visibility of women in popular culture and their increasing frustration with traditional gender roles. Simone de Beauvoir had written *Le deuxieme sexe* in 1949, well before women's place in French society came to be broadly considered. A long decade later, women were making a number of important challenges to the male status quo: in 1964, Betty Friedan's *Feminine Mystique* was translated into French, and Andrée Michel and Geneviève Texier published *La Condition de la Française d'Aujourd'hui*; in 1965, a new television show entitled *Les femmes aussi* aired, which targeted women as its primary audience; and in 1967, Ménie Grégoire began hosting a radio show for women that allowed listeners to ask her for help with their problems. Grégoire also noticed the changing place of women in her 1965 book *Le métier en femme*, where she wrote that women were now living in a time when they had to "invent" their own models and "upset" the models that were familiar to them. She noticed that women no longer knew exactly what was expected of them, "or what we expect of ourselves, or what to tell our daughters . . . but we can no longer ignore the fact that we are undergoing a transformation: the old image is fading, a new one is forming."[51]

Still, as jazz fans, women were portrayed differently from their male counterparts throughout the 1950s and 1960s. In an article on the Newport Jazz Festival, *Jazz Magazine* correspondent Marilyn Horne included four pictures of women, writing beside them "four feminine reactions: hysteria, exuberance, ecstasy, and indifference."[52] These four responses to jazz differed from the very "cerebral" reaction many men had to the music. Women, as jazz enthusiasts, were seen as more likely to express these extreme emotions, or otherwise be indifferent. Jazz writers certainly would not have used the same language to describe men's reactions to the music, because male behavior was the norm. Female responses, on the other hand, garnered attention only because people understood them to deviate from the male standard.

At times, the mainstream press acknowledged women as jazz fans, as when *Elle* or the Catholic women's weekly *Le Pélerin du 20e siècle* published articles on jazz for their readers. In 1962, *Elle* included a small piece on Roland Kirk in its "Quoi de neuf?" series, which covered a variety of subjects ranging from fashion, theater, movies, and music, to medicine. *Le Pélerin du 20e siècle*, a magazine that appealed to women primarily as wives and mothers, published an article on Louis Armstrong in 1965. These periodicals, and others like them, recognized that some among their female readership were attracted to learning more about jazz and supported this pursuit, however haphazardly. Unfortunately, the scope of their articles could not compete with magazines like *Jazz Hot* or *Jazz Magazine* that were less woman-friendly in their approach.

Other mainstream publications could be less supportive of women's interest in jazz, even warning that the music could potentially be dangerous to both women and children. In 1959, the Bordeaux paper *Sud-Ouest* published an article that blamed jazz for a woman's "fall." This article asked if it was a coincidence that "Marie-Thérèse D . . . 's life divided from the moment her passion for jazz took an excessive form." After developing numerous relationships in the jazz community, she fell "head over heels in love with a gangster" and then "followed a tenor saxophone player from Lionel Hampton's orchestra to the United States."[53] Obviously, this account strengthened the idea among some that jazz could tempt a vulnerable woman to abandon both her family and value system, echoing long-held ideas that women needed to be protected not only from certain types of modern culture and practices but even from themselves. Remember that in the interwar period, the Catholic Church and others had warned about the moral and physical dangers of jazz. Even if few people in postwar France still saw jazz as threatening—and certainly no one was any longer claiming that jazz could bring bodily harm—there remained an important continuity of beliefs about jazz, its otherness, and the potential threat it posed to "respectable" women.

A writer for *France Dimanche* also bolstered popular ideas about jazz's harmful capacities in a 1967 article on music and infants. This writer claimed that "an eight-day-old baby can suddenly stop being agitated when listening to a song with a melodious voice."[54] Female voices were supposedly the most soothing and four-month-old babies preferred Mozart. "IN

CONTRAST, THE SYNCOPATED RYTHMES OF JAZZ OVEREXCITE THEM AND MAKE THEM UNBEARABLE . . . An Armstrong recording increases their agitation" (capitalized text original).[55] This writer sent out a warning to parents to avoid exposing their young children to jazz. Mothers who were jazz fans could not continue to embrace this music without jeopardizing their children's welfare. Such views did nothing to encourage women to participate in the French jazz community and further validated jazz's maleness by making jazz seem dangerous to women and children.

Women tended to be aware of their disadvantageous and minority position in the French jazz public. One *Jazz Magazine* reader, in a letter to the cartoonist and commentator Siné, asked in 1967, "You who know men (and also women it appears) and jazz, how do you explain the small number of jazz fans of the feminine sex? I adore Roland Kirk, Pharaoh Sanders, and Guiseppi Logan. I am a woman. Am I a monster?"[56] Siné, in his usual style, responded sarcastically and caustically, "I don't know: you would have to send a photo! It is true, in effect, that the majority of women who are interested in intelligent things are ugly. At jazz concerts and at political meetings, there is not, in general, one to up the other." Of course, he was quick to also sarcastically point out that this did not apply to men: "For example, we at *Jazz-Mag*, are all handsome (especially me)."[57] Siné deprecated women in his columns in *Jazz Magazine*, revealing his own misogynist tendencies. In another issue, a woman wrote to him complaining about her husband's obsession with jazz and his free-spending jazz habit. Siné responded, "Madame, it is not a stereo system (*chaîne*) that your husband must buy immediately, but a bicycle chain."[58] A cartoon of a man getting ready to hit a kneeling, supplicant woman with a bicycle chain accompanied this reply. In his cartoons, Siné also drew naked, large-breasted women in front of libidinous men. In doing so, he initiated a double form of the male gaze—one within the drawing itself and one emanating from the live reader. One of the results of Siné's work was that he introduced a strong bias against women into French jazz discourse. Critics and fans so infrequently devoted time to discussing female artists or fans that this negativity contributed in a significant way to the overall characterization of women within French jazz circles.

Women were certainly aware of Siné's obsessive connection between them and sexuality, as well as his reinforcement of jazz's masculinity. One reader of *Jazz Magazine* wrote the following in a letter to him in 1967: "I am a young woman passionate about jazz. I am equally interested in men . . . Also, against custom, I am not going to send you my photo—I can assure you that I am pretty—but I am going to ask you to send me one, or two, of Jean-Pierre Binchet (in a swimsuit, that would be perfect) or, by default if he refuses, one of yourself, my dear Siné."[59] In refusing to send a picture of herself, this reader refused to be objectified by Siné, and in asking to have a picture of either Jean-Pierre Binchet or Siné, turned this fixation on the physical back onto Siné himself. This woman rejected her role as sexual object, asserting her own sexual desires and mocking Siné simultaneously.

Significantly, the lack of visible participation in jazz on the part of mainstream young women was influenced by the reality that this music was defined by male culture, so that female participation remained on the fringes. On the stage, women gained respect by being vocalists but rarely as instrumentalists, and it was these latter artists who won the most critical and popular acclaim for their artistic virtuosity. Nonetheless, as these letters to Siné attest, avid female jazz fans did exist. Some, like these women, wrote in to jazz periodicals to express their opinions or to ask questions, giving themselves a voice in a male-dominated culture. At times, photographers captured images of female jazz fans on film, and young male fans looked to find romance and/or female companionship within the jazz community. Young men wrote letters to *Jazz Mazagine* in search of pen pals of the opposite sex who shared their interest in jazz.[60] In truth, many young women admitted to first learning about jazz not through their own initiative but through the men in their lives, and not unpredictably, married couples seemed to share similar opinions about jazz. Of the married individuals who responded to the 1959 *Jazz Magazine* poll, two-thirds shared an *entente jazzistique* with their spouses.

THE JAZZWOMAN

The French professional jazz scene inherited gendered elements from its American counterpart. In the United States, jazz musicians learned their art through exposure to other jazz artists, making the music's culture not only distinctive but also at times hermetic by denying equal access and recognition to women. Perhaps in reaction to the fact that American culture historically ignored and underpaid jazz musicians, male jazz artists protected their own sense of community, nourishing and accepting the centrality of men in their cultural circle. In the United States, club owners, booking agents, bandleaders, musicians, and critics were almost all men, making the jazz profession a male-dominated one. It was no mistake that the word "jazzman" became a common way to identify a jazz artist on both sides of the Atlantic.[61] As Robin Kelley has reasoned, "The creation of an alternative culture can simultaneously challenge and reinforce existing power relations."[62] Leaders of the American jazz scene, while challenging the dominance of white American culture and eventually racial prejudice itself, still reinforced a status quo that favored male power and prestige.

The jazz scene offered few professional opportunities for women. Several factors explained women's overwhelming invisibility in jazz. Women lacked a number of "masculine" qualities understood by many to be necessary to a successful jazz career. They might not possess a showy self-confidence on stage or the ability to show their "chops" in the same way as a male performer. They might not be able to travel or to step away from home and family obligations, or to work in nightclubs that were often equated with alcohol, drugs, and crime.[63] The women who succeeded in this atmosphere often paid a price by losing their social respectability, whether they were in the United States or in France.

In addition to these variables that discouraged women from working as jazz artists, there was also the issue of economic competition because a large number of talented musicians (male and female) competed for a limited number of jobs. In the United States, African-American women felt pressure to not compete with black men for jobs, because this would be seen as challenging the men's standing. White jazzmen were also hesitant to embrace female jazz artists, sometimes becoming hostile over the idea of sharing the same stage with them, especially during the swing and big band eras.[64] Despite this widespread bias against jazzwomen, important female artists did become respected musicians in their own right.

From jazz's beginnings at the turn of the century in the United States, women made a place for themselves within this singular musical idiom, but it was only in the 1980s that a number of American writers first started focusing at length on women's contributions to jazz: Antoinette Handy wrote *Black Women in American Bands and Orchestras* and *The International Sweethearts of Rhythm*; Sally Placksin published *American Women in Jazz: 1900 to the Present, Their Works, Lives and Music*; and Linda Dahl wrote *Stormy Weather: The Music and Lives of a Century of Jazz Women*. In *Swing Shift: "All-Girl" Bands of the 1940s*, Sherrie Tucker showed that in the 1940s alone there were hundreds of female swing bands in the United States whose existence, like that of so many other jazzwomen, has been left out of the jazz historiography until rather recently.[65] The omission of women from the larger story of jazz for so many decades illustrated a discomfort with these pathbreaking women who participated on jazz stages when doing so went against traditional expectations and understandings of the music and of gender roles. Women instrumentalists disrupted the male/female jazz divide where men were to operate the instruments and women were to be vocalists and have sex appeal. Women were expected to sing and to dance, so when they played instruments instead they were understood to be engaging in a masculine behavior and were seen as aberrations.[66] Nonetheless, jazzwomen in the United States and in France worked as instrumentalists, singers, and even as critics but they did so within an arena created, controlled, and dominated by their male contemporaries.[67]

When American women achieved fame or recognition as jazz artists, they were more often than not vocalists, even if some female instrumentalists, like Lil Hardin Armstrong or Mary Lou Williams, became famous for their work.[68] Both jazz's subculture and American mainstream culture limited the accepted participation of jazzwomen by defining what instruments and activities corresponded with femininity. The majority of female jazz musicians performed on the piano where they were able to distinguish themselves on an instrument that had historically been connected to the female sphere—young middle-class women in the nineteenth and early twentieth centuries were frequently taught piano as part of their education. In jazz, instruments carried gendered meanings, contributing to women's restriction to specifically defined roles.[69] The brass, reeds, and percussion instruments were typically construed as "masculine," while strings and the flute were characterized as "feminine." Despite being an acceptable instrument for women, the piano did not necessarily fall easily into this rubric of male and female spheres. At the beginning of his career, Jelly Roll Morton had reportedly had reservations about playing the piano because he feared "being misunderstood." However, as the piano moved from being a background rhythm instrument into one used by soloists like Morton, it was masculinized, making it more difficult for female jazz pianists to distinguish themselves or to even find work.[70] Despite these challenges and their general invisibility in the jazz canon, American women continued their careers as jazz musicians in a variety of ways—as single artists, in bands, on television, in nightclubs, in schools, in churches—regardless of whether they were married or had children.[71]

The French jazz community reinforced this masculine side of jazz that had been fostered in the United States. When the writer Claude Samuel examined "the great jazzmen" in his 1962 book *Panorama de l'art musical contemporain*, he completely neglected to mention any female musicians. The term "jazzmen" alone excluded women from membership in this category of "greats" and Samuel did not choose to treat female vocalists in another section. Out of the forty-five artists he mentioned, ranging from the pioneer jazz musician King Oliver to the modern John Coltrane, Samuel listed one Frenchman—Django Reinhardt—as well as musicians widely known for their voices such as Fats Waller and Count Basie, but he did not allude to a single female.[72] This easy exclusion of women from jazz could also be seen in a letter written by a *Jazz Magazine* reader to Siné five years later. Taking the idea from American jazz fans who had playfully campaigned under the banner "Dizzy for President," this reader advocated a new French government formed by members of the French jazz community. Out of the eight ministerial posts he mentioned, all were to be filled by men: Michel Hausser, Guy Lafitte, Hugues Panassié, Lucien Malson, André Hodeir, André Francis, Bernard Peiffer, and Jean-Louis Comolli.[73] In his response, Siné suggested that he himself be made Prime Minister and then went on to mention seven more men who could fill governmental positions: Eddie Barclay, Ben Benjamin, Alain Gerber, Guy de Fatto, René Urtreger, Jean-Claude Naude, and Henri Renaud.[74] Members of the jazz community like Samuel and Siné both helped perpetuate the assumption that had started in the United States that jazz was a male music.

This often unstated bias against women manifested itself in more direct forms of exclusion and judgment. The Riems newspaper *L'Union* reported that "the head of a large jazz band categorically refused to hire women. Not because of misogyny. To the contrary. If the woman is pretty, he says, that is the trouble and spreads disorder among his musicians. If she is ugly, that is depressing, cutting off inspiration and making his players glum."[75] According to this bandleader's logic, women could only cause problems if allowed membership in his group. He did not seem at all concerned about a woman's lack or abundance of musical gifts, only her physical appearance and sexual allure. This type of reasoning led some men to conclude that jazz must remain a male domain in order to protect it from the damaging effects of sexual tension. In his fictional work *The Worlds of Jazz*, André Hodeir expressed the idea that, for women, family life would ultimately take precedence over musical careers. He wrote the following about a fictional singer: "She's left us. Marriage that's what every girl has in mind opportunity knocked and bang. When she starts wiping her kids' behinds she'll forget all the lyrics even her favorites."[76] Undoubtedly, women did have to juggle family life and professions and many chose to sacrifice the latter because the jazz musician's lifestyle, especially with its late hours, was in numerous ways antithetical to family life. Yet to assume that all women would make this choice and that they would then forget all about the music was both short-sighted and insidious. In such ways, French critics, writers, and fans consistently excluded women from jazz, revealing a predilection to ignore women's musical talent and to assume their lack of importance.

Some members of the French jazz community recognized the difficulties women had as professional jazz musicians as well as the problems they had in overcoming societal prejudices, even though these same people could also help reinforce women's limited place in the music. In an article on the saxophonist and singer Elvira Redd, a writer for *Jazz Magazine* noted her uniqueness in the musical world, calling her "this kind of monster (woman-saxophonist and saxophonist-singer) that one exhibits more frequently in fairs than in concert halls." Despite his poor choice in words, this writer did express how rare women who played the saxophone and sang were, acknowledging "the obstacles that explain the rarity of *jazzwomen*," and recognizing that both appearance and gender identity harmed women's careers. In discussing the growing recognition for Redd among critics, this writer stated, "Of course, she [was] a woman and ugly, but, little by little, listeners closed their eyes."[77] This writer acknowledged Redd's musical talents despite his chauvinism and his choosing to call Redd "a monster" and "ugly." But few musicians like Redd succeeded, and not many listeners, in France or in the

United States, were willing to consistently separate a woman's musical talents from her gender and physical appearance.

Despite both consistent prejudice and exclusion, female vocalists excelled, becoming popular on both sides of the Atlantic and gaining recognition from fans, critics, and general audiences. Of course, men also sang, and the musician perhaps most famous for his voice was Louis Armstrong, although he was first and foremost regarded for his instrumental abilities and musical inventiveness. Some male singers, like Fats Waller or Ray Charles, tended to create musics that pushed beyond the boundaries of jazz and were better characterized as blues, rhythm-and-blues, or gospel. But within the genre of jazz, French listeners tended to appreciate women more widely for their voices than they did men. One *Jazz Magazine* journalist wrote in 1955, "All fans obviously have a small predilection for female singers [over male ones]," and in 1961, a writer for *Jazz Hip* asserted that "if the weaker sex has not made any major contributions to the instrumental sphere of jazz, the same cannot be said about the vocal sphere. In quality and in number, female singers are effectively equal if not superior to their male colleagues."[78]

Of female vocalists, Americans in general, but African Americans in particular, were the most popular. In 1955, one writer for *Jazz Magazine* claimed that among vocalists, "artists of color are unbeatable; not one white female singer is truly a jazz musician, they seem to prefer the 'Hollywood' romance style."[79] Jazz critics most commonly evoked the names of Ella Fitzgerald, Billie Holiday, and Sarah Vaughan when they spoke of female jazz singers, calling them the "three greats"[80] and claiming that these three names "reappear with a remarkable consistency at the top of the elected hierarchy of singers."[81] Jacques Hess maintained, "Sarah is the young lady, Billie the woman, Ella the mother, a reassuring, lovable mother who has kept her good nature and tenderness from her twenties."[82]

In discussing Fitzgerald, Holiday, Vaughan, or any other female vocalists, French jazz writers used a strongly-gendered discourse. As early as 1938, Hugues Panassié wrote after a trip to New York about "the beauty of the American woman" and the black women whom he found "really astonishing" there.[83] This rather early fascination with black female bodies expressed a form of philo-racism and reinforced French men's appreciation for Josephine Baker (who will be discussed at greater length in chapter 3). This captivation with black women's bodies did not disappear in the 1950s and 1960s. Despite the fact that Vaughan was commended for her "invention" and Holiday her "versatility,"[84] critics in the 1950s and 1960s frequently focused on sexuality when it came to these musicians. In describing Billie Holiday's voice, André Clergeat wrote, "She is ingratiating, perverse, enveloping, extremely sensual, with a self-conscious and studied sensuality, similar to an uncontrollable charm that, when one is under its power, never releases you."[85] After Alain Gerber said of Carmen McRae, "[She] deserves this name—artist—because her art is a *representation* of life," he went on to praise her "eroticism." He wrote,

> Not the simple, good-natured and rather elementary eroticism of Sarah, which quickly goes flat, or the jesting eroticism of Ella, but an eroticism more subtly tied to the body, impregnable, resistant to tenderness, to miseries, to modesty, to the magic of the music. There is the raucousness of this voice, choking in high pitch, hoarse in low pitch, gravelly sometimes and vibrantly vulgar.[86]

When the critic André Hodeir wrote *The Worlds of Jazz* in 1972, he still focused on female musicians' sexuality. Of the fictional singer he called "F," Hodeir wrote, "That sexy F and her velvet voice, she put sex into everything, maybe we thought so more than the audience, we saw her do her grind from behind."[87] French commentators in the postwar period did not limit their discussions of women's sexuality to African-American women, but also portrayed white female jazz musicians as overtly sexual. Philippe Carles, in reviewing Lilian Terry, asked, "Have I already said that Lilian Terry is beautiful? Tall, brunette, divinely robust, adorably thin, 'she wavers, she hesitates; in a word, she is woman' (Racine)." By invoking a quote from Racine, Carles also labeled Terry as possessing some sort of enduring and timeless feminine nature, reinforcing notions of gender differences. He also described Anita O'Day as "mannered, sophisticated, lascivious, sensual (sexy), languid, aggressive."[88] Despite the fact that critics admired female artists' talent and musical abilities, they consistently stressed and praised the erotic appeal of these women. For these men, jazzwomen's sexuality was an important part of their music and could not be separated from evaluations of artistic talent. Little had changed from the time when Josephine Baker had first taken the stage. Encouragingly, they were no longer aggressively linked to an imagined African primitivism or asked to dance in banana skirts, but they remained prized for their female bodies more than for their musical prowess.

Ella Fitzgerald was the most consistent exception to this tendency and writers focused less direct attention on her sexuality. Carles, who was so interested in Terry and O'Day's sensual sides, wrote of Fitzgerald, "Her voice remains her strongest strength: she changes register with ease and shows herself capable of producing notes that other women cannot. She twitters, whispers, murmurs, hums, grunts or vocalizes, in a perfect way, smooth, without danger. With regularity."[89] More than any other jazzwoman of the period, Fitzgerald provoked wide public attention in France. However, unlike her contemporaries, she was not objectified for her beauty but occasionally because of her perceived lack of it, generating overtly-gendered discussions among members of the French jazz community.

Fitzgerald came to France as a member of Norman Granz's JATP tours almost yearly during the 1950s and 1960s, and at times, she also performed at various jazz festivals like the one held annually in Antibes.[90] Perhaps because of her very regular presence in France, Fitzgerald received constant notice from the French press. Critics praised her for her "dynamism,"[91] as well as her "extraordinary voice, supple like a tenor sax."[92] One writer went so far as to call her "the idol of Paris."[93] Yet despite this unhesitant admiration for her musical gifts, French writers also at times focused attention on Fitzgerald's body, distinguishing her music from her appearance.

In the tabloid *Ici Paris*, one writer focused an entire article on Fitzgerald's weight. According to this anonymous writer, despite the fact that she earned "a million each day" and had "hundreds of thousands of admirers," her life was "agony" because of her size. The article went on to say,

> Ella Fitzgerald is fat. She weighs 126 kilos. Her enormous chest shaking with sobs, she herself said, "I am an elephant in human form." Ella is only 42 years old, but she has already wanted to die several times. She no longer wants to see herself in a mirror. Before bed, she undresses in complete darkness. *Ella Fitzgerald horrifies herself.* [italics original][94]

The writer also recounted Fitzgerald's two failed marriages, one to the American Ray Brown, the other to a Swede, "as white, as thin, as blond as she herself was black and large. . . . The thing that the Swede loved in Ella was her voice. Only her voice."[95] The truthfulness of the information in this article was obviously suspect as *Ici Paris* was not a reliable news source but rather a sensationalist tabloid. Nonetheless, this author, while calling Fitzgerald "the incomparable and unequaled priestess of jazz," still chose to negatively emphasize her physical appearance, making her both an object of ridicule and pity and disparaging her talent.

A female writer for *Jazz Hip*, Monique Aldebert, approached the subject of Fitzgerald's appearance differently, depicting the singer as "charming, touching, moving, Ella, even by the contrast between her physical appearance and her voice. We all know it, this young and fresh voice of an amused and amusing child. For so many years already, how can she stay invulnerable to the influence of time?"[96] Aldebert constructed this perpetual youthfulness in Fitzgerald's voice in contrast to her physically being a "large woman." For her, Fitzgerald's lack of beauty increased the power of her music.

> This emotion is so much more pure because it reaches us without the help of any extra-musical contributions, because Ella does not possess the physical assets from which emanate the aggressive and intrusive sexuality of the women who know that they are beautiful, desirable, and who use this towards and sometimes against their personalities. (sexy at all cost . . .).[97]

Aldebert held that Fitzgerald was first and foremost a musician, making a strong distinction between Fitzgerald and women who were, or allowed themselves to be, easily objectified because of their appearance and sexuality. Aldebert continued,

> Her sole means of expression is her voice through which she expresses all of her musical assets. Ella swings, Ella goes back inside, Ella vocalizes, Ella confounds us with her ease, but *above all*, do not forget, Ella is a musician. [italics original][98]

Aldebert admired Fitzgerald's ability to constantly create through her music as well as her "inventive and emotional power." Importantly, Aldebert was a woman and a woman working within the very male-defined sphere of jazz criticism. Her thoughts about Fitzgerald were also appropriately situated in the mid-1960s when French women were becoming more aggressive in affirming their own rights, asserting their independence from male definitions of them. Aldebert applauded efforts to recognize Fitzgerald for her musical talent alone and encouraged the separation between music and sex appeal when it came to evaluating female jazz musicians. If male and female musicians were to create and promote their music on an equal basis, listeners had to judge both with the same criteria. Unfortunately, Aldebert was a lone voice of protest within a community that continued to stress the sexuality of female artists.

Illustrating the French jazz public's bias against women, one of Siné's male readers wrote to him in 1967,

> In "Jazzmag," allusions are frequently made, as soon as a female singer is introduced, to sensuality. One talks about the sensuality of Sarah Vaughan, about that of Carmen McRae, about the troubles created among critics by Anita O'Day. I have the impression that the members of your team don't think about anything but sex. . . . Regarding Billie Holiday, one always speaks of the woman, of love. I find that a little disgusting in a jazz revue where only musical problems should be grappled with.[99]

This reader observed just how sexual jazz critics' discussions of women tended to be and he chose to voice his objections. But this reader did not do so out of a desire to see women treated more fairly; he did so to protect a male realm. He ended his letter by writing, "Personally, ladies' voices have never especially given me a thrill: I find moreover that these singers are, on the whole, not very beautiful."[100] According to this letter, then, women perhaps did not belong in discussions of "musical problems" as they were not musically or sexually appealing to this reader. Significantly, this reader recognized the gendered character of jazz discussions and the inclusion of references to female "sensuality" by critics reviewing women, references that were absent when these critics wrote about male musicians. To avoid these sexual allusions, it seems the reader supported limiting the discussions of jazz to musicians whom he found worthy of attention: men.

French critics analyzed jazzwomen differently because they were women. As will be further discussed in chapter 3, black male bodies were admired for their physical aptitude and musical prowess, revealing that French critics were not immune to the enduring myth of black male sexual power. Yet the sexualizing lens through which women were viewed did not grant them a perceived advantage: it reduced them to sexual objects and trivialized their musical talent. French audiences certainly judged the physical traits of black jazzmen, but their music was neither accepted nor dismissed based on a stated sexual desirability. Predominantly white male French jazz fans used sexualized language to discuss both male and female jazz artists. In doing so with men, they revealed a fascination with black male bodies. With women, they expressed an inability to see jazz artists of different genders as equal to one another. White male jazz musicians were the only artists immune from this sexualized discourse that could reduce black men to being superior physical specimens and women to the objects of physical desire. In both cases, the bodies of jazz musicians became canvases on which white French jazz fans projected different types of desire based on skin color and sex: the desire to emulate and the desire to possess.

JAZZWOMEN *FRANÇAISES*

In general, not many French female musicians played or created jazz. One writer for *Jazz Magazine* wrote, "In France, few female vocalists devote themselves to jazz," and another admitted that "vocal jazz has only a limited success in France."[101] Some women, however small in number, did still choose to work within this music: Anita Love, who was the wife of trumpet player Guy Longnon;[102] Simone Chevalier, who performed at American military bases and in Madrid before appearing in France in the early 1960s;[103] and the very well-respected Mimi Perrin, who created the group the Double Six in 1956. Yet, with the exception of Perrin, these women and others like them did not receive the same amount of attention from French critics and fans as American female musicians. When the jazz community did discuss them, it paid surprisingly little attention to their sensuality and predominantly focused on their talent. Perhaps because there were so few of them, once a French woman achieved success in jazz, critics were likely to offer their professional respect. But we cannot avoid asking if French women were treated differently from their African-American counterparts because they were white. Was it more difficult for French critics to objectify their white countrywomen? Especially if they had professional or personal relationships with these women? French jazzwomen certainly reached much smaller audiences than *les américaines* who commanded global attention. One writer called Chevalier "a courageous, extremely gifted young woman who stubbornly keeps singing a repertoire that interests only a small fringe of the public."[104] The critic Jean Tronchot said of Chevalier: "[She] possesses a pretty voice and what's more, is a true jazz singer, something rather rare in France. She is better known abroad than here, for example in Holland, where she could easily compete with Rita Reys."[105] Chevalier, unlike many American singers, could not only sing in her native language but also in English, Italian, Spanish, and German, yet unfortunately still secured little commercial notice in France. With the exception of small references made to them periodically by members of the jazz community, French critics and fans seldom paid attention to musicians like Love or Chavalier. Perhaps they just did not think French jazzwomen were worth their time. If most French female jazz artists were largely ignored, Mimi Perrin was the exception to this rule.

Perrin was a member of the French group the Double Six that she founded in 1956, having left teaching to pursue a career in jazz. One French critic described her as a "pianist with a delicate touch, a singer long influenced by Billy Holiday, 'her goddess for ever and always.'"[106] After reportedly hearing on the radio the song "Sing a Song of Basie" by the American group the Lambert-Hendricks-Ross Trio, Perrin decided "to undertake a similar production, but in French."[107] She had already met the American Quincy Jones who was in Paris at the time and began convincing him to help her on the project. She also assembled a team including the sound engineer Jean-Michel Pou-Dubois, an instrumental rhythmic section, and five other singers—one other woman and four men—for whom, with her, the band was named.[108] The Double Six's first album was well received in France, as well as in the United States and Canada. One of the songs from this first album appeared for several weeks on the Hit Parade and the band performed at the Toronto Jazz Festival just before its second album was released, which, according to Phillipe Adler, was "more varied in its repertoire [and was] even more successful than the first."[109]

For decades, critics recognized Perrin and her group as unique among French jazz vocalists. In 1986, the critic Jean Wagner wrote of Perrin's group, "Even if France does not lack female vocalists who are sensitive to the jazz universe, soloists are lacking. . . . There is a single exception, that of the Double Six."[110] Throughout her career, Perrin was compared to the Lambert-Hendricks-Ross Trio's Annie Ross. Because each was the leading female musician of her band and the Double Six had used one of the American group's songs on their first album, the comparison seemed appropriate. However, French critics seemed to prefer the Double Six, perhaps because they sang in French and therefore were more easily understood, perhaps because the group shared the critics' nationality, or perhaps because as listeners they appreciated the aesthetic qualities of the music more. Philippe Adler, in praising Perrin's group, claimed that the Double Six's first record "in certain ways, appeared more advanced, more complete, more perfected than that of its American rival."[111] In the same vein, a writer for *Jazz Hip* asserted that

> in the first place, Mimi Perrin is not to the Double Six what Annie Ross is to the Lambert-Hendricks-Ross Trio. While Annie is only the third component of a trio whose foundations were laid long ago by Dave Lambert and Jon Hendricks, Mimi Perrin is the creator, songwriter, and adapter, in a word, the soul of this remarkable instrument of six pairs of vocal chords that is the Double Six.[112]

Interestingly enough, this same writer also chose to end his article by discussing Perrin's private life. He told his readers that she was a Parisian, about thirty-three years old, married to "a chemical engineer and bassist in his spare time," and the mother of an eight-year-old "who knows more about music and jazz than ninety-five percent of the people who read me." Here this article diverged from ones written about male musicians. This writer used Perrin's family life to help define and characterize her, while a male musician's existence outside of the realm of music was rarely discussed. Critics and fans alike widely respected Perrin's musical talent and creativity, but they still could portray her in a way that contrasted with depictions of male musicians. In the late 1960s, the Double Six's activities came to an end when Perrin herself became sick. From that time forward, she devoted herself to translations, not creating music, but she remained prominent as a musician in the minds of French jazz enthusiasts.[113]

Despite male dominance in jazz criticism, some French women worked as critics. By 1961, *Jazz Hip* reported on some of these female jazz professionals, writing that Madeleine Gautier "was alone for a longtime in a male domain. Others did finally come to relieve her. Among them, Martine Morel, pianist and Jelly Roll Morton fanatic, whose vibrant chronicles in *Jazz Hot* have not been forgotten, and, recently, Barbara Belgrave, who joined the *Jazz Magazine* team."[114] These women were often connected to jazz not only through their professional lives but also through personal ties. Gautier was married to Hugues Panassié, Belgrave was pianist Georges Arvanitas' partner, and Arlette Leloir—who wrote for *Jazz Hot* in the mid-1960s—was the wife of the jazz photographer J.-P. Leloir. Women who worked as jazz critics independent of the men in their lives were rare. This, of course, was also the case with musicians—even Mimi Perrin's husband was "a bassist in his spare time." Women often admitted being first exposed to jazz through their male friends and relatives, and a small minority of them then chose to work within this male-defined world.[115]

The critic Barbara Belgrave explained why women were not more involved in jazz as fans, critics, or musicians.

> In a general way, women are not interested in jazz or only rarely, with the exception of some musicians' companions. I believe that this comes from the fact that jazz is a virile art. Its creative function from the time of its birth is an act of man. A woman's feeling for jazz is therefore dependent on her masculinity. One can say that it is almost a question of men. That being so, I am sure that women are superior in immediate appreciation. In general, their instantaneous judgment hits the nail right on the head.[116]

For Belgrave, the masculine nature of jazz made it difficult for women to find or to create a space for themselves in this tightly-woven community, even if their immediate instincts seemed to be better than men's.

Men and women were thought to appreciate components of the jazz culture differently, so articles written by women tended to be aimed exclusively at a female audience. *Jazz Hot* called its female subscribers "Madame Jazote" and introduced one of Arlette Leloir's articles by writing, "Wanting to satisfy its female readers, *Jazz Hot* has not hesitated to entrust Arlette Leloir . . . with the jazz-fashion column for the occasion of the Wagram festival."[117] In this article, Leloir discussed the decor of the Salle Wagram as well as the audience's clothing, from women's "spiked heels" and "low-cut dresses" to men's "somber dress, blazer, white shirt, tie."[118] In the entire article, she did not once directly address or analyze the music, but only discussed fashion—that which the magazine assumed would interest its female readership more than the actual music.

Leloir's articles reinforced the idea that women were connected to jazz through men. In a 1965 piece, Leloir described how a young man first exposed her to jazz in the summer of 1950 in Lavandou. This man, to whom she gave the pseudonym "Jacques" and who "with his curly hair, his suntan, seemed to me nearly black," spoke "for a very long time about something totally unknown to my ears: jazz!" According to Leloir, "I admired his knowledge, his erudition of a musical world that I had ignored and that, therefore, seemed very complicated to me." Her initial exposure to jazz that summer went hand in hand with her romantic interests in Jacques and, at one point, she wrote, "Either I was becoming a jazz fan or I was amorous of him." After she returned to Paris at the end of the summer, she bought jazz records, magazines, and books, "wanting to get some of the vacation back."[119] Ironically, she discovered that much of Jacques' learned discussions of jazz were taken directly from André Hodeir's *Hommes et problèmes de jazz*, which she continued to study and read. But the initial appeal of the music was created through her romantic interests and she indicated that the music had seemed "complicated" to her, assuming that without Jacques she would have not become a jazz fan nor been able to initially understand the music. Leloir, of course, went on to marry a well-known French photographer of jazz musicians, reinforcing her connections to the music. Importantly, her nascent discovery of the music and the ensuing affiliation to it were thoroughly informed by her relationships with men. Writing from London, she once explained, "Because a woman must follow her husband, and because [J.-P.] Leloir decided to go to London, I am in London."[120] From the first moment of exposure and continuing into her adult life, Leloir's association with jazz depended to some degree on men.

The French jazz public perpetuated its male identity far into the postwar period. By adopting the sexual stereotypes that had been created along with the music in the United States, French jazz devotees reinforced their ties to a masculine identity. These critics and fans also objectified women's bodies and consistently focused on female vocalists' sexuality, placing primacy on their physical appearance, rather than their music. Some women, like Madeleine Gautier, Barbara Belgrave, and Annette Leloir, did successfully work as critics but their writing reflected their distance from the center of (male) jazz criticism. Perrin was the most notable female exception in the French jazz circle and she prevailed in creating and leading her own successful band, winning the respect of critics and fans alike. Unfortunately, misogynistic tendencies entered into the rhetoric surrounding jazz and the strongly-gendered discourse could not help but have lasting, damaging repercussions, excluding women from an equal membership in French jazz circles. Throughout the 1950s and 1960s, jazz—much like the French nation itself—continued to be a male domain.

NOTES

1. These two types of jazz audience also existed in postwar Germany. See Ursel Schlicht, "'Better a Jazz Album than Lipstick'(Lieber Jazzplatte als Lippenstift): The 1956 *Jazz Podium* Series Reveals Images of Jazz in Gender in Postwar Germany," *Big Ears: Listening for Gender in Jazz Studies*, eds. Nichole T. Rustin and Sherrie Tucker (Durham, NC: Duke University Press, 2008), 296.

2. Rebecca J. Pulju, *Women and Mass Consumer Society in Postwar France* (New York: Cambridge University Press, 2011), 100; and Jean-Pierre Rioux, *The Fourth Republic, 1944–1958*, trans. Godfrey Rogers (New York: Cambridge University Press, 1987), 351. For more information about fertility rates see Richard Ivans Jobs, *Riding the New Wave: Youth and the Rejuvenation of France After the Second World War* (Stanford, CA: Stanford University Press, 2007), as well as James F. McMillan, *Twentieth Century France: Politics and Society, 1889–1991* (London: Edward Arnold, 1992).

3. "Le boom de 'Salut les Copains,'" *Candide* (8 November 1962), 4; and Gloria Emerson, "France is getting younger to the cry of 'I am Free,'" *New York Times* (28 December 1965), 30.

4. Jean-François Sirinelli, *Les baby-boomers: Une génération, 1945–1969* (Paris: Fayard, 2003), 9.

5. Mat Pires, "The Popular Music Press," *Popular Music in France from Chanson to Techno: Culture, Identity and Society*, eds. Hugh Dauncey and Steve Cannon (Burlington, VT: Ashgate, 2003), 77.

6. Susan K. Foley, *Women in France Since 1789* (New York: Palgrave MacMillan, 2004), 251.

7. Claire Duchen, *Women's Rights and Women's Lives in France 1944–1968* (New York: Routledge, 1994), 191.

8. Victoria de Grazia, *Irresistible Empire: America's Advance through 20th-Century Europe* (Cambridge, MA: Belknap Press of Harvard University Press, 2005), 363. The pill became legal in France in 1967.

9. Axel Schildt and Detlef Siegfried, "Introduction: Youth, Consumption, and Politics in the Age of Radical Change," *Between Marx and Coca-Cola: Youth Cultures in Changing European Societies, 1960–1980*, eds. Axel Schildt and Detlef Siegfried (New York: Berghahn Books, 2006), 5.

10. Quoted in Jobs, 176–7.

11. Susan Weiner, *Enfantes terribles: Youth and Femininity in the Mass Media in France, 1945–1968* (Baltimore: Johns Hopkins University Press, 2001), 163.

12. *L'Express*, 16 October 1958.

13. "Françoise Sagan: The *Paris Review* Interview, August 1956," *Bonjour Tristesse*, Françoise Sagan, trans. Irene Ash (New York: Harper Perennial, 2001), 8.

14. Sagan, 35.

15. Jobs, 212, 218–19. Françoise Sagan, *Bonjour Tristesse*, trans. Irene Ash (New York: Harper Perennial, 2001).

16. Colin Nettelbeck, *Dancing with DeBeauvoir: Jazz and the French* (Carlton, Victoria: Melbourne University Press, 2004), 74.

17. Wiener, 146.

18. Jean-Louis Ginibre, "Editorial," *Jazz Magazine* 117 (April 1965), 15.

19. Tom Perchard also discusses this trend in *After Django: Making Jazz in Postwar France* (Ann Arbor: University of Michigan Press, 2015), 81.

20. Lucien Malson, "Qui aime le jazz?" *Arts* (7–13 February 1962), 1.

21. Daniel Humair, "Jazz à la carte," *Jazz Hot* 161 (January 1961), 36.

22. Boris Vian, "Le jazz: réflexions sur notre public," *Combat* (20 May 1948), 4. The Lorientais to whom Vian refers were named after the jazz club Le Lorientais and indicated fans who appreciated "hot" jazz immediately following the war.

23. Fred Appel, "L'universalité du jazz," *Jazz Hot* 116 (December 1956), 10; Henri Renaud, "New York reste vraiment la ville du jazz," *Jazz Hot* 148 (November 1959), 16; and Lucien Malson, "Le Jazz ne doit plus rester une maladie de l'adolescence," *Arts* 782 (July 1960), 13.

24. Robert Beauvais, "Jazz at Pleyel," *Arts* (20–26 October 1954), 5. Also on the typical fan, Raymond Queneau, "Rendez-vous de juillet," *Bâtons, chiffres et lettres* (Paris: Gallimard, 1965), 152.

25. "Voici l'amateur de jazz type," *Jazz Magazine* 21 (November 1956), 7.

26. "Qui êtes-vous?" *Jazz Magazine* 51 (August–September 1959), 17, 18.

27. "Qui êtes-vous?" 17, 18.

28. "Attitudes à l'égard des nations étrangers: les Etats-Unis," *Sondages: revue française de l'opinion publique*, nos. 1 and 2 (1958), 78.

29. Ibid., 79.

30. Mick Bouchard, "Comment l'on vient au jazz," *Jazz Bulletin* 12 (March 1957), 5.

31. André Hodeir, "Jazz," *Panorama de l'art musical contemporain*, ed. Claude Samuel (Paris: Éditions Gallimard, 1962), 120.

32. Lucien Malson, "Qui aime le jazz?" *Arts* (7–13 February 1962), 1.

33. Ibid.

34. Pierre Bourdieu and Jean-Claude Passeron, *Les Héritiers: les étudiants et la culture* (Paris: Les Éditions de Minuit, 1964), 30.

35. Ibid., 63.

36. Pierre Bourdieu, Jean-Claude Passeron, and Michel Éliard *Les étudiants and leurs études* (Paris: Mouton, 1964), 102–3, 146–7.

37. Lucien Malson, "Les étudiants et la connaissance du jazz," *Les Cahiers du Jazz* 12 (fourth trimester 1965), 44–5.

38. Jobs, 229.

39. Geneviève Dormann, "Les Jeunes filles réduites à rien," *Arts* 758 (18–24 January 1961), 3.

40. Article 24 of the Constitution of 1946 stated: "The Nation guarantees woman the exercise of her functions as female citizen and worker in conditions that allow her to fulfill her role as mother and her social mission." Foley, 243.

41. In 1964, two of the *Grandes Écoles* (the École Polytechnique and the École des Mines) were still closed to women, and by the early 1960s, only a handful of women had entered the others. Preparatory courses were not as available to girls; some schools used unofficial quotas to limit the number of accepted girls; and teachers tended to encourage their best female students to pursue teaching rather than admittance to a *Grandes Écoles*. See Duchen, 143.

42. Duchen, 151–54. Also see Linda Clark, *Schooling the Daughters of Marianne: Textbooks and the Socialization of Girls in Modern French Primary Schools* (Albany: State University of New York Press, 1984).

43. Pulju, 104; and Foley, 257–65. For more on women during this period, see Anne-Marie Sohn, *Âge Tendre et tête de bois: Histoire des jeunes des années 1960* (Paris: Hachette Littéraures, 2001); and Sylvie Chaperon, *Les années Beavoir, 1945–1970* (Paris: Fayard, 2000).

44. Pulju, 96. I am using the term *citizen consumer* as Pulju uses it. She borrows the term from Lizabeth Cohen's analysis of the situation in the United States in *A Consumer's Republic: The Politics of Mass Consumption in Postwar America* (New York: Alfred A. Knopf, 2003). Importantly, Pulju notes, "Articles about the home and full-time homemakers dominated in the 1950s. In the 1960s, fashion grew more prominent and articles on marital infidelity, the pill, and the female body began to appear in women's journals." Pulju, 220. Also see de Grazia's "Chapter 9: A Model Mrs. Consumer," 416–57.

45. de Grazia, 361. This information is from the 1955 poll *Enquête sure les tendances de la consummation des salariés urbaine: vous gagnez 20% de plus, qu'en faites-vous?* (Paris: Imprimerie Nationale, 1955).

46. Ann Taylor Allen, *Women in Twentieth-Century Europe* (New York: Palgrave Macmillan, 2008), 85.

47. Weiner, 17. Interestingly, when Gréco married her first husband in 1953, *Elle* published a detailed article on her marriage, showing her serving dinner to her husband and emphasizing the many new consumer goods she now owned as a wife: a refrigerator, a dryer, a table. So even an *enfant terrible* could become a domestic consumer and model wife. See "Juliette Gréco: la mariée de 25 juin," *Elle*, 6 July 1953, 17–19.

48. Foley, 252. For a thorough discussion of the *copains*, see Jonathyne Briggs, *Sounds French: Globalization, Cultural Communities, and Pop Music, 1958–1980* (New York: Oxford University Press, 2015).

49. Susan Weiner, *Enfantes Terribles: Youth and Femininity in the Mass Media in France, 1945–1968* (Baltimore: Johns Hopkins University Press, 2001), 150–1, 141.

50. Quoted in Jeremy F. Lane, *Jazz and Machine-Age Imperialism: Music, "Race," and Intellectuals in France, 1918–1945* (Ann Arbor: University of Michigan Press, 2013), 185.

51. Duchen, 117; Andrée Michel and Geneviève Texier, *La Condition de la Française d'Aujourd'hui* (Paris: Éditions Gonthier, 1964); and Ménie Grégoire, *Le métier de femme* (Paris: Plon, 1965), 8.

52. Marilyn Horne, "Newport Jazz Festival," *Jazz Magazine* 30 (September 1957), 12.

53. Cited by Frank Tenot, "Le scandale des 'ballets jazz,'" *Jazz Magazine* 46 (March 1959), 14.

54. "La musique fait du bien . . . à bébé." *France Dimanche* (21–27 March 1967), 15.

55. Ibid.

56. Joële Pergaud, letter to "Sinépistolier," *Jazz Magazine* 141 (April 1967).

57. Siné, "Sinépistolier," *Jazz Magazine* 141 (April 1967).

58. Siné, "Sinépistolier," *Jazz Magazine* 139 (February 1967), 11.

59. Pauline Carré, letter to "Sinépistolier," *Jazz Magazine* 142 (May 1967), 9.

60. See for example "Nous cherchons des correspondants, des musiciens, des amis . . . " *Jazz Magazine* 11 (November 1955), 38; and *Jazz Magazine* 19 (July–August 1956), 34.

61. Linda Dahl, *Stormy Weather: The Music and Lives of a Century of Jazzwomen* (New York: Limelight Editions: 1989), ix–x.

62. Robin D. G. Kelley, "'We Are Not What We Seem': Rethinking Black Working-Class Opposition in the Jim Crow South," *Journal of American History*, vol. 80, no. 1 (June 1993), 88.

63. Ibid., x.

64. Ibid., x.

65. Antoinette Handy, *The International Sweethearts of Rhythm* (Metuchen, NJ: Scarecrow Press, 1983) and *Black Women in American Bands and Orchestras*, Second Edition (Metuchen, NJ: Scarecrow Press, 1999); Sally Placksin, *American Women in Jazz: 1900 to the Present, Their Words, Lives and Music* (New York: Wideview, 1982); and Sherrie Tucker, *Swing Shift: "All-Girl" Bands of the 1940s* (Durham, NC: Duke University Press, 2000).

66. Tucker, 6.

67. Tucker also points out that, "although jazz is historically an African American cultural formation, its histories have been penned primarily by white men. Although often fanatically well intentioned, most of these white male journalists, aficionados, and musicologists have mostly not been positioned in ways conducive to challenging origin stories, periodization, or canons produced by white brokers of black culture." Tucker, 14.

68. Jill McManus, "Women Jazz Composers and Arrangers," *The Musical Woman: An International Perspective*, eds. Judith Lang Zaimont, Catherine Overhauser, and Jane Gottleib (Westport, CT: Greenwood Press, 1984), 197.

69. Jane Hassinger, "Close Harmony: Early Jazz Styles in the Music of the New Orleans Boswell Sisters," *Women and Music in Cross-Cultural Perspective*, ed. Ellen Koskoff (Westport, CT: Greenwood Press, 1987), 196. For more on the gendered nature of musical creation and representation, see Marcia L. Citron, "Feminist Approaches to Musicology," *Cecelia Reclaimed: Feminist Perpsectives on Gender and Music*, ed. Susan C. Cook and Judy S. Tsou (Urbana: University of Illinois Press, 1994), 15–34; and Susan McClary, *Feminine Endings: Music, Gender, and Sexuality* (Minneapolis: University of Minnesota Press, 1991).

70. Hassinger, 197.

71. Tucker, 322. For a closer look at jazzwomen in the United States since the 1970s, see Leslie Gourse, *Madame Jazz: Contemporary Women Instrumentalists* (New York: Oxford University Press, 1996).

72. Claude Samuel, *Panorama de l'art musical contemporain* (Paris: Éditions Gallimard, 1962), 161–73.

73. Philippe Chatrier letter in "Sinépistolier," *Jazz Magazine* 142 (May 1967), 8.

74. Siné, "Sinépistolier," *Jazz Magazine* 142 (May 1967), 8.

75. Cited by Siné, "Le Débloc-Notes de l'adadémicien," *Jazz Hot* 215 (December 1965).

76. André Hodeir, *The Worlds of Jazz*, trans. Noël Burch (New York: Grove Press, 1972), 54.

77. "Vi Redd ou le saxe fort," *Jazz Magazine* 148 (November 1967), 30.

78. "Petite histoire du jazz (VII): le jazz vocal," *Jazz Magazine* 7 (June 1955), 17; and Kurt Mohr, "Feminorama du jazz," *Jazz Hip* 25 (July 1961), 6.

79. "Petite histoire du jazz (VII): le jazz vocal," *Jazz Magazine* 7 (June 1955), 17.

80. André Clergeat, "L'une des trois grandes: Billie Holiday," *France U.S.A.: organe mensuel des relations Franco-Américaines* (March 1958), 2.

81. Pierre Fallan, "Bienvenue à Ella Fitzgerald," *Jazz Magazine* 24 (February 1957), 26.

82. Quoted in "Paris a reçu une bonne tournée," *Jazz Magazine* 28 (June 1957), 21–23.

83. Hugues Panassié, *Cinq mois à New-York* (Paris: Éditions Corrêa, 1947), 140.

84. Pierre Fallan, "Bienvenue à Ella Fitzgerald," *Jazz Magazine* 24 (February 1957), 26.

85. André Clergeat, "L'une des trois grandes: Billie Holiday," *France U.S.A.: organe mensuel des relations Franco-Américaines* (March 1958), 2.

86. Alain Gerber, "À la recherche de Carmen," *Jazz Magazine* 135 (October 1966), 35.

87. André Hodeir, *The Worlds of Jazz*, 53.

88. Philippe Carles, "Antibes 007: Les dames," *Jazz Magazine* 134 (September 1966), 22–23.

89. Ibid.

90. Michle Dorigné, *Jazz 2* (Paris: l'Ecole des loisires, 1970), 164, 168. In 1963, Vaughan performed in Antibes as well, and in 1967, she also sang at the Paris Jazz Festival.

91. Pierre Fallan, "Bienvenue à Ella Fitzgerald," *Jazz Magazine* 24 (February 1957), 26.
92. Michel Dorigné, *Jazz 2*, 164.
93. "Paris a reçu une bonne tournée," *Jazz Magazine* 28 (June 1957), 21.
94. "J'ai honte d'être laide," *Ici Paris* (19–25 April, 1961), 5.
95. Ibid.
96. Monique Aldebert, "Ella," *Jazz Hip* 37 (1965), 32.
97. Ibid., 33.
98. Ibid.
99. Max Dantin, letter to "Sinépistolier," *Jazz Magazine* 138 (January 1967), 15.
100. Ibid. Siné responded to this letter by calling Dantin gay.
101. "Questions et réponses . . ." *Jazz Magazine* 23 (January 1957), 7; and "Test: pièges pour Simone," *Jazz Magazine* 108 (July 1964), 40.
102. Ibid.
103. Jean Tronchot, "Jazz Notes," *Jazz Hot* 176 (May 1962), 30.
104. "Test: pièges pour Simone," *Jazz Magazine* 108 (July 1964), 40.
105. Jean Tronchot, "Jazz Notes," 30.
106. Philippe Adler, "Jazz vocal," *Informations et Documents* 152 (1 December 1961), 24.
107. Ibid.
108. The group's membership changed: Claudine Barge, Christine Legrand, Ward Single, Robert Smart, Monique and Louis Aldebert, Jean-Claude Briodin, Eddie Louiss, and Claude Germain all served as members at one time or another between 1956 and 1965. Jean Wagner, *Le Guide du jazz* (Paris: Syros, 1986), 232.
109. Adler, "Jazz vocal," 24.
110. Jean Wagner, *Le Guide du jazz* (Paris: Syros, 1986), 232.
111. Adler, "Jazz vocal," 24.
112. R.L., "France: Mimi Perrin," *Jazz Hip* 25 (July 1961), 12.
113. Also see Jean-Dominique Brierre, *Le jazz français de 1900 à aujourd'hui* (Paris: Éditions Hors Collection, 2000), 73–74.
114. "Jazz et les femmes," *Jazz Hip* 25 (July 1961), 25.
115. Robin Kelley has written about the important husband-wife jazz partnerships in the United States, arguing that not only did couples like Nellie and Thelonious Monk have stable, nurturing relationships, but that women like Lorraine Willis Gillespie and Anita Cooper Evans appreciated jazz before they met their husbands. Additionally, these women often handled the business side of their husbands' careers by managing tours and bookings as well as publishing contracts. See Robin Kelley, "The Jazz Wife: Muse and Manager," *New York Times* (21 July 2002), 24.
116. Barbara Belgrave, "Jazz et les femmes," *Jazz Hip* 25 (July 1961), 26.
117. Arlette Leloir, "Madame Jazote," *Jazz Hot* 195 (February 1964), 8.
118. Ibid.
119. Ibid., 42–43.
120. Arlette Leloir, "Un coup de soleil au coeur," *Jazz Hot* 201 (September 1964), 7–8.

Chapter Three

The Question and Politics of Race

Jazz's history in postwar France is inseparable from the subjects of race, nation, civil rights, and postcolonialism. On the simplest level, French critics and fans of the 1950s engaged in considerable debate about the color of musicians' skin and their ability or inability to play well. Although these debates continued into the 1960s, they became less frequent, so that by the middle of the decade only a small minority of the French jazz community continued to insist that the best players were black. For politically-minded listeners of these first postwar decades, race also remained a subject of vital interest, not because of a belief in the intrinsic talents of black players but because fans were shocked and distressed first by the realities of Jim Crow in the United States and then by the hardships that American blacks faced before and during the civil rights movement. The result was that, for some, jazz became a motivating force that led to social criticism and even to political engagement. In the 1960s, a number of French jazz enthusiasts chose to support talented white musicians from the United States and France, denying racial essentialists their arguments, and also elected to endorse the struggle for civil rights in the United States and labeled themselves antiracists. As France and the calendar moved further away from the experience of the Second World War, the French jazz community's ideas about blackness evolved as the music and the musicians themselves changed along with the social realities of the nation. Their discussions revealed a deep-seated French ambivalence over the subject of race, one that remains wholly unrectified in the present day.

BECOMING A DIVERSE NATION

Despite the fact that French jazz critics and fans concentrated on issues directly relevant to African Americans, their arguments and beliefs shed important light on emergent concepts of difference within the hexagon. Today, France owns a history of colonization and its accompanying racism, as well as both a long history of anti-Semitism and a progressively more entrenched form of anti-Arab discrimination. Yet few people of color lived within its borders until the first several decades after the war when the need for unskilled labor to fuel the economic growth of the *trente glorieuses* permanently brought large numbers West Africans, Caribbeans, and North Africans to the French mainland for the first time. With the arrival of increasing numbers of immigrants from the former colonies, France became a more ethnically, racially, and religiously diverse place, invariably raising tensions about who was and who was not a legitimate member of the nation.

In the ensuing decades of the postwar era, ideas about national belonging developed in different directions and, significantly, these disparate views still inform French politics today. On one side of the divide is an argument that essentializes the concept of Frenchness, insisting on integration, the idea that all immigrant and ethnic groups assimilate and adopt the national culture as defined by *les vrais français*.[1] Even less understanding of difference is an opinion expressed by the xenophobic far right that all of those without intrinsic, familial, and *true* ties to the nation have no place within its borders. According to this line of thought, French culture is homogenous, closed to outside influence and forms, and individuals are unable to assimilate new cultures or move beyond their cultures of origin.[2]

On the other end of the spectrum is a conviction that the nation can and does successfully absorb practices, beliefs, and peoples from across the globe without damaging or diluting its essential character. In writing about France at the end of the twentieth century, historian Herman Lebovics asserted that "postmodern multiplicity" threatened the French self-image of national life. This was the case despite the fact that the country has always borrowed and absorbed foreign cultural products and practices, and has seen its role as an international arbiter of culture as being intrinsic to its identity.[3] As Lebovics importantly points out, a long French tradition of incorporating the foreign into the national dates back to the Renaissance. In the case of jazz in France, "difference" existed within French culture for most of the twentieth century, demonstrating an eagerness to integrate and adopt the foreign (as well as the "primitive" and "exotic"). Members of the French jazz community in the 1950s and 1960s argued that jazz could enrich the national culture, one that was in their eyes increasingly stagnant and lacking in creativity and the new. These fans strongly believed that the energy and innovation of this American music could not only be successfully appropriated, but absorbed by French culture to positive ends.[4]

It is meaningful to note that French individuals who view their national culture as receptive to the foreign do not necessarily encourage the idea of multiculturalism or *métissage* (the mixing of cultures). To be sure, there are members of the *franco-français* majority who support the existence of minority cultures as well as a "right to difference" within the French nation; the Socialist Party first gave them a powerful voice on the political stage in the 1980s. However, the notion of multiculturalism remains highly contested as critics express a concern that by honoring and nourishing distinct foreign traditions within France the general unifying force of French culture is weakened. These critics fear that the social cohesion of the nation is threatened without the commonalities that result from sharing a united cultural patrimony. The splintering of the nation into distinct ethnic, religious, and cultural groups (labeled as *communautarisme*) is seen as dangerous to the French republican goal of integration.

In the postwar era, those interested in the cause of citizenship in France, and in protecting and promoting either a hermetic or more open national culture, all needed time to absorb the new realities created by decolonization and extra-European immigration. Certain members of the French jazz public contributed the message of inclusion to a debate that took ever more damaging turns on the other end of the political spectrum as time went on.[5] The story of jazz in the 1950s and 1960s took place when white French citizens—whether they were politicians, farmers, workers, or students—were grasping and grappling with the reality of racial, and ethnic diversity within French borders, not, as in earlier eras, in a colonized or exoticized world beyond. Certainly this subject matter was not new to people of North African, Caribbean, or African decent for whom racism was a lived reality. If white listeners chose to discuss or contend with the subjects of race, racism, and ethnic belonging, jazz gave them a means to do so. This by no means meant that the majority of jazz fans wrestled with the subject of race. Most of them were white, and like too many of their fellow countrymen, they had the luxury of ignoring the prejudices and inequalities that were part of the fabric of the French nation.

WHAT DOES IT MEAN TO BE A CITIZEN?

French ideas about national belonging, both exclusionary and inclusive ones, have been informed by a traditional republican assertion that race and ethnicity do not deserve a place in discussions of citizenship or national belonging, only culture does. As part and parcel of the French republican heritage dating from 1789 was a belief introduced above: that French citizenship and culture were irrevocably linked to one another so that belonging to the nation meant accepting, adopting, and owning the national culture and its value system as one's own.[6] According to this concept, race had nothing to do with being a citizen.

European immigrants to France have historically assimilated into the nation through their exposure to its school system, its army, and its unions. Until the 1980s, ethnic minorities did not have recourse to representative intermediary organizations, like the American National Association for the Advancement of Colored People (NAACP), to work as their advocates in the government and court system, and this prevented ethnic politics from gaining a foothold in France.[7] Some French jazz critics and fans, because of their awareness of racial politics in the United States, addressed the subject of civil rights before many of their white French contemporaries. By the late 1960s, they were directly addressing the reality of racism in France and urging their countrymen to recognize, resist, and contest bias on their own soil. However, in this period, none of them lobbied for the creation of civil rights organizations in France, and, in reality, the vast majority of jazz devotees did not show a concern for the growing minority populations and their hardships within France. Nonetheless, the language that jazz critics used and the support that they gave to the American cause in the 1950s reflected early postwar French ideas about both discrimination and equality. Importantly, these men were not the first individuals to take up an antiracist agenda: activists of African and Antillean heritage had been involved in the cause of civil rights in France for decades and did much more to advance the cause of antiracism than white French jazz critics ever did.[8] However, most members of the *franco-français* majority did not take up an earnest public discussion of civil rights on a large scale.[9] I am interested in exploring how antiracist thought evolved among white French citizens, who were rather oblivious when it came to recognizing and addressing discrimination in their own country. French jazz enthusiasts are one window into better understanding a nascent and slow-to-mature white French interest in civil rights.

It is imperative to point out that the American and French views of ethnicity significantly vary from one another and that the two countries have historically taken very distinct approaches to racial, ethnic, and cultural differences. The American political and social model allows people to hold allegiances to both the United States and a "home" of origin, giving them hyphenated identities (for instance, as Italian Americans, African Americans, or Polish Americans), while the French model insists on eradicating any other social, political, or cultural ties beyond an affiliation with France.[10] According to French expectations, an immigrant must do away with connections to another homeland and adopt the French cultural heritage as his or her own to complete the process of becoming French. Unlike the American census, the French one divides the population into only two categories—

"French" and "foreigner"—and ignores ethnic differences that the American system highlights so consistently between White, Hispanic, Black or African American, Asian, American Indian, and the like.

According to the political scientist Donald Horowitz, from the time of the Revolution, attaining equality meant that society needed to eradicate blood privileges and that citizens had to remove any indications of their origin beyond France.[11] Yet, as Dominic Thomas has argued, because of this official racial invisibility, discussions about difference have become more complicated at a time when people agree that French assimilation, insertion, and integration policies are largely ineffective.[12] By limiting their recognition of ethnic differences to a framework that focuses only on the processes of immigration and then assimilation, the French have a tendency to overlook the reality of diversity that shapes their culture.[13] As I have already pointed out, foreign cultural products have been successfully, even at times enthusiastically, absorbed into the national patrimony over the course of centuries. A question for the contemporary age is whether the French can make peace with the concept of *communautarisme* and with the reality of diverse and international cultures coexisting with one another but not necessarily assimilating and disappearing into the nation's larger dominant cultural narrative.[14] For an American audience, this relentless focus on culture might seem exhausting and unnecessary, because cultural practice and discrimination are not automatically and essentially linked in the United States. But in France they are, for culture, i.e. *la civilisation française*, was constructed to replace Catholicism as the bond of republican belief and practice.

Current and past observers of the postwar era have noted that discrimination against certain ethnic groups in France exists, but disagreement remains over how to label prejudices that single out North Africans for their religious and cultural practices, but might spare Antilleans who are viewed primarily as French. Various academics and observers have labeled these discriminatory practices "cultural fundamentalism," "cultural racism," and "culturalism," and have even discussed both the creation of a "national racism" in France and the "racialization of culture."[15] As early as 1956, the Martinique intellectual and revolutionary Frantz Fanon wrote, "Racism which wants to be rational, individual, determined, genotypic and phenotypic, is changing into cultural racism. The target of racism is no longer the individual man, but a certain way of life."[16] All of these observers express the same thought: culture was and is used as a reason for seeing ethnic groups as outsiders and justifying intolerance against them. But a victim's experience of this type of bias is no different from the experience of discrimination based on race, and the prejudices that begin with culture are undeniably racialized. How else can one explain the fact that people of North African descent encounter prejudice in France today regardless of their own cultural choices and practices? Racism uses the color of a person's skin to define and to prejudge his or her intelligence, physical capabilities, economic situation, social place, and, often in France, religion. The problem of exclusion and discrimination based on race exists. Studying the reception of jazz in the postwar years uncovers early debates over difference based on both race and culture, and reveals crucial tensions in French ideas at a time when immigrants from the former colonies were just beginning to make their presence felt on a national scale. Traditionally, the history of racism is mostly one of the political right and the history of antiracism is predominantly one of the political left, but looking at the latter's promotion and acceptance of jazz provides new insights into the way race was conceived in the early postwar period and problematizes the strong dichotomy between racism and antiracism, racism and cultural fundamentalism.

THE AFRICAN AND THE AMERICAN

Jazz emanated from African, African-American, and European musical traditions that coalesced into a new form of music in turn-of-the-twentieth-century New Orleans; an obvious and stated reason for the French interest in jazz during the 1950s was that it had originated from the efforts and creativity of black musicians. French audiences of this decade often professed that "black" jazz was the most authentic jazz and they consistently portrayed it as superior to the music played by white jazzmen.[17] The African-American experience of slavery and the endemic racial inequality that characterized American society were central to the music's evolution. For Europeans, jazz represented a new way of approaching music as its unique use of syncopation, as well as rhythmic and melodic tension, made it radically different from other contemporary sounds. In 1956, Lucien Malson maintained that it was "not a simple dance rhythm, a music closed in on itself, but a new way of thinking about music."[18]

This way of approaching jazz in terms of black and white had its roots in the interwar period when jazz first made its way to France. When the Harlem Hellfighters, Mitchell's Jazz Kings, and Will Marion Cook's Southern Syncopated Orchestra toured after World War I, they physically brought jazz to France and broadened its popularity there. At this time, Parisian modernists, including Jean Cocteau, Darius Milhaud, Igor Stravinsky, and Eric Satie, also undertook the task of incorporating jazz into their own music.[19] For these men, an interest in jazz was part of a larger fascination with black culture that focused on music, poetry, literature, and art from Africa and the Americas, and which contemporaries labeled "Negrophilia."[20] General audiences as well as elite commentators and artists expressed a belief in a unified and immutable black identity that was shared by the people of Africa and the members of the African diaspora no matter where they lived on the globe.[21]

A cadre of musicians known as Les Six actively searched out novel sounds in Parisian popular culture and brought the rhythms and melodies of jazz into their modernist music.[22] They were drawn to these previously unheard sounds because as artists they were pursuing ways to invigorate a seemingly exhausted French culture. So they visited not only music halls but also circuses and movie houses, all in an effort to find creative stimulation for their works. As a member of Les Six, the composer Milhaud found jazz especially appealing because he understood its roots to be a fusion of the African and the American. For him, time in the United States had not erased an inherent connection to Africa for black Americans. He tellingly wrote in 1924, "Primitive African qualities have kept their place deep in the nature of the American negro." The music of African Americans was characterized as spontaneous, creative, emotional, and free in contrast to entrenched and rational traditional European music. Yet these modernist musicians did not remain fascinated with African-American music for long. Because of jazz's growing popularity and ubiquity in Parisian entertainment, the French avant-garde became more disinterested in it as the 1920s moved forward. They no longer equated jazz with the cutting edge of interwar culture.[23]

Despite a stated support and attraction for all things connected to the *nègre*, the connotations and stereotypes that accompanied negrophilia had damaging repercussions at the same time that they helped the French define themselves in the face of a foreign other. Brett Berliner has written that "the tam-tam, nudity, and animality became representative of the exotic primitive nègre and served an important function for the French: these images delimited French cultural categories, creating an ordered cosmos for the French to inhabit." Images representing black subjects could represent "the savage, the dirty, the cannibal, the lazy, the happy, the sexualized . . . all in a form greater than a fiction, in a myth."[24] The myth of the nègre provided a counterbalance to a tired and entrenched French culture, and proved useful to interwar French men and women who were seeking out ways to stimulate not only themselves through exposure to the exotic, but French culture as well. French audiences most often focused on individuals and cultural products from Africa in this period, but they also had an active interest in African Americans.

Two of the most important examples of French cultural products co-opting African-American art in the 1920s were the 1923 ballet *La création du monde*, whose music was composed by Darius Milhaud, and *La Revue nègre*, the music hall show in which the African-American expatriate Josephine Baker began performing in 1925. For subject matter, *La création du monde* focused on Bantu creation mythologies and its music intentionally integrated elements of jazz. In describing his work on the ballet, Milhaud wrote, "[It] offered me the opportunity to make use of the jazz elements I had so seriously studied. I composed my orchestra like those in Harlem, with seventeen solo musicians, and I utilized the jazz style without reserve, blending it with a classical sentiment."[25] Despite his desire to integrate jazz into the music for *La creation du monde*, Milhaud was unfamiliar with the social and cultural context of jazz and used oversimplified means of classification, as when he labeled white jazz "mechanical" and black jazz "primitive." He traced jazz to "the darkest corners of the negro soul" and to "savage" Africa, even though he was unfamiliar with actual African music.[26]

Displaying a similar concentration on a perceived jazz culture, Baker was often accompanied by *La Revue nègre*'s jazz band when she performed, and just like Milhaud's *La creation du monde*, Baker's work adopted elements that were promoted and understood as African. She became most famous for her *danse sauvage*, which was designed by her French producer to fit notions of the day about blackness, sensuality, and the exotic.[27] This producer expected observers to equate Baker with an uncivilized African native in a simplistic and reductionist way as she danced in a sparse feathered costume before them. In 1926, Baker wore her signature banana skirt in a show at the Folies Bergère, reinforcing her connection to a primitivism that was based on her skin color and perceived sexuality.

Baker eventually rejected the image that portrayed her as an African native. But despite her own intentional rebuff of the *danse sauvage* and its racialized meanings, for countless French observers, Baker endured as a quintessential symbol of the era. She brought to her French audiences a vision of Africa and the "savage" that had been invented by Europeans and Americans to fill their own cultural void and needs. In the 1920s, Baker's shows, directed by men, connected her to an imagined erotic, primal, untamed "other" that corresponded with the colonial mentality as well as ideas about things "black." According to the theater manager of the Théatre Champs-Élysées, André Daven, Baker was "eroticism personified. The simplicity of her emotions, her savage grace, were deeply moving. She laughed, she cried, then from her supple throat came a song, crystal clear at first, then with a hoarseness that caught at the heart."[28] Not surprisingly, Baker was initially chosen in 1931 to be the queen of the Colonial Exposition in Paris, which showcased the French colonies from May to December of that year. In the face of protests asserting her American background, the offer was rescinded, yet the link her French fans made between her and Africa had already been expressed.[29]

Despite Baker's fame and popularity, much of what she symbolized distressed a cadre of French journalists and writers who were bent on excluding *jazz nègre-saxon* from the patrimony, their vexation illustrating that not all were caught up in this cultural trend of embracing blackness and the foreign.[30] By the early 1930s, Baker had stopped performing the *danse sauvage* to pursue a career more in line with traditional French music hall entertainment and in 1937 she became a French citizen. Baker's cosmopolitan identity helped to make her more popular because depending on the situation she could bring Africa, the Caribbean, the United States, or France to her audiences' minds.[31] Despite her eventual rejection of the primitive and the African as defining components of her public persona, she still continued to represent both the Jazz Age and a conception of blackness for many in France, whether they sought to embrace or to disallow its assumed qualities.[32]

In her physique and in her performances, she culturally represented both America *and* Africa for interwar French spectators.[33] Critics depicted her as a civilized French colonial subject who retained the primitive qualities of Africa at the same time as she built a life for herself in France. Baker's French admirers emphasized that she was able to pursue professional and personal opportunities in France that would not have been available to her in the United States because of racial prejudice. In doing so, they could claim France's moral superiority regarding race relations and also extol the benefits of the colonial civilizing mission.[34] Throughout the interwar period, Baker's identity could not be extracted from a connection to Africa or to America, and her audiences' perceptions of her reflected their own ideas about France's place in the world.

For the most part, French supporters of jazz during the 1920s endorsed what they understood to be "black" because blackness lay outside the perceived boundaries of an ingrained and less vigorous, less emotional, white culture that they wanted either to transform or to reject outright. Artists often chose the representational qualities they found in black music over the ones they found in American white music, and French modernists made a strong distinction between "authentic" black jazz and the white commercial jazz produced by Tin Pan Alley in the United States. Milhaud himself believed that blacks resisted blending their culture into the hegemonic American one by retaining "the African" in their forms of expression.[35] In 1924, he wrote, "Primitive African qualities have kept their place deep in the nature of the American negro."[36] As Matthew Jordan has shown, because of the strong artistic link to an African source, "black" jazz defied a perceived sophistication and homogenization of western culture that these modernists strove to avoid.[37] Those interested in jazz in the 1920s saw the music as firmly linked to the African, regarding it as something that derived from "the black soul."[38] Jazz retained important connections to the primitiveness of African musics for these French listeners who mostly elided any difference between African Americans and Africans. According to this mindset, both groups had incontrovertible qualities that included an affinity for music and dance as well as a gift for rhythm, spontaneity, and creativity, qualities that set them apart from white Americans or Europeans.[39]

In this historical moment, French audiences were already contending with the cultural hybridity jazz brought to forms of entertainment; well before the postwar period that is the focus of this study, observers and jazz enthusiasts embraced musics and dance styles connected to jazz precisely because they were perceived as foreign, emotional, and instinctual. In the words of Jeffrey Jackson, many intellectuals and artists "thought that cultures outside Europe offered the hope of regenerating a seemingly dead Western imagination that had been exhausted by the war."[40] For these fans of the 1920s, the African was an intrinsic component of jazz, informing and defining the music's origins and inventiveness.

By the middle of the 1920s, a variety of new labels were used to describe both the fascination with black art and the interminglings that led to the evolution of different black cultural forms. In 1924, one French observer, commenting on all that was novel about the early twentieth century, highlighted a *negromania* that welcomed all things with a perceived connection to blackness.[41] By the second half of the decade, a number of French intellectuals and musicians explored using previously unheard words and phrases to capture the fact that jazz emanated not only from an African source but from a very American one as well. In 1926, the French ethnographer André Schaeffner created a neologism to describe the culture in which jazz was born: *Afro-Américain*.[42] Along these same lines, the pianist and composer Jean Wiéner referred to the *musique négro-américaine* that impacted his work.[43] In 1929, the writer and ethnographer Michel Leiris fashioned yet another word to describe the cultural origins of jazz: *Aframérique*. In doing so, Leiris underscored the fused and mixed nature of the cultural world that produced jazz.[44] Notably, some among the French recognized that jazz did not evolve from an exclusively African culture but from one that at its core was a combination of different cultural sources. Eventually, the initial interwar understanding of jazz as especially connected to the African evolved into one that celebrated the art as *both* African and American. But doing so did not mean rejecting primitivist stereotypes. Conceptions of blackness that highlighted the emotional, the virile, the exotic, and the physical remained very much alive. In the minds of men like Leiris, "primitive" African culture was retained by African Americans as well as elevated through their contact with the West.

Of course, not all among the French liked the new sounds of *jazz nègre*, and some inserted into their cultural agenda a focus on the difference between the music of black artists and white French ones. The French composer and pianist Maurice Delage in 1926 wrote about how French jazz musicians, specifically Clement Doucet and Jean Wiéner, assimilated the language of this music to make it their own. For Delage, it was important to distinguish the "frenetic" or "epileptic" sounds of black jazz from the "polyphonic refinement" and "measured fantasy" of French jazz pieces that valued melody and harmony over the primacy of rhythm. Through this conceptual lens, Delage defined white French jazz with values and an outlook that were diametrically opposed to black jazz, and those like him envisioned a musical and cultural evolution that progressed from the initially primitive and exotic into the more civilized.[45] According to Delage, jazz, as it left its black roots and origins to be played and mastered by French musicians, was following this assumed trajectory for the good of the music.

In the 1930s, economic depression resulted in fewer African-American jazzmen touring in France, so that white French musicians had increased exposure. To be sure, there had been popular white musicians in France in the 1920s. For example, the bandleaders Jack Hylton from Great Britain and Paul Whiteman from the United States had both enjoyed success as performers in France during this decade. Despite the fact that their French listeners continued to acknowledge the African-American origins of the music that these men and their orchestras played, Hylton, Whiteman, and others like them did initiate an acceptance of white jazz among French fans. By the 1930s, orchestral jazz performed by white artists in music halls became the most prevalent means of listening to the music live, and white artists became more broadly known through records and radio shows as well. By the end of the decade, one of the most highly regarded jazz bands in the country was French, the Quintette du Hot Club de France, headlined by the guitarist Django Reinhardt and the violinist Stéphane Grappelli. Because of world events well beyond the confines of the jazz world—namely economic depression and then the Second World War—the direct influence of African-American musicians on the imaginings and realities of jazz in France did not disappear but lessened until the postwar period began. In many ways, the postwar jazz community picked up precisely where the one from the late 1920s left off.

Like his contemporaries, the critic Hugues Panassié's impressions regarding jazz were profoundly impacted by racial conceptions. He attributed to race the ability to swing and to play "hot," labeling the music "Negro swing." Because he saw jazz as emanating from a black worldview, he believed that black musicians not only played differently from white ones but in a far superior way. Throughout the interwar period, Panassié maintained that white players could play "real" jazz only if they embraced the emotion and the spirit that black musicians possessed.[46] As we will see shortly, these ideas surrounding jazz and race, which were promulgated by Panassié, changed little with the progression of time and, if anything, hardened into a more stringently racialized viewpoint.

Importantly, these conceptions of jazz that predated the Second World War, ones that not only welcomed but actively endorsed at first the African, then the African American, and finally what was understood to be *le noire*, far outlived the popularity of some interwar forms of the music, and eventually helped generate an interpretation that continued to shape how later devotees appreciated and promoted jazz.[47]

MUSIC IN BLACK AND WHITE

In light of the various attributes assigned to black musicians in the period before the war, it is not surprising that many postwar French admirers of jazz were interested in the color of a musician's skin. In 1946, the critic Claude Sautet wrote an article for *Combat* entitled "The Quarrel of the whites and the blacks" that discussed the relevance of race to the music of jazz. He thought that "from the technical point of view, whites have nothing to learn from blacks." A white musician like Benny Goodman possessed the actual ability he needed, he *could* play, but he lacked, according to Sautet, the inspiration or the capacity to inspire enthusiasm in others. Sautet professed that white musicians "do not know how to express themselves with sufficient heat, persuasion, sincerity, abandonment." Benny Goodman's "Pick a Rib" was "a technical success, fun, agreeable, and of very good taste, but nothing more: it does not captivate." For Sautet, the majority of whites did not have the "communicative power" of black players, but he did acknowledge exceptions to the rule.[48] Obviously he was not a Benny Goodman fan, but he admired the talent of Bix Beiderbecke, Milton Mezzrow, and the Quintette du Hot Club de France.

Non-French jazz critics readily highlighted the French tendency to praise black musicians at the expense of white ones. The British critic Leonard Feather thought that this behavior was discriminatory and he took offense at the commonly held opinion in France that black jazz artists were more "authentic" than white ones. He claimed that despite the fact that this belief could be guided unconsciously, it still represented a "true" prejudice against white musicians.[49] Unlike French jazz admirers of the early postwar period, Feather did not believe that there was a white style or a black style of playing and composing music. For him, race was irrelevant.

Certainly, many French critics did not agree. Charles Delaunay argued that "the majority of *true creators* are black, from the pioneers of New Orleans up until the modern champions of the school of 'bop.'" He recognized that European fans often discriminated against both American and European white jazz musicians, and often preferred "black musicians of an inferior class." For the French fan, however, blackness guaranteed a type of legitimacy and vitality that seemed to be missing in white musicians:

> [The] black musician, in a general way, is more spectacular, and . . . he shows to be more at ease, more relaxed (sometimes even inclined to a certain easy showing-off), than the white musician. For excellent that he is, the latter shows himself to be often uneasy, and seems to be bored. And the spectator does not like this.[50]

French jazz fans consistently essentialized blackness during the decade of the 1950s. Some stated that music was a fundamental part of the black personality, that blacks had "an inner taste for music."[51] People could love this music for its "intrinsic beauty," or as "a means to dance," but "the true fans are those sensitive to this music with the same intensity as the Blacks who gave it birth."[52] In this way, jazz was necessarily connected to blackness and these French fans thought that to be black meant to be emotional, virile, rhythmic, and active. A white jazz musician was more cerebral, refined, and polished, and he thus defied the essence of jazz. This fascination with black male bodies revealed the enduring myth of black male sexual power that made the black jazzman someone to imitate and admire. The white jazzman could never possess the same physical prowess, ability, or allure of a black musician: the latter's preeminence was not learned but an intrinsic part of his biological makeup.

French commentators argued that blacks had different physical characteristics that made them more athletically adept, enhancing their capacity to play musical instruments that required strength and endurance. André Hodeir found it

> astonishing to see that in important athletic tests of speed and jumping, that is to say in areas that require relaxation and flexibility, things that are so necessary in jazz, one always notes a certain superiority of black athletes. For example, in all the Olympic Games for twenty or thirty years the final of the 100 meters is invariably run with four or five blacks out of six runners. Transposed onto the plane of jazz, this supremacy is the same, I believe.[53]

He used this reasoning (along with data taken from an American psychoanalyst not mentioned by name) to explain why "the black drummer is, in nine cases out of ten, superior to the white one." Hodeir stated, "It seems to me that one especially finds good white jazz players on instruments which are physically less demanding. And where one commonly admits the superiority of blacks, it is precisely in the cases where the physical effort is the greatest."[54] Just as female jazz artists were objectified for their sex appeal, black jazzmen could be reduced to being physically superior specimens admired by white French audiences for their exceptional endurance and physical power.

Sometimes French critics singled out and criticized white jazz musicians for what they saw as their unimpressive talent. When Gerry Mulligan went to France in 1956 several writers gave him unfavorable reviews, one calling him "the bad white" who was not only "anti-natural" but also "commercial" as well.[55] A Patrice Sylvian review in *L'Aurore* described the "blonde, timid" Mulligan as playing with an "affectation of sophisticated nonchalance, bordering on boredom." Sylvian obviously did not care for Mulligan's performance, but interestingly enough, he liked Mulligan's records and he wrote that listening to them "gives a completely different impression and allows one to appreciate his real capacities" as a "brilliant baritone saxophonist" and "remarkable arranger."[56] This was unusual. Ordinarily, jazz fans insisted that live jazz was preferable to recorded music because it maintained the crucial link between musician and audience.[57] It is noteworthy that Sylvian also insisted on calling Mulligan "blonde," perhaps illustrating that it was precisely Mulligan's appearance, of which his whiteness was a part, which made him unappealing to French observers during a live show.

In this period, French jazz enthusiasts largely assumed and accepted the "fact" that French jazz musicians were not as talented as African-American ones. Before the war, the French Roma musician Django Reinhardt had achieved international recognition for his talents on the guitar, but he was alone so far in achieving this: the worldwide jazz community had recognized neither the genius nor the originality of another French musician. As a result, people questioned whether French jazz musicians were relevant to the music's growth and popularity in France. As early as 1950, *Jazz Hot* asked French critics and musicians, "Is there a jazz in France?" The writer and saxophone player Michel de Villers replied negatively. He thought that French jazz musicians were largely "imitators more or less weak-willed who, by nature, prefer the waltz." They were also white and therefore removed from authentic jazz by both their nationality and their race. According to de Villers, white Frenchmen were unable to have "a thing in common with the black folklore of Harlem."[58] Using the example of the American musician Charlie Singleton, de Villers also claimed that black musicians were more pleasing to the eye. "That is to say that Charlie Singleton, with a tenor, standing on stage, looks like a good musician, he is agreeable to look at. Even if a French musician had played exactly the same thing that night, one would have found him quite bad."[59] In this case, a Frenchman avowed that a black American musician was simply more enjoyable to watch than one of his white countrymen. Surprisingly, de Villers himself was a jazz musician.

Some French writers still hesitated to unconditionally confirm the superiority of American musicians. André Clergeat alleged that in terms of numbers, it made no sense to compare American and French musicians. According to him, a country of 45 million people could never produce as many great musicians as a country of 150 million. "This is not to express an anti-French theory recognizing the superiority of those who overrun us, whatever the reasons are for this superiority."[60] Here, de Villers agreed. He too thought that no one wanted to affirm an actual American advantage. American musicians benefited from the size and strength of their country and from the fact that they lived in the place where the jazz tradition had been founded.

The question of race did not recede in importance as the reputation of white musicians grew, and by the mid-1950s, increasing numbers of white (mostly American) musicians were entering the jazz scene in both the United States and France. In 1954, the French weekly *Arts* wrote, "The enormous progress made by white musicians, in number and in quality, has put into doubt, for many fans, the traditional ideas on 'jazz, the black art.'" The magazine asked two critics, Frank Ténot and Jacques Hess, to respond to the question, "Jazz, is it still a black art?" Ténot replied, "Yes, because the Black plays with all of his body," while Hess stated, "No, because it has become a global phenomenon."[61] Both critics defended at length their conflicting opinions and, in doing so, they opened up a debate about the differences between race and culture.

Ténot held that black musicians "are more suited to the execution of this art than whites are." Whites, even though they had come to play "at the sides of their [black] mentors," had not "yet produced any masterpieces of their own as important as those of Blacks, or any personalities on the same level as the half-a-dozen great black masters." At one point Ténot asked, "What white has the timbre of Sarah Vaughan?" directly implying the physical superiority of black voices over white ones. Because of this black prominence in jazz, Ténot was extremely concerned about the would-be influence of white musicians. For him, it was impossible to know in advance the impact white players would have on this music and therefore their importance to the story of jazz moving forward. The future held two possibilities in his mind. Either "a good number of new black masters will put their names down following the old black 'geniuses'" or "Whites and Blacks will equally divide the lead places in the framework of an art that will be different from today's." If white musicians came to hold a distinguished place, the music would fall into a new category of music and perhaps no longer be jazz. The first of these two possible futures, with black musicians alone advancing the music, was the preferable one for Ténot, and he claimed that it was also the most probable because of the successes black jazzmen had already achieved in this musical culture. Ténot went on to say, "I have too much admiration and love for the music of the great black masters of jazz from Louis Armstrong to Charlie Parker to be able to make a clean break between them and the production of these last five years."[62] For him, no common links existed between the music of black and white musicians. If white jazz held a dominant and celebrated position, it would carry the music away from its blackness and its roots.

Viewing things quite differently, Jacques Hess opposed using race to explain any musician's talent or abilities. He wrote, "It is evident that one is not born a jazz musician. One becomes one through a series of diverse responses . . . to the calls of a certain cultural milieu." For Hess, a musician was created by the culture surrounding him. He conceded that it "would be ridiculous to deny the historical supremacy of black Americans" but he insisted that it had to be determined whether this was an "essential," "natural," and "actual" supremacy:

Sociologically, we have good reasons to respond no. If one asks that only musical phenomenon influence this opinion one sees: first that the proportion of very good white musicians, arrangers and composers is actually a good deal more considerable than any other period in the history of jazz. Second, that this proportion, in the course of time, is going to grow.[63]

Hess, aware that he was contradicting others, predicted that "Hodeir and Ténot will ask me to cite for them a white genius, and will advance, from another direction, this famous [belief about the] natural relaxation of the black American." Hess thought that this argument about "natural relaxation" was potentially destructive. "Even if one admitted—something I am not ready to do—that this ability to relax found a complete explanation in morphology and the nervous system of a race, it still must be developed, it falls on each person to give it meaning, and I am persuaded that motivations of the cultural order enter into this."[64]

Hess also asserted that jazz devotees needed to address a second issue, namely "'Jazz and the Jews.' (One indeed knows the impressive proportion of Jewish jazzmen)." Hess was undoubtedly referring to Jewish musicians like Milton Mezzrow who was extremely popular in France, even if some jazz professionals might have distrusted him because of his close association to Hugues Panassié. Hess did not go on to discuss the subject of Jewish jazzmen at any length but claimed that he wanted to make people "reflect" on the difficulties surrounding the subject of race. He concluded his remarks by stating, "To the question: 'Jazz, is it still a black art?' one can respond with a yes. But this yes is not definitive."[65]

A united front organized itself in opposition to Hess, making him a frequent target in articles written by Lucien Malson, arguably the most influential jazz critic in the postwar period. Malson had studied sociology as well as American cultural anthropology as a student at the University of Bordeaux where he had come under the influence of sociologist Jean Stoezel. Stoezel made a considerable impact on the young Malson, who in a 1996 interview asserted that the professor had made him conscious of the variability of cultures and how difficult it was to attach an essence to man.[66] Much of Malson's professional life was informed by the studies he undertook at Bordeaux and he spent substantial amounts of time discussing the subject of race, while also focusing his energies on expanding the reach of jazz in France. As discussed in chapter 1, in addition to writing articles on jazz for various periodicals, Malson was the head of the Bureau de Jazz of Radiodiffusion-Télévision Française throughout the 1960s and was the author of several important books on jazz as well.

Because of Malson's prominent place in the postwar jazz community, it makes sense that he weighed in on the debate revolving around Hess, jazz, and race. In criticism of Hess, he wrote, "Hess claims that . . . white jazz and black jazz are not easily discerned from one another, that blacks were for a long time superior to whites but that, now, things tend to change. For Hess, white jazz today is at least as good as black jazz."[67] In 1954, Malson openly agreed with Ténot's belief that black jazz musicians were superior to white ones, yet he did so by employing an argument that stressed culture, not race, and cited UNESCO documents that declared "man is a history." According to Malson, the problem with Hess' reasoning was that he ignored the fact that life for blacks in the United States was in many ways defined by a certain "sociological constellation." The experience of living as a black man gave black musicians a certain edge over white artists in Malson's view and he stated, "It seems evident to us that the majority of first-rank musicians today are still black."[68]

In 1955, Malson explained in more detail what he exactly meant by "sociological constellation." He used the following example to illustrate how different the worlds of black and white were in the United States: "There are 160 Baptist churches in New York where black children are brought very young, where black children experience a certain way of singing, experience syncopation and aesthetic hubris. It is one thing among many that differentiates black education from white education." Malson was against relying on any sort of biological determinism (something that Hodeir and Ténot both seemed persuaded by at this point) but instead wanted to focus on factors such as education and experience. He declared that it was necessary "to create a sociology, but also to make a psychoanalysis of the black" and "to study many things." He went on to say, "What is certain in my mind, is that the gifts of the black do not reside in his skin, in his neurons."[69] Others certainly agreed with Malson on the importance of culture and the centrality of black musicians. For instance, Charles Delaunay wrote that it was understandable that the jazz of men like Art Blakey and Max Roach was aggressive: "It is normal because their social position demands that [the music] be aggressive."[70]

Due to the sustained emphasis on black musicians' talents, some French jazz musicians, especially during the 1950s, felt unappreciated and reacted passionately to this constant characterization of jazz as black. These artists wanted to create a space for "white" jazz. The guitarist Olivier Despax argued that black musicians were defined by a spirit that whites lacked, "a kind of ferocity of rhythm, a violence that one finally calls swing," and that they had "a brutal sensibility, absolutely not the sensibility of whites." Despax wanted to distance himself from this "black" jazz and connect with the white tradition he saw in American West Coast jazz. Blues defined African-American jazz and Despax claimed that when a person listened to jazz he was filled with "savage" longings and automatically desired to scream. In opposition to this "savage," "physical" music, he preferred the more "cerebral" jazz that was "specifically white." He insisted that "white jazz must not imitate black jazz. . . . [We] will not achieve it because blacks have something that we do not have and will never have."[71]

The absolute bifurcation of jazz into black and white was seldom motivated by antiblack sentiments as most French jazz players and fans wanted to make a connection with what they considered black. But in musicians such as Despax, one can sense a strong tension over the subject of race and a clear desire to be associated with whiteness. For him, the problem he found in belonging to the world of jazz was not one of nationality, for he readily admitted his admiration of the white American musicians Johnny Richards and Stan Kenton. Being French did not prohibit him from emulating these two Americans. Rather Despax's problem was almost exclusively with race because he would never play to the "black" side of jazz. Despax's opinion, however, was not the norm. Just as in the 1920s, the "blackness" of jazz continued to be precisely what made it appealing to the majority of French postwar listeners.

Lucien Malson did recognize, though, sentiments similar to Despax's in other French musicians, musicians who "find in white jazz a particular quality. It is more cerebral, more refined, more polished. There are those people who sometimes say 'that stinks of black' when they listen to jazz music."[72] Malson disapproved of this way of thinking and suggested that these individuals were perhaps not legitimate fans. He agreed that jazz could be made "less sensual" (the equivalent of "less black" in this strongly-divided mindset) without the music losing its essence. But to call for such a thing was not to embrace jazz in Malson's view. In a 1954 article for *Les Temps Modernes* he asserted, "The problem of the place of Whites in jazz is complex." Despite the fact that he thought "the essential aesthetic of jazz is black," he held that white musicians were successfully learning to assimilate "the language of jazz." He felt that

> it is often impossible to distinguish, from listening to a record, a white musician from a black musician. If Whites have played nothing but minor roles in jazz up until today, if there have not been great creators—except maybe Bix Beiderbecke—the absence of white artists of the first order is easily explained: Blacks devoted themselves to authentic jazz in much greater numbers; they grappled with the practice of jazz from the youngest ages; Whites came late.[73]

He asserted that the situation was changing because one found among white players "a large number of excellent artists and increasingly frequent contacts between musicians of the two races." He thought that white involvement could become more important to jazz in the "near future" and asked, "Can one say that modern jazz is better suited for 'pale faces'? It is very debatable. The new music is *equally* practiced by Blacks and Whites" (italics original).[74] Unlike some of his contemporaries in the 1950s, Malson did not attribute sensuality, musical talent, or intellectual acumen to biology and race, but ultimately he did defend the qualities of jazz that others considered "black" because they gave the music its richness and novelty. In doing so, he perhaps for a time contributed to the perpetuation of the racialized framework of jazz, until the advent of the 1960s when he more forcefully turned his attention to disrupting people's understandings of jazz that depended on skin color.

Like Malson, other members of the French jazz public in the 1950s wanted to shield the music from opinions like those expressed by the white musician Olivier Despax. A *Jazz Magazine* subscriber from Nice wrote a letter to the editor in 1955 asking for advice about how to defend jazz from harsh criticism. He wrote, "How does one respond to people who say that jazz is a music of 'Negroes,' a bestial music and one without harmony, a music that whites cannot play because they are not beasts?" Director of publications Jacques Souplet harshly condemned the opinions reflected in this subscriber's question. For Souplet, people could dislike jazz on musical grounds and prefer classical music, for instance, but "sensible" and "tolerant" ones would be "respectful of the tastes of others." Furthermore, such caustic opinions, according to Souplet, had not had any currency for the last "quarter of a century."[75]

At times, jazz critics cautioned against grouping entire groups of people into the same racial category. Charles Delaunay wrote that it was an "absolutely grotesque error to think that all black Americans are endowed with the gift for jazz, that all blacks love and understand jazz and that all blacks are extraordinary dancers."[76] Yet, overall, these men reinforced the notion that blackness and musical prowess went hand in hand. Because of this, many thought that jazz offered French and European musics something refreshing and alive without threatening older musical and cultural traditions. André Hodeir asserted that, for him, undoubtedly, the essence of jazz was contained in a certain "Negro spirit." In his 1956 book *Jazz: Its Evolution and Its Essence*, Hodeir admitted that for a long time he had been convinced that the only way to appreciate jazz was to acquire a way of feeling like "the Negros" and to completely abandon European culture. But, but by the time he wrote his 1956 history, he was searching for an intermediary position between African-American and European cultures; he hoped that jazz could serve as a compliment to his culture.[77] For Hodeir, Europeans could adopt American jazz without risking the loss of their Europeanness.

The opinions of *Jazz Magazine* readers on the subject of race coincided with the views of professional critics and at times could also reflect the primitivist interpretations inherited from the interwar period. In 1959, the magazine asked its readers to answer a thirty-two-part questionnaire, and three of the questions dealt directly with the question of race. In all, 2,435 individuals responded to the poll. Replying to the question, "Do you think that white musicians are as gifted as blacks?" 78 percent replied "no." One twenty-six-year-old respondent gave many of the same reasons critics did: in terms of numbers alone the most important "creators" were black, and black musicians had "the initiative in the direction of 'progress' in jazz." This reader went on to say that the talent of African Americans was not exclusively based on race.

> Jazz is not felt by an African who is not influenced by western culture. That this man would indirectly find a resonance with his "racial" origins (ecstasy, rhythm) is possible, but it would be necessary for him to have processed crucial pieces of European culture for the assimilation of forms that imprison these elements born in far-off Africa.[78]

In the mind of this respondent, "primitive" African music needed contact with European music in order to reach the more elevated plane of jazz. This notion of hybridity reflected an abiding sense among the French that jazz had dual roots, but that the African (represented here in a very predictable way as "ecstasy" and "rhythm") had to be mediated through European culture to be rightly expressed. Bound up in an appreciation for "black" music was a persistent belief in European (and French) superiority over the African as well as a desire to harness the emotion and the virility of jazz's "racial" origins.

The responses to the two other "race" questions in this 1959 questionnaire were in line with the opinions of French critics, reflecting shared notions of race and musical talent. Eighty-two percent of the readers replied "no" to the question, "Do you think that French musicians are in the same class as black Americans?" Just like their professional counterparts, the great majority of readers thought that French musicians could not compete with African-American musicians. And, finally, in response to the question, "Do you think that French musicians are in the same class as white American musicians?" a convincing majority (77 percent) responded "yes."[79] When African Americans were taken out of the equation and white French musicians were competing only with white Americans, most French fans thought that their countrymen held their own.

In 1961, a *Jazz Hot* reader by the name of J. Lebienvenu wrote into the magazine, claiming that "white jazz is maybe more calculated, more rational, than black jazz" and that "the white musician seems to improvise less freely, with less looseness, less relaxation, than the black jazzman."[80] Michel de Villers also willingly noted that perhaps blacks did relax better, although he argued that "the freedom of improvisation is a personal factor, independent of race." He concluded, "I have the impression that to create a list of instinctive musicians and musicians who were transformed would result in a rather nice mix of races."[81] This opinion of de Villers was very different from his position a decade earlier that black musicians deserved their greater popularity because of their race and that they were more agreeable to watch. Although the tension over the subject of black and white artists remained alive in the early 1960s, as these letters show, the majority of jazz critics began moving away from a strongly-racialized dichotomy that depended on biological explanations of difference. Some writers and fans even strove to abandon altogether the conception of jazz that depended on race.

The intense focus on race waned as jazz enthusiasts became less likely to connect a musician's talent to the color of his skin, reflecting a wariness of appearing racist but also a recognition that white Americans and Frenchmen were crucial contributors to the international and national jazz scenes. In 1963, *Jazz Magazine* reader Georges Fiogbe wrote, "It is false that the majority of jazz amateurs systematically prefer a particular musician because he is black." Fiogbe admired and appreciated various white musicians: "Stan Getz, Gerry Mulligan, Barney Wilen and a number of [others] . . . whose talents are recognized." Stressing that Django was not black, he queried, "Who is going to contest his greatness?" Importantly, two of the four musicians this reader mentioned were French musicians: Barney Wilen and Django Reinhardt. By the time this letter was written in 1963, French jazz musicians enjoyed a more expansive audience than they had in the 1950s. Their growing reputation and the French jazz public's recognition of their talent contributed to the disruption of the demarcation between black and white. Fiogbe noted that "for the *true* amateur, there is neither racism nor a complete preference: only different tastes" (italics original).[82] In the 1960s, the French jazz community came to appreciate more varied forms of jazz that included the music of American musicians—white and black—and white French musicians. Fans also began to look further than jazz to rhythm and blues and gospel: Georges Fiogbe was not only a follower of Stan Getz and Barney Wilen, but he also professed to love Ray Charles. For listeners like him, the borders between jazz and rhythm and blues were not clear when it came to artists like Charles, and the nebulous distinction many made between these two musics reflected a tendency to appreciate a wider variety of both sounds and musicians. Accepting white musicians went hand in hand with this broader trend. As mixed and ever-changing genres became more common, and French musicians received additional popular and critical acclaim, growing numbers of French jazz fans came to see race as a less relevant marker of musical talent. In reality, for jazz to be an important component of *French* culture, it could not rely on black artists alone but had to be ably played and created by French jazzmen as well. Erasing the importance of race to jazz not only moved French jazz audiences away from relying on racial stereotypes, but doing so allowed French artists to better compete with their African-American colleagues for the hearts and minds of French listeners.

During the 1960s, Lucien Malson continued to devote himself to invalidating the category of race both within and outside the world of jazz. In

1964, he wrote a book that did not focus on jazz at all. Entitled *Les enfants sauvages, mythe et réalité*, it addressed the problem of "wild children" who were deprived of human contact during their earliest years and who therefore became "inhuman and monstrous." He concluded in this book that "man . . . is nothing without society." One reviewer wrote that through *Les Infants sauvages*, "Malson proves that there is not a racial nature, that the human species is one and all have the same evolutionary factors, of which education through the social milieu, parents or school are not the least important."[83]

In his works on jazz itself, Malson now emphasized the irrelevance and fictionality of race, maintaining that the very notion "was imprecise, blurred, changing" as well as a continuing link with Fascism.[84] In 1966, he directly questioned the racial designation "black" by asking, "Blacks, Frank Stozier, Kid Ory, Jackie McLean, Albert Stinson, Ira Sullivan? Half-black, a quarter black, an eighth black? But why always black? Why not half-white, three-quarters white, seven-eighths white? Why speak first of black 'blood' when there are just a few drops?"[85] Society could not use the word "black" to explain the heritage of every person with dark skin; Malson saw that the term was a social construction used to define individuals and groups in a limiting and detrimental way. He went on to argue in another 1966 article that skin color, the basis on which all black people were assigned to a distinct race, was superficial. He did admit that "in jazz criticism we also speak of Blacks, and of their 'race' because the word does designate a visible biological trait that American society established in fundamental measure. This is not a serious wrong, if we are aware of the limits of the term."[86] Malson, despite his criticism of racialized categories and his awareness of the dangers that came along with them, still used the category "black" in his own work to discuss African Americans. But he tried to move people away from believing that skin color defined anyone's capabilities, musical or otherwise, and sought to elevate the discussion onto the plane of culture, where the place and prominence of African-American musicians could be discussed separately from the subject of race.

Malson responded to the opinion that "jazz is essentially a racial phenomenon and that *the* black race exists," by asking, "How, indeed, within this simplistic point of view, can the talent of musicians not be inversely proportional to the amount of white blood in their veins? Why then would the apparently white, but brilliant musicians, such as Lester, Django and, while we're at it, Bix Beiderbecke, not have some rights to be considered black?"[87] In order to make his point, Malson used blackness here as a cultural marker and not a physical one, basically asking why talented white musicians should not be called "black" since they had earned their place within the cultural milieu of jazz. By using these famous and well-respected white musicians as examples, he intended to upend the pervasiveness of racial labels and show that musical creativity had nothing to do with race, that it was inane to continue to insist that the color of a person's skin was connected to artistic talent.

Although individuals like Malson did not believe that skin color determined musical skill, many continued to perpetuate the notion that African Americans possessed some sort of cultural exceptionalism against which the majority of whites could not compete. Ultimately, Malson and others argued that African-American jazz musicians were the supreme architects and practitioners of the music, not because of their physical makeup, but because of a unique cultural vantage point that created a distinct and unparalleled aesthetic understanding. Importantly, during the 1960s they observed that increasing numbers of white musicians were taking advantage of the cultural heritage and offerings of jazz, becoming well-respected jazzmen themselves. As the postwar period advanced, the preponderance of critics and fans moved past a reliance on racial categories to determine the legitimacy and value of a musician's art. Hugues Panassié was once again the noted exception.

As discussed in chapter 1, in 1947, Panassié split with the majority of French jazz critics over the subject of bebop. He refused to recognize it as jazz and excluded people who did so from membership in the Hot Clubs. The music he supported and continued to champion for decades was New Orleans jazz, and he was one of the proponents of revivalism, the movement that tried to bring the "original" sounds of New Orleans back to life. For Panassié and his followers, this meant insisting throughout the 1950s, 1960s, and beyond, on the importance of a musician's blackness. In his magazine *Le Bulletin du Hot Club de France*, he unfailingly wrote and published articles on the significance of race, a subject that other jazz critics increasingly refused to entertain.

In *The Wretched of the Earth*, Frantz Fanon wrote about "white jazz specialists" like Panassié without mentioning the critic's name. Fanon noticed that when jazz evolved into new styles, certain aficionados could not reconcile their sclerotic vision of the music with bebop or other forward-looking forms of their art. This betrayed a prejudice on their part against black musicians who pushed beyond the realm of tradition and societal expectations. Fanon wrote, "The fact is that in their eyes jazz should only be the despairing, broken-down nostalgia of an old Negro who is trapped between five glasses of whiskey, the curse of his race, and racial hatred of the white men. As soon as the Negro comes to an understanding of himself, and understands the rest of the world differently, when he gives birth to hope and forces back the racist universe, it is clear that his trumpet sounds more clearly and his voice less hoarsely." Fanon recognized in the new genres of jazz, something completely different from Panassié. He saw "in them one of the consequences of the defeat, slow but sure, of the southern world of the United States. And it is not utopian to suppose that in fifty years' time the type of jazz howl hiccupped by a poor misfortunate Negro will be upheld only by the whites who believe in it as an expression of négritude and who are faithful to this arrested image of a type of relationship."[88]

Despite the criticism aimed at him from his fellow white French critics and from an internationally-known black intellectual like Fanon, Panassié persisted in forwarding his ideas about black musicians that showed his intellectual take on race had not changed since the 1930s.[89] In the political realm, he remained critical of democracy and universal suffrage, and it is not surprising that Fanon linked Panassie's mindset with that of the colonizer and the racist. His conception of blackness remained cemented in time even as the world, French society, and jazz changed around him. In the early 1960s, Panassié's magazine still claimed that there was an "essential difference" between blacks and whites[90] and that blacks who abandoned their nature and "conformed to the white manner of playing" had been subjected to "intellectual colonialism."[91] In 1965, Panassié argued in his book *La Bataille du Jazz* that only "true blacks" could create "true jazz."[92] Throughout his adult life, he remained committed to preserving the connection between blackness, jazz, and authenticity, but by the end of the 1960s he was largely alone in doing so. His opinions had become both aesthetically and socially obsolete; much to his chagrin he had lost *la bataille du jazz* in France.

In constructing their own ideas about what it meant to be an African American, French supporters of jazz in the 1950s fostered a notion of this music that envisioned its creators as different from white Europeans and Americans. Black musicians were admired for having sometimes acquired, sometimes inherent, characteristics that whites did not possess. French listeners stressed the emotion, rhythm, aggression, and sexuality of jazz, musical assets that the French (and whites in general) supposedly lacked. Jazz's otherness and position outside the mainstream of American cultural life was what, in many ways, made it appealing to the French; notably, other cultural imports from the United States were not so uncritically accepted in this era.[93] Nevertheless, in the 1960s, most French critics tended to move away from this racialized discourse, emphasizing the importance of culture and recognizing the talents of white American and French musicians. In the end, the frequent debates about the reasons for black musical talent showed the ambiguous and imprecise line dividing understandings of racial and cultural identity, taking us back to the issues raised at the outset of this chapter about racism and cultural fundamentalism. Conceptions of cultural difference, even if they excluded racial justifications, potentially led to stereotypes and discriminatory practices, contributing to a mentality that prejudged individual capabilities based on appearances and perceived cultural belonging. Through their debates, the jazz enthusiasts of the 1950s and 1960s illuminated how relying on culture to explain difference did not necessarily erase the reality of racialized beliefs, but at times excused the practice of putting blanket labels on whole groups of people. Significantly, jazz critics did end up altering their strong and unbending ideas about black and white musicians so that by the middle of the 1960s most of them were resisting formulaic understandings based either on race or on culture. Yet racial stereotypes could be found well into the 1970s among jazz writers who persisted in envisioning black and white musicians as having their own distinct characteristics: while African-American artists were expected to play emotional or instinctual music, white musicians were thought to be the best suited to play music in the intellectual and occidental tradition.[94] Although becoming less frequent and more veiled, the practice of creating racial and cultural boundaries between musicians based on skin color did not vanish. When French individuals rejected biological definition of race in favor of cultural explanations for difference, the ideas that informed racial prejudice did not disappear but instead came to be used again under the new guise of cultural difference.

Beyond progressive political outlooks, French jazz enthusiasts had another motive in erasing racial determinates from jazz: jazz could be more easily integrated into the French cultural patrimony if its authenticity did not depend on blackness. The French critics and fans who insisted in the 1960s that the connection between race and artistic creation were irrelevant indicated an important shift in thinking, even if multiple ways of envisioning the interplay of race, culture, and nation persist into the present day. We should remember that even in contemporary France the practice of focusing on cultural difference has not disappeared when it comes to individuals contending with the subject of national belonging and trying to understand and pronounce who belongs and who does not. The process is the same whether someone is trying to determine an individual's musical talent or an individual's place in the nation, as people are judged and placed on one side of the divide or another: white or black, true jazz musician or imitator, French or foreign. Today, many of those with a right-wing political agenda in France have not moved beyond using the cultural in their attempts to deny citizenship, rights, and national membership to entire ethnic enclaves, much as early postwar jazz enthusiasts sought to deny an authentic connection to jazz for those who were not black.

FIGHTING THE WHITE (AMERICAN) MENACE

Distinct from the subjects of racial and cultural exceptionalism, but crucial to French jazz critics and eventually fans, was the political cause of supporting African Americans and their quest for civil rights in the United States. In the postwar period, the French jazz cognoscenti were intent on illuminating the deficiencies inherent in American society. This was apparent on two different levels: an aesthetic one that involved contrasting jazz to other forms of American mass culture, and a political one that included not only affirming blackness but denouncing racism and segregation in the United States.[95] As part of this political expression of jazz appreciation, French periodicals, books, radio programs, television, and other mediums of photojournalism all addressed the reality of discrimination, Jim Crow laws, and police brutality in the United States.[96] In the 1950s, jazz magazines recommended that their audiences read American works like the *Jim Crow Guide to the U.S.A* by Stetson Kennedy, *Segregation: the Inner Conflict of the South* by Robert Penn Warren, and Big Bill Broonzy's autobiography.[97] On the radio, programs hosted by Hugues Panassié, Sim Copans, André Francis, Lucien Malson, and others exposed their listeners to the issue of American racism. In the 1960s, jazz writers closely examined the activities undertaken by Martin Luther King, Jr., Malcolm X, SNCC, and CORE. The television work of Jean-Christophe Averty in the late 1950s and the 1960s most certainly brought the issue of race to its viewers through programs like *Harlem sur Seine*, part of the *Cinq colonnes à la une* series, which aired in 1962 and portrayed the lives of African Americans in Paris.[98]

The coverage the French jazz public gave to American discrimination was an extension of a historical pattern: French social observers had been critical of American racism as early as the 1800s. Alexis de Toqueville pointed to the problem of race in the United States in his *Democracy in America* of 1835. More than a century later, French social scientists who studied the United States almost without fail pointed to racism as a fundamental American weakness.[99] In the 1950s and 1960s, the mainstream French media regularly reported on the racialized situations existing in the United States, but jazz critics tended to be more vocal and direct in condemning the American status quo. Because this music was historically connected to blackness, jazz enthusiasts had the potential to become socially aware: political causes taken up by American musicians created an ideological framework for the music's supporters in France. In the United States, jazz musicians actively challenged both domestic and international forms of racial discrimination, and leading members of the French jazz public followed their example.[100] The heightened political awareness on the part of American jazzmen reinforced the desire among French jazz critics to protest American racist practices. Of course, this did not mean that the average jazz fan became an antiracist. There was no causal relationship between musical taste and ethical behavior and many jazz enthusiasts were not involved in advocating for political and social equality in the United States or in France. Nonetheless, these same jazz fans could not pick up a copy of *Jazz Magazine* or *Jazz Hot* without reading about racial discrimination in the United States and how American musicians were involved in challenging the status quo.

Writers for jazz periodicals consistently delved into issues relating to American prejudice. As early as 1948, Boris Vian, who was a member of the Ligue Internationale Contre le Racisme et l'Antisémitisme, wrote that even though the United States was passing new laws against racial discrimination and lynchings, officials in the South were guilty of denying African-American artists the respect they deserved.[101] As the postwar period wore on, it became ever more apparent to French observers that the racial situation in the United States was not, in fact, improving, and jazz writers regularly pointed out instances of American bigotry. In 1957, *Jazz Hot* took particular interest in the controversy over the integration of public schools in the South, especially in the fact that Louis Armstrong had "severely condemned the hesitant attitude of President Eisenhower in this affair" and had declared that the president "lacked guts."[102] When the New York police took away Miles Davis' work permit at a nightclub after an altercation, *Jazz Hot* branded the entire episode an "inadmissible racial manifestation."[103] *Jazz Magazine* covered the story as well, and after recounting the "multiple wounds" caused by the "brutal attack" on Davis, the periodical stated, "Here is what can happen to you if your face does not please a New York policeman—especially if you are black and the policeman is white."[104] Critics also compiled stories that illustrated how jazz musicians' careers were damaged by racism. In 1957, Nat King Cole's television show on NBC could not find a commercial sponsor and Cole was only paid $2,500 a week. Yet according to *Jazz Magazine*, the show was almost as popular as *The $64,000 Question*. The magazine asserted that "the only reason that Nat King Cole has not found financial backing is Jim Crow, in other words, racism."[105] According to its American correspondent, "TV [in the United States] holds artists of color at a distance."[106] Concerts in the United States could be interrupted or canceled because of racial conflicts and these incidents were relayed to French readers. In 1955, *Jazz Magazine* told subscribers that the Houston police, "the enemies of freedom between blacks and whites," had arrested Norman Granz, Illinois Jacquet, Ella Fitzgerald, Dizzy Gillespie, and Georgianna Henry (Ella Fitzgerald's secretary) "for breaking the law forbidding interracial playing."[107] Two years later, a journalist from *Jazz Magazine* wrote that "a stick of dynamite thrown from a car exploded during a concert given by Louis Armstrong and his orchestra in Knoxville (Tennessee) February 19." This writer was "pleased" to report that no one was hurt and that the show was not interrupted. The complicated question of who had set off the explosion uncovered some of the existing tensions over race in the United States. There was suspicion that it

> was a move of intimidation on the part of a racist group who was against black music. Nevertheless, since segregation was practiced in this concert hall, the 2,000 white spectators separated from the 1,000 blacks, it is possible that is was blacks, angry that Louis was playing in halls where races were separated, who protested in this way.[108]

This writer noted that frustration and anger over racist treatment could likely lead blacks to violent and destructive means of protest. French observers were well aware that musicians performed in segregated venues in the United States, but they did not automatically condemn African Americans who played in these places; instead, they at times even expressed sympathy with the quandaries of black artists. A 1956 *Jazz Hot* article stated that "Louis Armstrong is annoyed with the black press. He played recently in an Indianapolis dancing hall where blacks are forbidden. Armstrong disclosed that he 'did not hesitate to play for racist listeners. . . . I play everywhere my manager books me.'"[109] This article, as well as the one about the mysterious concert explosion, did not overtly criticize Armstrong for playing in locations that denied African Americans equal access, but instead empathized with his predicament. Armstrong obviously needed to perform to earn a living but ironically, when he did, he also risked coming into conflict with members of his own community who reproached him for not doing enough to challenge Jim Crow. In situations like these, French commentators prided themselves on seeing the complexity of Armstrong's dilemma, bemoaning a social situation that legitimated discrimination, violence, and segregation.

French writers commended American musicians whose political actions challenged intolerance. In 1957, *Jazz Hot* reported that "a committee to combat the effects of racism within the Federation of American Musicians was formed by the Hollywood local of the union."[110] In the spring of 1959, *Jazz Magazine* ran a story entitled "Brubeck and Jim Crow." According to the unnamed writer, Dave Brubeck, who was white, had lost a number of jobs because his bassist Eugene Wright was black: a March 4th concert at the University of Georgia was canceled; "the best TV contract of his career" was taken away; and a week-long $75,000 tour in Johannesburg, South Africa was called off as well. Brubeck responded in the following way, "All that I know is that they could pay me $1,000,000 and that would not make me turn Gene away because of his color. One does not buy self respect!"[111] Approving fans and critics could obviously commend Brubeck for his antiracist values and his challenge to the status quo, as well as his refusal to betray his ideals for monetary reasons.

In each of these situations, French writers expressed a social critique of the United States. The black musicians who had created jazz, kept the music alive, and perpetuated its originality were collectively treated as outcasts in America. These French critics were interested in exposing to their readers negative American stereotypes about the U.S. black population. In a 1954 article on Fats Waller, one writer asserted that although this musician had achieved great success, "he remained for many Americans an inferior being, the 'dirty black' that one uses as a bafoon."[112] In a piece on the New York jazz scene several years later, Daniel Filipacchi began by discussing the fear among white Americans of getting lost in the "black part" of Central Park, a fear that revealed assumed prejudices regarding African-American communities, crime, and violence. Importantly, Filipacchi pointed out that he, a white Frenchman, had no such fears about going into a black neighborhood, making the not-so-subtle effort to cast the French, rather than white Americans, as the antiracists.[113]

During the 1960s, the American jazz scene became increasingly politicized as more musicians became involved in the civil rights movement. American artists in all fields of entertainment used their influence to educate the public about civil rights causes and to stop the practice of segregation. These efforts were lauded by French writers and a wide variety of actions were reported in this context: Dinah Washington asking people to boycott buying her records in the South to show their disproval of racial segregation;[114] Norman Granz forming a committee to ensure that jazz musicians would only play in unsegregated performance spaces;[115] Duke Ellington refusing a concert date in Little Rock, Arkansas, because of the racial segregation that continued to be practiced there;[116] Mahalia Jackson working to organize a benefit in Chicago for the Southern Christian Leadership Conference; Lena Horne and Harry Belafonte arranging a meeting about segregation with Robert Kennedy, then the Attorney General;[117] and black and white jazz musicians and vocalists participating directly in the March on Washington.[118] By staying informed about the actions of American musicians, French listeners were exposed to the strong political stances of many American performers. Most importantly, leaders of the jazz community told fans to sympathize with these actions of protest and become political themselves. The pervasiveness of articles on the subject of American racism stemmed from the obvious reality that jazz musicians experienced its affects on their careers as well as on their personal lives. Listening to this music *could* affect a person's politics and *could* lead him or her to stand against bigotry and injustice. Of course, listening to jazz did not automatically make people antiracist and certainly many fans harbored no such political sentiments or intentions. But the editors and writers of *Jazz Magazine* and *Jazz Hot* (who also controlled radio programming, wrote books, and contributed to mainstream publications) pushed fans to take a stand against racism and prejudice.

At times, French writers could be critical of African Americans if their actions were judged to be insufficiently political. In 1965, Dominique Eudes interviewed Duke Ellington for the men's magazine *Lui*. In this interview, Eudes repeatedly pushed Ellington on the issue of race and put forward statements and questions such as: "All black musical and cultural contributions have been integrated by American culture, but the problem is that Blacks themselves have not been integrated"; "Is it . . . easier for a White to become rich than it is for a Black?"; and, "In what way do you think that jazz can be a song of revolt?" In his responses, Ellington did not strongly condemn the United States for its racism. Instead, he said things like: "I don't think that a country exists in the world where no difference is made between a Black and a White. In the United States, there is simply more publicity around all of these histories"; "I know tons of Whites who don't have anything at all. It is not so very easy [to make money] and also a lot of them live less well than Blacks. Me, I don't know this world of segregation. I have always been respected because I was respectable, people paid me and there was nothing else. For Cab Calloway, it was the same thing"; and, "[Jazz] was a diversion," having nothing to do with revolt. As the interview progressed, Eudes' tone betrayed a sense of disappointment and frustration, but not one of hostility, and the article ran with the lead, "Duke Ellington sees the black problem in the United States from a very personal and very unexpected standpoint."[119] A month later, when excerpts from the article appeared in *Jazz Hot*, the political and social commentator and cartoonist Siné, who wrote for both *Jazz Hot* and *Jazz Magazine* in the 1960s, directly criticized Ellington. He wrote, "Monsieur Duke Ellington, you are a liar. By rubbing your skin white you have blackened your soul and the result has probably gone beyond your expectations! You are now the universal color of bastards: the color of shit."[120]

By the mid-1960s, individuals like Siné did not tolerate any ambivalence on the part of African Americans (or anyone) when it came to acknowledging and combating instances of American racism. Certainly the majority of French fans did not voice an opinion as disparaging and cynical as Siné's when they saw a lack of political engagement on the part of musicians. However, jazz critics pushed fans to see racism in the United States as a reality and a problem to resist; they wanted musical appreciation to be informed by political considerations.

In the political culture that coincided with and then followed the events of 1968, jazz became associated more closely with political radicalism. Free jazz was connected to the politics of Black Power and French supporters of this music tended to embrace this link. Eric Drott has observed that for politically-engaged French listeners, free jazz's implied connection to African-American protest as well as its anticommercial nature made the genre more attractive than rock or contemporary forms of classical music.[121] At times there was an explicit yearning on the part of the French free jazz community to have the music be associated with political awareness and action. Jedediah Sklower has highlighted the fact that "free jazzmen français" used their music to benefit political causes, "notably under the banners of third-worldism and anti-imperialism."[122] Along these same lines, the French musician François Tusques told an interviewer that "all the French 'free' musicians were very much anchored in the left (some were members of the Communist Party)."[123] The problem for French free jazz musicians was that they were not the original creators of this music nor were they in truth fighting the same fight as African Americans in the United

States. In 1968, Michel Portal admitted that French free jazzmen "play a stolen music" and then went on to say that free jazz was a "black music" that came from a "precise political and ideological situation" that did not belong to the French.[124]

By occupying a more privileged social position than African Americans, French free jazz supporters had a tendency to perhaps overcompensate and to make the music more blatantly political than American musicians even wanted it to be. When asked by a French critic about his group's political connections, the American artist Joseph Jarman of the Association for the Advancement of Creative Musicians (AACM) replied, "We don't have any affiliation with political groups. . . . All we can say is that the only thing that interests us is: music, music, music."[125] Members of the African-American jazz community held widely varying opinions, some of which focused on black nationalism, anticolonialism, integration, or anticommercialism and some of which were deliberately apolitical like Jarman's in this particular quote. In general, French jazz devotees were inclined to overlook the different political positions that American jazz artists held in their efforts as jazz fans to support the civil rights of African Americans.[126] French jazz audiences used jazz to fill their own political and ideological needs. Of course, free jazz artists were on record protesting against segregation and pushing for civil rights but they were also on record, as in the case of Jarman here, stipulating an apolitical outlook. Jazzmen were never a monolithic group and free jazz musicians were no exception to this rule. What the French jazz public was prone to doing was overlooking the idiosyncratic political worldview of American artists and seeing them as a homogenous whole. Particularly for French fans of free jazz, art could not be separated from a politics that endorsed at the very least racial equality, if not broader social and economic equality as well.

From the 1950s on, members of the French jazz public conflated diverse viewpoints and opinions into a singular and undifferentiated one that politicized African-American musicians. The most political among French jazz enthusiasts supported the drive for civil rights in the United States, often without making a distinction between the goals, ideologies, and practices of different African-American organizations and individuals, and without accepting that some African-American artists did not even want to be overtly political. In the politically-charged atmosphere of the late 1960s, French jazz fans with viewpoints on the far left of the political spectrum might have adopted the cause of African Americans because they did not have a similar indigenous group to support. As activists, they were searching for a purpose and ended up championing African Americans. Drott interestingly posits this view that *gauchistes* after 1968, in the absence of a radical French industrial proletariat, needed a group that could fill the role of Marxian revolutionaries, and African Americans were used to satisfy this ideological and political void. The tendency to see African Americans as well positioned to drive social change (because of their long history of subjugation) became more acute because no equivalent group of people could be found in France.[127]

This leftist French audience, which was most supportive of both free jazz and the ideology of Black Power, entered into a decades-long tradition of defending black Americans. As young and vocal activists in post-1968 France, they were not only more assertive in expressing their political voices than earlier generations of jazz fans, they were also smaller in number due to their unconventional taste in music. At a time when these French politicians were searching for campaigns to promote, they honed in on the injustices, needs, and actions of black Americans. Eventually, French leftists would find political and social motivation closer to home, especially in social movements that rose up in the wake of decolonization, but until the injustices of French racism became more widely recognized, supporting justice and equality for African Americans was an entrenched component of their political cause.

LE RACISME FRANÇAIS

At this point, it is important to ask how French jazz fans who were disturbed by American racism addressed cases of discrimination closer home. As France evolved into a multiracial and multicultural society in the postwar era, the jazz scene encapsulated a cosmopolitanism that welcomed global forms of artistic expression and ethnic belonging. The American drummer Famoudou Don Moyere described how artists from across the globe came together in France in the late 1960s, asserting, "You know the Paris scene, it was people from all over the world. I was playing a lot with the drummers from Guinea, Senegal, and Ivory Coast. [Saxophonist] Manu Dibango had just come up from Cameroon."[128] The long-famous Josephine Baker, following her vision of racial equality and universal brotherhood, founded a utopian movement she called the Rainbow Tribe (*Tribu arc-en-ciel*). Beginning in the second half of the 1950s, she adopted into this "tribe" twelve children from Korean, Columbian, French, Jewish, Algerian, Finish, Venezuelan, Côte d'Ivoirian, and Moroccan backgrounds and brought them to live with her in her French home.[129] By the 1960s, Baker, whose connection to jazz went back decades, was projecting her ideal of cultural and religious diversity onto a France whose white citizens were just beginning to wrestle in earnest with their evolving and divergent thoughts about race, culture, and national belonging. Jazz critics and musicians tended to embrace the inclusive microcosm represented by Moyere's description and Baker's family, but there were others among the French who viewed non-Europeans as illegitimate members of the nation.

Even though the realities of French society were changing, in general American instances of discrimination were much more prominently discussed than issues surrounding French bigotry. From the vantage point of the twenty-first century, Pap Ndiaye has noted that African-American culture has been studied extensively in France, substituting for a national examination of France's own minority groups.[130] For decades, the French avoided acknowledging or directly analyzing French prejudices based on race. Focusing on American shortcomings was a more comforting and common move because observers could simultaneously bring the global superpower down a peg and make French social norms appear preferable. During the late 1950s, as the Algerian War waged on and the conflict in Indochina had only recently come to a close, racism in France was an undeniable reality, and jazz fans were led to become at least minimally aware of it.[131] Yet, despite a slow but growing cognizance of indigenous forms of racism, French observers persisted in highlighting American inequitable practices and not French ones.[132] The American jazzman Sidney Bechet lived in France in the 1950s and also toured in North Africa with French musicians. When discussing the issue of racism of both sides of the Atlantic, Bechet asserted, "The French have no call to crow over Americans . . . I've been in Dakar and I've seen what they do to Negroes there, and Frenchmen are no better than anyone else."[133] Like Bechet, some of the most cogent French social observers could not help noticing parallels between American and French forms of prejudice.

By the early 1950s, the topic of French bigotry had not been widely discussed in France outside the subject of anti-Semitism. The fact was that few ethnic minorities had yet moved to the metropole. Of course, men and women from the former French colonies lived in interwar France and had been doing so for decades, but these individuals were largely members of the educated elite and remained for the most part in Paris. Close to 200,000 African soldiers had served in France during the Great War but most of them returned to French West Africa at war's end. For contemporary historians, discovering the actual numbers of black residents in France during any era is difficult, as the French census has never included racial categories. But an official 1926 census did record 2,580 black Africans living in France, even though there were probably close to twice as many. Most likely, 10,000 black Antilleans also lived within the borders of metropolitan France.[134] Keeping in mind that the nation had a population of somewhere around forty million, these numbers were small. The racial makeup of the hexagon changed most dramatically in the 1960s when hundreds of thousands of Caribbean workers made their way to France to find employment in both private and public sector jobs. Mass migration from black Africa happened a bit later, but Tyler Stovall has shown that by the end of the 1960s, Africans were frequently residents of Paris and other French cities.[135]

In the 1960s, growing numbers of jazz writers began exposing instances of French racism, especially cases that were somehow connected to jazz. In 1966, a writer for Hugues Panassié's *Le Bulletin du Hot Club de France* cited one such example: a black musician living in Paris was told when he tried to rent an apartment, "Oh! You are black. . . . We don't rent to blacks." The article claimed that this was not the first time such a thing had happened in France but that "several hotels in Paris (and in the provinces) had notoriously refused to let rooms to black jazzmen." The article went on to say, "This is, after all, 1966, but in this country where so many people gladly criticize the United States for its racism, these same people become strangely myopic when it concerns seeing what passes under their own noses."[145]

In 1969, members of the African-American musicians collective the Association for the Advancement of Creative Musicians (AACM) moved to Paris. The men stayed roughly a year and then, by 1971, had returned to the United States. One of the AACM musicians, Wadada Leo Smith, later recalled that these black artists experienced discrimination in a variety of forms during their time in France. Smith remembered his difficulties in finding a place to live the following way:

> A lot of places in the city had problems renting to black guys. Some of the places I went to, they were kind of like some of those places in America where you call up and talk about them, have somebody call and talk about them, then you go to deal it and it doesn't exist any more. One of the real estate people told me directly that certain areas, you could live in. You could live in an area where the Arabs lived in. Certain areas, you could get a place, but somebody would have to get it for you. I finally got a place at the end of town, Porte d'Orléans, good neighborhood. . . . I rented from a British guy that was an absentee.[146]

This recollection illustrates that the lived reality of African Americans in Paris was in some ways not that different from life in the United States. Some observers at the time linked this to the changed social and racial atmosphere existent in the wake of the Algerian War. The British journalist Val Wilmer wrote about her time spent in Paris during this era in her memoir entitled *Mama Said There'd Be Days Like This: My Life in the Jazz World*. In this book, Wilmer noted,

> By 1970 the racial climate had changed considerably from the tolerant one that had seemed so attractive to expatriate Blacks of an earlier generation. Following the war in Algeria, open hostility was directed against North Africans and anyone with a dark skin not dressed conservative. And the black man/pimp: white woman/whore stereotype persisted wherever interracial couples were found. Taxis in Pigalle were a problem. My aid was enlisted to hail a cab by a musician *en route* to a concert; he skulked in a doorway while I stopped it. "He'll think I'm one of them Algerians," was his jocular comment.[147]

The postcolonial mindset converged with and informed an increased racial awareness in France in the later half of the 1960s, when some French nationals also became more mindful of their country's modes of intolerance as increased immigration from beyond Europe diversified the metropole. For the first decade and a half after the end of World War II, few people recognized or were willing to admit that racial discrimination was real in France. As the 1960s advanced, with rising numbers of people of African, North African, and Asian descent in the country, and the raw memories of colonial loss informing people's reaction to non-European immigrants, foreign observers like Smith and Wilmer, as well as some members of the *franco-français* majority, became more cognizant of distinctly French prejudices.

During the 1960s letters to jazz periodicals discussed French jazz club owners and employees discriminating against individuals for reasons of race as well as for motives based on class. Three complaints, in 1960, 1961, and 1967, were made about one club in particular: the Caveau de la Huchette. *Jazz Hot* critic Michel de Villers, responding to the first two letters, did not take the 1960 accusation of racism all that seriously. A "Monsieur Combes" had written to say that blacks were not allowed into the Huchette. De Villers claimed that this was not racism—an individual was refused entry because he was "a bore." The person could also be black and be a bore but his blackness would not be the reason for denying his admittance. De Villers chose to ignore the possibility that the Huchette might use race to size up potential patrons. Instead, he wrote, "I agree with [French jazzman] Maxim Saury that some very fine brawls stirred up by some Blacks at the Huchette were started because of their exclusion. It does not have anything to do with racism."[148] For de Villers at this point, race did not justify selectively choosing who was and who was not permitted in the club and he thought that only behavior caused blacks to be denied entry. In 1961, he attenuated his position a bit when Pierre Toco, the head of a boarding house (Maître d'Internat) who happened to be black, was not granted entry or membership into the Huchette. The club sent the following letter to Toco: "The Admissions Committee of the Huchette University Club informs you that your request cannot be filled for the current academic year, the number of enrolled members being already greater than our limit." Whenever Toco attempted to go to the club, he was asked whether or not he was a member. He made two more requests for membership but each time received the same response. What eventually made this racist in the minds of both Toco and de Villers was that the former's white colleague, who was also not a member at the Huchette, had never been asked for proof of his membership when arriving at the establishment. De Viller's comments were not without racist overtones themselves when he stated, "I know, having myself observed it, that certain blacks conduct themselves badly at jazz clubs." Yet, he went on to say that "this fact does not authorize in any case a general racial policy."[149] He held back from directly criticizing the Huchette though, stating that he was waiting to hear its side of the story (which was never published in the magazine).

A *Jazz Magazine* reader, Zenzis Abdou, made still another complaint against the Huchette in 1967, writing, "It appears that jazz fans . . . are not racists. But this seems to be strongly compromised when there are no Blacks at the 'Caveau de la Huchette,' where, each night, Blacks (and they alone) are refused entry in being asked for their membership card, impossible to obtain even if they naively make the request." The politically-radical cartoonist and columnist Siné responded to Abdou by first stating that no jazz fan "steps foot in the Caveau de la Huchette," it not being a place where good, authentic jazz was performed. However, he went on to acknowledge that this did "not prevent, of course, true jazz fans from being able to be racists, like the rest of the world." Siné made a point to connect this racist practice at the Huchette with world politics. For him, all bigotry was an "injustice" and he hoped that Abdou, like the blacks of South Africa, would rise up one day. He finished his response in a rather dramatic voice: "That which will begin in South Africa will continue everywhere to finish at the Caveau de la Huchette. Your day of glory has not yet arrived. I hope to live it with you."[150] Siné was on the far left of the political spectrum and not only supported civil rights causes like those in South Africa and the United States, but also the cause of the communist revolutionaries in Cuba.[151] He had also supported the Algerian cause during the Algerian War, and in 1962, had created his own magazine, *Siné Massacre*, where he voiced anticolonial, anticlerical, and anticapitalist views. In addition, he contributed political cartoons to the weekly periodical *Révolution africaine*, founded in 1963 in Algeria by former members of the Front de Libération Nationale (FLN).[152] The politics of men like Siné depended on the belief that all people deserved "freedom" irrespective of race or social class. His colleague Lucien Malson stated that "one cannot be for the emancipation of Negroes and for the upholding of kings, for racial freedom and for social inequality, for the liberation of the citizen and for the humiliation of man. It is necessary to make a total choice."[153]

As critics like Malson and Siné were openly antiracist and proworking class, it made sense for readers to write to them with their grievances. While many expressed complaints about race, others focused on class. One such reader was a self-described member of the working class who had just returned from the army when he tried to go to a jazz club in the Saint-Michel quarter (perhaps the Huchette). He was not allowed in because he did not have a student identification card. He wrote to *Jazz Magazine*, "This is racism. If I am black, Jewish, or a proletariat, do I not have the right to love jazz?"[154] Examining this letter in conjunction with the others concerning the Huchette calls into question the broadmindedness of French jazz audiences beyond the rather close-knit circle of critics. Obviously, in some clubs there was a preconceived notion of who should and who should not be admitted; sometimes race caused people to be turned away and at other times assumptions about their social class did. The jazz scene in France remained a largely white and middle class one. Although "others" were usually granted entry, in a number of cases they appeared to be barred from participating in the creation, perpetuation, and enjoyment of jazz.

As shown above, the letters submitted by fans to the editors of jazz periodicals offer important insights into the French jazz milieu as they give a voice to a group of people who were frequently written about, but infrequently heard. Their concerns and observances repeatedly led the readers of *Jazz Magazine* and *Jazz Hot* back to the subject of racism. In 1966, Claude Chiron of Paris wrote the following in his letter:

> The French in another time had the enviable reputation of being the least racist people on earth, black musicians in Paris frequently affirmed this. Was it the arrival of the West Indians and Africans, students and workers, who changed everything? The West Indians are French citizens, and the Africans come to ask us for the help that we promised them during colonization. The sub-proletariats are Africans, West Indians, and North Africans.[155]

Chiron went on to say that "we need them as much or maybe more than they need us and we need the Spanish and Portuguese workers who are not treated much better."[156] Chiron saw the contradictions and unfairness that existed within French society. The French needed the former colonized to fill labor shortages and asked them to come and work in France, but upon arriving, these immigrants were then met with scorn and injustice. People from Africa, Asia, and the Caribbean were doubly oppressed by the French, first through colonization and then through the racism, discrimination, and exploitation of the postcolonial era. The philosopher Étienne Balibar has observed that these immigrants "appear as the result of colonization and decolonization and thus succeed in concentrating upon themselves both the continuation of imperial scorn and the resentment that is felt by the citizens of a fallen power, if not a vague phantasmatic longing for revenge."[157] The feelings of social, political, and economic insecurity that accompanied the early postwar and postcolonial years in France helped to bring a latent racism to the surface of French society. Members of the jazz scene were quick to notice this occurrence and Chiron thought that the situation could very easily worsen. He finished his letter with the following statement: "Attention: Jim Crow is in the process of moving into French society and in the most underhanded of ways. Of course, there will not be official segregation, but maybe there will be persecution, 'quarantines,' an inconspicuous hate."[158] Lucien Malson was at this point in time serving as the editor and respondent of *Jazz Hot*'s "Courrier des Lecteurs" page and his response concurred with Chiron's letter:

> We always think that racism is an American or South African malady, but the bastards are among us. The seemingly kind French are not better than others. If ten percent of our population had skin that was black, "azobé" or "okoumé" passing through shades of teak, from "angélique" or from "wacapou," we would have vigorous neo-nazis.[159]

Malson made a point of saying that racism was "the absolute moral evil."[160]

Proponents of jazz tended to believe that this music could be used to combat racism and they placed themselves, as supporters of the music, on the left of the political spectrum; for those on the far left jazz was part of their radicalism. Michel de Villers wrote in 1963, "It is an established fact that, in general, it is the people on the Left all across the world who sincerely love jazz; but this is without a doubt because, in capitalist countries, jazz and leftism are two anti-conformist attitudes." Because of its "universal" qualities, jazz was thought to have the ability to bring people beyond their immediate differences to a place of common understanding. In de Villers words, jazz "has been able to become an excellent remedy against racism." As a solution, of course, jazz did not and could not always work, because the music was only "a remedy, not a certificate" that proved tolerance in those who appreciated it.[161]

In valuing a music that had itself embraced such variance from the beginning, in adopting musical elements from Africa, Europe, and the United States, some argued that listeners could tap into some sort of collective identity and move beyond racial prejudice through jazz. At least that was what many French critics hoped would happen among the music's supporters. In some instances perhaps it did. The *négrophilia* that fueled the early interwar fascination with jazz became less direct in the postwar years but a fascination with black bodies undoubtedly remained present through the 1950s. The wars in Indochina and Algeria, increased immigration from beyond Europe, colonial and postcolonial struggles against exploitation, and the American civil rights movement all contributed to shifting notions about race that led some among the French to adopt the cause of antiracism. That French men and women tended to project racist qualities onto the United States did not mean that discrimination or categorization based on skin color did not exist in France. They most certainly did. But most French individuals seemed more adept at rejecting racism on an abstract level when the discussion revolved around the United States than at recognizing the same insidious habits within their own country. The problematic figure of Hugues Panassié illustrated through his own actions the philosophical inconsistency of rallying for African-American rights but then insisting that black jazzmen play their music and perform in only certain unchanging and essentialized ways. Even though he continued to support right-wing political causes and insisted on the existence a fundamental black personality, he used his support for jazz to prove (unconvincingly from a twenty-first-century standpoint) that he was not a racist.

Those drawn to jazz had varying ideas on race, ranging from those who did not ponder the question of skin color but enjoyed listening to a music emanating from an African-American tradition, to those who believed that musical talent depended on blackness, to those who thought that race was irrelevant and should be avoided as a means of explaining musical talent. Sometimes these various thoughts coexisted within one individual; race was not easily understood or explained and certainly did not exist within a simple binary system. The very essence of jazz was complicated: it remained within a framework defined by both race and culture, black and white, racism and antiracism, the national and the cosmopolitan. The music was important for bringing these tensions closer to the surface of French society where they could be examined. Unfortunately, skin color did not disappear as a means of defining groups of people in France and, in the end, the jazz public might have only served to foreshadow the growing racism of the postwar period. Nevertheless, the music gave people who were willing to do so, a means of looking beyond themselves and embracing the multicultural during a time of significant change and uncertainty.

NOTES

1. For conceptions of this idea from the first half of the twentieth century, see Herman Lebovics, *True France: The Wars Over Cultural Identity, 1900–1945* (Ithaca, NY: Cornell University Press, 1992).

2. Herman Lebovics, *Bringing the Empire Back Home: France in the Global Age* (Durham, NC: Duke University Press, 2004), 135. In the 1980s, Jean-Marie Le Pen coined a new word—*differentialism*—to help codify this belief. In making his cultural stance known, he distorted the Socialist belief in multiculturalism. Lebovics describes the resulting mentality, "The immigrants from North and West Africa were not French. They cannot become French. Many of them do not want to be French. Kick them out!"

3. Herman Lebovics, *Mona Lisa's Escort: André Malraux and the Reinvention of French Culture* (Ithaca, NY: Cornell University Press, 1999), 4.

4. To better understand the place of jazz in French culture during the *first half* of the twentieth century and to see how it moved from a contested to a widely embraced music, see Matthew F. Jordan's study, *Le Jazz: Jazz and French Cultural Identity* (Urbana: University of Illinois Press, 2010).

5. This is an obvious reference to the politics of Jean-Marie Le Pen and his National Front party that began in the 1970s and became famous for its platform "France for the French." Le Pen himself ran for president five times before his last run in 2007, often garnering more than ten percent of the vote. His politics are xenophobic and exclusionary and he has admitted being a racist. His daughter, Marine Le Pen—who is now head of the National Front Party and has presidential aspirations of her own—suspended him from the party in 2015.

6. For a juridical look at the issue of French citizenship from the time of the Revolution through the twentieth century, see Patrick Weil, *Qu'est-ce qu'un français? Histoire de la Nationalité française depuis la Révolution* (Paris: Éditions Grasset et Fasquelle, 2002). There are a variety of works on the subject of immigration and ethnicity. See, for instance, Miriam Feldblum, "Paradoxes of Ethnic Politics: the Case of Franco-Maghrebis in France," *Ethnic and Racial Studies*, vol. 16, no. 1 (January 1993), 52–74; and Catherine Wihtol de Wenden, "From

Migrants to Citizens: Muslims in France," *Politics and Religion in France and the United States*, eds. Alec G. Hargreaves, John Kelsay, and Sumner B. Twiss (Lanham, MD: Lexington Books, 2007), 139–53. In his *Ethnicity and Equality: France in the Balance* (Lincoln: University of Nebraska Press, 2007), the French intellectual Azouz Begag tries to move productively beyond the limiting and unrealistic conception of citizenship that denies ethnic groups national legitimacy.

    7. See Gérard Noiriel, *Le Creuset français: Histoire de l'immigration XIXe–XXe siècles* (Paris: Éditions du Seuill, 1988).

    8. For more on early civil rights activism in France, see Philippe Dewitte, *Deux siècles d'immigration en France* (Paris: La Documentation Française, 2003).

    9. A central moment in creating awareness and spurring action for minority civil rights in France came with Harlem Désir's foundation of SOS Racisme in 1985.

    10. See Verene Stolke, "Talking Culture: New Boundaries, New Rhetorics of Exclusion in Europe," *Current Anthropology*, vol. 36, no. 1 (February 1995), 1–23; Maxim Silverman, *Deconstructing the Nation: Immigration, Racism and Citizenship in Modern France* (London: Routledge, 1992); Michèle Lamont, "The Rhetoric of Racism and Anti-Racism in France and the United States" (1996 manuscript); and David Beriss, *Black Skins, French Voices: Caribbean Ethnicity and Activism in Urban France* (Boulder, CO: Westview Press, 2004).

    11. Donald L. Horowitz, "Immigration and Group Relations in France and America," *Immigrants in Two Democracies: French and American Experience*, eds. Donald L. Horowitz and Gérard Noiriel (New York: New York University Press, 1992), 18.

    12. Dominic Thomas, *Africa and France: Postcolonial Cultures, Migration, and Racism* (Bloomington: Indiana University Press, 2013), 60.

    13. Miriam Feldblum conveys this idea in her article cited above.

    14. For a concise and excellent explanation of *communautarisme* and *intégration* in present-day France, see Alec G. Hargreaves, "Translator's Introduction," Azouz Begag, *Ethnicity and Equality: France in the Balance* (Lincoln: University of Nebraska Press, 2007), vii–xxii. He writes, "In reality minorities have been prevented from participating in French society not by the cultural differences but by the prejudices and roadblocks placed in their way by members of the majority ethnic population." For two other studies that reassess Frenchness in a contemporary context, especially after the 2005 riots, see Dominic Thomas, *Black France: Colonialism, Immigration, and Transnationalism* (Bloomington: Indiana Univeristy Press, 2006) and *Frenchness and the African Diaspora*, eds. Charles Tshimanga, Didier Gondola, and Peter J. Bloom (Bloomington: Indiana University Press, 2009). Also refer to the Alec G. Hargreaves, *Multi-Ethnic France: Immigration, Politics, Culture and Society*, 2nd ed. (New York: Routledge, 2007), as he has updated the book to take recent developments into consideration.

    15. Stolke, 1–23; Etienne Balibar and Immanuel Wallerstein, *Race, Nation, and Class: Ambiguous Identities* (London: Verso, 1991); and Silverman.

    16. Frantz Fanon, "Racism and Culture," *Présence Africaine* 8–9–10 (June–November 1956), 123.

    17. I acknowledge the problems of using the terms *black* and *white* to discuss musical talent or to make any other broad generalizations about groups of people. I only do so because these French observers, critics, musicians, and fans used these labels, using the word *black* in reference to, almost solely, African Americans.

    18. Lucien Malson, "L'universalité du jazz," *Jazz Hot* 116 (December 1956), 10.

    19. For the place of both jazz and conceptions of blackness in modernism see Petrine Archer-Shaw, *Negrophilia: Avant-Gard Paris and Black Culture in the 1920s* (London: Thames & Hudson, 2000) and Jody Blake, *Le Tumulte Noir: Modernist Art and Popular Entertainment in Jazz-Age Paris, 1900–1930* (University Park: Pennsylvania State University Press, 1999). Also Bernard Gendron's "Fetishes and Motorcars: Negrophilia in French Modernism," *Cultural Studies* 2 (May 1990), 141–55; "Jamming at Le Boeuf: Jazz and the Paris Avant-Garde," *Discourse* 12 (Fall–Winter 1989–1990): 3–27; and *Between Montmartre and the Mudd Club: Popular Music and the Avant-Garde* (Chicago: University of Chicago Press, 2002).

    20. The international black cultural movement known as *négritude* had a significant place in France as well, positively influencing French views of "black" cultures in Europe, Africa, and

the Americas. See Dominic Thomas, *Black France: Colonialism, Immigration, and Transnationalism* (Bloomington: Indiana University Press, 2007); Brent Hayes Edwards, *The Practice of Diaspora: Literature, Translation, and the Rise of Black Internationalism* (Cambridge, MA: Harvard University Press, 2003); and Lilyan Kesteloot, *Black Writers in French: a Literary History of Negritude*, trans. Ellen Conroy Kennedy (Philadelphia: Temple University Press, 1974). Jean-Paul Sartre communicated his own support of *négritude* after World War II in "Black Orpheus," *"What is Literature?" and Other Essays*, trans. John MarCombie (Cambridge, MA: Harvard University Press, 1988), 291–330 and in "Présence noire," *Présence Africain* 1 (1947), 44–46.

21. Jeremy F. Lane, *Jazz and Machine-Age Imperialism: Music, "Race," and Intellectuals in France, 1918–1945* (Ann Arbor: University of Michigan Press, 2013), 15.

22. The members of Les Six were Georges Auric, Louis Durey, Arthur Honegger, Darius Milhaud, Francis Poulenc, and Germaine Tailleferre (Tailleferre was the only woman in the group).

23. Jackson, 117–21. I have used Jackson's translation of Milhaud. Also see Darius Milhaud, "The Jazz Band and Negro Music," *Living Age*, 18 October 1924, 172.

24. Brett A. Berliner, *Ambivalent Desire: The Exotic Black Other in Jazz-Age France* (Amherst: University of Massachusetts Press, 2002), 122 and 124.

25. Darius Milhaud, *Notes sans musique* (Paris: René Julliard, 1949), 152. Quoted in Jordan, 77.

26. Bernard Gendron, *Between Montmartre and the Mudd Club: Popular Music and the Avant-Garde* (Chicago: University of Chicago Press, 2002), 94.

27. Jeffrey H. Jackson, *Making Jazz French: Music and Modern Life in Interwar Paris* (Durham, NC: Duke University Press, 2003), 113.

28. Quoted by Josephine Baker and Jo Bouillon, *Josephine*, trans. Mariana Fitzpatrick (New York: Paragon House Publishers, 1988), 51.

29. There was an important contingent of black women living in Paris in the 1920s and 1930s from the Antilles who disproved of Baker's overly sexual performances. The Nardal sisters, who were from a middle-class Martinican family and who lived in Paris during the interwar years, were publically critical of the sexualized and frenetic projection of black culture created by the French jazz scene. Instead of jazz dancing, they favored the Antillean beguine. As black francophone intellectuals, they were interested in a transatlantic discourse of "race uplift," and in their view Baker and other aspects of jazz culture disrupted their agenda. See Rachel Anne Gillet, "Jazz women, gender politics, and the Francophone Atlantic," *Atlantic Studies: Global Currents*, Vol. 10, No. 1 (2013), 109–130, http://dx.doi.org/10.1080/14788810.2013.766494; and Lane.

30. Jordan, 111.

31. Elizabeth Ezra, *The Colonial Unconscious: Race and Culture in Interwar France* (Ithaca, NY: Cornell University Press, 2000), 99.

32. For more on this subject, see Tyler Stovall, *Paris Noire: African Americans in the City of Light* (New York: Houghton Mifflin Company, 1996), 54

33. The identities that played into French receptions of jazz were of course complicated by French involvement in the Americas and Africa. This nourished understandings of the music that depended on the "Black Atlantic" and its crisscrossings of identification and meaning. For more on the Black Atlantic, see Paul Gilroy, *The Black Atlantic: Modernity and Double Consciousness* (Cambridge, MA: Harvard University Press, 1993).

34. Jennifer Anne Boittin, "Chapter 1: Josephine Baker: Colonial Woman," *Colonial Metropolis: The Urban Grounds of Anti-Imperialism and Feminism in Interwar Paris* (Lincoln: University of Nebraska Press, 2010), 1–36.

35. It is worth pointing out that in the United States at this time white jazz bands, like those led by Paul Whiteman, won the major record deals and performance contracts, not African-American bands. See Jordan, 73–76.

36. Jackson, 117.

37. Jordan, 76–77.

38. Jackson, 89.

39. Ibid., 87–91; and Gendron, 106.

40. Jackson, 94.
41. Jackson, 35.
42. Jordan, 119. See André Schaeffner, "Notes sur la musique des Afro-Américaines," *Le Ménéstrel* no. 88 (August 6, 1926), 299. Schaeffner also cowrote and published with musical editor André Coeuroy the first French monograph on jazz, *Le jazz* (Paris: Éditions Claude Aveline, 1926). Interestingly enough, by 1935, Schaeffner lamented the passing of the authentic, original, primitive jazz; with disapproval he claimed that the music had become a form of commercial mass culture. See Jordan, 140.
43. Jackson, 119. Wiéner made this comment in his 1978 autobiography looking back on his interwar musical creations. See Jean Wiéner, *Allegro appassionato* (Paris: P. Belfond, 1978).
44. Jordan, 137–38.
45. Maurice Delage, "La Musique du jazz," *Revue Pleyel* (April 1926), 19. Quoted in Jordan, 113–17.
46. Jackson, 175. Nicely illustrating the continuity of his thoughts about a "true" jazz, Panassié published an entire book on the topic in the 1940s. See Hugues Panassié, *The Real Jazz*, trans. Anne Sorelle Williams (New York: Smith & Durrell, 1942).
47. As Jordan points out, there were also among the French those who actively rejected jazz in the interwar period, largely conservative and protectionist writers and politicians as well as Catholic leaders and those who wished to reject Americanization and internationalism. Despite the broad popularity and success of productions like *La Revue Nègre*, a number of critics saw jazz as a defiance of proper French entertainment.
48. Claude Sautet, "La Querelle des blancs et des noirs," *Combat* (5 December 1946), 2.
49. Leonard Feather, "Préjugés," *Jazz Hot* 45 (June 1950), 11.
50. Charles Delaunay, "Préjugés ou malentendus," *Jazz Hot* 45 (June 1950), 12.
51. Frank Tenot, "Les chants religieux du peuple noir des Etats-Unis," *Jazz Hot* 88 (May 1954), 14.
52. Delaunay, "Préjugés," 9.
53. André Hodeir, "Jazz noir; Jazz Blanc," *Jazz Hot* 102 (September 1955), 9.
54. Ibid.
55. Jean-Louis Martin, "Le mal blanc," *Le Bulletin du Hot Club de France* 57 (April 1956), 29.
56. Patrice Sylvian, "Les disques: variétés," *L'Aurore* (6 March 1956), 4.
57. Reflecting on Walter Benjamin's understanding of "aura" is instructive here. See Walter Benjamin, "The Work of Art in the Age of Mechanical Reproduction," *Illuminations*, ed. Hannah Arendt, trans. Harry Zohn (New York: Schocken Books, 1969), 217–51.
58. Michel de Villers, "Jazz français 1950," *Jazz Hot* 42 (March 1950).
59. Michel de Villers, "Prejugés et sens critique," *Jazz Hot* 114 (October 1956), 8.
60. André Clergeat, "Préjugés et sens critique," *Jazz Hot* 114 (October 1956), 8.
61. "Le jazz est-il toujours un art negre?" *Arts* 475 (August 4–10, 1954), 5.
62. Frank Tenot, "Oui, parce que le Noir joue avec tout son corps," *Arts* 475 (August 4–10, 1954), 5.
63. Jacques Hess, "Non, parce qu'il est devenu un phénomène mondial," *Arts* 475 (August 4–10, 1954), 5.
64. Ibid.
65. Ibid.
66. Loudovic Tournès, *New Orleans sur Seine: Histoire du jazz en France* (Paris: Fayard, 1999), 114–15.
67. Lucien Malson, "Jazz noir; Jazz blanc," *Jazz Hot* 102 (September 1955), 8.
68. Lucien Malson, "La musique noire serait-elle grise?" *Jazz Hot* 94 (December 1954), 9–10.
69. Malson, "Jazz noir," 8.
70. Charles Delaunay, "Jazz noir; Jazz blanc," *Jazz Magazine* 102 (September 1955), 32.
71. Olivier Despax and Gérard Brémond (interviewer), "Olivier Despax: un jeune qui voit blanc," *Jazz Hot* (May 1959), 14.
72. Malson, "Jazz noir," 9.
73. Lucien Malson, "Le Jazz ne meurt pas," *Les Temps Modernes* 99 (February 1954), 1469.

74. Ibid.
75. "Questions et réponses," *Jazz Magazine* 11 (November 1955), 38.
76. Delaunay, "Jazz noir," 9.
77. André Hodeir, *Jazz: Its Evolution and Its Essence*, trans. David Noakes (New York: Grove Press, 1956), 10.
78. 78. "Qui êtes-vous?" *Jazz Magazine* 51 (August–September 1959), 19.
79. Ibid.
80. J. Lebienvenu, "Courrier des lecteurs," *Jazz Hot* 167 (July–August 1961), 4.
81. Michel de Villers, "Courrier des lecteurs," *Jazz Hot* 167 (July–August 1961), 4.
82. Georges Fiogbe, "L'impossible unamité," *Jazz Magazine* 95 (June 1963), 7.
83. François-René Cristiani, "Livre," *Jazz Hot* 201 (September 1964), 9. Malson's book was recently reissued; see Lucien Malson, *Les enfants sauvage* (Paris: Bibliothèques 10–18, 2002).
84. Jean-Jacques Patrice, "Le courrier pour une définition de la négritude," *Les Cahiers du jazz* 15 (first trimester, 1967), 103.
85. Lucien Malson, "A la recherche de l'homme noir," *Les Cahiers du jazz* 13 (1966), 16.
86. Lucien Malson, "Courrier des lecteurs," *Jazz Hot* 221 (June 1966), 15.
87. Lucien Malson, "La recherche de l'homme noir," *Les Cahiers du jazz* 13 (1966), 17.
88. Frantz Fanon, *The Wretched of the Earth*, trans. Constance Farrington (New York: Grove Press, 1963), 243.
89. See Lane for more about Panassie's views in the 1930s, especially Lane's chapter entitled "Jazz as Antidote to the Machine Age: From Hugues Panassié to Léopold Sédar Senghor," 90–125.
90. "Revue de Presse," *Le Bulletin du Hot Club de France* 133 (December 1963), 32.
91. "Revue de Presse," *Le Bulletin du Hot Club de France* 115 (February 1962), 31.
92. See Frank Tenot, "Jazz Informations," *Jazz Magazine* 121 (August 1965).
93. For a detailed analysis of the French opposition to American culture in the postwar world, see especially Richard Kuisel, *Seducing the French: the Dilemma of Americanization* (Berkeley: University of California Press, 1993).
94. To better understand how French jazz writers still conveyed prevalent social stereotypes through the 1970s, see Stephen Lehman, "I Love You With An Asterisk: African-American Experimental Music and the French Jazz Press, 1970–1980," *Critical Studies in Improvisation*, vol. 1, no. 2 (2005), 38–53.
95. This is an argument I have made in my previous work. See Elizabeth Vihlen, "Sounding French: Jazz in Postwar France," PhD dissertation, SUNY Stony Brook, 2000, as well as Elizabeth Vihlen, "Jammin' on the Champs Elysées: Jazz, France, and the 1950s," *"Here, There and Everywhere": The Foreign Politics of American Popular Culture*, eds. Reinhold Wagnleitner and Elaine Tyler May (Hanover, NH: University Press of New England, 2000), 149–62. Ludovic Tournès also writes about these subjects in "La réinterprétation du jazz: un phénomène de contre-américanisation dans la France d'après guerre (1945–1960)," in *Play it Again Sim . . . : Hommages à Sim Copans*, special edition of *Revue française d'études américaines* (December 2001), 74.
96. This was something that also happened in the United States beginning by the mid-1940s when "the virtually all-white jazz journals were boasting of their progressive racial attitudes, as well as that of white musicians, while denouncing Jim Crow practices in nightclubs, record companies, and the rest of society." Bernard Gendron, *Between Montmartre and the Mudd Club: Popular Music and the Avant-Garde* (Chicago: University of Chicago Press, 2002), 137.
97. Jean-Paul Sartre first published this book by Kennedy in 1956 in Paris.
98. A. D., "Harlem sur Seine?" *Jazz Hot* 177 (June 1962), 7.
99. See for instance, Daniel Guérin, *Où va le peuple américaine?* (Paris: René Julliard, 1951); André Seigfried, *America at Mid-Century*, trans. Margaret Ledésert (New York: Harcourt, Brace and Company, 1955); Daniel Guérin, *Décolonization du noir américan* (Paris: Les Éditions de Minuit, 1963); and Philippe Carles and Jean-Louis Comolli, *Free Jazz/Black Power* (Paris: Gallimard, 2000).
100. For more on the American context, see Kevin Gaines, "Duke Ellington, *Black, Brown and Beige*, and the Cultural Politics of Race," *Music and the Racial Imagination*, eds. Ronald Radano and Philip V. Bohlman (Chicago: University of Chicago Press, 2000), 599.

101. Tournès, "La reinterpretation du jazz," 78.
102. "Jazz actualités: Eisenhower vu par Armstrong," *Jazz Hot* 125 (October 1957), 28. Also see "Les querelles raciste rebondisent aux U.S.A.," *Jazz Magazine* 32 (November 1957), 10–11.
103. "Jazz à la carte," *Jazz Hot* 147 (October 1959), 30.
104. L.F., "Sauvage agression contre Miles Davis," *Jazz Magazine* 52 (October 1959), 13.
105. "Jim Crow contre Nat King Cole," *Jazz Magazine* 31 (October 1957), 12.
106. Yetty Lee, "Flashes," *Jazz Magazine* 5 (April 1955), 10.
107. "Flashes: Américains de dernière minute," *Jazz Magazine* 11 (November 1955), 11.
108. "Attentat contre Satchmo," *Jazz Magazine* 26 (April 1957), 11.
109. Nat Hentoff, "Armstrong et Jim Crow," *Jazz Hot* 113 (September 1956), 26. Hentoff is an American critic, so we can see his comments here as linking the perspectives of jazz aficionados from both the United States and France.
110. "Nouvelles d'Amérique," *Jazz Hot* 124 (September 1957), 22–23.
111. "Brubeck et Jim Crow," *Jazz Magazine* 47 (April 1959), 13.
112. "Fats Waller," *Jazz Magazine* 1 (December 1954), 5.
113. Daniel Filipacchi, "En direct de New York: coup d'oeil de Daniel Filipacchi sur le jazz américain," *Jazz Magazine* 32 (November 1957), 27.
114. "Flashes," *Jazz Magazine* 67 (February 1961), 14.
115. "Jazz à la carte," *Jazz Hot* 171 (December 1961), 9; "Jazz Informations," *Jazz Magazine* 78 (January 1962), 13.
116. "Jazz à la carte," *Jazz Hot* 169 (October 1961), 5.
117. "Jazz Informations," *Jazz Magazine* 96 (July 1963), 15.
118. Jean-Louis Ginibre, "La lutte finale," *Jazz Magazine* 99 (October 1963), 14.
119. Dominique Eudes, "Le globe-trotter de Harlem," *Lui* 18 (June 1965), 50, 52, 64.
120. Siné, "Le bloc-notes de l'Académicien," *Jazz Hot* 211 (July–August 1965).
121. Eric Drott, *Music and the Elusive Revolution: Cultural Politics and Political Culture in France, 1968–1981* (Berkeley: University of California Press, 2011), 115.
122. Jedediah Sklower, *Free Jazz, la catastrophe féconde: Une histoire du mond éclaté du jazz en France (1960–1982)* (Paris: L'Harmattan, 2006), 170.
123. Vincent Cotro, *Chants libres: Le free jazz en France, 1960–1975* (Paris: Éditions Outre Mesure, 1999), 113. Here, Cotro cites his own 1997 interview with François Tusques.
124. See Cotro, 61; and *Jazz Hot* 241 (May–June 1968).
125. Daniel Caux, "A.A.C.M. Chicago," *Jazz Hot* 254 (October 1969), 17 and 19. I have used the translation cited in Drott, 116.
126. In addition to Drott, also see Lehman.
127. Drott, 116–17. Beyond the scope of my book's timeframe, in 1971, Philippe Carles and Jean-Louis Comolli wrote the book *Free Jazz/Black Power*, in which they expressed their Marxist view that African Americans were among the broad global class of the exploited. They wrote, "We consider that this contradiction between the value systems of whites and blacks, at work in the colonization of jazz and the resistance to this colonization, is but one moment in the principal contradiction between the colonizers and the colonized, exploiters and exploited: between capitalism and its victims." See Carles and Comolli, *Free Jazz/Black Power* (Paris: Gallimard, 2000), 39. I have used the English translation from Drott, 133.
128. Quoted in George E. Lewis, *A Power Stronger than Itself: The AACM and American Experimental Music* (Chicago: University of Chicago Press, 2008), 246.
129. Bennetta Jules-Rosette, *Josephine Baker in Art and Life: The Icon and the Image* (Urbana: University of Illinois Press, 2007), 184–91.
130. Pap Ndiaye, *La Condition noire: Essai sur une minorité française* (Paris: Calmann-Lévy, 2008).
131. I made this argument in "Sounding French" as well. Also see Tournès, "La réinterprétation du jazz," 80.
132. Tom Perchard also notices this trend in *After Django: Making Jazz in Postwar France* (Ann Arbor: University of Michigan Press, 2015), 187.
133. Quoted in John Chilton, *Sidney Bechet: The Wizard of Jazz* (New York: Oxford University Press, 1987), 252.

134. Berliner, 2. Also see Philippe Dewitte, *Les Mouvements nègre en France 1919-1939* (Paris: Éditions L'Harmattan, 1985) who uses police reports to estimate the number of Africans in France.

135. Tyler Stovall, "'No Green Pastures:' The African Americanization of France," *Empire Lost: France and Its Other Worlds*, ed. Elisabeth Mudimbe-Boyi (Lanham, MD: Lexington Books, 2009), 74.

136. For more on the African-American community in France, see Tyler Stovall, *Paris Noire: African Americans in the City of Light* (New York: Houghton Mifflin Company, 1996); Michel Fabre, *From Harlem to Paris: Black American Writers in France, 1940-1980* (Urbana: University of Illinois Press, 1991); Ursula Broschke, *Paris without Regret: James Baldwin, Kenny Clarke, Chester Hines, and Donald Byrd* (Iowa City: University of Iowa Press, 1986); Bill Moody, *The Jazz Exiles: American Musicians Abroad* (Reno: University of Nevada Press, 1993); and James Campbell, *Exiled in Paris: Richard Wright, James Baldwin, Samuel Becket, and Others on the Left Bank* (Berkeley: University of California Press, 2003).

137. In discussing the 1920s, Brett Berliner has argued that there is a "myth of a racially tolerant, indeed unprejudiced France" based on the treatment of African Americans there. He points out that there were actually few African Americans and that they "generally stayed for short periods of time, and, most significantly, were talented, artistic, and, in French eyes, civilized individuals. Since they rarely competed with Frenchmen for jobs, it was easy to embrace them, especially when commodified on a stage." See Berliner, 237.

138. Colin Nettelbeck, *Dancing with DeBeauvoir: Jazz and the French* (Carlton, Victoria: Melbourne University Press, 2004), 195

139. Lucien Malson, "Les Noirs," *Jazz Hot* 52 (February 1951), 7.

140. Frank Ténot, "L'Oncle Tom et le Jazz," *Jazz Magazine* 14 (February 1956), 6.

141. Lucien Malson, "Les Noirs," *Jazz Hot* 55 (May 1951), 11.

142. Malson, "Les Noirs," *Jazz Hot* 52 (February 1951), 7.

143. Malson, "Les Noirs," *Jazz Hot* 56 (June 1951), 11.

144. Ténot, "L'Oncle Tom," 6.

145. "Incident raciste," *Le Bulletin du Hot Club de France* 154 (January 1966), 11.

146. Lewis, 226. Lewis interviewed Wadada Leo Smith in La Jolla, California on March 7, 1999.

147. Val Wilmer, *Mama Said There'd Be Days Like This: My Life in the Jazz World* (London: Women's Press, 1980), 192. Also see Lewis, 255.

148. Michel de Villers, "Courrier des lecteurs," *Jazz Hot* 159 (November 1960), 5.

149. "Courrier des lecteurs," *Jazz Hot* 161 (January 1961), 5.

150. "Siné," *Jazz Magazine* 148 (November 1967), 41.

151. Philippe Koechlin, "Siné: Moi, j'aime quand ça chauffe!" *Jazz Hot* 176 (may 1962), 14–18.

152. See the 1963 issues of *Révolution africaine* where he published a regular series of political cartoons entitled "La semaine politique de Siné."

153. Lucien Malson, "Courrier des Lecteurs," *Jazz Hot* 225 (November 1966), 15.

154. "Questions et réponses: racisme?" *Jazz Magazine* 52 (October 1959), 9.

155. Claude Chiron, "Courrier des lecteurs," *Jazz Hot* 225 (Novemeber 1966), 15.

156. Ibid.

157. Etienne Balibar, "Racism and Nationalism," *Race, Nation, and Class: Ambiguous Identities*, ed. Etienne Balibar and Immanuel Wallerstein (New York: Verso, 1991), 41–42. Azouz Begag makes much that same point in saying, "Today policies on urban issues, integration, equal opportunities, and law and order are all impregnated by the legacy of colonialism. Anti-Arab racism is often grounded in rancorous sentiments that say: 'You kicked us out of Algeria in 1962; you're going to take over here now.'" Azouz Begag, *Ethnicity and Equality: France in the Balance* (Lincoln: University of Nebraska Press, 2007), 109.

158. Chiron, 15.

159. Lucien Malson, "Courrier des Lecteurs," *Jazz Hot* 225 (November 1966), 15.

160. Malson wrote several other similar letters in response to readers in the mid-1960s when he hosted the "Courrier des Lecteurs" column. See for example, "Courrier des Lecteurs," *Jazz Hot* 211 (July–August 1965), 19; and "Courrier des Lecteurs," *Jazz Hot* 210 (June 1965), 13.

161. Michel de Villers, "Courrier des Lecteurs," *Jazz Hot* 192 (November 1963), 4.

Chapter Four

More than an American Music

In the first two decades following World War II, the French faced an ever more powerful United States, so that American culture, politics, and economics directly influenced French ways of life. With the Marshall Plan and American economic hegemony following the war, French leaders and citizens confronted expanding American capabilities in a variety of areas, while simultaneously watching their own nation lose its place in world affairs. France's financial and political might slipped away after a less-than-glorious record during the war, and as overseas colonies—symbols of French global power—became independent. In the face of these challenges, French people were concerned with fostering a distinct national identity. However, despite a clear interest in nurturing an idiosyncratic French culture, French jazz enthusiasts advanced an American music. Although the jazz public was predominantly male and located on the left of the political spectrum, it rarely advocated socialism or communism in an outward fashion; but it did consistently and openly denigrate American capitalism, consumerism, and racism. The Cold War directly swayed French politics in the 1950s, unleashing debates over communism and capitalism, and the Soviet way versus the American way, as individuals worked to stake out their own place among these debates. In this politicized context, culture was not distinct from politics. Despite the fact that jazz was an American creation, many of its French fans actually used it as a vehicle through which they could express their criticisms of the United States and selectively appropriate "America."

THE MEANING OF "AMERICA"

French identity after World War II emphasized the nation's role in promoting and protecting international culture, and with this particular aim in mind, the

Ministry of Culture was founded in 1959 under the leadership of André Malraux. French leaders asserted that France's place in global affairs largely hinged on the prominent place the nation gave to the arts. Facing the United States' economic and military resources, they claimed that the French high regard for artistic creation made their country great.[1] Although these same individuals worked to develop France's financial and military assets, they also tied the nation's strength to its cultural endowment. Through the medium of jazz, the French could both embrace and renounce different aspects of American culture and society, while supporting a unique American art form and its wide-reaching potential.

French jazz audiences deliberately sanctioned or rejected different aspects of U.S. culture, since a complete endorsement would have meant lending their approval to American social, economic, and cultural models. These fans accepted jazz while they and their countrymen concomitantly criticized other aspects of American society. Since well before the war, French commentators like George Duhamel had disparaged American fast food, football, Fords, and Hollywood.[2] Following World War II, French anti-Americanism first peaked in the early 1950s due to the wide-ranging influence of communists and leftist intellectuals, and then it peaked again in the 1960s, under the leadership of Charles de Gaulle and his followers.[3] Until 1956, when Soviet behavior changed the status quo, French communists and public intellectuals eschewed American capitalism and militarism while they continued to be optimistic about the future of the Soviet model.[4] Over the ensuing years, Gaullists were the most insistent critics of the United States, as they worked to maintain French sovereignty on diplomatic, military, economic, and cultural fronts. In doing so, they were an important pillar of anti-American discourse during the Fifth Republic.

Despite these powerful political objections to the American way, American culture continued to make inroads into French life. Hollywood movies were widely watched in France by the 1950s. Two world wars and an aggressive American export policy had given the Americans global dominance in the film industry, and some genres, like film noir, were given critical acclaim.[5] Coca-Cola became a major presence in the French soft drink market in the 1950s; after 1945, Disney reached French viewers through movies, comics, and television; the periodical *Sélection du Reader's Digest* began appearing in France in 1947; and products made by American companies like Revlon or Proctor & Gamble became ubiquitous over the ensuing postwar decades.[6] Nonetheless, individuals, political parties, and trade organizations often rejected these envoys of American consumer culture because they were seen as a threat to a traditional French way of life or to certain professions and livelihoods. Jazz, on the other hand, was promoted by its postwar French audience with a distinct enthusiasm that included no reservations about the music's potential negative impact on French national culture, even among communists, leftist intellectuals, or Gaullists. While Levi's jeans and American cigarettes like Camel eventually became youthful and countercultural symbols of America, they still did not carry the same stated symbolic weight or political meanings of jazz.[7]

Supporters of jazz were manifestly interested in the United States, so that French articles and books on the music dealt with American history, politics, social issues, and culture, focusing on artists such as Charlie Parker, Miles Davis, Dizzy Gillespie, Louis Armstrong, Bud Powell, and Sidney Bechet. Jazz critics were also mindful of French musicians like Claude Luter, Guy Lafitte, and Michel Legrand but wrote about them much less frequently than about their American counterparts. In monthly columns, French writers covered news and gossip coming from the United States, and in advertisements the influence of both American business and culture was apparent. The American record companies Capital and Atlantic used references to the United States in their French sales pitches, putting forth such proclamations as "At the same time as in the U.S.A!" and "The most dynamic American trademarks" in their advertisements.[8] References to the United States were also popular in French marketing strategies. A. Courtois promoted one of its trumpets as "adopted by the best American and French musicians," and Selmer showcased its instruments by using famous jazz stars like Louis Armstrong and Benny Goodman in their ads.[9] In French jazz periodicals, writers referred to the American jazz magazine *Down Beat* as "our *confrère*" and discussed articles appearing in a variety of American magazines—*Jazz Review*, *Billboard Magazine*, *Ebony*, *The Record Changer*, and *Metronome*. In addition, critics reviewed American movies that touched the subject of jazz, such as *Pete Kelly's Blues*, *The Benny Goodman Story*, and *The Cool World*. French jazz fans were abundantly aware of the American jazz scene—especially the one in New York—and read about important festivals like the Newport Jazz Festival in French publications. For these French jazz audiences, understanding and promoting American jazz was an indispensable element of their musical appreciation.

THE JAZZ EXCEPTION

During a time of national self-doubt, one reason the French jazz community found this music so acceptable was that it came from an African-American tradition, a topic discussed at length in chapter 3. Because French jazz fans had long asserted that African Americans were both the architects and best practitioners of jazz, a strong distinction had been made between jazz and the rest of mainstream American culture. In postwar France, audiences would not equate jazz with other American cultural exports like Hollywood movies, *Reader's Digest*, or Coca-Cola. They saw jazz as a music that was distinct from any European or white American contemporary music, and this otherness, in many ways, made jazz appealing as well as benign as a cultural threat.[10] As we saw in chapter 1, starting in the interwar period, French musicians, fans, and critics had made a connection in their minds between jazz and blackness, jazz and the primitive, jazz and the other. Among the French, there had never been a fear of African political, social, or cultural hegemony: Africans were a colonized, and therefore controlled, exoticized other, whose music and art (and labor and natural resources) could be harnessed and elevated by the West. Jazz appreciation's roots in primitivism in the 1920s made it quite distinct from other American cultural products in the postwar period. The music's supporters had long seen jazz as a means of invigorating French culture and had never seen it as a threat to traditional French ways of life.

As also discussed in chapter 1, the French jazz public had long seen jazz as a musical hybrid that reflected and communicated the "African" *and* the "American." For jazz critics, this meant that understanding jazz involved knowing the country of its birth, and they often traveled to the United States, relaying their experiences to readers back home in France. In their work, they portrayed the United States and France as diverging from one another in social, cultural, and economic matters, and their appreciation for the United States coexisted with distrust. When French writers wrote about jazz, they communicated their misgivings about American commercialism and consumerism, while also bemoaning the economic plight of American musicians, many of whom were unable to make enough money to support themselves. French critics pushed members of the French jazz public to advocate for equality and artistic advancement, not profit making, and they made it clear that they did not support American capitalism and its corresponding values. In contrast to how the "African" side of jazz was historically and problematically embraced for its "primitivism," French critics worked to mitigate and control the strength of the "American" side.

Hugues Panassié was the first critic to go abroad for an extended period of time. In 1937, he spent five months in New York, and after the war, in 1947, published his account in *Cinq mois à New-York*. Later French visitors reported their own experiences in much the same way as Panassié—by reviewing jazz clubs, discussing encounters with individual musicians, and making an explicit effort to analyze different aspects of American society, especially the problem of racism. Despite Panassié's condemnation of American racism and his dislike of American food and wine, he otherwise came away from his 1938 visit with positive feelings about the country. He told readers that he tried to remain open-minded about American life, writing that "if, in American life, things shocked me, I am perfectly aware that an American can also perhaps be shocked by certain aspects of French life; and I am even more aware that I am myself irritated by plenty of the customs of my countrymen."[11] In the late 1940s, Panassié returned to the United States and reported his findings in *La Revue du Jazz*. He expressed his disappointment in the new, modern sounds of bebop, asserting that "after several days spent in New York, one is astonished by the number of excellent musicians found there! . . . and the paucity of good jazz that one hears."[12] Yet, he continued to preserve his contacts with American artists like Louis Armstrong and kept telling his readers about the new "goings-on" in the United States. Despite his more traditional aesthetic tastes and antidemocratic political leanings, he continued to stress the importance of sustaining the French jazz community's link with America.

Other French jazz professionals went to the United States in the postwar decades to experience the jazz scene as well. Early in 1957, André Hodeir spent several months in New York, and described the city as

> an immense pot, bubbling pell-mell with the most diverse ingredients. One rediscovers this impression with each new thing: the architecture—the cooking (where salt food mixes with sugar in the most strange way)—the people that one meets. But from this unexpected mixture emerges an extraordinary life. . . . One better understands a certain unfinished side of jazz when one sees the milieu in which it develops: the lack of unity in the majority of works is more easily explained.[13]

According to Hodeir, seeing the American way of life, and especially how it was lived out in New York, helped jazz audiences to better understand their music. In 1957, Daniel Filipacchi also went to New York to report on American jazz, and like Hodeir, found a new understanding for the music. For instance, he pointed out that Duke Ellington's song "Air-conditioned Jungle" now made sense to him: "The air-conditioned jungle is New York. These small machines that you hear discretely humming in all windows are in America what the huge shade trees are to the inhabitants of the jungle. One comes to find refuge near them."[14] Whether this interpretation of Ellington's song title was correct, Filipacchi—like Hodeir and Panassié before him—found when he came to New York what were for him crucial influences on the music.

French criticisms of American society easily came to the surface in discussions about jazz, one frequent subject of interest being American consumerism. French commentators habitually expressed their dissatisfaction with the postwar consumer society that American corporations and politicians were intent on exporting to other parts of the globe. Central to this relatively new way of life was the idea that the production of manufactured goods in high numbers meant higher profits for businesses as well as lower costs for the consumers.[15] In the minds of many Frenchmen, however, American consumerism was equated with social conformity: everyone striving to own the same products and define themselves through material goods. By the 1950s, the gospel of consumption had not only taken a very strong hold in America but was also beginning to make an important impact on European countries. These countries had opened their borders to American investment, products, and ways of doing business, allowing standardized products, new spending patterns, higher wages, and increased social mobility to make inroads on their own economic and social systems.[16] In many ways, consumerism came to define postwar society, and its materialistic outlook pushed people to orient their lives around buying new cars, household appliances, clothes, and even jazz records.

An emphasis on profit-making was a central component of this consumer society, and this put French jazz fans in a dilemma, because they wanted both to avoid the American hyper-concern with money-making and to see musicians themselves financially succeed. Ideally, fans thought jazz should be a live, improvised music, not one that depended on recordings or rehearsed concerts. Critics, characterizing improvisation as "free" and "paraphrased," claimed that jazz did not readily comply with marketplace standardization.[17] However, jazz musicians had no way of receiving appropriate compensation unless they conceded to some demands of the mass market, and French critics mourned the fact that many musicians lived in poverty.

On the whole, American jazz artists did not benefit from their nation's wealth in the first decades after the Second World War and many of them lived in destitute conditions at one time or another. In 1956, Félix Manskleid of *Jazz Magazine* wrote that the United States was experiencing an "era of prosperity without parallel in its history" but that its musicians were "the sole Americans not to benefit from this situation." This, at a time when the jazz community claimed that interest in the music had "never been greater." According to Manskleid, only 33 percent of the 252,512 members of the American Federation of Musicians could subsist on the money they earned playing music, while the others had to rely on "a second occupation or job." For more than a decade, hotels, restaurants, and dance halls had been moving away from having live entertainment in their establishments. "According to expert opinion this state of affairs was caused by two things: first, what Americans call the 'technological' revolution, then the twenty percent federal tax applied to cabarets."[18] Even when a musician got a job, he reportedly only made $3,454 a year (1.200.00 francs). As recorded music replaced live music, musicians found themselves out of work. Both black and white artists often coped with the need to earn a living by giving into the demands of the marketplace. An American correspondent for *Jazz Hot* noted that "the one regular job that a black musician can hope to find is in a rhythm-and-blues band, or again—and this is worse—in a rock and roll band. It goes without saying that this is not an agreeable experience for a young jazzman."[19] In the eyes of French jazz lovers, American musicians were given neither the creative recognition nor the monetary rewards that they deserved, and that the American population could afford.

Vocal members of the French jazz community felt that music as an art was endangered by its exposure to commercial values, but this did not change the fact that many musicians had to surrender to commercialism in some way to make a living. Some commentators were critical of this capitulation, while others saw it as a financial necessity. Hugues Panassié wrote, "I deplore commercialism, I even fight against it, but I cannot condemn musicians who are its victims" and he encouraged jazz fans not to be too judgmental.[20] At times, musicians also voiced their dissatisfaction with their need to be commercially viable, and searched for solutions to the problem. In a 1955 interview, Sarah Vaughan claimed,

> Jazz fans reproach me for the success of a commercial recording. They think that I intend to abandon jazz. They are wrong: I am the only artist to have signed recording contracts with two different firms. The reason? I record commercial successes for one and jazz for the other. One popular record, one record for the music.[21]

Like Vaughan, French commentators saw commercialism and jazz as incompatible, so that "commercial" jazz was antithetical to the music's meaning. To remain within the confines defined by many as "true" jazz, musicians had to avoid both overexposure and reliance on the recording industry. The ideal was live performance and continuous artistic creativity.

Jazz became dislocated from its folkloric and noncommercial base as technological capabilities increased. By the mid-1950s, fans could listen to jazz on a wide variety of radio shows and see musicians playing on television. Movies also incorporated jazz in their soundtracks, and in this atmosphere the musical "hit" was born. In his monthly *Jazz Magazine* column, Frank Ténot bemoaned this development when he wrote,

> You all know what a "hit" is in variety entertainment: it is the unyielding appearance of the best seller, it is the piece of success, the vehicle that sells copies by the tens of thousands, the tune that saturates juke boxes, that poisons programs with record requests, the music that pays.[22]

When a song became a "hit," it lost the freshness and novelty that jazz fans considered so imperative. Georges Hilleret, a writer for the French equivalent of *T.V. Guide*—*Télé 7 jours*—expressed in 1965 the same concerns as Ténot, remarking that in the previous thirty-five years, because of the recording industry, the situations for musicians had drastically changed for the worse. He wrote,

> Toward 1930, there were, only in Paris, more than ten thousand musicians living off of their work. In 1965, there remain about twelve hundred, of which five hundred are completely unemployed. This fall is due to the vanishing opera houses, restaurant bands (hit by a luxury tax) and the appearance of talking movies, which ruined all cinema musicians with one blow.[23]

The result of this situation was that "France became a huge juke-box" as recorded music replaced live, leaving many musicians out of work. Recorded music was cheaper for restaurants and cafés and brought a high return to record companies, squeezing out small, commercially unsuccessful musicians. Other observers were also concerned about the increasing commercialization of jazz. André Hodeir worried that jazz musicians would play differently if they understood "the secret of large-scale commercial success: playing 'pretty' and [playing] a repertoire of old and new hit tunes."[24] For him, the resulting music would lose much of the rawness and emotion that French fans looked to find in jazz. Many saw the recording industry itself as the enemy because it openly represented a society that valued money above all else. Ténot warned, "Don't believe that these masters of recordings listen to the artists. They are only sensitive to the crystal-clear sound of coins falling into the music box, and their preferred reading is their bank account statement."[25]

The most crucial markers of a musician's commercial success were record sales. Best sellers ensured financial security for musicians, but for the most part jazz records did not enter this category, which remained primarily the domain of variety records and, in the 1960s, rock and roll. French jazz listeners depended on record collections because concerts were generally expensive and infrequent, especially for those who lived outside of Paris. Buying records was also costly for average fans, the majority of whom were in their teens and twenties. One *Jazz Magazine* reader from Marseilles wrote that as a fan

> for some ten years and, of course, as a collector of records, I am increasingly dismayed by the current price of LPs. Is there a way to change this? Jazz, which always wants to be more revolutionary, is it going to become paradoxically the privilege of a rich bourgeoisie? Since admission to national museums is frequently free, since artistic films and film screenings have reasonable admission ticket prices, should jazz be a luxury art?[26]

The politically radical Siné responded to this letter by saying that the only countries where records were affordable were China and Cuba, places where the governments were against jazz because of their Cold War politics. He claimed that "there are two ways to resolve the problem: fight to make France socialist . . . [or] rip-off the stores: it is the solution adopted by a lot of beatniks and provos: it is a lot faster and efficient! Me, if I chose the first solution, it is only because I have my records right here."[27] Because of their leftist politics, both the fan from Marseilles and Siné denounced commercial interests and high record prices, but more moderate observers were also bothered by the high cost of records. In discussions of record prices, the subject of Americanization was only thinly veiled; when Siné claimed outright support for Cuba and China, his unspoken criticism of American capitalism was apparent. Anti-Americanism for Siné, and others like him, did not so much mean protecting an older, more "authentic" French lifestyle, but advocating an economic, political, and social system that advocated equality and artistic advancement, not profit-making.

In a 1966 series on record companies, critic Philippe Koechlin interviewed three French record company executives about jazz records in France: Jean Tronchot from Philips, Henri Renaud from CBS, and André Poulain from Polydor. Not surprisingly, these men differed from Siné in their views on jazz and commercialism. Renaud openly maintained "that good music can sometimes be commercial" and Tronchot and Poulain agreed that jazz records' lack of commercial viability was a problem.[28] Jazz records did not sell well in comparison with other genres, especially those of variety and rock and roll. Tronchot asserted that, since about 1962, records sales had risen in the latter two categories while jazz sales remained stagnant because of a saturated market.[29] Poulain claimed that "when rhythmic music does not sell, one calls it jazz. When it sells, it is of course rock and roll or American variety or whatever else but one hurries to classify it under another name."[30] Out of these three represented companies, only Philips recorded French musicians, despite the fact other French record company executives expressed a wish to record their countrymen.[31] Basically, to record a musician in Paris cost significantly more "than to publish an LP already in existence in an American catalog. In order to be profitable, the records of French musicians must sell two or three times more than those of American origin." This was not necessarily because the French jazz public was less interested in French musicians, but because costs were higher and jazz fans were not numerous enough to buy a profitable number of records. And, of course, record companies expected some of the records they made to be "flops." "In jazz, the ratio between a 'failure' and a success is one to four or five (that is to say that the 'best-seller' sells four or five more than the unsuccessful record). In variety, the ratio can easily go to one to five hundred, or more!" This made publishing variety records less of a risk, because the hits easily paid for the failures. "In jazz, one cannot frequently do anything but cherish the hope that money won't be lost." According to one executive, the most profitable jazz records were those which appealed to the larger public, for instance, ones made by Ray Charles, Ella Fitzgerald, Dave Brubeck, Miles Davis, the Modern Jazz Quartet, Errol Garner, and the like. For records made in France by either French or American musicians to be profitable, they had to sell abroad.[32] The careers of these three executives depended on jazz records' commercial success. Their jobs were tightly connected to American corporations and they were willing to base their professional decisions around profit-making. Like Siné, they admired jazz and realized that record production was part of the capitalist system; unlike Siné, they sought a way to make the production of jazz work within a commercial society.

A 1956 Jazz at the Philharmonic (JATP) concert brought out many of the tensions that were a consequence of American consumerism in France. For twelve years, the American promoter Norman Granz had sponsored jazz concerts in the United States, Japan, Australia, and Europe, so that by the 1950s, the JATP had evolved into an initiative that backed close to 150 performances a year around the globe. The first JATP concert had been held in 1944 at the Los Angeles Philharmonic Auditorium, and from the beginning, the JATP was informed by Granz's left-leaning politics. The initial concert was a benefit for Mexican-American youths who had been wrongly convicted of murder in a 1942 Los Angeles case. In the words of an American contemporary, Granz was "a jazz fan and a strong liberal [who] decided that jazz should be listened to in the pleasantest surroundings by the largest possible number of people of all races, creeds, and colors."[33] His concerts challenged racial segregation by allowing integrated audiences in segregated Los Angeles performance spaces.[34] For Granz, the JATP was built upon a multiplicity of jazz genres, collaboration, and improvisation. In his own words, "The basic principle of the JATP was the mixture of styles, the jam-session."[35] Even though Granz was also a record producer for the Clef, Norgran, and Verve labels who was clearly interested in turning a profit through his jazz enterprises, the Swiss critic Kurt Mohr claimed that ideally the JATP concerts were also based on an "a priori anti-commercial aspect of jazz," indicating the contradictions inherent in the tours.[36] The JATP went to Europe every year after 1952 and Granz continued promoting performances there until the dissolution of the JATP in 1967.[37]

Both before and after the 1956 concert, public and professional opinions were largely "unanimous" in their praise of Granz's tours, resulting in audiences giving very few negative reviews of JATP performances.[38] In the 1960s, the jazz community became increasingly willing to criticize Granz's programs, although the JATP concerts continued to be well attended. Despite the fact that Granz's activities brought in over five million dollars in 1955, one French writer still called the JATP the "apotheosis of the jam session." Granz supported musicians and their art through his concerts as well as his record labels, and claimed to nourish the "hot" style of improvisation—its vehemence and heat, and the importance of the jam session.[39] During JATP concerts, French celebrities ranging from the jazz violinist Stéphane Grappelli to the popular singer Maurice Chevalier and the actor Eddie Constantine joined audiences and even tried to get autographs from the American performers.[40] At times, these audiences got a bit out of hand. In 1958, a writer for *Paris Journal* wrote that it was a tradition at these concerts for attendees to break chairs.[41] Two years later, a correspondent for *Les Lettres Françaises* reported that a long line of people waiting inside and outside of the Olympia "smashed all of the barriers and cheerfully waltzed the ticket booths in a completely unexpected . . . and rather dangerous dance!"[42] Frank Ténot wrote that

> in Paris, JATP concerts were occasions for disagreeable disorders. If Roy Eldridge was applauded, Bill Harris who followed him was booed. There would be a wrestling match. Norman Granz, who did not completely understand the moods of the ill-bred French public, would get angry and threaten to lower the curtain if the screaming did not stop. "*You're a typical French audience . . . I am going to stop the concert . . .*" And the charivari would become a riot. [italics originally in English][43]

From time to time, French critics did take aim at the format of the JATP concerts. In 1961, the musician and critic Michel de Villers announced that "the JATP is a false jam-session," and in 1963, critic Jacques André wrote an article entitled "Jazz in an armchair?" which directed attention at the ways the concerts were presented.[44] Yet, on the whole, French observers had positive things to report about the JATP and Granz. In 1953, the critic Gérard Legrand affirmed that in these concerts there was "little or no arranging, improvisation is queen again," and in 1956, *Jazz Magazine* correspondent Marilyn Horne praised Granz for his commitment to fighting racial segregation. *Paris Journal* deemed the 1958 concert in Cannes "a triumph," and a year later, in 1959, a writer praised Granz for making "important progress in French" and for presenting "the program in our language."[45]

French critics' varying reactions to the JATP illustrated their conditional acceptance of jazz performances. As long as Norman Granz promoted concerts that reinforced the French expectations of the music, audiences supported and even lauded his efforts, no matter how rowdy they might become at his concerts. But when critics sensed that JATP performances were becoming overly oriented toward profit-making, their objections were direct. This was the case with the 1956 Paris concert when, much to the chagrin of spectators, many aspects of the performance seemed blatantly commercial. According to André Hodeir, there was no psychological tension for players who performed at a "prefabricated jam-session" and he found it difficult to believe that an artist could "create during fixed hours."[46] Granz had inserted planned dances into the performance, defying what French critics understood to be an essential aspect of jazz—its undetermined nature. Michel de Villers deplored the fact that even the physical surroundings of this concert were unrealistic: "a chair, a cigarette, a glass of beer are prohibited from the scene." Because it was a predesigned spectacle, Granz gave different musicians specific roles to play during the concert: "Flip Phillips, for example, is there for 'heat' whether he likes it or not."[47] As a result of its "inauthenticity," the 1956 JATP concert did not receive critical acclaim in France. Charles Delaunay explained why:

> There is in my opinion a psychological deficiency on the part of Norman Granz, who, judging as an American, thinks that the European fan will always be satisfied with listening to some great musicians, those who were also there the year before. That which is valid for the United States where the tours are frequent and where the prices for concerts are more in line with the budget of Yankee fans, is not true in Europe where the fan only has the chance of attending rare tours and frequently at overly high prices. . . . [In Europe] one will have added maybe one or two new soloists. It is disappointing in advance.[48]

Delaunay assumed that the European, and especially French, jazz supporter was not as accustomed to the expense of these concerts or to their prefabricated conformity as an American fan presumably was. Delaunay's cohort expected originality, creativity, and improvisation from jazz, and when jazz concerts resembled American consumer society in all of its monotony and artificiality, they too were criticized. In the words of Delaunay, the JATP program seemed to be "losing its velocity in France."[49]

During no other time in the 1950s or 1960s, however, did commentators so uniformly object to the JATP, and the concerts, despite reservations and criticisms, continued to happen every year until 1967. In 1955, André Hodeir perhaps best clarified this seeming paradox: "In a season like this one, where the good jazz concerts are rare, one particularly appreciates that Mr. Granz's annual tour gives to the Parisian public the opportunity to listen to rather brilliant individuals. The quality of jazz produced by this jam session of stars is not forgotten."[50] When given the chance, most French fans readily attended a concert where some of the most famous American musicians were going to play, unless its format became far too formulaic and predictable. So, despite the harsh and direct reproof delivered by critics at the 1956 JATP tour, French jazz lovers did not have many other opportunities to attend the performances of American artists. Granz would sometimes have a dozen musicians touring with him, and the lure was irresistible. On the whole, French jazz aficionados appreciated the fact that Granz's concerts gave them the chance to see talented and well-known musicians. Nonetheless, if expectations were not met, professional critics did not hesitate to express their reservations and reproaches. These writers insisted on holding American performances to a certain standard, and in doing so, they reflected French cultural expectations that distrusted an intrinsic correlation between commercialism and art.

THE COLD WAR CONNECTION

The perception among some Americans during the Cold War was that jazz could "sell" their nation abroad. As early as 1949, the *New York Herald Tribune* claimed, "It appears that half the world is collecting American jazz records," while one of its readers asserted that "jazz continues to be one of our most exportable commodities—second, perhaps, only to dollars."[51] As a result of this mindset, beginning in 1956, Dwight Eisenhower's administration began using jazz as Cold War propaganda by diverting some of the $5 million earmarked for its program of cultural exchange to fund jazz concerts abroad.[52] Not surprisingly, Eisenhower and his State Department did not come up with this idea, but the initiative resulted from the efforts of a cadre of musicians, civil rights proponents, cultural critics, and politicians like the Democratic congressman Adam Clayton Powell, Jr. The government's intention to promote jazz tours abroad was announced by Powell in late 1955. The congressman, who was married to the jazz and classical musician Hazel Scott, had purportedly been pushing for these tours since the summer of 1954, and had convinced Theodore Streibert, the director of the United States Information Agency, to "utilize jazz as a weapon of the Cold War." Powell boasted, "We'll therefore call it the 'cool' war from now on." Composer Walter Bishop composed a song to commemorate the government's move entitled "Jazz is our secret weapon."[53]

Through "Goodwill Ambassador" tours, the concept of Cold War cultural containment was interwoven with promoting jazz. Dizzie Gillespie was the first lead musician to participate on one of these foreign visits and as his band toured in Latin America, the Middle East, and Southeast Asia, the goal was for it to represent the energy of "America's classical music" and democratic society for onlookers.[54] In subsequent years, other artists—including Louis Armstrong, Wilbur de Paris, Tony Scott, Herbie Mann, Randy Weston, and Benny Goodman—performed in Africa, Latin America, Eastern Europe, Asia, North and South Africa, and the Soviet Union, bringing the uniquely American sounds of jazz to audiences with little exposure to the music.[55]

The State Department program was imbued with irony as many of these jazz musicians were African-American artists whose official mission was to promote the ideas of American democracy abroad, at the very same time that the civil rights movement was making it abundantly clear that African Americans were denied basic freedoms and rights back home in the United States. Members of the State Department were interested in jazz because they felt the music represented distinctly American values such as freedom and individuality, and they believed that American musicians could convince foreign listeners that American ideals were superior to those of Soviet communism. U.S. government leaders strove to highlight the universal qualities of jazz to international audiences, but these State Department tours depended on the specific blackness of American jazzmen to project an inclusive image of the United States. This image of universal equality, of course, did not correlate with the current domestic reality in the United States, in which racial discrimination was very much part of the status quo.[56] The musicians, and often the foreign audiences, were well aware of racial inequality in the United States and this complicated the government's Cold War message about American values. The tours of the 1950s and 1960s took place during a distinct historical moment when forty new African and Asian nations were emerging from their colonial pasts, the Cold War was increasing global tensions, and the African-American civil rights movement was illustrating the entrenched inequalities existent in American society. Importantly, when global audiences welcomed jazz and other forms of American popular culture, this did not indicate their wholesale acceptance of American foreign policy. Listeners created meanings from these visits that fit their own politics and cultural frameworks. The U.S. government attempted to harness jazz's popularity to promote its own agenda as well as American culture and values, but musicians and supporters of jazz were aware of this manipulation on the part of the American government and had varying reactions to it.

In an effort to illustrate jazz's aesthetic distinctiveness and its ability to bridge cultural divides, the American government's French periodical *Informations et documents* communicated to readers the music's relevance and uniqueness on the world stage. In 1961, one of the periodical's journalists wrote, "[Jazz's] vitality and constant evolution express the diversity and the dynamism of American culture."[57] Because of the perceived success of the State Department tours, French readers were told in 1966 that President Dwight Eisenhower declared, "Jazz is one of our best diplomats."[58] That spring, Louis Armstrong had gone to Asia, reportedly performing to audiences of 60,000 to 80,000. When he returned, Senator Jacob K. Javits proclaimed,

> Communist newspapers have written about Louis Armstrong on their front pages and have had to admit that his concerts have achieved a success without precedence. That is what we owe to this very talented and profoundly "human" artist. He deserves thanks from the government of the United States and the gratitude of all Americans.[59]

This quote, taken from the pages of *Information et Documents*, illustrated to a French readership the global attraction of jazz and how the music appealed to peoples' humanity across geographical, political, and ideological barriers.

French jazz critics and journalists continually covered the events surrounding the State Department sponsorship of jazz. *Jazz Hot* published a detailed account of the initial 1956 Gillespie tour written by Marshall Stearns, the American musicologist who accompanied the performers. The magazine also printed a letter from Quincy Jones who had gone with Gillespie as an arranger and trumpet player, and various detailed photographic accounts of the trip.[60] Before the tour even took place, *Jazz Hot* referred to jazz bands as the United States' "secret army."[61] After Gillespie's return, *Jazz Magazine* reported that the American journalists had invited the musician to play at a May 25th dinner honoring President Eisenhower.[62] French journalists also informed readers about other important congratulatory reactions by American government officials to later concerts—for instance, that Congress was looking to give Louis Armstrong "a medal in recognition of service paid in favor of human relations and for his good work," and that after Benny Goodman's 1962 tour of the Soviet Union, Jacqueline Kennedy invited him and his orchestra to lead a jazz series at the White House.[63] By discussing such events, French commentators who covered the American jazz scene made sure French fans were cognizant about the U.S. government's use and endorsement of jazz.

French jazz enthusiasts did not directly benefit from the government-funded concerts promoted by the American State Department. In 1956, the *New York Times* declared that Europeans could not understand why more money was not being spent to give financial support to jazz artists abroad.[64] Undoubtedly, French fans would have been happy to see these State Department jazz tours come to France. As it was, the American government only sponsored concerts in areas where jazz was less well known and promoted. By the time the Goodwill Ambassador trips began, jazz had been long appreciated in France and other parts of Europe, where it had arrived at the end of World War I. In Western Europe, a jazz culture was already firmly established and had a network of support to ensure its continued viability and popularity.[65] Unfortunately for French fans, the tenacity of their own national jazz critics, concert promoters, club owners, and record producers in marketing jazz within the hexagon precluded the American government from sponsoring performances in France. The U.S. government thought that its jazz dollars could be better spent elsewhere, especially in the newly-independent nations in Africa, Asia, and the Middle East, where an interest in American jazz among the general populations was either newly minted or nonexistent.

Those French jazz devotees who adhered to the Communist Party line or who placed themselves on the radical political left found serious fault with the State Department tours. A married couple, M. and Mme. Bernard R. from Courbevoie, wrote to *Jazz Magazine* in 1956 that "the Dizzy tour in Asia, organized under the auspices of the American State Department, displeases [us]. That *Jazz Magazine* . . . allows itself to insert in its lines the more or less anticommunist goals which surround these concerts, that is inadmissible."[66] These particular fans disagreed with the American government using jazz for propagandistic purposes, but they were also disappointed with *Jazz Maga-*

zine for giving so much coverage to this American effort and for seeming to sanction U.S. foreign policy. Another reader wrote the magazine in 1959 about the danger of imposing art on other countries. "Communism has nothing to do with the art of Louis Armstrong nor does capitalism with Galina Oulanova. Each in its own proper domain, the two countries are equal."[67] This reader did not think that the United States should have used jazz for political ends, but should have allowed both Russian and American art to prosper in their own respective realms. Jazz supporters on the far left of the political spectrum, who remained committed to a Communist worldview, found it rather easy to criticize the American government's flagrant use of jazz as a means of promoting the American way in other countries.

Because of the Cold War and Soviet leaders' importance in international Communism, French Communists who followed the stated party platform paid close attention to Soviet thoughts on jazz. In general, Soviet leaders in the two decades following World War II denigrated jazz. In 1952, in France, readers of *Le Monde* were told that in the Soviet Union jazz was understood to be "music for big rich members of the bourgeoisie" as well as "a music of enslavement."[68] When Stalin died in 1953, the harsh Soviet stance on this music began to dissipate but tensions remained strained for decades to come and Soviet opinions on jazz colored people's impression of the music in all Eastern Bloc countries. In the German Democratic Republic, jazz (as well as rock and roll, beat, and boogie-woogie) were disparaged in the 1950s and early 1960s because political leaders feared that music coming from capitalist countries—that were untraditional and appealing to young audiences—would bring bourgeois culture into the country and thereby taint the nation's socialist future.[69] East German officials described genres like boogie-woogie and jazz as "decadent" and "degenerate" and asserted that these genres were part of "American cultural barbarism." Some also worried about the jazz fans' "sexual drives" when they danced. Interestingly enough, that fact that these musics were rooted in African-American culture did not convince authorities to approve of them, even though communist leaders recognized African Americans as an oppressed group and publicly condemned racism in the United States.[70]

Recognizing the critical and dismissive stance that the Soviets historically took toward jazz, Lucien Malson wrote in 1957, "One knows that during the Stalinist era, Negro-American music was officially considered corrosive. In extreme circumstances, theoreticians admitted that one listened to blacks sing or play in the Louisiana-tradition with sympathy, but they rejected jazz's other manifestations—products of bourgeois society without aesthetic value and completely pernicious."[71] Despite the general rejection of jazz, in the latter 1950s, Soviet leaders did allow music critics to "reconsider the problem of jazz." According to Malson, "nothing in Marxism prevented them from picking up this music, recognizing its human quality and finally seeing in its rhythmic virtue something besides a reflection of economic malaise."[72] For French critics like Malson, jazz and Marxism were not incompatible with one another and they hoped for a general reconciliation between Soviets and jazz. By the late 1950s, some Soviets citizens had a positive view of the music, something that was shown in a poll taken at the 1959 Moscow Trade Fair. At this fair, which had been put on by the American government as part of an agreement between the two superpowers, attendees were asked in a secret ballot what their favorite exhibit had been. Out of fifteen choices, Soviet fairgoers ranked Cinerama and jazz at the top.[73]

In 1961, another French observer welcomed the fact that "Soviet youth, who the regime has wanted to hold away from a music judged bourgeois and decadent, is free more and more to show its own tastes and impatience with official prohibitions."[74] A year later, in 1962, *Jazz Hot* quoted an official Soviet journal as saying that "jazz is not synonymous with imperialism. A saxophone is not an instrument of colonization. We must not forget that jazz was not born in bank safes, but on the miserable streets of black neighborhoods."[75] With Soviet leadership becoming less wary of jazz, came a slight "thaw" between the United States and the Soviet Union in relation to jazz, and in 1962, the U.S. State Department sent Benny Goodman on a tour of the Soviet Union. However, this tour did not mean that Soviet leaders or audiences unconditionally accepted jazz. There seemed to be abundant numbers of young and enthusiastic fans in Moscow and Leningrad, the alleged jazz capitals of Russia, but some of the concertgoers in St. Petersburg risked being arrested by going to see Goodman.[76] And even though Khrushchev himself went to a Goodman performance, this Soviet leader, like Stalin, continued to have serious problems with jazz. In 1963, he claimed, "When I hear jazz, it's as if I had gas on the stomach." Later that same year, the Soviet government would not allow Duke Ellington and Count Basie to tour in the country and Khrushchev maintained the hard line against jazz until his fall from power a year later in 1964.[77]

Open musical relations between the Soviet Union and France, on the other hand, began to develop as early as 1957. In July of that year, a number of French jazz musicians attended the sixth World Youth Festival (Festival Mondial de la Jeunesse) in Moscow, including Hubert Rostaing, Michel de Villers, and Christian Garros. The biggest French success was Michel Legrand's orchestra, which gave twenty concerts in Leningrad, Moscow, and Kiev. At the Kirov Stadium in Leningrad, some 110,000 fans reportedly attended his show. The president of the Loire-Atlantic Jazz-Club, Michel Prodeau, claimed that this tour "was in some way the communicative, visual confirmation of the existence of modern jazz, that it is a music interpreted with heat, passion, and emotion, by normal men, just like the Ukranian choruses or the Ninth by a great symphonic orchestra."[78] Soviet jazz fans praised members of the French jazz community, reinforcing French ideas about their important place in the international jazz world. One of the directors of the Leningrad Jazz Club told Prodeau,

> At the Club, we have listened to the records of Christian Chevalier and André Hodeir several times. Both of them have had a great success. We have put Christian Chevalier and [Stan] Kenton on the same level. André Hodeir is known here as being an eminent theoretician of jazz and a remarkable arranger. The music of André Hodeir enchanted our musicians. We all remember the excellent orchestra of Michel Legrand, the best jazz orchestra that has come to Leningrad. We very much appreciate the French musicians, and it is too bad that we know them so little.[79]

These flattering comments no doubt "enchanted" the French, whose musicians had not been given much critical acclaim by the international or domestic press by 1957. Of course, Leningrad Jazz Club members would have been unlikely to put the little-known pianist Chevalier and the famous Kenton on the same musical level if they had had easier means of exposure to American music. But the paucity of American jazz in the Soviet Union gave French artists the opportunity to advance their own reputation.

French musicians maintained the cultural link between the Soviet Union and France over the next several years. When they went to the Soviet Union part of their aim was to disrupt the view that jazz was an insidious, bourgeois, solely American music, and French jazz fans generally rejoiced when jazz could play its role as a universal cultural arbiter behind the Iron Curtain. In 1962, Claude Luter went to Moscow to represent French jazz at a musical exposition. Luter professed that for the Soviets, jazz was not just an American music but a Western one, saying, "Jazz is synonymous with freedom . . . for a Soviet, jazz represents before all else the West and is equated with the absence of intellectual constraints."[80] In this way, jazz exemplified intellectual freedom. By not characterizing the music as exclusively American, Luter elevated his status as a jazz musician and stressed his own importance in conveying the meanings of jazz to Soviet listeners. But he could not get around the reality that the West and the United States were often equated in the minds of those living behind the Iron Curtain, and he linked the experience of those living under communism to those who had lived in Occupied France during the war. He stated, "In the first place, it must be said that all that is 'western' has a particular attraction for the Russians, a little like it was for us under the Occupation, jazz, films, cigarettes . . . in fact anything that represented the United States with which we did not have the slightest contact anymore."[81] Luter placed himself in the American camp even if he chose not to be overtly political, and in fact saw himself as a cultural ambassador, bridging the gap between East and West. He even encouraged French fans to send "young Soviets" jazz records to better expose them to the music.[82] Regardless whether musicians like Luter or Legrand had *official* governmental sponsorship (they did not), they went to the Soviet Union at a time when it was difficult for Americans to do so, and while there, they devoted themselves to promoting a music which carried obvious political connotations.

French musicians and critics also tried to spread their influence into other countries behind the Iron Curtain, applauding those times when Eastern and Central Europeans seemed to embrace jazz. In 1957, when the Polish revue *Jazz* began publication, Frank Ténot participated in its inaugural issue by writing an article about the Parisian jazz scene since the Liberation. Lucien Malson found Ténot's collaboration with this magazine "comforting."[83] In 1961, *Jazz Magazine* happily proclaimed that "the young in Central Europe—Hungary, Poland, Czechoslovakia, East Germany, Yugoslavia—would suffice to demonstrate that beyond ideological frontiers, jazz succeeds in playing its role as a universal cultural phenomenon"[84] That same year, Czechoslovakia hosted the first Karlovy Vary Jazz Festival in the small town of that name, convincing French critics that jazz's audience in Eastern Europe was growing and that Communist leaders were becoming more accepting of the music. A French writer was pleased that during the Festival's technical discussions, "André Hodeir's name was brought up several times. They venerate him."[85]

Not surprisingly, French critics mourned situations that interfered with jazz's progression in Communist Europe. In 1968, organizers of the fifth International Prague Jazz Festival had to call off the event after the Soviet invasion. *Jazz Magazine* published the letter that these organizers sent to inform participants of the festival's cancellation. Although the French periodical did not directly condemn the Soviet Union's actions, by informing readers about this particular repercussion, the editorial board conveyed its belief that political repression was detrimental to jazz.[86]

French critics and fans found it problematic to criticize the propagandistic use of jazz on the part of the U.S. State Department because government funding of jazz abroad made the music cheaper and more accessible in other countries. So even though French jazz listeners sometimes criticized the American government's use of jazz to fill foreign-policy needs, these fans were also pleased with the exposure the Goodwill tours brought to the music. In the words of one *Jazz Magazine* critic, "We are simply happy to see the Americans give to jazz the place that it deserves in the cultural patrimony.... What interests us is the increasing importance of jazz in the 'official' life of the USA."[87] Despite the United States' self-serving cooptation of jazz, the government was for the first time publicly recognizing and exporting this music to other parts of the globe. Some members of the French jazz community, due to their general anti-Americanism and their affiliations with the Communist Party, did not hesitate to condemn this American use of jazz as propaganda. But for the most part, French jazz fans remained uncritical of this facet of American foreign policy because it furthered the interests and audiences of jazz, and French jazz musicians also toured behind the Iron Curtain to promote their music as well as their careers. In general, members of the French jazz public took advantage of Cold War tensions to advance both their own personal interests and jazz in general: they supported the American government's sponsorship of international concerts and also willingly went to Communist countries to expose both American and French jazz to a wider audience. However, they were interested in promoting neither the U.S. government's policies nor a positive image of America to others. Instead, they took advantage of distinct situations to sustain a music they saw not only as American, but also as their own.

UN AMÉRICAIN FRANÇAIS: SIDNEY BECHET

A number of American jazz artists chose to live in France after World War II, such as drummer Kenny Clarke, pianist Bud Powell, and trumpeter Bill Coleman, among others. However, French fans embraced clarinetist and soprano saxophonist Sidney Bechet more than any other expatriate musician of the postwar era, actually labeling him a "French star" and "the most Parisian of the American jazzmen."[88] The manner in which French jazz critics, musicians, and fans, as well as popular audiences, venerated Bechet revealed a desire to make this American artist "French." For French audiences, Bechet's choice to live his last decade in France made their country more relevant on the international plane of jazz, and indicated French superiority in terms of social, cultural, and economic life. For these reasons, Bechet received more critical and general acclaim in France than he ever did in the United States. One writer maintained that his recorded music was "the most beautiful and humane witness in the history of jazz."[89] Other than the French-Belgian gypsy Django Reinhardt, Bechet was unique in the way he captured national French attention.[90] From 1949 forward, he occupied a distinct place in French culture as both a jazz artist and a commercially successful musician, as both an American and an honorary Frenchman. The fame and popularity that he experienced in France came to him rather late, due to his performances in France after the Second World War and his eventual move to Paris. His earlier history in France was a bit more problematic.

Bechet first went to Europe in 1919 with Will Marion Cook's Southern Syncopated Orchestra when he was in his early twenties, playing initially in London and then later with a smaller band for several months in 1920 at the Apollo Theatre in Montmartre. The only European to give his musical ability any important critical notice at the time was the distinguished Swiss conductor Ernest Ansermet who wrote, "There is in the Southern Syncopated Orchestra an extraordinary clarinet virtuoso who is, so it seems, the first of his race to have composed perfectly formed blues on the clarinet. . . . I wish to set down the name of this artist of genius, as for myself, I shall never forget it—it is Sidney Bechet."[91] The rest of the European public, including the French, gave him little mention during that first visit. He returned to France again in the summer of 1925 and performed in the *Revue Nègre* at the Théâtre Champs-Elysées, the show that won Josephine Baker widespread acclaim in France. Over the next several years Bechet played in France, Belgium, Germany, and Russia, but back in Paris in 1928, he got into a gunfight with fellow American and banjo player Gilbert "Little Mike" McKendrick in Montmartre. Several people were injured in the altercation: the pianist Glover Compton was shot in the leg, the Australian dancer Dolores Giblins was shot in the lung, and a French woman Madame Radurea was shot in the neck.[92] Bechet and McKendrick were both arrested and spent eleven months in French prison. When Bechet was released, French authorities ordered him to leave the country and he did not return to France again until 1949.[93]

His initial 1949 visit was a brief one, lasting only for his time spent performing at the Paris Jazz Festival hosted by Charles Delaunay's Hot Club de Paris at the Salle Pleyel in May. He returned to France again in the fall of that year, with Delaunay as his manager, then again in the summer of 1950. During this stay, he played in Paris with Claude Luter's band at the Vieux Colombier. At this time, he did not seem intent on residing permanently in France and told a writer for *Melody Maker*, "I guess there will be some movement back and forth between here and the United States."[94] But by the end of the summer, he seemed to have decided to remain in France and ended up living there until his death in 1959. During that close to ten-year period, he participated in a social circle that included well-known actors and musicians such as Simone Signoret and Yves Montand, and when he was in Paris he performed in music halls with French celebrities that included the likes of Georges Brassens, Catherine Saubage, Marcel Mouloudji, Jacques Brel, and Charles Aznavour. In 1954, his ballet *La nuit est une sorcière* was staged in Paris, and in the middle of the 1950s he participated in eight different French films as a performer or as a composer, and sometimes as both. As a sign of his widespread popularity, he had his own fan club in France by 1956.[95] Through this professional activity, Bechet made an indelible mark on French imaginations and his admirers continued to talk about his importance long after his death. In 1989, Frank Ténot wrote, "Sacred Sidney! Jazz would not be as popular in France today if he had not passed through and stayed in our country. In ten years, he marked our country's sensibility with an unalterable imprint. One would have loved for it to have lasted a little longer."[96]

Bechet was born in New Orleans and lived there until after World War I when he started playing his music at clubs in New York, Chicago, and abroad. Despite his changing geographical location, he continued to play in the New Orleans style throughout his career. As the critic Guy Longnon wrote, "Modern jazz? He ignored it. . . . Sidney, tranquilly, was his own boss, he pursued his 'own way' without worrying about the rest. . . . [The modern musicians] were another generation."[97] In many ways, the popularity of New Orleans jazz in the 1930s and 1940s in France made Bechet's newfound success possible after the war. In the late 1940s, when bebop was pushing jazz into new realms in New York, a small but important group "of imitators sympathetic to and zealous about [bebop's early] ancestors" was solidifying in France around the work of Claude Abadie, Claude Luter, Pierre Braslavsky, later André Réwéliotty, Michel Attenoux, and Maxim Saury.[98] Despite Bechet's close connection to the music of New Orleans, the entire French jazz community, not just Hugues Panassié and other exclusive supporters of New Orleans jazz, championed his work. Interestingly enough, Bechet wrote a letter to Panassié criticizing him for his treatment of musicians: "I am not informed about the differences you have with Mr. Delaunay, but is it really too bad that musicians can be the victims of your childishness."[99] Certainly, Delaunay and other supporters of bebop did not discount Bechet's music because he played older, more traditional sounds. Instead, they upheld his work as much as, if not more than, Panassié did, and Delaunay worked as his agent in France.

Bechet played with American musicians during his decade in Paris, but more importantly to the French, he played with young French musicians and the New Orleans orchestras in Paris, especially influencing the French jazz artists Claude Luter, André Réwéliotty, Mowgli Jospin, and Pierre Braslavsky. French jazz fans were most aware of his work with Luter. In October of 1949, the two musicians recorded "Les Oignons," which achieved popular notice, actually becoming "a juke-box success accessible to all of the public" in France.[100] This song was based on a Creole nursery song and its simple verse and chorus structure was interspersed with silent breaks. When fans listened to the song, they often shouted, "Oignons!" during these breaks, fostering a sense of audience participation whether the music was live or recorded.[101] Unfortunately for some, "Les Oignons" and other songs like "Petite Fleur" (1952) and "Dans les Rues d'Antibes" (1952) were distinct from Bechet's original, more "authentic" music because of their broad appeal.[102]

Because of these songs, one reader of *Jazz Magazine* asserted that "Sidney Bechet was a musician, but a musician for the crowds of young adolescents between the ages of 15 and 18 who knew nothing of music. . . . To play pieces like 'Petite Fleur,' 'Les Oignons,' etc., it is not necessary to have first place in the conservatory."[103] As indicated by this reader, Bechet's most visible fans were teenagers who were not necessarily jazz fans themselves. In 1961, two years after Bechet died, a *Jazz-Magazine* contributor polled one hundred people and found that sixty-two of them "love or idolize Bechet."

Out of this sixty-two, "thirty-eight only like Bechet's jazz and are impervious to all other jazzmen (they are instead fond of Brenda Lee, Johnny Hallyday and other singers of this category, whom they consider jazz singers); seventeen willingly listen to New Orleans jazz but do not like rock n' roll; seven are 'eclectics' and appreciate all forms of jazz."[104] Ironically, despite the strong anticommercialism of the French jazz community, the fans who most supported Bechet did not listen to any other jazz musicians and basically supported his commercial recordings alone. Nevertheless, until he died, opinion polls placed him among the most appreciated jazz artists as well. For example, in a 1956 poll taken by the radio station Europe numéro 1, Bechet placed among the top four most popular jazz musicians, and two years later, Bechet still placed in the top eight.[105] Significantly, French jazz fans found much to appreciate in Bechet's music long after the American jazz community had ceased giving him critical notice. In 1958, Bechet certainly did not appear on any top-ten lists among American fans. In France, however, fans treated him differently because of his strong link to the French jazz scene and to the country itself.

The French adolescents who went to jazz concerts were known for their rambunctious behavior, and scenes could not only break out during JATP performances but also during Sidney Bechet concerts. On the occasion of selling Bechet's millionth record (or more precisely his 1,350,000th one), the record company Vogue held a free concert at the Olympia in Paris as a promotional event in October of 1955. The Olympia only held 1,800 people but as the concert neared, close to 5,000 people were waiting at its doors to see Bechet on stage. After the first 2,000 were admitted, the doors to the Olympia were closed, while the remaining 3,000 then "rushed at the police and smashed the windows of the surrounding stores."[106] *Franc-Tireur* claimed that after the concert the Olympia looked like

> the scene from a heartbreaking battlefield. A hundred broken or torn chairs, seats, originals from the balcony, strewn in the pit, debris of every sort. And, as compensation, refrigerators replaced the seats on the balcony, where 'fans' had hoisted them during intermission to serve as promontories. The portraits of celebrities were broken or lacerated. The only ones that survived were those precious ones of Edith Piaf, Anny Cordy, and Gilbert Bécaud.[107]

Two concertgoers were injured and twenty people were arrested, two of whom were held for "hitting and rebelling against police agents."[108] This somewhat disastrous concert obviously made a strong impression on the French public. Bechet himself wrote about it in his autobiography:

> I don't know if I'm glad or sorry that there were terrible scenes outside [the Olympia]. The people there were so anxious to get in that the police had to be called and there were scuffles and arrests and everything. I'm sorry that these

people who love the music should have got into trouble, but . . . hell, I'll play for them whenever they want me.[109]

The French jazz public remained rather silent on the Olympia concert but the *Combat* critic Jacques André maintained that these destructive concertgoers were "false fans" who demanded Bechet play his commercial hits like "Petite Fleur" while he was actually playing his older, less commercial music.[110] André emphasized that these disorderly youths were not "true" members of the jazz community. For him, they did not appreciate Bechet's jazz but his money-making hits instead. Beyond André, other French jazz critics opted to ignore the event lest it bring negative attention to their music.

Despite their lack of critical approval, Bechet's "juke-box hits" expanded his, as well as jazz's, overall audience in France. One of the most important ingredients of Bechet's popularity was that he attracted such a wide cross-section of French music fans: supporters of New Orleans jazz, advocates of bebop, listeners of variety music, the old and the young. Almost a decade after he died, in 1968, a Frenchman wrote, "Because Sidney was a radiant musician, his personality and authority imposed themselves on fans of diverse tastes."[111] The broad promotion that different segments of French society gave to Bechet allowed him to become an enduring fixture for his French supporters who permanently connected him to the success and lived experience of jazz in their country.

One particular French "memory" of Bechet stands out above all others: his life in Antibes-Juan-les-Pins. He lived in this town on the Côte d'Azur during the summers between 1950 and 1955, regularly playing at the Mediterranean version of the Vieux Colombier.[112] In 1951, in Antibes, he married a German woman, Elisabeth Ziegler, and for decades members of the jazz world wrote about this wedding with its long procession through town. The musician Claude Luter claimed that "in the memory of man, one had never seen its parallel. A true bacchic procession, a ceremony worthy of a king. Barrels full of wine or rum had been put all along the route: for certain, the men on the corners slept the coming night in the gutter."[113] Bechet himself also described this singular event in his autobiography:

> You see, M. Badel [down there in Antibes], he was remembering how in New Orleans every year we have a Mardi Gras and we have this Zulu parade. And it is the ambition of every guy in New Orleans to be the King of the Zulus. So Louis Armstrong, he happened to be King a year or two before, and it was in *Time* magazine and everything. So M. Badel, he asked me, "Would you like to be King for a day?" So I accepted it. I phoned my fiancée up and we accepted it. And it was one of the biggest things that's ever been seen since Aly Khan's marriage. We went right around the town, and there were bands on carts going around just like I remember from way back when I used to be in the second line [in New Orleans parades]. It was really something, and I am certainly

grateful to all those people and to all those musicianers who made it into a day I won't ever forget.[114]

In 1962, three years after Bechet died, the mayor of Antibes-Juan-les-Pins, Pierre Delmas, offered his own recollections about the clarinetist's wedding day and asserted that it had made a lasting impression on the town as well: "All of Juan-les-Pins adores jazz. You know, the marriage of Sidney Bechet marked us all! All the town participated in this party that was in the tradition of New Orleans carnivals!"[115] The 1951 wedding of Sidney and Elisabeth Bechet was an important local event for Antibes-Juan-les-Pins. Through this marriage celebration, members of the town expressed their admiration for Sidney Bechet and their preparedness to adopt outside traditions (in this case ones coming from New Orleans) to show Bechet's membership in their community. Despite the close historical connection between French and New Orleans culture, the French men and women of Antibes-Juan-les-Pins recognized this "Bacchic" procession as an American one. Sidney Bechet made them willing to disregard their own local marriage customs to advance a foreign practice, creating through this event an important piece of regional history.

When he lived there, Bechet was a notable person in the life of Antibes-Juan-les-Pins. In the words of the French jazzman Claude Luter, "he was one of the great figures" in the "official life" of the town.[116] According to many, in the years leading up to 1949, "the town had lost a lot of prestige: between 1949 and 1955, she came back to life, knew her golden age. The presence of Bechet coincided with this renaissance. . . . For the first time a jazzman attracted customers in a cabaret on the Côte [d'Azur]. Bechet was a 'figure.'"[117] Bechet's French biographer Raymond Mouly alleged that Bechet's presence in Antibes-Juan-les-Pins "contributed significantly to their rising tourism."[118] Because of the notoriety and tourist dollars Bechet brought to the community, the critic Philippe Adler maintained that "in Antibes, since Sidney Bechet passed through, the shoemaker, the policeman, fishmonger, and . . . the town councilor [all] love jazz!"[119] The economic activity that Bechet generated in this small southeastern town directly impacted people's pocketbooks. Notably, town members did not appreciate him for his music alone, but also because he brought important revenue as well as national and international recognition to the locale of Antibes-Juan-les-Pins. This has to be considered when understanding the townspeople's acceptance and seeming promotion of Sidney Bechet. Difference was welcomed when it brought francs and outside attention to a struggling French community.

Not surprisingly, even after his death, Bechet remained an important cultural figure in Antibes-Juan-les-Pins. A little more that a year after he died, the town created the Antibes Jazz Festival, and in July 1960, 250 musicians from seventeen different countries came to the small seaside area for this event.[120] Situated between Nice and Cannes and graced with a pine grove that looks out onto the Mediterranean, Antibes-Juan-les-Pins was an ideal spot to host an outdoor music festival. The festival honored Bechet in a number of ways: it held an afternoon parade and an evening concert and then erected a permanent stone statue of him. According to one observer, these actions "established Sidney Bechet as the legendary citizen of the town for posterity."[121] The town renamed the pine grove the Sidney Bechet Pine Forest and mayor Pierre Delmas "paid homage to the memory of the musician, and praised the virtues of the man." During the evening concert, "Claude Luter played among other songs of Sidney's, 'Petit Fleur,' with an emotion that did not escape anyone."[122] Within several years of its inception, the festival came to be known by the catchy name of *Jazz à Juan*, and today the event lasts for ten days. Over the years, many American jazz greats have taken the stage there: Charles Mingus, Miles Davis, Ella Fitzgerald, John Coltrane, Dizzy Gillespie, Stan Getz, Sonny Rollins, Sarah Vaughan. In addition to these musicians, French jazzmen like Michel Legrand and Michel Petrucciani have also made regular appearances in Antibes-Juan-les-Pins.[123] For well over fifty years, this community has celebrated Sidney Bechet and the fame he brought to the area as an important site of jazz performance. In the 1950s, jazz fans went to listen to Bechet at the Vieux Colombier; now, they go to Antibes to hear dozens of musicians from all over the world at a festival that was created as a means of indefinitely perpetuating his influence there.

Despite Bechet's fame and notoriety in Antibes-Juan-les-Pins, the musician spent the majority of his time while living in France in Paris, and in 1959, he died of cancer in the suburb of Garches. Like the majority of Frenchmen, he died a Catholic and *Paris Journal* pointed out that a Father Dublomb had helped him throughout "his terrible and terrifying sickness. The abbot Jacques Pé gave him his last rights."[124] Immediately after his death, members of the general Parisian population, along with Bechet's fellow musicians, friends, and family, began preparing for his funeral.

> The Prince of Jazz deserves a brilliant ceremony and we think that it would be right to revive here, in France, the rites of Harlem. For him alone. Certain instrumentalists have already had the idea of following his casket "with music." And we estimate that this would be an excellent initiative. The diocese of Versailles would not be opposed to it.[125]

So, just like the citizens of Antibes-Juan-les-Pins, people in Paris were willing to orchestrate another "American" procession to honor "him alone." François Mallet of *L'Express* wrote, "The death of Sidney Bechet brings an almost national bereavement. His name was, in France, as familiar as those of Edith Piaf or Yves Montand."[126] Raymond Mouly wrote a story for *Jazz*

Magazine on this occasion that included a number of references to his Europeanized identity. There was a picture of him holding baguettes under one arm as he spoke to a gendarme, and another of him speaking to surrounding Parisians at his café. The following words accompanied this latter picture: "He had become a Parisian like others. For his 'fans' he had founded the Club Sidney Bechet."[127] Mouly included a final picture of Bechet's funeral procession, writing, "His burial in a small town in a Parisian suburb was representative of the last years of his life *à la française*."[128] Bechet's admirers simultaneously viewed him as an American and as an important facet of postwar French culture, and, through his funeral, they honored both. On May 19, 1959, three thousand people went in the rain to his funeral and followed his casket to the grave site.[129]

Bechet's French supporters continued to accentuate his ties to France. Several months following his death, Charles Delaunay wrote, "For the public, Sidney personifies the essential virtues of jazz, youth and the power of expression of a new music."[130] That same year, a journalist for *Paris Journal* wrote,

> Sidney, a pure artist, loved Paris. He was married in 1949 . . . in Antibes. The best of his life was spent in Paris. The large city had adopted him. He had made it his homeland because it was what he loved: the symbol of equilibrium and the power of art.[131]

This writer ended his article claiming that each time Bechet had left Paris to go on tour, the musician had felt "sad." "Paris is sad today to leave him. A little bit of itself has left with Bechet."[132] French people chose to see in Bechet several specific qualities: artistic creativity, equilibrium, and a devotion to France. These qualities mirrored ones that French leaders chose to assert in the first several decades after the war: the nation's ability to draw on its wealth and history of artistic creativity; the French desire to find social, political, and economic equilibrium; and French citizens' national devotion. The relationship between Bechet and France was symbiotic. In France, Bechet found a place where people continued to admire and to promote his artistic ability even as he grew older and less innovative, and long after the American jazz scene had ceased to sustain his work. In Bechet, French fans had proof that American jazz musicians preferred France and that their country remained an important center of artistic inventiveness. Importantly, French leaders in the 1950s and 1960s promoted the idea that France was the cultural capital of the world, even if the United States had far greater economic, military, and increasingly cultural capability. With an artist like Bechet residing in France, contemporaries could claim that their nation enjoyed a unique place in the heart of a jazzman whom they understood to be simultaneously an American by birth and a Frenchman by choice.

Despite the determined and seemingly benign promotion Bechet received from his French admirers, there is a lingering question of how his blackness informed French opinions of him. Could his celebrity be separated from his race? Certainly, there was an element of amused condescension in some accounts about Bechet. As late as 1987, Charles Delaunay remembered this about Bechet's life in France,

> Sidney never became big-headed with the people. He liked to be recognized by them as he walked down the street, and when anyone shouted greetings to him he always shouted a friendly message back. People loved to hear him talk in French, even though it was always Creole. It never changed, or improved, it was what we would call 'petit nègre'. If he was in a bar he'd start up a conversation with anyone. Oh yes, he had a great appeal for the general public.[133]

Sandwiched between his expressions of outright praise for Bechet, Delaunay mentioned how the musician spoke in "petit nègre." In doing so, Delaunay elided any differences between Bechet (an American) and the French colonial subjects whom French popular culture had derogatorily portrayed as speaking in halting or improper French for decades. From the early 1900s, the "Y'a bon" slogan used for Banania made an ever-changing Senegalese soldier into a happy, servile, and inferior caricature in order to sell a chocolate and banana flavored breakfast drink.[134] In the early 1930s, *Tintin in the Congo* portrayed the Congolese people speaking in the French African pidgin dialect too.[135] These two well-known examples illustrate the fact that when Delaunay made this reference in 1987, it was ripe with racialized meaning. Yes, Bechet was praised for his geniality (which was in contrast to his difficult and at times combative reputation among some in the music industry) but neither this nor his musical success placed him on an equal footing with white Frenchmen. The careful public persona that Delaunay, as his agent, had crafted for Bechet reflected the confines of the white French colonial mind. Bechet was not a threat to French culture, but an acculturated outsider who could bring vitality, humor, and a sense of French superiority. By all accounts, it seems that Bechet lived well in France. The American pianist George Wein said this about his residency there: "There was no reason for Bechet to come back from France after he settled there. He was happy and was worshipped."[136] So, in the end, Bechet was worshipped but he was still not an equal.

BECOMING FRENCH

After World War II, the French confronted growing American influences not only in foreign affairs and economic matters but in the cultural realm as well.

In the first twenty-five years following the war, those belonging to the French jazz community made their own meanings for this very American music, defying American dominance and control in a variety of areas. Jazz critics insisted on emphasizing the importance of African Americans in the history of jazz, so that by supporting this American minority and condemning racism in the United States, they simultaneously criticized American society and supported an American music. These same critics also directly denounced American consumerism and values based on commercialism. For them, jazz, because of its consistent use of improvisation, existed outside of the boundaries of a strict consumer society. French writers thought that the marketplace could not easily capture and sell the essence of live performances. They quickly pointed out the dangers of "best sellers" as they not only put money into performers' pockets (which French jazz fans saw as a good thing) but they also gave high returns to the record companies who continued to push musicians to create sounds with the most popular appeal. French jazz critics did not think that artistic creativity should be controlled or manipulated by profit-making concerns and they quickly reprimanded American and Americanized companies who enforced commercial standards on musicians.

The Cold War helped to define the cultural values of the postwar era, and with firmly-entrenched debates over the American and Soviet political, social, and economic systems informing a wide variety of opinions, it is not surprising that French jazz devotees manipulated American and Soviet Cold War policies to advance this music. In general, they supported the American State Department's jazz tours abroad as well as other efforts by Washington to bring the music to a global audience. American leaders may not have been jazz fans themselves, but they recognized its propagandistic virtues. As a result, they promoted an African-American, nonmainstream music as a means of selling the American way in places like Latin America, Asia, Africa, and Eastern Europe. Although critical of the politics behind the American government's sponsorship of jazz, members of the French jazz public applauded the fact that the music was receiving broader notice and support both within and outside of the United States. At a time when Communist leadership in Eastern Bloc countries did not readily welcome American artists, French musicians and critics went as ambassadors of jazz. They forwarded the cause of both American and French jazz in the Soviet Union and in the Soviet satellite nations, taking advantage of a tense political situation to advocate their music.

Through these negotiations on the political and cultural terrain, French supporters of jazz did not view this music simply as an American creation but as an art form that had become part of their own cultural milieu.[137] The French jazz community did not move to endorse "America" when its members embraced jazz. Instead, fans created their own meanings for the music, and despite the fact that jazz undoubtedly remained American, French audiences used jazz to mediate American influences on their own culture, rejecting aspects of American racism and consumerism, and attenuating French support of American global politics. With a musician like Sidney Bechet, the French simultaneously revered an American musician and revealed a long-lasting tendency to distort the character and behavior of blacks in a way that made them appear nonthreatening to French culture. Bechet was unique, an individual, and French commentators never stopped stressing that point. Exceptions were made for him—Bacchic processions happened on the Côte d'Azur and "rites of Harlem" happened in Paris—but these exceptions were for him alone and observers took pleasure in relating the ways in which he acted as a (white) Frenchman. Bechet could not become fully equal to his French contemporaries while living in a time and a place that remained informed and defined by a colonial mentality. The French could act on their believed superiority to both colonial subjects and to Americans through their relationship with Bechet, because his identity was connected to both of them through his racial belonging and his passport. To be French in these decades following World War II meant pushing back against a United States whose postwar power seemed irreconcilable with continued French global leadership. To be French also meant trying to maintain control over a quickly disintegrating colonial empire, something to which we turn to in greater detail in chapter 6. But first, we need to better understand what French jazz meant for critics, musicians, and listeners who were contending with their national identity in the postwar world.

NOTES

1. See Herman Lebovics, *Mona Lisa's Escort: André Malraux and the Reinvention of French Culture* (Ithaca, NY: Cornell University Press, 1999). Lebovics asserts, "Although the economy continued rapidly to modernize in the Gaullist years, French costs of labor, land, and capital were still not low enough to make its exports of non-luxury goods particularly competitive. Nor, despite de Gaulle's aspirations for French *grandeur*, was the Fifth Republic (yet) politically a major force in the world. France set out to deploy its ample cultural capital to gain an edge in as many of the ways that international power is measured as possible" (159).

2. Georges Duhamel, *America the Menace: Scenes from the Life of the Future*, trans. Charles Miner Thompson (Boston: Houghton Mifflin Co., 1931). For more on Anti-Americanism as a cultural phenomenon, see Seth D. Armus, *French Anti-Americanism (1930–1948): Critical Moments in a Complex History* (Lanham, MD: Lexington Books, 2010).

3. Richard Kuisel, *The French Way: How France Embraced and Rejected American Values and Power* (Princeton, NJ: Princeton University Press, 2012), 66. Also see Sophie Meunier, "Anti-Americanism in France," *French Politics, Culture and Society* 23 (2005), 126–41.

4. See the seminal book on this phenomenon, Tony Judt, *Past Imperfect: French Intellectuals, 1944–1956* (Berkeley: University of California Press, 1992). Intellectual illusions about the Soviet Union finally ended with Khrushchev's Secret Speech of 1956.

5. Through the Blum-Byrnes agreement of 1946, the American government insisted that French markets remain open to American movies as a condition of economic aid. The French movie industry's response brought an end to the agreement, but Blum-Byrnes still had lasting

ramifications. See Patricia Hubert-Lacombe, *Le cinéma français dans la guerre froide, 1946–1956* (Paris: Harmattan, 1996); John Trumpbour, *Selling Hollywood to the World: U.S. and European Struggles for Mastery of the Global Film Industry, 1920–1950* (Cambridge, MA: Cambridge University Press, 2002); Jean-Pierre Jeancolas, "L'arrangement Blum-Byrnes à l'épreuve des faits: les relations (cinématographiques) franco-américaines de 1944 à 1948," *Bulletin de l'Association française de recherches sur l'histoire du cinéma* 13 (1992); Laurent Creton, *Histoire économique du cinéma français* (Paris: CNRS Éditions, 2004); and Michel Margairaz, "Autour des accords Blum-Byrnes," *Histoire, économie, société* 3 (1982), 439–70.

6. Kuisel, *The French Way*, 157; Brian Angus McKenzie, *Remaking France: Americanization, Public Diplomacy, and the Marshall Plan* (New York: Berghahn Books, 2008), 208; and Victoria de Grazia, *Irresistable Empire: America's Advance through 20th-Century Europe* (Cambridge, MA: Belknap Press of Harvard University Press, 2005). For more on Hollywood, see Richard F. Kuisel, "The French Cinema and Hollywood: A Case Study of Americanization," *Transactions, Transgressions, Transformations: American Culture in Western Europe and Japan*, eds. Heide Fehrenbach and Uta G. Poiger (New York: Berghahn Books, 2000), 208–23. On the subject of Americanization in France and Europe, see Frank Castigliola, *France and the United States: the Cold Alliance since World War II* (New York: Twayne, 1992); Denis Lacorne, Jacques Rupnik, and Marie-France Toinet, eds. *The Rise and Fall of Anti-Americanism: a Century of French Perceptions*, trans. Gerry Turner (New York: St. Martin's Press, 1990); Irwin M. Wall, *The United States and the Making of Postwar France, 1945–1954* (New York: Cambridge University Press, 2002); *French Historical Studies* vol. 19, no. 2 (Fall 1995) that is devoted to "Working on France in American Universities: Interdisciplinary Perspectives"; Rob Kroes, R. W. Rydell, D. F. J. Bosscher, eds. *Cultural Transmissions and Receptions: American Mass Culture in Europe* (Amsterdam: VU University Press, 1993); and Rob Kroes, *If You've Seen One, You've Seen the Mall: Europeans and American Mass Culture* (Urbana: University of Illinois Press, 1996).

7. For more on a variety of American products in France during this era, see Barnett Singer, *The Americanization of France: Searching for Happiness after the Algerian War* (Lanham, MD: Rowman and Littlefield Publishers, 2013), 159, 254n24. For more on the process of Americanization across Europe, see Harm G. Schröter, *Americanization of the European Economy: A Compact Survey of American Economic Influence in Europe since the 1880s* (Dordrecht, the Netherlands: Springer, 2005).

8. *Jazz Hot* 98 (April 1955), 30–31; and *Jazz Hot* 148 (November 1959), 3.

9. *Jazz Hot* 97 (March 1955), 7. Selmer ads also used French musicians like Guy Lafitte at times, but American musicians were far more prevalent. *Jazz Hot* 145 (July–August 1959); and *Jazz Hot* 148 (November 1959).

10. The position of the French jazz community in this era was dramatically different from that of West Germans. Uta G. Poiger has written, "West German promoters of jazz had for the most part convinced the West German public by the late 1950s that jazz was an art music and not responsible for male aggression and female sexual expressiveness. At the same time, references to the fact that most American jazz musicians were African-American or Jews were largely missing from West German commentaries on jazz." See Uta G. Poiger, "American Music, Cold War Liberalism, and German Identities," *Transactions, Transgressions, Transformations: American Culture in Western Europe and Japan*, eds. Heide Fehrenbach and Uta G. Poiger (New York: Berghahn Books, 2000), 140. Also see Uta G. Poiger, *Jazz, Rock, and Rebels: Cold War Politics and American Culture in a Divided Germany* (Berkeley: University of California Press, 2000); and "Fear and Fascination: American Popular Culture in a Divided Germany, 1945–1968," *Kazaaam! Splat! Ploof! The American Impact on European Popular Culture since 1945*, eds. Sabrina P. Ramet and Gordana P. Crnković (Lanham, MD: Rowman & Littlefield Publisher Inc., 2003), 55–68.

11. Hugues Panassié, *Cinq mois à New-York* (Paris: Éditions Corrêa, 1947), 10.

12. Hugues Panassié, "Premières impressions d'Amérique," *La Revue du Jazz* 4 (April 1949), 111.

13. André Hodeir, "Impressions de New York (I)," *Jazz Hot* 119 March 1957), 13. Also see "Impressions de New York (II)," *Jazz Hot* 120 (April 1957), 24; and "Impressions de New York (III)," *Jazz Hot* 121 (May 1957), 7–8.

14. Daniel Filipacchi, "En Direct de New York," *Jazz Magazine* 31 (October 1957), 26. For another similar account of New York, see François Postif, "New York in jazz time," *Jazz Hot* 161 (January 1961), 22–23.

15. Rob Kroes has warned against using the term *Americanization* to describe patterns of consumption that might have arrived in Europe without the United States' involvement. He has pointed out, "America served to give a name and face to forces of cultural change that would otherwise have been anonymous and seemingly beyond control." See Rob Kroes, "American Mass Culture and European Youth Culture," *Between Marx and Coca-Cola: Youth Cultures in Changing European Societies, 1960–1980*, eds. Axel Schildt and Detlef Siegfried (New York: Berghahn Books, 2006), 82. Mary Nolan has seconded this concern by discussing Americanization as "actual or imagined." See Mary Nolan, *The Transatlantic Century: Europe and America, 1890–2010* (New York: Cambridge University Press, 2012), 230.

16. Richard Kuisel, *Seducing the French: the Dilemma of Americanization* (Berkeley: University of California Press, 1993), 3; and Axel Schildt and Detlef Siegfried, "Introduction: Youth, Consumption, and Politics in the Age of Radical Change," *Between Marx and Coca-Cola: Youth Cultures in Changing European Societies, 1960–1980*, eds. Axel Schildt and Detlef Siegfried (New York :Berghahn Books, 2006), 13.

17. "L'éxique du jazz," *Jazz Hot* 110 (May 1956), 34.

18. Félix Manskleid, "L'Age d'or aux U.S. mais pas pour les musiciens," *Jazz Magazine* 13 (January 1956), 8.

19. Alfred Appel, Jr., "L'école du New-York," *Jazz Hot* 128 (January 1958), 14.

20. Hugues Panassié, *Jazz Panorama* (Paris: Éditions Deux-Rives, 1950), 66.

21. Yetty Lee, "Flashes," *Jazz Magazine* 4 (March 1955), 10.

22. Frank Ténot, "Les Pieds dans le plat," *Jazz Magazine* 31 (October 1957), 11.

23. Georges Hilleret, "Ci-gît la musique français victime du play-back," *Télé 7 jours* 264 (10–16 April 1965), 10.

24. André Hodeir, "Le Jazz américain est en pleine santé mais il n'y a pas de nouveau Bird," *Jazz Hot* 123 (July–August 1957), 10.

25. Ténot, "Les Pieds dans le plat," 11.

26. Pascal Paone, Letter to "Sinépistolier," *Jazz Magazine* 143 (June 1967), 60.

27. Siné, "Sinépistolier," *Jazz Magazine* 143 (June 1967), 60.

28. Henri Renaud, "Le jazz et la vinylite (II)," *Jazz Hot* 217 (February 1966), 11.

29. Jean Tronchot, "Le jazz et la vinylite," *Jazz Hot* 216 (January 1966), 12.

30. André Poulain, "Le jazz et la vinylite (III)," *Jazz Hot* 218 (March 1966), 12.

31. Henri Renaud, "Le jazz et la vinylite (II)," 11. According to Koechlin, Philips was "the only record label to do so rather regularly." Philippe Koechlin, "Le jazz et la vinylite," *Jazz Hot* 216 (January 1966), 12.

32. Jean Tronchot, "Le jazz et la vinylite," *Jazz Hot* 216 (January 1966), 12.

33. Whitney Balliett, "Pandemonium Pays Off," *Saturday Review*, 25 September 1954, 45. Quoted in John Gennari, *Blowin' Hot and Cool: Jazz and its Critics* (Chicago: University of Chicago Press, 2006), 211.

34. Eric Porter, *What Is This Thing Called Jazz? African American Musicians as Artists, Critics, and Activists* (Berkeley: University of California Press, 2002), 86. Also see Scott DeVeux, "The Emergence of the Jazz Concert, 1935–1945," *American Music* 7 (Spring 1989), 6–29; and *The Birth of Be-Bop: A Social and Musical History* (Berkeley: University of California Press, 1997).

35. L.F., "La fin du JATP?" *Jazz Magazine* 145 (August 1967), 15.

36. Gennari, 211. Also see Michel Ruppli, *The Clef/Verve Labels: A Discography (The Norman Granz Era, Volume 1)* (New York: Greenwood Press, 1986); and Kurt Mohr, "Le J.A.T.P.," *Jazz Hot* 107 (February 1956), 7.

37. On the end of the JATP tours, see L. F., "La fin du JATP?" Even though the JATP disbanded in 1967, the series did resume for a couple years during the 1970s. See Gennari, 211.

38. "J.A.T.P. aux Champs-Elysées," *Jazz Magazine* 4 (March 1955), 31.

39. "Jazz at the Philharmonic ou l'apothéose de la Jam-Session," *Jazz Magazine* 3 (February 1955), 30.

40. "J.A.T.P. aux Champs-Elysées," *Jazz Magazine* 4 (March 1955), 31.

41. "Rendez-vous mondial du jazz à Cannes," *Paris Journal* (11 July 1958), 1.
42. Agnès Navarre, "À l'Olympia J.A.T.P. jazz," *Les Lettres Françaises* (1–7 December 1960), 7.
43. Frank Ténot, *Jazz* (Paris: Armand et Georges Israël, 1983), 22.
44. Michel de Villers, "Courrier des lecteurs," *Jazz Hot* 161 (January 1961), 7; and Jacques André, "Jazz dans un fauteuil?" *Combat* (25 March 1963), 8.
45. Gérard Legrand, *Puissances du jazz* (Paris: Arcanes, 1953), 176; Marilyn Horne, "Amateur de jazz, mécène et businessman Norman Granz," *Jazz Magazine* 14 (February 1956), 13–15; and "Un J.A.T.P. de derrière les coulisses," *Jazz Magazine* 49 (June 1959), 25–35.
46. André Hodeir, "Le J.A.T.P.," *Jazz Hot* 107 (February 1956), 7, 9.
47. Michel de Villers, "Le J.A.T.P.," *Jazz Hot* 107 (February 1956), 7, 9.
48. Charles Delaunay, "Le J.A.T.P.," *Jazz Hot* 107 (February 1956), 9.
49. Ibid.
50. André Hodeir, "Les concerts J.A.T.P.," *Arts* (23 February–1 March 1955), 4.
51. John O'Reilly, "Disk Jockey of 'Voice' Winning Good Will for U.S. World Over," *New York Herald Tribune* (27 October 1949), 1; and Kay C. Thompson, letter to the editor, *New York Herald Tribune* (29 October 1949), 10.
52. Penny M. Von Eschen, *Satchmo Blows Up the World: Jazz Ambassadors Play the Cold War* (Cambridge, MA: Harvard University Press, 2004), 5. Also Leonard Feather, "Le gouvernement U.S.: le jazz sera notre meilleur ambassadeur," *Jazz Magazine* 13 (January 1956), 4.
53. Leonard Feather, "Le gouvernement U.S.: le jazz sera notre meilleur ambassadeur," *Jazz Magazine* 13 (January 1956), 4. Also see "Dizzy a reformé son grand orchestre," *Jazz Magazine* 15 (March 1956), 5; Nat Hentoff, "Le grand orchestre de Gillespie," *Jazz Hot* 109 (April 1956), 21; Leonard Feather, "Le bilan de la tournée de Monsieur l'ambassadeur Dizzy," *Jazz Magazine* 19 (July–August 1956), 10–11; and "Mission diplomatique," *Informations et documents* 230 (1 August 1966), 36.
54. Lisa E. Davenport, *Jazz Diplomacy: Promoting America in the Cold War Era* (Jackson: University Press of Mississippi, 2009), 47.
55. The Goodwill Ambassador tours also sent athletes like Jesse Owens and Gilbert Cruter (a world-class high jumper), as well as the Harlem Globetrotters to foreign locals. See Amy Bass, *Not the Triumph but the Struggle: The 1968 Olympics and the Making of the Black Athlete* (Minneapolis: University of Minnesota Press, 2002), as well as Penny Von Eschen, *Race Against Empire: Black Americans and Anticolonialism 1937–1957* (Ithaca, NY: Cornell University Press, 1997). For more about the jazz tours from the French perspective, see "Dizzy à Ike: continuez à exporter du jazz," *Jazz Magazine* 20 (September 1956), 9; "Les frères de Paris nouveaux ambassadeurs américains," *Jazz Magazine* 26 (April 1957), 8; "Wilbur de Paris chez le négus," *Jazz Hot* 124 (September 1957); "Jazz et propagande," *Jazz Hot* 128 (January 1958), 40; "Herbie Mann en A.F.N.," *Jazz Magazine* 60 (June 1960), 10; "Louis Armstrong ambassadeur U.S. en Afrique," *Jazz Magazine* 64 (November 1960), 15–16; "Benny Goodman ira à Moscou," *Jazz Magazine* 81 (April 1962), 16–17; "Phil et Zoot à Moscou," *Jazz Magazine* 82 (May 1962), 15; and Philippe Koechlin, "Benny gaga," *Jazz Hot* 181 (November 1962), 10.
56. For more on the State Department tours, see Stephen A. Crist, "Jazz as Democracy? Dave Brubeck and Cold War Politics," *The Journal of Musicology*, vol. 26, no. 2 (Spring 2009), 133–74; and Graham Carr, "Diplomatic Notes: American Musicians and Cold War Politics in the Near and Middle East, 1954–60," *Popular Music History* 1 (2004), 37–63.
57. Russel B. Nye, "Jazz d'aujourd'hui," *Informations et documents* 138 (1 March 1961), 19.
58. "Mission diplomatique," *Informations et documents* 230 (1 August 1966), 36.
59. Ibid.
60. See "Dizzy en Asie," *Jazz Hot* 111 (June 1956), 12–13; and Marshall Stearns, "Dizzy en Asie," *Jazz Hot* 112 (July 1956), 14.
61. Nat Hentoff, "Nouvelles d'Amérique: Armé sécrète," *Jazz Hot* 106 (January 1956), 26–7.
62. "A son retour Dizzy a joué pour Ike," *Jazz Magazine* 18 (June 1956), 6.
63. "Jazz à la carte," *Jazz Hot* 170 (November 1961): 9; and "Flashes," *Jazz Magazine* 87 (October 1962), 14.

64. Felix Helair, Jr., "The United States has a Secret Sonic Weapon—Jazz," *The New York Times* (6 August 1955).
65. Von Eschen, *Satchmo*, 8.
66. M. and Mme. Bernard R., "Questions et réponses," *Jazz Magazine* 21 (November 1956).
67. Nicelle Samuel, "Vivent les ballets russes!" *Jazz Magazine* 54 (December 1959), 5.
68. See "Le jazz banni en U.R.S.S.," *Le Monde* (3 May 1952). Also see "Flashes," *Jazz Magazine* 6 (May 1955), 6, on the negative Soviet view of the saxophone in jazz.
69. Günter Mayer, "Popular Music in the GDR," *Journal of Popular Culture*, vol. 18:3 (Winter 1984), 157.
70. Poiger, 129–30.
71. Lucien Malson, "A l'Est, du nouveau," *Jazz Magazine* 25 (March 1957), 10.
72. Ibid.
73. de Grazia, 456.
74. "Du swing tartare?" *Jazz Magazine* 69 (April 1961), 17.
75. Quoted by S. M., "Derrière le rideau de fer," *Jazz Hot* 178 (July–August, 1962), 10.
76. Davenport, 118.
77. See S. Frederick Starr, *Red and Hot: The Fate of Jazz in the Soviet Union* (New York: Limelight Editions, 1985). Also, "L'U.R.S.S. a refusé une tournée Duke Ellington et Count Basie patronée par le State Department," *Jazz Hot* 187 (May 1963), 10. The French jazz periodicals widely covered Goodman's tour. See "Benny Goodman ira à Moscou," *Jazz Magazine* 81 (April 1962), 16–17; "Phil et Zoot à Moscou," *Jazz Magazine* 82 (May 1962), 15; Jean-Louis Ginibre, "Les raisons d'un choix," *Jazz Magazine* 86 (September 1962), 15; and Philippe Koechlin, "Benny gaga," *Jazz Hot* 181 (November 1962), 10.
78. Michle Prodeau, "Le jazz en U.R.S.S.," *Jazz Hot* 154 (May 1960), 18. This article covered events that had happened in 1957. No reason was given for the three-year delay in publication.
79. Fima Barban, quoted by Prodeau, 18.
80. Claude Luter, quoted by Francis Dreyfus, "Luter à Moscou," *Jazz Magazine* 78 (January 1962), 27.
81. Claude Luter, "Quelques instants avec Claude Luter," *Jazz Hot* 172 (January 1962), 32.
82. Claude Luter, "Luter à Moscou," *Jazz Magazine* 78 (January 1962), 28.
83. Lucien Malson, "A l'Est, du nouveau," *Jazz Magazine* 25 (March 1957), 11.
84. "Du swing tartare?" *Jazz Magazine* 69 (April 1961), 17.
85. S. M., "Derrière le rideau de fer," *Jazz Hot* 178 (July–August 1962), 10.
86. "Un festival annule," *Jazz Magazine* 160 (November 1968), 17. The letter was as follows: "L'entrée d'armées étrangères sur le territoire de la Tchécoslovaquie et l'occupation temporaire de quelque-uns de nos centres culturels ont retardé les préparatifs du 5e Festival International de jazz de Prague à un dégré tel qu'il ne peut avoir lieu. L'organisation du festival et les constructeurs d'instruments de musique de notre pays, pleinement conscients de leurs devoirs envers le jazz, important domaine d'activité culturelle et artistique, dès que la situation le permettra prépareront le festival de l'année prochaine qui s'inscrira dans le tradition de haute qualité artistique obtenue par les précédents. Pour prouver que la situation tend à se "normaliser" également dans le domaine du jazz, les organisateurs ont l'intention de mettre sur pied—pour la deuxième quinzaine de décembre—un concert groupant des orchestres et des solistes de jazz tchèque. Nous serons heureux de conserver le contact avec tous nos amis étrangers amateurs de jazz et les informerons du développement futur de nos activités." (Les organisateurs du 5e Festival de Prague.)
87. "Questions et réponses," *Jazz Magazine* 21 (November 1956).
88. For more on postwar expatriates, see Tyler Stovall, *Paris Noire: African Americans in the City of Light* (New York: Houghton Mifflin Company, 1996); Michel Fabre, *From Harlem to Paris: Black American Writers in France, 1940–1980* (Urbana: University of Illinois Press, 1991); Ursula Broschke, *Paris without Regret: James Baldwin, Kenny Clarke, Chester Himes, and Donald Byrd* (Iowa City: University of Iowa Press, 1986); and James Campbell, *Exiled in Paris: Richard Wright, James Baldwin, Samuel Becket, and Others on the Left Bank* (Berkeley: University of California Press, 2003). The specific quotes about Bechet can be found in

François Mallet, "Jazz: Sidney Bechet, vedette française," *L'Express* (21 May 1959), 35; and Michel Dorigné, *Jazz 1* (Paris: L'École SA, 1968), 132.

89. Gerald Gohier, "Dans un pavillon de Garches Sidney Bechet le prince noir du jazz agonise," *Paris Journal* (14 May 1959), 6. Tom Perchard has pointed out that Bechet was "revered as a singular representative—a living icon—of a past time." See his *After Django: Making Jazz in Postwar France* (Ann Arbor: University of Michigan Press, 2015), 43.

90. After Bechet's death, writers, fans, musicians, and advertisers sometimes simultaneously referred to him and Reinhardt. For instance, Vogue ran an advertisement proclaiming "Homage to two giants of Jazz" to promote a collection of five records including both of their "best recordings." See *Jazz Hot* 253 (September 1969), 6.

91. Quoted by Sidney Bechet, *Treat it Gentle* (New York: Hill & Wang, 1960), 127. Bechet's autobiography was published in France as *La musique c'est ma vie*, trans. Yvonne and Maurice Cullaz (Paris: La Table Ronde, 1977).

92. Chilton, 84.

93. Bechet, 149–56. Also see Harold Flakser, "Bechet, 1928–1931," *Jazz Magazine* 74 (September 1961), 32.

94. Quoted in Chilton, 234.

95. Colin Nettelbeck, *Dancing with DeBeauvoir: Jazz and the French* (Carlton, Victoria: Melbourne University Press, 2004), 70.

96. Frank Ténot, "La Traversée éblouissante," in Fabrice Zammarchi's *Sidney Bechet* (Paris: Éditions Filipacchi, 1989), 13.

97. Guy Longnon, "Sidney Bechet," *Jazz [Hip]* 15 (July 1959), 6.

98. François Mallet, "Sidney Bechet, vedette française," *L'Express* (21 May 1959), 36.

99. Sidney Bechet, "Une lettre de Sidney Bechet," *La Revue de Jazz*, 2nd series, n. 1 (July 1952), 14.

100. Philippe Carles, André Clergeat, and Jean-Louis Comolli, *Dictionnaire du jazz* (Paris: Robert Laffont, 1988): 79. Also see Sidney Bechet, *Treat it Gentle*, 194.

101. Alyn Shipton, "The New Orleans Revival in Britain and France," *Eurojazzland: Jazz and European Sources, Dynamic, and Contexts*, eds. Luca Cerchiari, Laurent Cugny, and Franz Kerschbaumer (Boston: Northeastern University Press, 2012), 268.

102. Ibid.

103. "Chèr Frère Jazz," *Jazz Magazine* 64 (November 1960), 5. Importantly, *Jazz Magazine* received and published a number of letters from its readers protesting this view of Bechet; they called him a "true creator" and asserted "his genius." See "Cher Frère Jazz," *Jazz Magazine* 66 (January 1961), 5, 7.

104. Charlie Pesin, "Le Gallup et Bechet," *Jazz Magazine* 73 (August 1961), 7.

105. "Europe N°1 a consultué les amateurs français," *Jazz Magazine* 21 (November 1956); and "27.000 amateurs européens ont designé les 10 jazzmen de l'année," *Jazz Magazine* 37 (May 1958).

106. Antoine Golea, "Un phénomène d'hystérie collective: Sidney Bechet et ses 'fans,'" *Témoignage Chrétien* (28 October 1955), 5.

107. "Quand les 'fans' de Bechet déchainent," *Franc-Tireur* (21 October 1955), 10.

108. Jacqueline Cartier, "Le concert Sydney Bechet dégénère en émeute," *L'Aurore* (20 October 1955), 2.

109. Bechet, *Treat it Gentle*, 200.

110. Jacques André, "Le jazz et ses faux amateurs," *Combat* (21 October 1955), 2.

111. Bernard Niquet, "Le hérault de la nouvelle-orléans," *Jazz Hot* 240 (April 1968), 11.

112. This was the southern counterpart to Annet Badel's Vieux Colombier where young existentialists gathered in Saint-Germain-des-Près and where Bechet established his "Parisian home base." See Christian Béthune, *Sidney Bechet* (Marseille: Éditions Parenthèses: 1997), 127.

113. Claude Luter, "Bechet, citoyen de Juan," *Arts* 782 (July 1960), 14.

114. Bechet, *Treat it Gentle*, 197.

115. Pierre Delmas, interviewed by Philippe Adler, "Vive Monsieur le Maire," *Jazz Hot* 179 (September 1962):, 8.

116. Claude Luter, "Bechet, citoyen de Juan," *Arts* 782 (July 1960), 14.

117. Ibid.

118. Raymond Mouly, "L'hommage de Juan-les-Pins," *Jazz Magazine* 62 (September 1960), 18.

119. Philippe Adler, "Vive Monsieur le Maire!" *Jazz Hot* 179 (September 1962), 8.

120. Mowgli Jospin, "Vibrant hommage à Sidney Bechet dans la nouvelle babel du jazz," *Le Figaro* (12 July 1960), 13.

121. Mouly, "L'hommage," 18.

122. Ibid. For another account of these events, see Charles Delaunay, "Antibes et Juan-les-Pins à l'heure du jazz," *Jazz Hot* 157 (September 1960), 21. Bechet's popularity extended beyond Antibes and Paris. In 1975, the town of Nancy named one of its streets Rue Sidney Bechet. See Xavier Brocker, *Le Roman vrai du jazz en Lorraine 1917–1991* (Jarville-La Malgrange: Éditions de l'Est, 1991), 31.

123. "History of the Jazz à Juan festival," Jazz à Juan, accessed April 12, 2016, www.jazzajuan.com/HISTOIREDUFESTIVAL.aspx.

124. "Sidney Bechet," *Paris Journal* (15 May 1959), 10.

125. "Sidney Bechet, Prince du Jazz n'a jamais su lire une partition," *Paris Journal* (15 May 1959), 10.

126. François Mallet, "Sidney Bechet, vedette française," *L'Express* (21 May 1959), 35.

127. Raymond Mouly, "Notre ami Sidney," *Jazz Magazine* 50 (July 1959), 17.

128. Ibid., 24.

129. Béthune, *Sidney Bechet*, 158.

130. Charles Delaunay, "Sidney Bechet," *Jazz [Hip]* 15 (July 1959), 4.

131. "Sidney Bechet," *Paris Journal* (15 May 1959), 10.

132. Ibid. This article wrongly claimed that Bechet married a Frenchwoman in accentuating his ties to France. During his time in France, Bechet did have a long-term relationship with a Frenchwoman with whom he had a child, but they never married.

133. Chilton, 251.

134. Simone Brown, *Dark Matter: On the Surveillance of Blackness* (Durham, NC: Duke University Press, 2015); and Peter J. Bloom, *French Colonial Documentary: Mythologies of Humanitarianism* (Minneapolis: University of Minnesota Press, 2008), 41–42.

135. Hergé, *The Adventures of Tintin: Tintin in the Congo* (Copenhagen, Denmark: Egmont, 2005).

136. Whitney Balliet, *American Musicians: Fifty-Six Portraits in Jazz* (New York: Oxford University Press, 1986), 33.

137. I agree with Rob Kroes that Americanization "should be the story of an American cultural language traveling and of other people acquiring that language. What they actually say in it, is a different story altogether." See Kroes, "American Mass Culture and European Youth Culture," 105.

Chapter Five

Red, White, and Blue Notes: French Jazz

Postwar French jazz musicians created a space for their art not only within an international framework defined by the hegemony of the United States, but they also worked to build recognition for their work within French national culture. They faced hardships from a variety of fronts. Jazz enthusiasts made constant comparisons between them and their better-known and better-respected American counterparts, and record companies, concert promoters, and club owners frequently hesitated to promote or to hire them, creating a shortage of work for them in France. Facing these challenges, French jazzmen still worked to build an audience for their music and to earn professional respect from their fellow citizens. Through organization and a willingness to perform in France and abroad, musicians did what they could defend and to sustain *jazz français*.

THE QUESTION OF *JAZZ FRANÇAIS*

In the 1950s and 1960s, but especially in the latter decade, the jazz community concerned itself with the question of a national jazz. By the 1960s, French musicians like Martial Solal had won both domestic and international attention for their talents, sparking an interest among listeners about the question of French jazz. Even before the growing prominence of Solal and others, and dating from the mid-1930s, the guitarist Django Reinhardt had permanently contributed to people's notions of French jazz and its relevance to both American jazz and French national culture. In the postwar period, jazz critics, musicians, and fans nevertheless struggled to define a French form of the music, and in the process, frequently referred to the musical heritage left by Reinhardt.

In 1960, the Marseilles-based *Jazz Hip* asked a number of prominent members of the French jazz scene to discuss French jazz. In doing so, these critics and musicians revealed important understandings about the music. Most agreed with Michel de Villers when he stated, "French jazz is jazz played by musicians of the French language."[1] This simple definition allowed members of the jazz community to discuss a "French jazz" without having to claim that it was aesthetically unique. The majority of critics and musicians agreed that this music did not have its own distinguishing sound, causing some of them to dismiss the idea of a French jazz altogether. The pianist André Persiany asserted, "In my opinion, French jazz is a myth," and Michel de Villers agreed, claiming, "French jazz does not exist. . . . Jazz musicians across the entire globe refer to the same Muses—Armstrong, Parker, Monk and company. . . . Musically, therefore, it is impossible to separate French jazz from American jazz or Belgian jazz."[2] Charles Delaunay reiterated this point, proclaiming that "this entity [French jazz] obviously refers to the entirety of French musicians and not to a musical essence that is purely French, since, until the contrary can be proven, all jazz musicians have until now drawn their inspiration from the great creators who—with the exception maybe of Django Reinhardt—were Americans, and more accurately black."[3] Persiany, de Villers, and Delaunay all identified the problem of separating French jazz from its American and international counterparts: French musicians had not established a separate genre of the music that listeners could easily identify as French. Instead, these musicians drew on the American sources of the music and depended on them for both foundational and creative purposes.

Through the 1960s, musicians and critics continued to discuss the question of French jazz. Pianist, composer, and avid supporter of native French musicians Jef Gilson wrote in 1965, "In reality, the exchanges between Europe and the United States since the last war have been too numerous and too frequent for a European tendency in jazz to be able to truly express itself."[4] Like his counterparts five years earlier, Gilson recognized that the constant cultural exchange between the United States and France prevented a French jazz from emerging. Gilson actually saw no constructive reason to divide jazz into national categories, asserting that the opposition between American and French jazz "would appear archaic to us, if it arose, for the same reason that political regionalism or even nationalism do."[5] Despite recognizing the absence of a singular French jazz, Gilson remained one of the period's strongest supporters of French jazz musicians. Although he did not think French jazz itself was musically idiosyncratic, he nonetheless fought for the recognition of French artists.

Other critics discussed the problem of labeling a genre of jazz distinctively French. In 1965, Jean Wagner asked,

> What is French jazz? That whose creators live in France? In that case, Kenny Clarke is the greatest French drummer. And I don't dare to consider the case of Bud Powell. . . . Another hypotheses: French jazz is created by musicians of French origin? A more absurd definition still: between the Algerian Solal, the Swiss Humair and the Flemish Pedersen, I don't see more than a single thing in common between them—the use of the same language—which on the level we are interested in, is very superficial. Maybe one could speak of French jazz when there exists in France a distinct aesthetic movement as important as West Coast or Hard Bop or Funky![6]

According to Wagner, jazz could not be considered markedly French on the basis of a musician's residency, his perceived national affiliation, or his language because a musician who lived, worked, and created in France might very well be foreign. He could potentially be American like Clarke or Powell, Swiss like Humair, or Flemish like Pedersen. It is interesting that Wagner classified Solal as foreign because the musician was indeed French: he was a *pied-noir* who grew up in Algiers and moved to Paris in 1950. With the label "Algerian," Wagner alluded to the uncertainties surrounding national identification following the Algerian War when millions of *colons* moved to France, a subject that will be further discussed in relation to jazz in chapter 6. These men and women had lived in Algeria for several generations and had French citizenship, but many of them had ancestors who came from beyond France, from places like Spain, Italy, and Malta. The historian Philip Naylor has shown that by 1954, nearly half of the *colons* were not of French origin.[7] Uncertainties and tensions over membership in the nation certainly spilled over into the jazz world as individuals discussed the various citizenships of musicians. And here, Wagner seemed to deny Solal full identification with France because of his Algerian birth.[8] Importantly, Wagner, like his colleagues, not only dismissed the idea of "French jazz" based on passports and birthplaces, but also because the music did not inhabit a precise aesthetic realm. French musicians played a variety of jazz, ranging from New Orleans to the avant-garde but they still had not created a "school" of their own.

Conflicting notions obviously informed jazz fans' ideas about French jazz. On the one hand, critics and fans recognized that there were important French musicians who deserved attention and respect. On the other hand, they also observed that these musicians had not invented a musical genre that could be distinctly recognized. French musicians, like their American counterparts, played varied forms of the music, and had not established a specifically national jazz sound. Lastly, French commentators felt tempted to discuss *French jazz* because it was the only means by which they could give their countrymen credit for their music and their craft. At times though, these writers still insisted that a certain Frenchness manifested itself in the music of these jazzmen, regardless of the music's diversity and the influence of American jazz. Despite obvious reservations, critics, fans, and musicians all discussed *French jazz*. Historian Ludovic Tournès has contended with the meaning of this term and in doing so illustrated the challenges associated with establishing a precise definition. He argued that the work of French jazzmen reflected that they were not content to only imitate American artists but did their part to help construct "the musical evolution of jazz," revealing "one of the most tangible signs of an acculturation of black American music in our country." For him, the term "French jazz" made "no reference to a hypothetical 'school' or to any 'style' typical of the hexagon" but simply sanctioned "the affirmation, in France, of a group of musicians recognizing the language of jazz."[9] Tournès' broad definition of French jazz allowed the phrase to serve a useful purpose: it highlighted jazz's important place in postwar culture, emphasized the active participation of French musicians in promoting and creating this music, and recognized that there was no actual French school of jazz.

From the vantage point of 1964, the critics Philippe Carles and Jean-Louis Comolli claimed that 1954 was the most important year for *jazz français*. Before that, members of the jazz public had certainly made important achievements: Hugues Panassié founded the Hot Club de France in the 1930s; Django Reinhardt's Quintette du Hot Club de France had come into existence in 1934; in 1945, André Hodeir wrote *Le Jazz, cet inconnu*, and in 1948, published *Introduction à la musique de jazz*; by the end of the 1940s, Martial Solal began his musical career. Yet, in 1964, Carles and Comolli asserted that 1954 was French jazz's landmark year because of the groundbreaking new works generated by Hodeir, Solal, and the young musician Jean-Luc Ponty. In 1954, Hodeir published *Hommes et problèmes du jazz* where he inaugurated "a lucid, responsible, ambitious criticism"; Solal appeared on the French jazz scene with his first compositions and trio performances; and the young French jazz artist Jean-Luc Ponty published his first record in 1954—*Jazz Long Playing*.[10] The most unusual part of Carles and Comolli's argument was that jazz criticism was an intrinsic and crucial component of French jazz. For them, French jazz included the written works of men like André Hodeir whose articles and books on jazz continued to reach an international audience throughout the postwar period. Hodeir had importantly put a French mark on jazz criticism, and these writers claimed that he and his cohort had been the first to affirm jazz's universality and to theorize jazz. They implied that the French had contributed to jazz through their written analyses of the music, thereby enriching all of jazz through the written word.

Comolli and Carles also envisioned jazz as a universal music, thereby unintentionally complicating their image of French jazz. In a postwar age that had witnessed the birth of the United Nations, UNESCO, and the Universal Declaration of Human Rights, these two writers reflected a western mentality that believed in the universal, a belief enshrined in French history with the Declaration of the Rights of Man. French critics, fans, and musicians could be citizens in a musical world that transcended national identity, and yet they resisted the pull of the universal and insisted on holding on to their Frenchness. This pull between the national and the universal has been evident in French history since the time of the Revolution and members of the French jazz community were not immune to this conflicted sense of identity. They wanted to participate in and help to develop a universal cultural form while simultaneously making their own unique contributions and protecting their status as Frenchmen. Tom Perchard has shown that French jazz musicians in the 1970s finally began to develop their own unique aesthetic practices, carrying the cause of French jazz beyond the scope of this book but illustrating the enduring interest musicians and activists would have in creating and sustaining *jazz français*.[11]

THE EXAMPLE OF DJANGO REINHARDT

The French-Belgian-Roma jazzman Django Reinhardt loomed large in discussions of French jazz. Reinhardt, born in 1910 near Charleroi in Belgium, spent a part of his early years in Italy and North Africa but grew up primarily in France, spending the majority of his life there after the age of ten. But due to his family's constant migrations he could have just as easily been born in France or Italy. Until he was twenty-four, he did not have a passport or any type of national identity papers as he lived largely outside the confines of traditional and mainstream European society.[12] He never received a formal education and remained largely illiterate throughout his life, only learning to write his name and phonetically-spelled French words as an adult. He never read well enough to review his own professional contracts and his French was always spoken with a distinct accent. During his lifetime, he did not primarily identify with French culture but with the Roma: the Romany language was his first language and he frequently lived in Roma encampments both on the outskirts of Paris and in the provinces long after his fame and personal wealth made living elsewhere possible.

Reinhardt's musical roots were firmly planted in Roma culture, leading him as a child to take up the banjo and then the guitar, which were not conventional jazz instruments. When he was twelve years old, he started playing traditional French and Roma musics in Parisian dance halls but by the time he was sixteen he had heard the new sounds of jazz and began working this music into his own repertoire. He found regular employment as a musician until 1928, when his left hand was badly burned in a fire. Because of this injury, he had to painstakingly teach himself to play the guitar by only using three fingers on his left hand—his middle and index fingers and his thumb—which contributed to his distinctive way of playing. The contemporary jazz critic Michael Dregni has described his playing in this way:

> Two fingers on six strings, forced to move at least twice the speed of anyone else's four fingers and then faster yet as he threw in flourished and single-finger chromatic dashes all the way up the fretboard on one string and then continuing across the strings, flaunting and then flouting his handicap.[13]

In 1930, he began looking for work again but had difficulty finding a job as a jazz musician because clubs wanted to hire African-American musicians, not Roma guitarists.[14] Reinhardt persisted in finding employment where he could, sometimes even in Parisian Russian cabarets, and continued to develop his art as a jazz musician. In 1934, he big break arrived when he became the leading member of a new band—the Quintette du Hot Club de France—whose other members were Stéphane Grappelli on violin, Roger Chaput on guitar, Louis Vola on bass, and Reinhardt's brother Joseph who also played the guitar. Charles Delaunay, a friend of Reinhardt's who took part in founding the Quintette as well as in promoting Reinhardt's music for years to come, wrote in his 1961 book entitled *Django Reinhardt* that before the Quintette, jazz had been "a cacophony," "a series of discords," "reserved for Negroes, or, as was said, 'for savages.'" The Quintette's use of string instruments made jazz a "more delicate music" that could now "be more easily assimilated by outsiders."[15]

As the years and then decades passed, the Quintette began to hold a unique place in French jazz history because its fans saw it as legitimizing both white and French musicians, and perhaps even certain Roma ones. During World War II, the group's membership shifted to accommodate the changes brought on by the war. Stéphane Grappelli, who was the Quintette's second most important member, lived in London at a time when other members were also unable to maintain their ties to the band. As a result, Reinhardt founded the Nouveau Quintette du Hot Club de France that focused his musical energies on swing. This new band's most significant difference from the original was a result of Reinhardt's replacement of Grappelli with the clarinetist Hubert Rostaing, as it brought the ensemble away from its strong reliance on string instruments.[16] Throughout the war years, Reinhardt, despite his Roma ethnicity, was able to find not only regular work but celebrity and wealth in occupied Paris.[17] After the war, Reinhardt reestablished many of his prewar ties in the jazz world and continued creating new sounds and playing them for audiences throughout France, Europe, and even in the United States before a cerebral hemorrhage caused his death on May 15, 1953. By then he was already becoming a legend of French jazz.

The French jazz community had a tendency to fixate itself on Reinhardt's Roma background and, in many ways, critics, musicians, and fans used his "race" and cultural background to explain part, if not at times all, of his musical talent. Of course, the Roma had long experienced discrimination in France, with the first anti-gypsy laws being passed in France as far back as 1539.[18] By the time Reinhardt was born, stereotypes about his ethnic group were well-entrenched: gypsies were thought to be criminals and beggars who were not only portrayed as dirty but dangerous to the health and welfare of others. The Third Republic passed laws to control their nomadic ways and starting in 1913 required them to have anthropometric identity cards showing a number of their physical traits, such as head size, chest measurement, length of right ear, and eye color; the cards also included an individual's fingerprints and two photographs. In 1940, the Third Republic forbid the Roma to move from place to place, and the Vichy government retained the same policy. During the Occupation, the French oversaw more than forty concentration camps for the Roma to ensure that they had a fixed residence.[19]

Paired with this long history of French discrimination against the Roma that both predated and coincided with his fame, Reinhardt's celebrity in Occupied France is surprising, especially since jazz critics and promoters highlighted his Roma heritage, often showing that they had the same racial biases as the rest of their countrymen. Charles Delaunay described the Roma group to which Reinhardt belonged in the following way:

> The facial features, tawny complexion and dark almond-shaped eyes of the Romanies betray their Hindu origin, sharply differentiating them from the Continent's other races, from whose influence they have remained free. Consumed with a desire for liberty, unable to settle down in the countries through which they pass or to submit to their laws, these tribes wander from place to place, preserving their age-old customs, living on air, odd jobs, the occasional concert-show, or by their wits, but more certainly than anything else off the profits of their thieving. Work is not their strong point; in fact, they regard it as debasing. And whilst the women have to look after the family welfare, all the men have to do is to see they are smartly turned out. As a result, the men are frequently proud and lazy.[20]

In addition to these physical and cultural characteristics, Delaunay also argued that the Romas excelled musically, writing,

> Though rough and uneducated, the Romanies often show, if not, as we have seen, a natural facility, a least a certain liking for music—a racial trait that probably has its origin in national forms such as the Hungarian czardas or the Spanish flamencos. Leading an indolent life, the men often take up an instrument, generally stringed, such as the violin, mandolin, guitar or zither. Preserving a folk tradition down through the years, the old men like to recall their

own youth and transmit a musical past, rich in color to the younger generation.[21]

Delaunay thought that Reinhardt's musical acumen was due in large part to his gypsy heritage, and he conflated the racial with the cultural in his construction of Reinhardt's persona. Although he considered Reinhardt "white," Delaunay most certainly also regarded the musician as other because of his ethnic origins. He wrote, "Django Reinhardt was one of the very few white jazzmen to possess the exceptional attack and swing that are the birthright of the best colored musicians." He also described the musician as "primitive and artist at one and the same time."[22]

Other jazz aficionados took an interest in Reinhardt's racial background as well. Gérard Legrand, who actually thought Reinhardt was "overrated," still wrote about the connection between his race and music. In his 1953 book *Puissances du jazz*, Legrand claimed, "The accursed races are made to understand one another, and without a doubt Django was an excellent accompanist for musicians more restless than powerful, like Bill Coleman and Dicky Wells," both of whom where African-American jazz artists.[23] Critic Hugues Panassié asserted that "[Django] keeps from his gypsy origins a musical temperament that makes him very different from all other musicians,"[24] while Jef Gilson maintained that "it would be interesting to study the remarkable career of Django in explaining how his Manouche or (Hungarian) gypsy or (Spanish) gypsy origins, which I know, allowed him to make himself immune to exclusively American influences."[25] Frank Ténot continued to argue long after Rienhardt's death that the musician's Roma inheritance was extremely relevant to his music. In 1977, he asserted "[Reinhardt's] music, a unique case in the context of jazz, is the fruit of the marriage between the gypsy sensibility and the influence of the jazz masters of the thirties: Eddie Lang, Armstrong, Tatum, Carter, Hawkins, Ellington."[26] Eleven years later, Ténot described these two elements of Reinhardt's music as "folklores born in the ghettos on the margins of official culture."[27] In focusing such pointed attention on Reinhardt's Roma heritage, critics betrayed their own understandings about this ethnic group and their belief that gypsies were not only culturally but also sometimes racially distinct from the French. According to these writers, this difference contributed in large part to Reinhardt's musical talent. His ethnic heritage allowed him to be both French and gypsy simultaneously, contributing to French jazz fans' appreciation of his musical singularities. According to this line of thought, the gypsy in Reinhardt gave him his musical talent, while the Frenchman in him allowed jazz fans to focus on his French national belonging, which they shared with him, and to promote him as the most important French jazz musician.

The critic Michel-Claude Jalard wrote an article on "Django and the gypsy school of jazz" where he asserted that within the gypsy community there was "a folklore that was naturally drawn to jazz like the blues, spirituals, and black preaching." Jalard went on to discuss the differences between the social conditions of the African-American and gypsy communities.

> The black American, in fighting against segregation, demands racial and civil equality, that is to say, integration. The gypsy, on the other hand, who lives on the margins of society, longs for people to respect his ethnic and moral uniqueness and for a statute that would legitimately sanction this. In a similar way, jazz will be for the black American a means by which he can make himself recognized by whites by bringing his spontaneous expression to a universal aesthetic level—one characterized by "European civilization." So, inversely, the gypsy without a determined folklore, will play for himself, in using to his advantage all the formal elements of the society whose margins on which he lives.[28]

Despite the differences between gypsy and African-American culture, Jalard emphasized that they both existed on the margins of society (the former largely because of choice, the latter because of racial discrimination). Yet this difference gave them a unique cultural vantage point whose potential for aesthetic uniqueness was considerable. Jalard, like others among the French, thought that culture could and should be used to bridge societal gaps, especially in France. He wrote,

> Jazz seems the most natural bridge which can be cast between gypsies and the society on whose margins they live: jazz is in effect an art full of future that is beginning to assure itself of a universal audience; but it is also an art of improvisation and of the actual moment.[29]

Jalard wrote this article in 1959 when a larger minority presence was only beginning to make itself felt in France. In the following decades, French jazz enthusiasts became increasingly supportive of ideas like Jalard's because they stressed the societal relevance of culture and its ability to foster national unity. Because Jalard chose to raise jazz to a universal level, he hesitated to portray Reinhardt exclusively as a "gypsy." He asserted, "As a matter of fact, Django, he is at this moment less the extraordinary 'gypsy' guitarist than the jazz musician par excellence."[30] Jalard was very concerned with "the social problem posed by gypsies and the rhythmic disparities of their integration into modern society."[31] In some ways, he saw jazz as a solution to this disjuncture, hoping that through mediums such as jazz, gypsies could be brought into the larger national community.

Others noted the combination in Django's music of the particular—represented by the Roma or the African-American background—and the universal. French fans, critics, and musicians all stressed the universal promises of jazz, and argued that this music had the ability to appeal to and to unite people across racial, national, and linguistic barriers. In 1954, the French jazzman Alix Combelle claimed that "Django, he was universal in music."[32] In 1968, fifteen years after Reinhardt's death, the critic Alain Balalas argued that Reinhardt's music evoked both its idiosyncratic and catholic roots. Balalas asserted,

> Django is one of the most important, and curious, and custom-made jazz musicians. Born of that of Louis Armstrong, Benny Carter and Duke Ellington, his music awakens, all in being of a very black spirit, of strange echoes, as if it had found again, not only the accent of the great black soloists but also something older, more universal, a song born beyond the barriers of race, common to all the people in suffering, in anticipation of redemption, something which would be like the essence even of music—completely pure.[33]

Through Reinhardt, French jazz fans thought they could unite one of their own "national" musicians with both the music's African-American foundations and its universal promise and appeal.

Importantly, French supporters of jazz saw Django Reinhardt as occupying a unique and honored place not only in French jazz but in the entire history of the music. In 1950, three years before Reinhardt's death, the *Le Monde* critic Pierre Drouin claimed that "one can count on the fingers of one hand the French musicians who have enriched jazz's heritage with their personal mark. Django Reinhardt is among them, and maybe the most original. His guitar conquered America as it did Europe."[34] Before his own death, and a year after Reinhardt's, Boris Vian wrote, "He was the greatest of French jazz musicians; one of the greatest musicians in all of jazz."[35] Hugues Panassié expanded on this praise of Reinhardt, arguing that American guitarists did not consider Reinhardt "their equal, but as their master." Panassié claimed to have heard "the best jazz musicians from the other side of the Atlantic exclaim: 'Django is a genius' or 'A musician like Django, only one or two is born each century.'"[36] Panassié, who so infrequently celebrated French musicians, also compared Reinhardt to the one musician he admired above all others, claiming, "Django makes his guitar speak like Louis Armstrong makes his trumpet speak."[37] Coming from another critic this compliment would have been much less significant, as only Panassié continued to push the music of Louis Armstrong above the music of all other musicians throughout the postwar period. That he chose to equate Reinhardt and Armstrong here shows his considerable esteem for the former's musical talent. On the occasion of Reinhardt's death, Panassié maintained that "Django is certainly the greatest musician Europe has given to jazz. He was the first European 'jazzman' to acquire international fame, and he is the *only* European who influenced black musicians."[38] Almost ten years after Reinhardt's death, the critic Claude Samuel wrote in his *Panorama de l'art musical contemporain* that Reinhardt was perhaps the only European soloist "who had aroused the admiration of American jazzmen."[39]

Members of the French jazz community debated whether Django had created an actual "school" through his music. Most of them agreed that his influence was significant but that he had not led jazz off into a completely new direction or created a new genre of jazz. Michel de Villers maintained that

> from the instrumental point of view, this influence is undeniable: one senses him in Charlie Christian. . . . From the musical point of view I admit that Django did not make the same impact that was made by a Louis Armstrong or a Charlie Parker, but it must be said that he was much less known because, living outside of America, his music was circulated rather little.[40]

The musician Louis Vola, who had played bass with the Quintette, asserted in 1963 that Reinhardt's music had made a lasting impression. He told an interviewer, "I must say that, until now, I have not known a guitarist who, when he spoke of Django, said that [the music] had aged; I know, I think, all the guitarists of Paris; 'eh! well,' one hears them all say: 'I listen to Django's records, they are always extraordinary.' Everybody truly talks about Django."[41] When the French critic Jacques Gaspard asked Kenny Clarke, the American musician who had been living in France for over a decade, if he thought Reinhardt had had an influence on jazz musicians, Clarke replied, "Oh, yes, on all the guitarists of the world, I think."[42]

Within the French Roma community, Reinhardt also had an enduring impact as young musicians chose to both largely follow his musical style and to play his instrument, the guitar. In 1965, the critic Philippe Adler wrote an article on Reinhardt's thirteen-year-old nephew Boulou, who was a young prodigy on the guitar. He wrote, "Boulou is a swinging product 'Made in France.'"[43] In addition to recognizing Reinhardt's solid and lasting musical influence on French gypsy jazzmen, jazz devotees also repeatedly noted his influence on the music itself. Like his nephew Boulou, Reinhardt had been "Made in France" and his supporters continued to emphasize this. Michel-Claude Jalard asserted that "there is therefore, in jazz, a Django tradition, more robust particularly in France, and especially among his racial brothers, but which has sometimes influenced American guitarists or those who quote, above all else, these last ones."[44] Reinhardt's supporters continued to contend that his music had been both consequential and pathbreaking. In 1986, the critic Jean Wagner declared that "musically, he was the first jazz guitarist to have given an individual aesthetic dimension to his instrument." And at the turn of the twenty-first century, Jean-Dominique Brierre wrote in his book *Le jazz français* that "King Django" had crossed "the French musical landscape like a meteor."[45]

Jazz audiences honored Reinhardt's contribution to French jazz long after he died. To commemorate the first anniversary of his death, French jazz musicians gave a concert in his name at the Salle Playel where they interpreted his most famous works.[46] Four years later, in 1958, filmmaker Paul Paviot made a short film about him, entitled *Django Reinhardt*, which retraced the musician's life. A number of French jazzmen assisted Paviot in this endeavor, including Stéphane Grappelli, Alix Combelle, André Ekyan, Eugène Vées, Emmanuel Soudieux, and Joseph Reinhardt.[47] In May of the following year, concert promoters organized a Nuit du Jazz in Rouen with the theme "Homage to Django Reinhardt." Seven French musicians, among whom were Stéphane Grappelli and Sacha Distel, participated in the concert.[48] On the tenth anniversary of his death, French jazz aficionados commemorated Reinhardt in a number of ways. *Jazz Hot* put his picture on the cover of their May issue along with the words "Ten years ago . . . "[49] More importantly, the record company Philips released an original record, *Hommage à Django* on which a variety of French jazz musicians collaborated, the most famous of whom were Sacha Distel and Claude Bolling. The critic Aris Destombes said in his review of this album that these two musicians "knew how to draw the most from the orchestra and from the [musical] themes to pay homage, with fervor and respect, to the greatest soloist that France had until recently possessed."[50] A final tribute to Reinhardt was made that year when the Belgian town of Liberchies, where the musician had been born, hosted the Festival International de jazz Django Reinhardt.[51]

Fifteen years after his death, the mayor of Samois-sur-Seine, where Reinhardt had spent his last years, organized "a day entirely consecrated to the memory of the guitarist." According to a *Jazz Magazine* correspondent, Maurice-Louis Blanc, four or five thousand people came to Samois for this event. In addition to a religious service and the city putting a plaque on the house where Reinhardt had lived, an array of French musicians performed at a concert lasting from the afternoon until eight o'clock at night. In the words of this correspondent, "French jazz, on May 19, remembered its first master."[52] Since 1983, a Festival Django Reinhardt has taken place each spring in Samois-sur-Seine.[53]

Throughout the postwar period, Django Reinhardt remained, despite his death, an important fixture of French jazz. In fact, his persona took on a kind of mythical status. In 1957, the critic Pierre Bompar wrote about Reinhardt in a way that emphasized stereotypes about both the guitarist and the Roma community and that also oversimplified and romanticized his musical achievements. Bompar wrote, "Free, tender but exuberant, passionate and a little romantic in his music like in his life. That was Django Reinhardt, vagabond of jazz and modern minstrel."[54] Ten years after his death, Madeleine Gautier wrote, "Django belonged to the race of free men: he did not analyze himself. He remains for those who knew and loved him, at the same time both secretive and naïve, tough and infinitely sensitive, of a sensible intelligence and a freshness of incomparable soul."[55] Due in large part to such remarks, observers began noting in the late 1950s that his life was taking on legendary proportions. In 1958, *Jazz Magazine* published an eight-part series that lasted from its January issue until its October one entitled "The Legend of Django Reinhardt." In this series, Yves Salgues recounted the famous details of Reinhardt's life: his gypsy beginnings and heritage; the fire that had deformed his left hand; the free-spending, carefree lifestyle he had led; his time as the leader of the Quintette du Hot Club de France; his later interest in painting; his untimely death at the age of forty-three.[56] Through such accounts, jazz enthusiasts constructed an image of Reinhardt that depended on his differences from mainstream French life. The critic Demètre Ioakimidis stated in 1962, "Django Reinhardt was a very great musician, one of the true original creators of the music of jazz. He was also a character with a capital "C." From this fact, a legend was created around him."[57] In 1963, the musician Daniel Humair also noted this, claiming that "there is a Django myth; there is a legend."[58] Because his life had been flavored with experiences alien to most of his fans, members of the French jazz community told and retold the story of his life, making both his music and his life loom large in the story of French jazz itself.

In debating whether a markedly French form of jazz existed, critics ceaselessly evoked the name Django Reinhardt. In 1965, Jean Wagner labeled Reinhardt and Martial Solal the "two greats of French jazz." He then went on to question, however, if they had anything in common, "either on the level of musical language or anything at all? One of them took pleasure in a nearly Slavic nostalgia, the other is Mediterranean. In other words, there is not, on the aesthetic level, any French jazz."[59] Twenty-one years later, in 1986, Wagner again broached the subject of Reinhardt and a distinct French genre of jazz, this time choosing to discuss Reinhardt and the jazz violinist Stéphane Grappelli. He identified these musicians as

> two of the most personal improvisers in the history of jazz, one of romantic tragedy completely filled with a European-colored nostalgia, the other of the typically adventurous Mediterranean spirit who never stopped searching for roundabout paths where the most vivid flowers formed bouquets of iridescent color. It was apparent that the two of them would not have had the same discourse had they not lived in France.[60]

Here Wagner claimed that a certain *Frenchness* determined the music of these two jazzmen, and he argued that their music would not have been the same "had they not lived in France."

Multiple meanings and identities converged as fans listened to Django Reinhardt's music. The fact that Reinhardt was a member of the Roma ethnic group and had actually been born in Belgium did not prevent his listeners and admirers from labeling him as French and celebrating his membership in the French nation, reflecting a cosmopolitan component to French identity that embraced foreign cultural affiliations. Reinhardt's ethnic heritage allowed him to be both French and Roma simultaneously, contributing to fans' appreciation of his musical talent and eliding the long history of discrimination that the Roma people experienced (and continue to experience) in France. According to the pervading line of thought around Reinhardt, the gypsy in him shaped his inimitable artistic vision, while his passport—again not obtained until he was twenty-four—allowed French jazz audiences to focus on his national belonging, which they shared with him, and to promote him as the most important of French jazz musicians. Although he died in 1953, French critics and listeners continued to forward his musical legacy and in doing so exposed a multiplicity of racial, cultural, and national meanings, not only for his music and his own personal identity, but for what it meant to be French in an evermore ethnically and culturally diverse world. Reinhardt was not upheld as an example of a nonethnic Frenchmen who became French through his education or adoption of French ways and values, quite the contrary. His fans loved him precisely because he remained a gypsy and brought his Roma culture to them through jazz. Reinhardt's admirers required him to be culturally foreign, but this did not mean that they saw him as their equal.

THE AMERICAN COMPARISON

A major difficulty in defining an unmistakable French form of jazz was the impossibility of extracting it from the original American music. As the American academic George Lewis has written, "European jazz musicians were said to inhabit a landscape in which aesthetic, methodological, and stylistic direction flowed for the overwhelming part from the metropole of America to the tributaries in their own lands."[61] Because of this reality, French jazzmen unambiguously conceded that American jazz influenced them. In 1956, the tenor saxophonist Jean-Claude Fohrenbach told an interviewer,

> I was first very influenced by Coleman Hawkins, then, two years ago when cool music started to spill into France, I was tempted by and interested in this new style. But I realized that the important tendencies of cool did not correspond with either my temperament or my conception of jazz. . . . I am always looking for new things. That is why I prefer to listen to black musicians. They alone can teach us what we lack.[62]

Fohrenbach acknowledged that his musical style depended a great deal on new innovations emanating from the United States. Instead of finding musical inspiration from both French and American musicians, he looked almost exclusively to American "black musicians" to find and to correct deficiencies in his own art. He then chose whether or not to integrate these American innovations into his own musical repertoire. Other French musicians followed this same process. For instance, the twenty-four-year-old tenor saxophone player François Jeanneau was said to "not hide his musical affection for John Coltrane."[63] In general, French musicians found considerable inspiration from American artists and no one who played this music could rightfully divorce his or her own art from the American genre that originally brought it to life.

Because of the constant musical reference to jazzmen from the other side of the Atlantic, French musicians at times adopted American-sounding pseudonyms to sell more records. For example, the Algerian-born Raphaël Schécroun gave himself the name Errol Parker. Michel de Villers was disgusted by this situation and blamed fans for their strong prejudices about a musician's nationality. He wrote, "Don't you think that Schécroun would prefer to record under his own name? Is he not forced to use this strategy because of the profound stupidity of the average fan? All of this would not be necessary if the record buyer didn't attach a greater importance to the sound of the record sleeve than to the sound of the band." De Villers then went on to mention other musicians who had changed their names to American-sounding ones: Virginie Morgan, Earl Cadillac, Peter Moore, Johnny Hallyday, and Frank Morgan.[64] Clearly, their American counterparts influenced French musicians, and at times these less-appreciated European artists felt the need to adopt Anglicized names in order to compete on a more equal footing with their better-respected colleagues.

Because of the prominence of American musicians, supporters of jazz continually compared the work of French and American musicians. In 1958, Frank Ténot constructed an imaginary conversation between two French fans in his *Jazz Magazine* column. One of the two participants in the conversation asserted the following: "You are unfair to French musicians, you don't talk about anything but American musicians. . . . You devote articles and photos to foreign artists no better than ours." The other participant responded by claiming that American musicians themselves were only concerned with events in New York, that the records of French artists sold poorly as "the public loves Basie, Dizzy, Miles, Armstrong" and that "when we put a French musician on the cover, the magazine sells less."[65] This type of dialogue continued among members of the jazz public throughout the 1960s as enthusiasts tried to give their national musicians respect and wider recognition but found they constantly came up against arguments that French musicians did not sell and that the public was most concerned with American artists.

French listeners, at times, communicated rather destructive opinions about their own countrymen when evaluating French and American jazz. In 1960, the musician Marcel Zanini declared, "France is, in my opinion, a country which has numerous musicians of great talent, but which does not have one group that can compete with American orchestras."[66] For others like Zanini, French artists simply could not rival American ones. Martial Solal, who was one of the few French jazzmen to earn the respect of French and American fans alike, explored the negative sentiments that fans, critics, and musicians all shared about French jazz. He thought that the French had a "pro-American complex" in relation to the music and he argued that "the French public is not very expert in jazz matters." According to him, this was "due to the fact that, even with experience, the public takes for gospel everything that comes from the other side of the Atlantic."[67] For Solal, French jazz was caught in a destructive cycle: fans tended to be interested solely in American music; critics responded by writing almost exclusively about Americans; and fans, as a result, were denied access to information about French jazz, further augmenting their devotion to the American music. Solal, like Zanini, also noted that the art of American musicians was consistently stronger than that of French jazzmen. But he thought this was in part the case because of the petty atmosphere that existed within the French jazz community and because the musicians themselves bought into the idea of American superiority.

Other critics noticed this detrimental tendency among French jazz musicians. Jef Gilson wrote that the crisis in French jazz was partly due "to the 'complexes' French musicians have because they imagine (even when they strongly claim the contrary): (a) that they do not ever equal American musicians; (b) that the public will not admit this fact to them; (c) that the public will tolerate them if need be only if they obediently find their inspiration from American idols."[68] In 1961, the critic Catherine Pierre pointed out the inclination among French musicians to see themselves as subordinate to Americans, contending, "It is commonly said that French jazz lacks creators; it is not in maintaining an inferiority complex among our musicians that we will see the rise of a new Django!"[69] Like Solal, Gilson and Pierre both observed a "pro-American complex" among musicians. Gilson argued that for these jazzmen to succeed, they had to distance themselves from their dependency on American music, that they "must *coûte que coûte* make a 'personal' music, their only chance to break through. There is not one example of a musician who 'copies' becoming truly famous. Django owed his international success to being truly himself."[70] Critics insisted that in merely imitating American sounds, French musicians were not only buying into the belief that American musicians were better, but they were reinforcing this belief by being so unoriginal themselves.

Listeners appreciated jazz because it was so different from French popular music, and, as discussed in chapter 3, they embraced with a type of philoracism the African Americans who had created the music in the first place. Certainly the importance of American musicians could not be denied, but jazz audiences harmed the prospects of French jazzmen and their ability to compete with Americans in their own national market by negatively prejudging them in relation to their overseas counterparts. As a result, one feature of the jazz landscape remained unchanged: listeners continued to regard African Americans as the ultimate jazz performers and French artists as substandard by comparison.

Despite this pervasive sense of French jazz inferiority, beginning in the late 1950s, and picking up momentum in the 1960s, a number of jazz devotees began a crusade to make French jazz more popular. Some critics began asserting that to judge a musician solely on the basis of his national affiliation was absurd. In 1960, Michel de Villers claimed that listeners should stop comparing French jazz to American forms of the music. Instead, he argued, all jazz should be judged on an equal basis. He wrote, "The time has come to put an end to a myth: that of a French jazz different from the other which would be THE TRUE one. We only look for one thing: the quality of jazzmen, without passports" (capitalized text original).[71] In the early 1960s, critics like de Villers pushed listeners to move beyond national considerations and only evaluate musicians based on their art. Of course, successfully convincing jazz fans to do this would benefit French artists.

French jazzmen had been long concerned with the perceived favoritism audiences and employers gave to African Americans. The pianist Stéphane Mougin argued as early as 1932 that French cabaret and music hall owners preferred to hire black Americans over Frenchmen. Writing for the early jazz periodical *Jazz-Tango-Dancing*, he condemned the *Négromanie* that guaranteed respect and jobs for even "bad" black musicians at the expense of white French ones.[72] Jeffrey Jackson has pointed out that "Mougin's remarks constituted one of the first sustained and thoughtful arguments to separate the discussion of jazz music from the race of the performer." And Mougin's agenda had one purpose: to make audiences more receptive to French jazz musicians so that the latter could find work.[73]

Decades later, other observers argued that fans limited their aesthetic purview by not paying attention to the work of French musicians, some of whom, they contended, equaled American ones. In 1960, the critic Raymond Mouly maintained that

> if it is true that on the whole, jazz coming from the United States is superior to that which is played in France, it is also true that every curious fan, if he wanted to go through the trouble, could find among [French] nationals ten or twelve musicians capable of affecting him as much as the idols. It is stupid, under the pretext that these men are less numerous, to deprive them of being listened to.[74]

A year later, a reader of *Jazz Magazine* echoed Mouly, asking,

> Who would deny French jazz is of quality? What I want to say is that certain of our jazzmen are worth as much as their colleagues across the Atlantic. The population of young jazz fans is incapable of recognizing this objective fact. French jazz does not sell. . . . The still novice jazz fan will buy Monk exclusively, but the true music lover, he will buy Monk *and* Arvanitas *and* Solal. Something else is obvious: we don't talk enough about French jazzmen. I accidentally discovered Arvanitas listening to an advertised Kréma record: today this excellent pianist is an integral part of my collection.[75]

For this jazz fan, having a well-rounded appreciation for the music meant listening to more than Americans, and his record collection obviously included the works of both American and French performers. Like his contemporaries, this listener did not claim that French jazz was in any way superior to the American music, but that there were a certain number of French artists whose work deserved equal recognition and respect. Jazz enthusiasts seemed largely to be arguing the same thing: that American musicians were of course the most important actors on the jazz scene but that there were a number of French musicians who were just as creative, inventive, and talented who deserved the same measure of exposure.

In a 1960 issue of *Jazz Hip*, both musicians and critics acknowledged that national jazzmen faced a dismal state of affairs. The well-known saxophonist Guy Lafitte asserted, "If it is delicate to discuss the situation of jazz in France, it could become explosive to discuss the condition of the French jazz musician."[76] As a performer, Lafitte himself had to make a living within a form of art whose supporters frequently judged him and his fellow Frenchmen as minimally important. Not surprisingly, Lafitte and others like him chose to address the disquieting situation confronting them and the difficulties they faced in earning a living whether they were in Paris or the provinces. Because jazz musicians could not easily find employment, most of them (not unlike many of their American counterparts) had to find supplemental work, either outside of the world of music or in more popular "variety" bands or by performing abroad. In his *Jazz Magazine* column, Frank Ténot wrote that "men like Solal, Lafitte, Wilen, Urtreger, Arvanitas, Michelot, Guérin, Hausser, etc. wake each morning asking themselves if tomorrow they will be able to still get by remaining jazzmen. They don't ask for a lot: simply to earn a living without playing mambos or being forced to become expatriates."[77] Observers recognized that French jazz artists, in choosing their profession, met with difficult prospects, making it hard for them to support themselves. As a result of this situation, some began questioning the status quo and pushing record companies, the press, promoters, and fans to change their way of approaching and treating French jazzmen.

When addressing the circumstances of French musicians, commentators took frequent aim at record companies and their lack of promotions for these artists. By criticizing corporations, they bought into a top-down understanding of cultural dissemination, arguing that fans' musical ideas were strongly affected by advertisements and the availability of records in stores. A major problem with record companies, according to some, was that they promoted American records at the expense of French ones. In 1963, Roger Luccioni, a consistent advocate of French jazz, argued that "record companies mislead themselves when they sink sometimes considerable sums of money into their advertising campaigns to push records, sometimes second-rate American ones, and don't condescend to give one centime to first-rate French productions."[78] Some found the disparity between what record companies were willing to spend to promote American and French productions offending, and because of insufficient promotions, fans could not easily find access to recordings by French artists even if they made a point of looking for them. In all actuality, French jazz records did not sell well in comparison to their American equivalents. Most argued that this was not the fault of musicians or due to a general lack of talent, but was caused by the cumulative neglect of the recording industry, the lack of publicity by the press, and the limited opportunities for French musicians to perform live. Luccioni explained that French artists were also hurt by the high cost of records. He argued that "a fan who—we suppose—devotes 20 or 30 N.F. in his monthly budget for buying records, will prefer—and one cannot decently blame him—to buy himself an American product."[79]

Solutions to this problem were clearly not easy to come by. Of course, people urged record companies to alter their polices but these companies were not going to do so without some financial incentive. Because of the resulting predicament, some jazz enthusiasts looked to the government to initiate change. In 1965, Jef Gilson called for a legislative bill that would "make recordings producing less than a thousand copies exempt from the 'value added tax.' One could in this way facilitate the publishing of works reputed unsellable in spite of their notable cultural value and being otherwise proclaimed."[80] Gilson hoped that government officials could in this way subsidize "limited editions" of artistically important records, offering both publishing houses and musicians the opportunity to record their chosen works without exclusive concern for the bottom line. These subsidized records, Gilson hoped, would also improve people's opinions of French jazz by giving them easier access to the music. In the end, the government passed no legislation to help pay for the production of French jazz records. The government did take part in improving the situation for French musicians by sponsoring more jazz radio programming and concerts in the 1960s, and this effort increased in the subsequent decades. But the government took no active role in subsidizing jazz recordings.

Critics did not place all of the blame for the unpopularity of French musicians and the paucity of French jazz records on the record companies or lack of government aid. They also faulted jazz periodicals that did not devote adequate attention to French jazz. Roger Luccioni found fault with the specialized jazz press for its neglect of this music, asserting that "we think it's absolutely unfair that a large review devote more than a third of its pages to a John Coltrane and not one single line to French jazz."[81] Again, because critics believed that jazz fans were largely influenced by that to which they were exposed, they held that jazz magazines were harming the prospects of French musicians by not giving them coverage on their pages. Martial Solal argued that "when a jazz fan from the provinces opens a jazz magazine, he begins by believing what he reads inside."[82] Solal held that if the jazz press made no mention of French versions of the music, the fans would believe that only the American creations were worth considering or buying.

Some fans agreed with Solal and pressed jazz periodicals to devote less time to American news and more time to French musicians. *Jazz Hot* received a letter from a reader who wrote,

> That the Modern Jazz Quartet is playing in New York or Chicago does not interest me. And I would love to know who it does interest. On the other hand, a well established 'Jazz à la carte' for France and Europe, that surely interests all of your readers. In the same way I would love to find articles about and interviews with French and European jazzmen more frequently in your review.[83]

A *Jazz Magazine* reader sent a letter arguing a similar point, contending that

> the French public is without a doubt guilty of not being interested in its jazzmen. But who then keeps this public regularly informed on the life of national jazz, concerts of some French jazzman in Paris or in the provinces? Who gives reports on some orchestra after a gala, . . . a cabaret party? Such information is conspicuous by its rarity in your review. . . . Let's get going on a good cause, let's talk about Michel Attenoux, Hubert Fol, Guy Longnon, Gérard Badini, Claude Gousset, Maurice Martin and all the others . . . and don't forget to keep us informed on the next Antibes festival.[84]

Such reprimands revealed a growing frustration among fans about the inadequate recognition given to French jazz. Listeners who were interested in their fellow countrymen's music were the most likely to become advocates of French jazz. They had the ability to prod magazine editors, concert promoters, and record producers (precisely those individuals who had the most control over jazz's distribution and information networks in France) to give French musicians increased credit and exposure. These fans were not numerous or assertive enough to make the magazines change their format though. In 1963, Martial Solal wrote, "Never will the idea of doing a review entirely devoted to French jazz sell to [*Jazz Hot* and *Jazz Magazine*]."[85] Again, the problem of *selling* returned: news about American jazzmen simply moved more magazines.

Professional critics and the recording industry were at times closely aligned with one another, a situation which potentially reinforced French jazz's disadvantage. Roger Luccioni alleged that "the majority of the critics of the specialized French press are employed by a record firm."[86] Daniel Humair backed this assertion, writing, "We must not forget that the majority of critics are above all sellers of records."[87] Of course, not all prominent commentators had close allegiances with record companies, but whether they did or did not have economic and professional ties with this industry, they persuaded people to purchase or to not to purchase records in their articles and reviews. By not frequently writing about the recordings of French musicians, critics unquestionably contributed to poor sales. Unless listeners were particularly assertive in investigating French jazz, there was no easy means by which they could consistently learn about the music and its creators. So, in many ways, professional commentators and record companies were equally to blame for generating a discouraging atmosphere for French jazz musicians.

In the early 1960s, the popularity of both American and French jazz was threatened from yet another front: rock and roll's growing currency among the young. Young men in their teens and twenties were the most visible supporters of jazz because they were the most likely to be frequent concert-goers and record buyers. Observers felt that any infringement on jazz's popularity within this demographic group would be potentially harmful to jazz. And if jazz in general suffered, French jazz would be even more severely damaged. Jef Gilson took aim at "journalists who, addressing themselves to the young, create shameless propaganda for the most adulterated musical productions." He thought that this was "particularly serious" when it came to "ex-jazz fans trying to persuade themselves that remunerative actions in favor of yé-yé or neo yé-yé in the press and on the radio are well-founded."[88] Gilson called on the jazz press to do as much as it could to attract and retain readership by making writing more accessible and avoiding overly technical discussions and "incomprehensible *philosofofouillerie.*" In doing so and by publicizing the work of French artists, Gilson argued that French jazz periodicals could help keep jazz, and especially French jazz, alive. If French jazz was going to survive, new musicians had to continue to be advocates for the music's advancement, and this would be unlikely if, at the beginnings of their careers, artists had no hope of gaining support among fans.

THE STRUGGLE TO BE HEARD

When clubs did decide to hire jazz musicians, they often looked to Americans living in Paris like Sidney Bechet, Kenny Clarke, or Bud Powell. In order to stop this practice of hiring American jazzmen at the expense of

French ones, the musician Michel Hausser contended that fans must "shun certain Parisian jazz clubs which only hire American musicians, even if they are very mediocre, without a visa, without residence permits and especially without work permits! Will the authorities always close their eyes?" Hausser claimed that French musicians could contribute to the success of clubs, and that *caves* and cabarets need not depend on American musicians for financial reasons. He asserted, "A jazz club can very well stay alive with a French band. I have moreover proved it these last years with my band in transforming, with our music alone, a terrible bistro in the Latin Quarter into a respectable jazz club known today as far as the United States."[89] Protectionist impulses were long lasting in France, and French musicians had complained about foreign musicians putting them out of work as far back as the 1920s. When musicians like Hausser complained about losing jobs to American artists, they were reviving an old nativist move that pitted the French musician against foreign ones, even as jazz relied on a cosmopolitan identity for its very existence in France. Jazz was an imported music. Without the foreign, there would be no jazz.

From the late 1920s onward—as the use of the phonograph, the radio, and sound film expanded—musicians had been threatened by technology. One union in the interwar period, the Chambre Syndicale des Artistes Musiciens de Paris, had ordered members to refrain from playing in establishments that used radios, and the Syndicat des Musiciens de la Région Parisienne had asked patrons to avoid establishments that used record players.[90] Of course, as time wore on, cabarets and *caves* did not stop using these technologies, and a number of postwar observers claimed that French musicians were not given ample occasions to play their music live as bars, nightclubs, and cafés started to use jukeboxes and other types of recorded music.[91]

In the 1960s, supporters of live music began to notice an increasing preference among these establishments to use recorded music over live. In 1965, a writer for *Télé 7 Jours* noted this trend and wrote an article about the dangers created for French musicians by the increasing popularity of hi-fi stereos in public places and the prominence of foreign musicians. He claimed, "So, our artists are beginning to stop working. In ten years, how many French musicians will there be in France? The record and recorded music will prevent them from making a living. . . . We will give foreign artists acclaim. And we will say, with reason: 'The French are not musicians.'"[92] French jazzmen faced a number of substantial professional hurdles: they had few chances to perform in small public spaces like nightclubs; bar and restaurant owners at times discriminated against them by choosing to exclusively hire American musicians; and cheaper, recorded music began to replace live in these places, making it difficult to earn a living as a musician.

Concert performances did not offer French jazz artists sufficient public exposure either. Jazz concerts most frequently showcased American musicians, and when they did feature French ones, fans outside of Paris were rarely able to attend. Fans from the provinces repeatedly asked why more French jazzmen did not venture outside of Paris to perform. Responding to one such question, *Jazz Magazine* replied by asking, "How many towns in France are capable of organizing 600 people paying 500 francs to listen to a French jazz orchestra?"[93] When jazz enthusiasts wanted to go to French musicians' concerts, the majority did not have the money to buy expensive tickets and, as a result, these concerts frequently did not make a profit. Because concerts featuring French artists were both expensive and a financial risk for their organizers, few were arranged. The Paris-centered musicians also seemed unwilling to take full advantage of the provincial jazz fans who were an important base of potential support. These musicians preferred to perform in Paris or not at all, and provincial concert promoters opted to sponsor concerts featuring American artists because they were both less expensive to produce and more likely to attract a large audience.

In addition to these challenges, labor conflicts also harmed French jazz by making reciprocally-beneficial relationships difficult or impossible to maintain between musicians and their employers. Roger Luccioni explored this destructive disharmony between "employer" and "employee," defining "the employer" as "the head of a cabaret, the director of a music label, the organizer of concerts or the producer of a radio program. The employee is obviously the musician." He maintained that conflicts between the two groups damaged French jazz. Regarding "the employee," he argued that

> certain musicians who, in surrendering their gifts to a way of life frequently reprehensible, forget all professional integrity, don't honor their contracts, demand salaries that are clearly not in touch with their "commercial" value, and who further will sabotage work by accepting a wage "of poverty." We will not even dwell on certain good practices, such as the systematic and collective disparagement of colleagues.[94]

In Luccioni's opinion, employers were also guilty of not always acting in the best interest of the music. He asserted that many employers engaged in the same negative practices as musicians, but

> seem to be more to blame in the actual situation. How many are they, in effect, these heads of cabarets who, in obviously serving themselves break the laws of July 1901 on associations, call their "den" a "private club," excusing themselves in this way from costly expenses which have a name: Social Security, Performance Permit, Copyright . . . and even the minimum necessary contract whose SOLE beneficiary is the musician, who is then *exploited*. [italics original][95]

Like other labor conflicts, this one concerned pay, contracts, and professional respect. Musicians and employers who did not honor their agreements caused tensions within the jazz community. Because nontraditional lifestyles at times defined the jazz scene, strained relationships could obviously be exacerbated through alcohol or drug use or opposing value systems. Musicians could either demand too much money or work for too little, damaging their prospects of ever earning a living wage, while employers could "exploit" musicians by not paying social security taxes or honoring copyright laws. French jazz suffered because of its limited means to public exposure, and conflicts between musicians and those with the ability to hire them only further damaged the music's potential to succeed in the domestic market.

Due to the unfortunate situation caused by these various circumstances—the lack of publicity by record companies and the press, the scarce opportunities for musicians to perform live, the divisions within the French jazz community—some supporters of French jazz looked to fans as a possible solution. Observers were quick to note that the public, in general, did not give enough support to French artists, but they also felt that fans could change. Frank Ténot called upon these fans to help French jazzmen, telling them,

> It is up to you, dear readers, to help your compatriots who have chosen jazz as their profession to succeed completely. It is up to the public to free our artists from material predicaments, to encourage publishing firms and nightclub owners to hire our groups exclusively for jazz. It is only under these conditions that jazz will become prosperous here. . . . As for American musicians, a large part of their comfort and ease comes precisely from the fact that they have the opportunity to play regularly for a large public.[96]

Professional critics were not the only ones to recognize the potential power of fans to help French musicians become successful. An amateur enthusiast from the provincial town of Dieppe called on fans to rally around their fellow countrymen, writing, "The value of French jazz is not appreciated fairly in France. Records made in Paris sell badly and all our musicians are not esteemed by their own compatriots as they should be. We must help them."[97] In the end, the popularity of French jazz rested in the hands of young people who chose to pay for concerts and other live performances, and to buy records and magazines—or not.

Notwithstanding the distressing circumstances in which French musicians often lived and performed, members of the jazz community did at times recognize these artists for their musical talents. And although their music frequently met with a lack of commercial, popular, and professional success, critics, fans, and their fellow musicians could value these artists for aesthetic reasons. By the early 1960s, critics routinely noted the musical acumen of French jazzmen, despite the less than perfect conditions under which they often performed. In 1960, the record company Fontana released a new album *Jazz et Jazz* which had been recorded entirely in Paris. André Hodeir composed the music for the project; the performing artists were Kenny Clarke, Martial Solal, Raymond Guiot, Christian Legrand, and the Jazz Groupe de Paris with Roger Guérin and Pierre Michelot.[98] Because Fontana had produced, recorded, and released *Jazz et Jazz* in France, and because the artists who had participated in its creation were, with the exception of Kenny Clarke, exclusively French, the album was significant in expressing and shaping ideas about French jazz. Due to the constant comparisons that jazz fans made between French and American music, the jazz community had to address *Jazz et Jazz*'s relationship to music coming from the United States. The consensus among critics was that Hodeir's music was quite distinct from American jazz, as well as from imitative French creations that largely mirrored the sounds coming from the United States. The critic Nicole Hirsch went further than most and proclaimed Hodeir's music *more* varied and original than some products of American jazz, maintaining that "the record does not give an impression of monotony as is frequently the case with American productions."[99] Similarly, Aris Destombes also embraced the uniqueness of *Jazz et Jazz*, arguing that the album created a French space in jazz, differentiating it from other products of French musicians whose dialog was with universal or American jazz, not a French jazz. He claimed that "in my mind [the album] seizes the place of typically French productions, as opposed to that which is made by French soloists who express, with their temperament, universal jazz."[100] In their reactions to Hodeir's album, these critics expressed how interest in French jazz remained alive in the early 1960s. Beyond Django, this album showed fans the possibility of creating and nurturing jazz sounds that they as Frenchmen could call their own.

In another example of French jazz receiving positive critical acclaim, in 1962, *Jazz Magazine* reported a May 3rd Martial Solal, Guy Pedersen, and Daniel Humair concert at the Salle Gaveau. The periodical's correspondent contended that these musicians had proven through their performance that French jazz could rival American music in quality and importance. He went on to say that the concert's music was "a cruel disproof to jazz lovers of our country, jazz lovers too inclined not to appreciate anything but American jazz." Solal, Pedersen, and Humair's talent, in this writer's mind, also served as "a caustic lesson to certain French musicians who, to satisfy I don't know what masochism, take pleasure in mediocrity, stemming from powerlessness or laziness, all in denouncing with virulence the injustices of which they are the victims." In essence, this critic asserted that Solal, Pedersen, and Humair communicated a certain agency through their music that disrupted stereotypes about both French music and musicians, stereotypes that characterized them as victims of American superiority and other unfortunate situations. He went on to say,

> Rather than wallow in a neglect of tired heroes, Solal, Pedersen and Humair wanted to show that jazz was not any longer the exclusive property of some people born on the other side of the Atlantic. In this respect, the concert came to confirm what the record had already approved: the trio asserts itself as one of the best small formations that jazz has known.[101]

Despite the difficulties French jazz artists faced, members of the jazz public did periodically acknowledge their aesthetic achievements and were even occasionally willing to place French and American musicians on the same artistic plane. These were no small achievements for French jazzmen, but they would have to continue pushing for recognition, record contracts, and opportunities to perform in a world that continued to prefer musicians from the United States.

BUILDING A REPUTATION AND A UNION

As their professional work started to gain a measure of respect, French musicians worked to secure their own well-being by establishing a union in the mid-1960s to represent their interests. Through their actions, French jazzmen made it clear that they saw themselves as active and relevant participants in the national culture who deserved fair compensation and work conditions.

The union created by French jazzmen in the mid-1960s resulted from a decades-long initiative by orchestra and music hall musicians and, finally, jazz leaders. The government had enacted various laws since the 1930s to protect French musicians from foreign competition. In 1933, authorities put a law into place that established a ten-to-one ratio between French and foreign performers.[102] Three years later, in 1936, legislators allowed 30 percent of cabaret musicians to be foreign. Members of the French government were motivated to create such legislation because of the economic crisis and the severe unemployment caused by the Great Depression. At this time, French politicians were more than eager to protect native artists from their American and European competition, and several years later the law was made even more restrictive when foreign musicians were limited to 10 percent of a cabaret's musical workforce.[103] During World War II, the situation changed once again to favor French nationals over noncitizens. French performers benefited from the paucity of foreign artists, as Americans, Jews, and anyone affiliated with the Allies were legally excluded from playing music in Occupied France.

After the war, French policymakers made it easier for the first time in decades for foreign musicians to enter the country. The ordinance of November 2, 1945, allowed these artists to come to France as tourists (like any other foreign visitors) on a simple *permis de séjour temporaire*. Once in the country, they could then find work beyond legal channels without obtaining an official work permit. Some French musicians, who had enjoyed having a monopoly on the musical market during the war, were troubled that nonnatives were given easy admission into France and then employed by opportunistic nightclub owners. Even if American and European musicians chose to seek out legal work permits, immigration law at this time did not make distinctions among different professional categories and because of this, musicians were regulated by the same rules as all other workers. In these early postwar years, French audiences were hungry to hear the new musical sounds coming from America and the owners of cabarets and *caves* were more than willing to accommodate their patrons. Quite simply, hiring American musicians was good for business, and French performers were negatively impacted by this reality. As a result, in 1946, a group representing dance orchestras—some of whom were jazz musicians—asked the Ministère du Travail to limit the number of visas given to foreign artists, but the government took no action. In the summer of that year, a cohort of orchestra leaders agreed to no longer hire foreign musicians or French musicians who worked with foreigners.[104]

These 1946 actions were not the first efforts at organization to impact French jazz. A year earlier, in 1945, a number of musicians had created the Groupement Professionnel des Musiciens (GPM) du Hot Club de France. The *Bulletin du Hot Club de France* strove to make its readership aware of the obstacles French musicians faced. A writer for the periodical stressed that these artists decided to organize because they had been "hit by the suppression of dance music, exploited by unscrupulous organizers, ignored by Radiodiffusion Française, their rights threatened (rights won through talent and years of work and struggle) by anonymous newcomers without any professional worth, but supplied with capital or 'protections.'"[105] With the support of the Syndicat des Artistes Musiciens de Paris (SAMuP), this professional group sought both to establish and to reinforce solidarity among French jazz musicians. At their first meeting on February 28, 1945, Alex Renard, Alix Combelle, Michel Warlop, André Ekyan, Jerry Mengo, Claude Laurence, Charles Hary, and others "examined their work conditions in establishments, their participation in galas, and their relationship with Radiodiffusion Française."[106] The GPM pledged to organize its own events where French musicians could perform and refused to cooperate with Radiodiffusion Française unless this state organization changed its treatment of French musicians. Lastly, the GPM decided to take "social measures to assure musicians and their families against accidents or old age" and considered creating "relief and individual insurance funds."[107] With goals like improving French musicians' working conditions, increasing their public exposure, and creating a safety net for them, it is somewhat surprising that this group did not become influential among French jazzmen. Its strong affiliation with the Hot Club de France undoubtedly hurt its long-term potential. The *Bulletin du Hot*

Club de France was the official mouthpiece of the GPM and over the next several years, at a time when Hugues Panassié was increasingly distancing himself from the rest of French jazz professionals, the GPM's ability to spread its message to a varied audience certainly suffered. The GPM also chose a problematic time to come into being. Its members were mostly musicians who had been popular before and during the war and who continued to play traditional forms of jazz. In 1945, jazz fans were interested in the new sounds of bebop and in learning about the latest musical innovations coming from the United States from which they had been cut off for four years. This period was one of the most difficult for French jazzmen, making many of the GPM's goals unattainable. Cabaret owners, concert promoters, critics, and fans were generally not interested at this point in taking up the cause of French jazz. In the end, the GPM simply did not have the leverage it needed for bargaining power.

Employment prospects for French jazz musicians were limited by unions and labor laws in other countries like England, Belgium, and the United States that regulated the number of work permits granted to foreign musicians. This made it difficult for French performers to find legal employment abroad, when foreign jazzmen allegedly found rather easy employment in France. In 1955, the periodical *Arts* published an article claiming that

> several dozen foreign musicians without any originality have established themselves in France even though unions in other countries refuse work permits to French instrumentalists: Alix Combel and Fred Adison have not gotten work permits in Belgium even though the Belgian orchestra of Eddie de Latte appears at the Palais d'Hiver in Lyon. And yet, a union for French musicians exists.[108]

The GPM had fallen into obscurity by 1955, but the Syndicat des Artistes Musiciens de Paris (SAMuP) had not. Jazzmen had to compete with American musicians far more than most French performers, but their voice within the SAMuP was not loud enough to alter union initiatives. Eventually, jazzmen had to create their own distinct branch of the SAMuP to defend themselves.

A writer for the periodical *Télé 7 jours*, Georges Hilleret, claimed that "French musicians are too few in number to defend themselves effectively," while in other countries like Great Britain, the United States, and Canada, musicians were better treated. He wrote,

> The BBC simply does not allow the playback, except, for example, when an artist must sing and dance at the same time. . . . In the United States and Canada, unions for musicians are very powerful. They have obtained conditions that the French can only dream about: for example, an owner of a cabaret who uses nothing but records is required to hire a certain number of musi-

cians . . . even if he does not need them. On TV, the playback virtually does not exist, simply because it takes work away from musicians. . . . In addition, the defense of Anglo-Saxon musicians [in Great Britain] is fierce in regard to foreigners.[109]

Like many of his French contemporaries, Hilleret purported that French musicians fared badly when compared to artists working in other European or American countries, and he endorsed creating stronger union representation for them. He did not like that France welcomed "everyone" and that French musicians then had to compete with foreign musicians who did not pay taxes.[110]

As a result of this growing dissatisfaction with work conditions, in late 1965, French jazz musicians created the Syndicat des Artistes Musiciens de Jazz.[111] The official announcement of this new organization read as follows:

> Tuesday, October 26, the "Artistes Musiciens de jazz" of French nationality formed a union division affiliated with the Syndicat des Artistes Musiciens de Paris. It is a date that one could qualify as "historic" since jazz musicians have never had an official organization to represent them.[112]

Not surprisingly, this new union chose to not recognize its precursor, the GPM, but claimed to be the first such representative organization for French jazz musicians. The union's inaugural meeting had twenty-five musicians in attendance, while ten others had given their vote in absentia to all unanimous decisions. Michel Hausser and Guy Lafitte oversaw the majority of this first meeting and remained important spokesmen for the union over the next several years. The musicians in attendance elected Hausser as president and Lafitte as vice president. Stéphane Grappelli, Maxim Saury, Jean Tordo, Dominique Chanson, and René Urtreger were among the chosen union officers, and the elected substitutes for these last representatives included Jean-Luc Ponty, Roger Guérin, Claude Guilhot, Jean-Pierre Sasson, Yvan Julien, and Jacky Sanson. *Jazz Hot* wrote that the union's "defined program is rather simple but very vast: to defend the profession against all abuse (in particular, the control of foreign labor); the organization of the profession; close contact between the organization and concert producers, cabaret directors, business managers, the specialized press, etc."[113] The new union immediately sent a letter addressed to "Sirs, Directors of Cabarets or the Entrepreneurs of Shows, Galas, or Concerts, employing jazz musicians," which stated,

> One of our first objectives being to make people respect the decree of March 13, 1933, concerning the employment of foreign musicians, we request permission to watch over your establishment, or events of which you are the organizer, to observe the application of this decree; this with a *constructive* goal—to finally permit each of us to exercise with dignity his profession and

to avoid in this way the intervention of the public authorities that the Syndicat des Artistes Musiciens would be obliged to alert in case of an infraction.[114]

These musicians acknowledged their respect for American musicians such as Bill Coleman, Jimmy Gourley, and Kenny Clarke who lived in France at the time, but they wanted to protect themselves from the further encroachment of non-French musicians into the limited jazz market. They also did not want to be forced to play yé-yé or variety music to earn a living. To protect the modest number of jobs available to them, these artists decided to go after foreign musicians who threatened their work, electing to use the law which had been signed by President Albert Lebrun in 1933 stipulating that the ratio between French and foreign musicians had to be ten to one.[115] Hausser and Lafitte argued, "We equally hold on to having control over jazz clubs' programs, in order to avoid . . . seeing on a Club's poster 1 French musician for 10 foreigners, something unthinkable in any other country."[116] In order to control the number of nonnationals, the union lobbied to influence the Minister of Labor's decision to grant work permits to new arrivals. Hausser and Lafitte wanted to have the minister take into consideration the union's opinion on each new foreign musician before conferring a work permit.[117]

The actions of the section Syndicale des Artistes Musiciens de Jazz created controversy on both sides of the Atlantic. In late 1965, the *New York Herald Tribune* published an article entitled "Paris Musicians Seek Jobs of American Jazzmen" that criticized the union, claiming that the group's actions were specifically aimed at African Americans. Hausser and Lafitte responded to this article with a letter to the newspaper in which they asserted, "Our principal goal is not to get rid of American musicians, be they black or white, but to regulate, because of intense unemployment, the arrival of new foreign musicians, from wherever they come, on the Parisian jazz scene."[118] Hausser and Lafitte argued that they wanted to help Americans already playing in France legalize their status by getting them the proper work permits, not to destroy their chances for employment. Their main agenda was to control the number of new foreigners coming into the country so that French jazzmen did not lose their ability to find work.

Some participants in the French jazz public responded negatively to the union's goals and activities. The owners of jazz clubs and cabarets, of course, had mixed reactions to the new group. Michel Hausser admitted that "we have been able to make ourselves heard with certain bosses but others have given us the deaf ear in slandering us." Obviously, club owners felt that their business would be threatened if they could not consistently hire the musicians who made them the most money. Generally, these musicians tended to be American, but clubs also depended on the labor of musicians from other European countries like England, Sweden, Holland, and Belgium. Club owners who chose not to cooperate with the Syndicat des Artistes Musiciens de

Jazz damaged the union's ability to succeed. As a result, the union tried to express its sympathy for these individuals and to blame their difficult circumstances on the government, not on musician-inspired initiatives. Hausser argued that "the situation of a jazz club in France is terribly precarious and that has nothing to do with the action of the union but only with the numerous charges and taxes that it must pay."[119] As a result, the union also tried, however unsuccessfully, to change the fees and taxes levied by the government on these venues.

The cartoonist Siné was firmly opposed to the union and actually quit his job writing for *Jazz Hot* in October of 1966 because he disagreed with the magazine's support for the organization.[120] He maintained that the only criteria by which he wanted a musician's worth judged was aesthetic: whether he wanted to hear him play or not. He also thought that the union's activities were going to keep the better jazzmen from being heard in France. He explained to members of the union that

> jazz is the art of Afro-Americans and I think that no one here contests their supremacy. If certain Frenchmen succeed in this art, it is very much due to them, whom you have pillaged, plagiarized, imitated, or from whom you have been inspired. So please be more modest and less ungrateful. And it is you or at least some among you—because *I know at least a dozen French musicians, and not the most mediocre, who are against your union which is not representative*—who want to gag American jazz in France!" [italics original][121]

Lucien Malson also had problems with the union's desired control over who was heard in France and who was not, but he expressed his dissatisfaction in a more delicate way, asserting, "I do not believe that we have to impose someone's presence on listeners if they have not spontaneously wanted it, even if, objectively, they are wrong or if they are being cheated. Art does not have frontiers."[122] Siné and Malson both endorsed the right of jazz audiences to freely choose the live music they wanted to hear, regardless of the performing musician's national affiliation. An executive for Polydor records, André Poulain, opposed the union as well and asserted in 1966, "I am not so supportive of the French jazz musicians' union. A Solal, a Gilson, a Chautemps, do not need barriers to assert themselves, and I will also cite Humair, Arvanitas, the Double Six, Jean-Luc Ponty."[123] All of these commentators claimed that exceptional French musicians would be heard without the union resorting to legal actions against foreign musicians. They also feared that the union was curtailing freedom of expression in France by lobbying to make it difficult for foreign musicians to practice their art.

At times, jazz artists themselves dissented with the goals and opinions of the union. In 1968, in the atmosphere of the May upheavals and strikes, a number of anonymous musicians broke from the larger Syndicat des Artistes

Musiciens de Paris (SAMuP), claiming the group collaborated with the Gaullist government and had objectives at odds with their own. Representing Parisian musicians in general (not just jazz musicians), the SAMuP had lobbied de Gaulle's government since 1965 for concessions like wage increases, higher taxes on theaters using recorded music, and tax rebates for establishments that employed musicians. This Parisian group also thought that the government should create a professional license for performers. In a 1965 letter to de Gaulle, the SAMuP had decried the foreign and amateur competition professional musicians faced, saying, "Whereas other countries defend their musicians by every means, and practically forbid the entry of foreign labor, France opens wide its arms even to countries that turn away French orchestras."[124] Importantly, the SAMuP primarily represented classical musicians and music hall entertainers who wanted to protect their livelihoods from the encroachment of technology, non-French musicians, and new genres like rock and roll. The SAMuP did represent the interests of jazz musicians in this regard, especially those who played in the popular New Orleans style in traditional French performance spaces, but it was not overly interested in embracing new musics. Even though the SAMuP created a new branch devoted to rock as a result of May–June 1968, that "pop" division never received much support from the parent union in later years, and genres like free jazz were largely neglected.[125]

In 1968, during the musicians' strike, a number of these performers, including jazzmen, formed a radical protest group named Action Musique. Significantly, free jazz musicians made up the core of this new collaborative and they strongly opposed the policies advocated by Michel Hausser who was still the president of the jazz sector of the SAMuP. Action Musique explicitly opposed the use of a professional card because it was "a measure of segregation harmful to amateur and foreign musicians." The group welcomed all musicians—professional, amateur, and foreign—to practice their art.[126] Leaders of the group refused to define the boundaries of their music through professional licensing and did not want any part of a situation in which a government or a union dictated who could perform in public venues. For them, the professional card would be used as a tool of repression by the powers that be. Because many of the Action Musique participants were free jazz musicians whose artistic merit had already been called into question because of the avant-garde nature of their compositions, they were intent on protecting their freedom to choose how, when, and where to play their music for compensation.[127]

Action Musique also criticized the SAMuP for lobbying de Gaulle's government, which it had been doing since 1965. The organizers of Action Musique believed that negotiating with the Fifth Republic was unacceptable because doing so fostered the sense that de Gaulle's rule was legitimate. SAMuP leaders had attempted to hold a meeting with Minister of Cultural

Affairs André Malreaux on May 30, and in the process had engaged in discussions with his deputies. Even though the meeting with Malraux never happened, members of Action Musique saw this as undercutting the musicians' strike and as a blatant dismissal of the plight of other striking workers. This radical group claimed that the strike should recognize "the role of the musician in a capitalist society, where culture is an agent of the dominant class." Instead, they saw union leadership playing a power game with a government of which they disproved.[128] In their opinion, no compromises should be made in the interest of improving musicians' short-term circumstances at the expense of far-reaching social change.[129]

Later in 1968, another faction of dissenting jazzmen formed the Fédération des Musiciens de Jazz en France that—in line with Action Musique's goals—invited all jazz musicians in France, whether they be professional or amateurs, French or foreign, to join their organization. According to the magazine *Actuel*, the Fédération would provide publicity for its members through such mediums as posters, radio and television appearances, and would send promotional materials to "universities, theaters, maisons des jeunes, maisons de la culture, radio and television stations, festivals, town halls, etc., as well as to corresponding foreign organizations." In addition, the organization would provide members with rehearsal spaces and facilitate meetings between musicians and non-musicians.[130] The Fédération's goal was to establish a less-exclusionary organization to which jazzmen in France (not necessarily just French musicians) could belong. Instead of promoting itself as an enforcer of legislation and defender of French jazz, this group based its activities at the grassroots level, encouraging better relationships between musicians and their audiences as well as providing performance venues and marketing materials to members. Despite the higher visibility of the Syndicat des Artistes Musiciens de Jazz, some musicians dissented with its aims and chose to join other organizations that disrupted decades-old ideas about the legitimacy of musicians based on their passports, professional credentials, or conventional musical focus.

The creation of the Syndicat des Artistes Musiciens de Jazz showed the desire among French jazzmen to be recognized by their countrymen, but it also illustrated these musicians' expectation to be shown preferential treatment by club owners, concert promoters, the government, and fans solely because of their nationality. The union's members certainly saw themselves as legitimate jazz musicians with a *right* to be heard over foreigners in France. National identity interestingly played a very strong role in the union's arguments and goals. Because labor laws in the United States and much of Europe inhibited French jazzmen's ability to play beyond the boundaries of the hexagon, musicians like Hausser and Lafitte argued that France should use similar exclusionary laws to protect its own national musicians. They maintained that French jazzmen deserved both artistic recognition and adequate paychecks for their work. The creation of the Syndicat des Artistes Musiciens de Jazz illustrated that some of these musicians were willing to organize and to lobby the government to protect their music and their livelihoods. The union's foundation depended on its leading members having a clear conception of French jazz, on them tying their own fortunes to this music, and on them wanting to publicly defend it. Like the rest of the jazz community, their definition of French jazz was simple, yet it required that the music be played not only by French-speaking musicians, but by French citizens.

French jazzmen started off at a disadvantage when compared to their better-respected and better-known American colleagues. Because jazz was originally an African-American music, French audiences were more likely to buy tickets and records if the artist was American, and despite a growing multiplicity of jazz genres in the postwar period—ranging from New Orleans and bebop to cool and free jazz—French jazz did not come to signify its own aesthetic category by the end of the 1960s. Instead, musical innovation in jazz tended to unfold in the United States and then to migrate to other places around the globe. In France, Django Reinhardt disrupted this rule, as his inventiveness and idiosyncratic style earned him an international reputation before his death in 1953. For decades afterwards, the French jazz public used Reinhardt's example in defining and promoting French jazz, but the classification only meant jazz as played by French and French-speaking musicians. Earning a living was difficult for all jazz artists, whether black or white, American or European, and French musicians certainly did not find easy employment or publicity in their own country. French critics, record company executives, and concert promoters favored American artists over their fellow countrymen, and fans tended to follow along. French jazz's success, or lack of it, was caused by a number of different factors, which in the end either encouraged or dissuaded fans from buying French. Despite these multiple impediments, French jazz artists remained devoted to the music and continued to be vocal advocates for *le jazz français*. A lucky few of them were even able to attain professional success and recognition at home and abroad, achieving an important level of notoriety among their contemporaries.

NOTES

1. Michel de Villers, "Ce qu'ils en pensent," *Jazz Hip* 22 (rentrée 1960), 19.
2. Andre Persiany, "Ce qu'ils en pensent," *Jazz Hip* 22 (rentrée 1960), 17; and de Villers, "Ce qu'ils en pensent," 17–18.
3. Charles Delaunay, "Ce qu'ils en pensent," *Jazz Hip* 22 (rentrée 1960), 11.
4. Jef Gilson, "Le jazz français, mythe ou réalité" *Les Cahiers du Jazz* 11 (third trimester 1965), 3.
5. Ibid.

6. Jean Wagner, "Le jazz français? Rien que des musiciens . . ." *Les Cahiers du Jazz* 11 (third trimester, 1965).

7. Philip C. Naylor, *France and Algeria: A History of Decolonization and Transformation* (Gainesville: University of Florida Press, 2000), 14; Robert Aldrich, *Greater France: A History of French Overseas Expansion* (London: Macmillan Press, 1996), 123. Driving this point home, the *pied-noir* Albert Camus famously claimed, "The French of Algeria are a bastard race, made up of unforeseen mixtures. Spaniards and Alsatians, Italians, Maltese, Jews, and Greeks have come together there." Albert Camus, *Selected Essays and Notebooks*, ed. and trans. Philip Thody (Harmondsworth, UK: Penguin, 1979), 133.

8. Solal also had a Jewish father, something that excluded him from school in wartime Algiers when Nazi race laws extended to the colonies of Occupied France. John Fordham, "Piano Legend Martial Solal on Jazz, France and Godard," *The Guardian*, May 20, 2010, accessed January 3, 2013. http://www.guardian.co.uk/music/2010/may/20/martial-solal-jazz-piano.

9. Ludovic Tournès, *New Orleans sur Seine: Histoire du jazz en France* (Paris: Fayard, 1999), 223.

10. Philippe Carles and Jean-Louis Comolli, "10eme anniversaire: l'époque de la renaissance," *Jazz Magazine* 113 (December 1964), 88.

11. Tom Perchard, "Chapter 6: Looking for Something We Don't Yet Know: Towards a French Jazz," *After Django: Making Jazz in Postwar France* (Ann Arbor: University of Michigan Press, 2015), 190–233. Also see Jean-Dominique Brierre, *Le Jazz français de 1900 à aujourd'hui* (Paris: Éditions Hors Collection, 2000); and Philippe Coulangeon, *Les Musiciens de jazz en France* (Paris: L'Harmattan, 1999).

12. Michael Dregni, *Django: The Life and Music of a Gypsy Legend* (Oxford: Oxford University Press, 2004), 66. For more on the details of Reinhardt's biography, see Benjamin Givan, *The Music of Django Reinhardt* (Ann Arbor: University of Michigan Press, 2010); Michael Dregni, *Django Reinhardt and the Illustrated History of Gypsy Jazz* (Denver, CO: Speck Press, 2006); and Paul Balmer, *Stéphane Grappelli: With and Without Django* (London: Sanctuary, 2003).

13. Dregni, *Django: The Life*, 48.

14. Ibid., 49.

15. Charles Delaunay, *Django Reinhardt*, trans. Michael James (New York: Da Capo Press, 1982), 71. This Da Capo edition was an unabridged republication of the first edition published in London in 1961. It was later published in French under the title *Django mon frère*.

16. Other musicians also joined the Quintette: Pierre Fouad (on drums), Pierre Ferret (on guitar), and Emmanuel Soudieux (on bass).

17. Other musicians who played in Reinhardt's quintet over the years: Pierre Ferret (on guitar) and Emmanuel Soudieux (on bass).

18. Donald Kenrick and Grattan Puxon, *The Destiny of Europe's Gypsies* (New York: Basic Books, 1972).

19. Shannon L. Fogg, *The Politics of Everyday Life in Vichy France: Foreigners, Undesirables, and Strangers* (New York: Cambridge University Press, 2009), 86, 88, 93.

20. Delaunay, *Django Reinhardt*, 32.

21. Ibid., 37–38.

22. Ibid., 27, 64.

23. Gérard Legrand, *Puissances du jazz* (Paris: Arcances, 1953), 115.

24. Hugues Panassié, "Cinq grandes figures du jazz français," *Bulletin du Hot Club de France* (1945), 8.

25. Jef Gilson, "A propos de 'Jazz et Jazz,'" *Jazz Hot* 163 (March 1961), 17.

26. Frank Ténot, "Django Reinhardt," *Le Jazz*, eds. Frank Ténot and Philippe Carles (Paris: Librairie Larousse, 1977), 141.

27. Frank Ténot, "Reinhardt 'Django,'" *Dictionnaire du jazz*, eds. Philippe Carles, André Clergeat, and Jean-Louis Comolli (Paris: Robert Laffont, 1988), 853.

28. Michel-Claude Jalard, "Django et l'école tsigane du jazz," *Les Cahiers du jazz* 1 (fourth trimester 1959), 55–56.

29. Ibid., 58.

30. Ibid., 64.
31. Ibid., 73.
32. Alix Combelle, "En pensait à Django," *Bulletin du Hot Club de France* 38 (May 1954), 3.
33. Alain Balalas, "Django Reinhardt," *Bulletin du Hot Club de France* 178 (May–June 1968), 8.
34. Pierre Drouin, "'Expressions de jazz' au théâtre des Champs-Elysées," *Le Monde* (26 December 1950), 6.
35. Boris Vian, "Hommage à Django Reinhardt," *Arts* (9–15 June 1954), 3.
36. Hugues Panassié, "Cinq grandes figures du jazz français," *Bulletin du Hot Club de France* (1945), 8.
37. Ibid.
38. Hugues Panassié, "Django Reinhardt est mort," *Bulletin du Hot Club de France* 29 (June–July 1953), 7.
39. Claude Samuel, *Panorama de l'art musical contemporain* (Paris: Éditions Gallimard, 1962), 167.
40. Michel de Villers, "Spécial Jazz," *Arts* (23–9 March 1960), 14.
41. Jacques Gaspard, "Un blues gitan," *Jazz Hot* 187 (May 1963), 26.
42. Ibid., 27.
43. Philippe Adler, "Vive Boulou! Mesdames et Messieurs faits gaffe à Boulou!" *Jazz Hot* 207 (March 1965), 12.
44. Michel-Claude Jalard, "De Django et de divers," *Diaspason* no. 131 (December 1968), 56.
45. Jean Wagner, *Le guide du jazz* (Paris: Syros, 1986), 99; and Jean-Dominique Brierre, *Le jazz français de 1900 à aujourd'hui* (Paris: Éditions Hors Collection, 2000), 37.
46. Boris Vian, "Hommage à Django Reinhardt," *Arts* (9–15 June 1954), 3.
47. Bernard Courouble, "Première mondiale du film de Paul Paviot: 'Django Reinhardt,'" *Jazz [Hip]* 6 (May 1958), 14.
48. "Flashes," *Jazz Magazine* 48 (May 1959), 11. The other musicians were Géo Daly, Raymond Le Sénéchal, Paul Piguillem, Marcel Dutrieux, and Jean-Louis Viale. The concert was officially called the IVe Nuit du Jazz.
49. *Jazz Hot* 187 (May 1963).
50. Aris Destombes, "Hommage à Django Reinhardt," *Jazz Hot* 186 (April 1963), 16.
51. Jacques Lefebvre, "Festival Django Reihardt," *Jazz Magazine* 101 (December 1963), 21.
52. Maurice-Louis Blanc, "A propos de Django," *Jazz Magazine* 156–7 (July–August 1968), 13. The musicians who performed in this concert included Stéphane Grappelli, Raymond Fol, Joseph and Babik Reinhardt, Eugène Vées and his sons, Jean-Claude Naude's orchestra, les Guitars Unlimited, Claude Nougaro, Emile Carrara, Lous Vola, André Ekyan, Claude Guilhot, Dany Doriz, Hal Singer, Georges Arvanitas, Jacky Samson, Heinz Shäfer, Maurice Vander, Aldo Romano, Jean Bonal, Philippe Nedjar, and Eddy Louis.
53. Frank Ténot, "Reinhardt 'Django,'" *Dictionnaire du jazz*, eds. Philippe Carles, André Clergeat, and Jean-Louis Comolli (Paris: Robert Laffont, 1988), 852. For information on the current festival, see "Festival Django Reinhardt," http://www.festivaldjangoreinhardt.com/.
54. Pierre Bompar, "Django Reinhardt," *Jazz Bulletin* 14 (May 1957), 3.
55. Madeleine Gautier, "Django," *Bulletin du Hot Club de France* 128 (May–June 1963), 1.
56. See Yves Salgues, "La légende de Django Reinhardt," *Jazz Magazine* 33 (January 1958), 19–23; 34 (February 1958), 29–33; 35 (March 1958), 26–29, 45; 36 (April 1958), 25–27, 42; 37 (May 1958), 28–29, 41–42; 38 (June 1958), 26–27, 38; 39 (July 1958), 32–33, 42; 40 (August–September 1958), 28–30; and 41 (October 1958), 31–33.
57. Demètre Ioakimidis, "Django Reinhardt," *Jazz Hot* 175 (April 1962), 8.
58. Daniel Humair, "Un blues gitan," *Jazz Hot* 187 (May 1963), 27.
59. Jean Wagner, "Le jazz français? Rien que des musiciens . . ." *Les Cahiers du Jazz* 11 (third trimester, 1965), 7.
60. Jean Wagner, *Le guide du jazz* (Paris: Syros, 1986), 219.

61. George E. Lewis, *A Power Stronger than Itself: The AACM and American Experimental Music* (Chicago: University of Chicago Press, 2008), 247.
62. François Mallet, "Jean-Claude Fohrenbach au Tabou," *L'Express* (13 February 1956), 12.
63. Lucien Malson, "Le Jazz: Un espoir: Jeanneau," *Arts* (16–22 March 1960), 6.
64. Michel de Villers, "Courrier des lecteurs," *Jazz Hot* 164 (April 1961), 6.
65. Frank Ténot, "Les pieds dans le plat," *Jazz Magazine* 40 (August–September 1958), 13.
66. Marcel Zanini, "Ce qu'ils en pensent," *Jazz Hip* 22 (rentrée 1960), 16.
67. Martial Solal, "Table Ronde: le jazz français et ses problèmes," *Jazz Hip* 32 (Easter 1963), 12.
68. Jeff Gilson, "Cher Frère Jazz: Pour le jazz français," *Jazz Magazine* 60 (June 1960), 5.
69. Catherine Pierre, "Le Jazz: en attendant Django," *Le Monde* (20 December 1961), 17.
70. Jeff Gilson, "Cher Frère Jazz," 5.
71. Michel de Villers, "Ce qu'ils en pensent," *Jazz Hip* 22 (rentrée 1960), 19.
72. Stéphane Mougin, "Quelque mots entrenous," *Jazz-Tango-Dancing*, June 1932.
73. Jeffrey H. Jackson, *Making Jazz French: Music and Modern Life in Interwar Paris* (Durham, NC: Duke University Press, 2003), 150.
74. Raymond Mouly, "Ce qu'ils en pensent," *Jazz Hip* 22 (rentrée 1960), 20.
75. André Raux, "Chèr Frère Jazz: Le Jazz français se porte bien," *Jazz Magazine* 73 (August 1961), 5.
76. Guy Lafitte, "Ce qu'ils en pensent," *Jazz Hip* 22 (rentrée 1960), 24.
77. Frank Ténot, "Le Testament de Django," *Jazz Magazine* 57 (March 1960), 15.
78. Roger Luccioni, "Pourquoi un deuxième spécial France?" *Jazz Hip* 32 (Easter 1963), 9.
79. Roger Luccioni, "Le Jazz français en danger?" *Jazz Hip* 22 (rentrée 1960), 7–8.
80. Jef Gilson, "Le jazz français, mythe ou réalité?" *Les Cahiers du jazz* 11 (third trimester 1965), 5.
81. Roger Luccioni, "Pourquoi un deuxième spécial France?" *Jazz Hip* 32 (Easter 1963), 9.
82. Martial Solal, "Table Ronde: le jazz français et ses problèmes," *Jazz Hip* 32 (Easter 1963), 11.
83. J.-P. Martin, "Courrier des lecteurs," *Jazz Hot* 151 (February 1960).
84. Michel Mardignan, "Cher Frère Jazz: Parlez-nous de jazz français!" *Jazz Magazine* 70 (May 1961), 9.
85. Martial Solal, "Table Ronde," 11.
86. Roger Luccioni, "Pourquoi un deuxième spécial France?" *Jazz Hip* 32 (Easter 1963), 9.
87. Daniel Humair, "Table Ronde: le jazz français et ses problèmes," *Jazz Hip* 32 (Easter 1963), 11.
88. Jef Gilson, "Le jazz français, mythe ou réalité?" *Les Cahiers du jazz* 11 (third trimester 1965), 5.
89. Michel Hausser, "Réponse à Frank Ténot," *Jazz Hot* 153 (April 1960), 29.
90. Both instances are cited in Jackson, 151. "Compte rendu sténographique de la reunion des musiciens de cinema," *L'Artiste musicien de Paris*, March 1926, 82; and copy of a 1930 tract from Le Syndicat des Musiciens de la Région Parisienne, F7 13816, Archives Nationales.
91. Eric Drott, *Music and the Elusive Revolution: Cultural Politics and Political Culture in France, 1968–1981* (Berkeley: University of California Press, 2011), 55.
92. Georges Hilleret, "Ci-gît la musique français: victime du play-back," *Télé 7 jours* 264 (10–16 April 1965), 11.
93. "Cher Frère Jazz . . . " *Jazz Magazine* 59 (May 1960), 7.
94. Luccioni, "Le jazz français," 9.
95. Ibid.
96. Frank Ténot, "Le Jazz en France: nos musiciens cherchent un public," *Jazz Magazine* 25 (March 1957), 25.
97. M.A.S., "Questions et réponses," *Jazz Magazine* 34 (February 1958), 7.
98. "A propos 'Jazz et Jazz,'" *Jazz Hot* 163 (March 1961), 19.
99. Nicole Hirsch, "A propos 'Jazz et Jazz,'" *Jazz Hot* 163 (March 1961), 20.
100. Destombes, "A propos," 20.
101. "1 + 1 + 1 = 1," *Jazz Magazine* 83 (June 1962), 18.

102. Michel Hausser, "L'Art et le metier," *Jazz Hot* 217 (February 1966), 16.
103. Ludovic Tournès, *New Orleans sur Seine: Histoire du jazz en France* (Paris: Fayard, 1999), 230–31.
104. Tournès, 230–1. The *chefs d'orchestre* who signed a letter appearing in December's *Jazz Hot* pledging not to hire foreign musicians included Jacques Hélian, André Ekyan, Alix Combelle, and Hubert Rostaing among others.
105. "Un événement sensationnel: le groupement des musiciens français," *Bulletin du Hot Club de France* 2 (1945), 3. Of course, unions were not new to the world of French music. During the interwar period, Parisian jazz musicians had looked to organizations like the Chambre Syndicale des Artistes Musiciens de Paris to represent their interests but they did not have their own union of jazz musicians. See Jackson, 144–45, 151.
106. "Le coin du professionnel," *Bulletin du Hot Club de France* 2 (1945), 14.
107. Ibid.
108. "Bulletin de sante," *Arts* (16–22 February 1955), 4.
109. Georges Hilleret, "Ci-gît la musique français victime du play-back," *Télé 7 jours* 264 (10–16 April 1965), 10–11.
110. Ibid.
111. This organization was also frequently referred to as the Section Syndicale des Artistes Musiciens de Jazz.
112. "Jazzmen sydiqués," *Jazz Hot* 215 (December 1965), 9.
113. Ibid.
114. J.-L. G. (most likely Jean-Louis Ginibre), "Nos jazzmen se fachent," *Jazz Magazine* 125 (December 1965), 16.
115. Michel Hausser, "L'Art et le metier," *Jazz Hot* 217 (February 1966), 16.
116. Michel Hausser and Guy Lafitte, "Lettre ouverte au 'New York Herald Tribune,'" *Jazz Hot* 216 (January 1966), 8.
117. Guy Lafitte and Michel Hausser, "Les musiciens de jazz s'unissent," *L'Artiste-musicien de Paris* 64, no. 12 (Summer–Fall 1965), 63.
118. Ibid.
119. Michel Hausser, "L'Art et le metier," *Jazz Hot* 217 (February 1966), 16.
120. See Michel Hausser and Guy Lafitte, "Lettre ouverte au 'New York Herald Tribune,'" *Jazz Hot* 216 (January 1966), 8; and *Jazz Hot* 224 (October 1966), 6.
121. Siné, "L'Art et le metier," *Jazz Hot* 217 (February 1966), 18. Also see *Jazz Hot* 224 (October 1966), 6.
122. Lucien Malson, "L'Art et le metier," *Jazz Hot* 217 (February 1966), 18.
123. Philippe Koechlin, "Le jazz et la vinylite," *Jazz Hot* 218 (March 1966), 12.
124. Eric Drott, *Music and the Elusive Revolution: Cultural Politics and Political Culture in France, 1968–1981* (Berkeley: University of California Press, 2011), 56–57. I have used the translation by Drott. Arthur Haneuse and Fernand Frank, letter Charles de Gaulle, in *L'Artiste-musicien de Paris* 64, no. 10 (April 1965), 14–15.
125. Drott, 58.
126. "Les Musiciens et la révolution de mai," *Jazz Hot* 242 (August–September 1968), 16.
127. Drott, 60.
128. "Les musiciens et la revolution de mai," *Jazz Hot* 242 (August–September 1968), 14–15.
129. Drott, 61.
130. "Pour une Fédération libre de musiciens," *Actuel* 1 (October 1968): 2. The article only named one member, Claude Delcloo, whom people were asked to contact for further information about the Fédération.

Chapter Six

And What of Empire?

In the 1960s, French jazzmen expanded their efforts abroad by touring in overseas departments and territories, as well as in former colonial holdings, aspiring at times to represent not only jazz but France to their audiences. In this period, as independence movements brought about the formation of new nations across the globe, the French jazz community labeled jazz musicians born in various parts of the Union Française as French. These musicians were almost exclusively of European descent so that their legal and cultural affiliations with France were uncontested. Well-known African or Asian musicians from parts of the former French empire were rare, and the majority of French jazz artists continued to be white before and after the initiation of independence movements. International performances and tours by jazz musicians were complicated by the diverse circumstances that informed the process of decolonization across Africa, as different regions were impacted by a multitude of factors that accompanied independence. A century of colonialism, the Cold War, and economic debt left newly-independent African nations with an unstable present and an unsure future. Democracies often evolved into military dictatorships that suppressed civil society and relied on violence.[1] Each African nation and French department had a unique relationship with metropolitan France, and as a result, the initiatives of the French jazz community depended on varying local and international realities. In some places, like Algeria in the early 1960s, jazz concert audiences were white, European, urban, and often tied to the French military presence. In other locales like Martinique—which became a French overseas department in 1946—the target audiences were not only black and white, but were ideally from a variety of social backgrounds. Regardless of location, European jazz performers, fans, and even the French government used jazz as a unifying force between

France and its past and present imperial holdings during a tumultuous and often violent decade.

JAZZ IN *ALGÉRIE FRANÇAISE*

Since 1848, Algeria had held the status of a French department so it had long been considered by the government and by many French nationals to be an integral part of France. When Prime Minister Pierre Mendès-France declared in 1954 at the outset of the Algerian War, "Algeria is France, not a foreign country," the majority of French men and women agreed with him. The settlers in Algeria appreciated jazz in the same way as their counterparts in the metropole did, where it was a music most often enjoyed by middle-class, Parisian males. In Algeria, this meant that jazz fans were mostly privileged Europeans living in cities like Algiers or Oran. In terms of the nation's musical history, jazz initially had no historic roots in Algeria beyond the connections created by Europeans during the colonial period. In writing about Algerian music from the perspective of 1969, an African writer pointed out, "The field of Algerian music is quite large and well diversified, which is explained by the many contributions made by the different people who have alternately lived in Algeria." This writer claimed that the two most important genres in Algerian music were folkloric music and classical "Andalusian" music, and of course, made no mention of jazz.[2] Jazz had been brought into the country by Europeans, one of the many "different people" who had lived there over the centuries, and during the course of the 1960s finally came to be identified not with the French colonizers but with African Americans and Africa.

Before independence, the jazz community in Algeria was dominated by Europeans who relied on recorded music imported from either the United States or France. During the Algerian War, the Arab and Berber populations would find it easy to equate this music with French colonial rule, not with a music connected intrinsically to African or African-American culture. During his time in Algeria as a youth, the critic Philippe Carles listened to the program *À L'avant-garde du jazz*, hosted by the Frenchman Jean-Louis Mialy, the founder and president of the Hot Club d'Oran.[3] The most active participants in the Algerian jazz public at this time were French settlers and soldiers like Carles or Mialy, not members of the indigenous population.[4] Although Arabs and Berbers outnumbered the *colons* in Algeria by eight to one, French jazz enthusiasts rarely alluded to their existence. Even if jazz critics and fans back in France often labeled themselves antiracists in this period, they did not tend to challenge those who endorsed an *Algérie française*, question the goal of keeping Algeria an intrinsic part of France, or support Algerian nationals. Politics rarely entered into French discussions about jazz in Algeria during the war. Members of the jazz community did not differentiate themselves from the mainstream French public in this regard, as they refrained from criticizing the French effort to hold on to Algeria. In discussing French civilians during the war, Frantz Fanon wrote, "The war in Algeria is being waged conscientiously by all Frenchmen and the few criticisms expressed up to the present time by a few individuals mention only certain methods which 'are precipitating the loss of Algeria.' But the colonial reconquest in its essence, the armed expedition, the attempt to throttle the liberty of a people, are not condemned."[5] Through their silence, the French population, including jazz fans, tacitly endorsed their government's initial denial of the right to self-determination for the Algerian people.

The *colon* jazz musicians Martial Solal and Errol Parker were both born in Algeria in the 1920s and their lives signaled the importance of American and French jazz for those Europeans in Algeria who became enamored with the music. Additionally, these musicians' sense of national belonging reflected the blurred lines between claimed French and Algerian identities. Solal was born in Algiers in 1927 and, like so many of his contemporaries, first heard jazz as an adolescent on the radio. After he became a professional musician at the age of eighteen, he performed at the settler establishment l'Hôtel Aletti in Algiers as well as on Radio-Alger. During his military service as a young man he was stationed in Rabat, Morocco, and played the piano and the clarinet for Radio-Maroc. In 1950, he left North Africa for Paris where he continued pursuing his musical career away from his birthplace.[6]

The jazz pianist and drummer Errol Parker was born Raphaël Schécroun to a Jewish family in Oran in 1925. When he was fourteen, he "lived next to a movie theatre which always played the same record during intermissions, *I Know That You Know*, with Django Reinhardt, Rex Stewart and Barney Bigard." He also heard jazz through the radio, records, and friends, and by his late teens became a jazz piano player.[7] He served in the French army during World War II and then attended l'École des Beaux-Arts in Paris, where he studied sculpture. While a student, he worked as a musician to support himself, in Paris as well as on the French Riviera and in the Alps. In 1960, he changed his name to Errol Parker (Errol for Errol Garner, and Parker for Charlie Parker) to get around a recording contract with the Italian record label Ricordi. He never returned to Algeria to live, but remained in Paris, where he opened the nightclub le Ladybird in 1964, and then permanently relocated to New York in 1967 where "he finally switched to drums to realize his vision of a North African style of jazz drumming, with minimal cymbals and a conga drum in place of a snare."[8] In his autobiography, Parker identified himself as "Algerian" and emphasized his links to Africa, not to France, saying, "I come from a simple, acoustic, African tradition of just wood, skin and metal."[9]

Obviously, Solal and Parker's own identities were complicated by lives lived in Algeria, France, and other places, and they could easily identify with multiple homelands, but without exception they were pegged by the French jazz community as being valid members of the dominant *French* culture, even when they wanted to bring a North African approach to their music or understood themselves to be *Algerian*. Their experiences were exceptional because of their eventual celebrity in France, but they both had an organic connection to the settler community, and became jazz fans while they were adolescents living in Algiers and Oran, the most populous and Europeanized of colonial Algerian cities. Members of the *colon* community were the backbone of the jazz public before and during the Algerian War—they went to *caves*, attended concerts, joined jazz clubs, listened to radio programs, and bought available records—and Solal and Parker were part of this community.

In addition to settler jazz enthusiasts and celebrities like Solal and Parker, French soldiers played a visible and vocal role on the French-Algerian jazz scene, at times even eclipsing the settler fans in terms of influence. By the late 1950s, France had 600,000 troops in Algeria, and the vast majority of them were conscripts.[10] By the end of the war, an estimated 2.5 million French servicemen spent time in Algeria, many of them harboring resentment against the very same settler population they were obliged to protect.[11] This meant that members of the jazz public in Algeria did not necessarily enjoy easy camaraderie or mutual understanding. For many jazz fans serving in the military, there was a sense of estrangement from France and from their preferred cultural pursuits. Certainly, the jazz offerings in North Africa did not compare to those back in France. In 1959, a young soldier, Jean-Louis Gérard, wrote in to *Jazz Magazine* to say, "I would like to establish communication between isolated jazz fans like me." He indicated there were others like him in the "villages" and in the "*djebels*" (a variant of the Arab word for mountains, *jebels*). These fans were in "Oran, Algiers, Constantine, and territories in the south," and Gérard claimed, "Jazz would be a way for us 'to keep up morale.'"[12] Several months later, *Jazz Magazine* mentioned this soldier again, writing, "There are in North Africa, under our colors, a very large number of jazz fans." To foster their bond with jazz, the magazine suggested forming "an association of *jazzfans* in uniform. Young guys must also have concerts, shipments of records, meetings. They need to keep contact with the music that they love. We have their testimony: jazz programs also represent a means of keeping up morale."[13] *Jazz Magazine* published Gérard's name and address with the hope that other soldiers would contact him and possibly form "a club that will have the means of effectively intervening to help the isolated [fans]."

A year later, in the summer of 1960, an officer serving in North Africa, Maréchal-des-logis Pajon, wrote to say that "the radio is the simplest and easiest way to reach the largest number of people in the military." Because he was stationed in the Algerian city of Colomb-Béchar, he could listen to a military radio station during his free time at night. So each week he tuned into the program *Béchar-Jazz*. He regretted the fact that he and his cohort had "a tiny number of jazz records" and maintained that the "RTF has promised us records, but we have received nothing. . . . You see our extreme destitution! It is too bad, because the audience for Radio-Béchar is essentially military and jazz programs especially interest us. The station covers the northern part of the west Saharan zone, a part of Algeria and the south of Morocco." In response to Pajon's letter and claim that members of the military stationed in North Africa wanted to hear more jazz, *Jazz Magazine* called on its readers to send "LPs or 78s in good condition" to be used on the *Béchar-Jazz* program.[14] A large number of the drafted soldiers owned transistor radios. Because this type of radio was both portable and relatively inexpensive, parents often gave one to their sons as a going-away present before they left for Algeria. The military hierarchy even recommended transistor radios to young soldiers to help them stay entertained during their free hours while in the service, and if they did not already own one, these soldiers could buy a transistor through the army magazine *Bled*. The soldiers used the radio as a means of remaining connected to the metropole during their time in Algeria. As Susan Weiner has noted, "In the barracks and the infirmaries, everyone's ear was constantly pressed to his own personal transistor, each tuned in to his own favorite station—music and never news."[15]

In 1961, the conscript Henri Largier wrote a letter expressing how pleasantly surprised he had been by the number of jazz bands in Algiers. Not surprisingly, all of the musicians he mentioned had French names: Jean-Christian Michel, Jacques Sany, Jean-Pierre Cazeaux, and Pierre Siste. Siste even regularly appeared on television in Algiers and had performed recently in a local concert. Largier was disappointed that the audience at this concert was mostly made up of women who did not listen attentively but "with an absentminded and little informed ear" and who would no doubt "loudly" applaud the first rock and roll guitarist to arrive on the scene. His depiction of the jazz audience not only illustrated the intermingling of French soldiers and settlers during the war, belying any sense of tension between the two communities, but also reinforced the male nature of French jazz culture. For him, the young women did not have a complete understanding of the music, and to make matters worse, Largier assumed that they would applaud jazz and rock and roll equally, something that would be unacceptable to legitimate (and male) jazz fans who were understood to appreciate the aesthetic originality and complicated nature of the music. As a further indication of the mutually-dependent relationship between the military and jazz during the war, during this concert, Siste played with a quintet that included a soldier stationed in Algeria, Yves Honorat.[16] Not only were soldiers important audience members for radio broadcasts and concerts, but they were musicians as well. And, compared with settlers, these soldiers had more recent exposure to the jazz happenings in France, which they then brought with them to Algeria.

In 1962, one of these soldiers, Jean Crestet, worked as a reporter for *Jazz Magazine* and turned in a story about three of his fellow combatants who were also "modern" jazz musicians: drummer Georges Lalue, guitarist Jacky Giraudo, and vocalist Claude Meloni. Despite specializing in different instruments, they had been assigned to play the cymbals during their time as members of the 9th *Zouaves* military regiment. When their military service ended, the three men remained in Algiers to play jazz, and for Crestet, this filled a void for his fellow soldiers who craved to hear more of the music. He wrote, "In Algiers, in uniform and material and psychological conditions that one can only imagine, many young conscripts do not forget that they must have jazz." In the summer of 1962, a month before Algeria officially became an independent nation, this young Frenchman still seemed to hope for a return to some semblance of the colonial status quo and assumed that jazz and the French listeners who supported the music in North Africa would remain after the war. He stated that in this city, jazz "is part of these distractions that one hopes to find later, with the return of normal life, under the hot African sun."[17]

Crestet noted that jazz devotees in Algiers were resourceful. "Knowing to use with an ingenuity that never falters the smallest local resources—here a *cave*, there an old piano that someone fixed up—these fans have formed, little by little, ensembles that are extremely dynamic and likeable and that breath the spirit of pioneers." Crestet titled his article "A hard apprenticeship" to indicate the difficult realities facing the French jazz community in Algeria. "Cut off from a large public, these amateur musicians play above all for themselves, for the love of a music that brings them one of their only true joys."[18] He neglected to mention the Arabs and Berbers who made up the majority of the country's population, who had been engaged in a violent war for independence since 1954, and who clearly imagined a different future for their nation. For the French jazz public, these Algerian nationals went unnoticed while French colonials and soldiers sustained the "Algerian" jazz culture. Like much regarding the colonial mission, the viewpoints, desires, and talents of the Europeans remained privileged, while those of the colonized were ignored and rarely discussed.

Beyond the military and the settler populations, other French citizens living in Algeria also participated in sustaining jazz's place there. One such individual, Claude Zeppilli, wrote a letter to *Jazz Magazine* to tell readers about his rather unusual experience. A Frenchman from the mainland, he had gone to live in Algeria near the Sahara Desert because of his professional work in geophysics. Because he was already a jazz fan when he arrived, he felt compelled to find a way to remain connected to the music during his time away from the French mainland. After spending several months in Touggort, he founded a weekly jazz program broadcast by the radio station "Touggort Oasis." He was thrilled by this achievement and proudly exclaimed, "Jazz in the heart of the Sahara!" The towns of Hassi Messaoud and Hassi R'Mel provided additional opportunities to join other jazz aficionados, and the large number of soldiers who completed their service in the region contributed to the jazz public both as listeners and as musicians. Zeppilli declared that his radio program was a "frank success" and asserted that "numerous listeners had written him to ask for their favorite records." He produced his show with the fifty records he owned, which included those of Tommy Ladnier, Miles Davis, Duke Ellington, and the Jazz Messengers. He ended his letter by saying that he looked forward to returning to Paris, "because it is there that things are the best."[19]

Zepilli's correspondence from Algeria is thought provoking for a number of reasons. It not only showed a French jazz fan with no prior professional experience in the music industry founding a jazz radio show in a Saharan town, but it also illustrated the idealized centrality of African-American musicians in the French jazz fan's mind, because all of the artists he directly mentioned were not only from the United States but were black as well. Back in France, supporters of jazz publicly supported the American civil rights movement and influential critics declared themselves antiracists, activities that would be antithetical to supporting French colonial power. That supporters of jazz participated in bolstering the image of a strong French Algeria illustrates the complexity of cultural usage. These men harnessed the popularity of jazz, a music whose origins had more in common with the colonized than the colonizers, to shore up French morale and culture and to deny the obvious circumstances of politics and war. Despite this adulation of African-American musicians, which members of the French jazz public bought into whether they were in France or in places like Algeria, Paris remained the "best" cultural locale for men like Zeppilli, not New York or Chicago or New Orleans, and certainly not Algiers or Oran or Constantine. In a familiar move by members of the French jazz public, African-American musicians were lauded in a way that illustrated a particularly French way of appreciating the "black" genius. French critics and fans studied, discussed, and broadcast their understandings of jazz, and of the artists who created it, from the privileged center of the metropole—from Paris. And no members of the French jazz community noted the philosophical inconsistency of admiring one subaltern culture and people (jazz and African Americans) while subjugating other ones through colonial domination and war.

In 1960, during one of the tensest periods of the war, a number of well-known professional French musicians—including Stéphane Grappelli, André Persiany, Jean-Claude Pelletier, Michel Attenoux, Dominique Chanson, Pascal Groffe, and Philippe Combelle—participated in the Semaine du Jazz in Oran, along with American artists Mezz Mezzrow, Jack Butler, Billy Byers,

Kansas Fields, and Clay Douglas. The writer for the *Bulletin du Hot Club de France* who covered the event, Pierre Voran, asserted that the festival was "the first event of this kind in North Africa." For him, the "numerous amateur musicians from Algiers and Oran" who participated in the shows proved the "strong potential and an excellent spirit" among jazz fans in Algeria, and he hoped that "this first Festival which serves as a witness to the good health of jazz in Algeria, will serve as a model for other events to come."[20] Besides noting that the organizer of the event, Rémy Amoros, had proven his "courage" in putting the festival together, Voran seemed oblivious to the turmoil engulfing the North African country and the tensions surrounding the rule of de Gaulle's new Fifth Republic. For him, bearing witness to "the health of jazz in Algeria" was akin to confirming the potency of French rule there. By this time, Oran was the only Algerian city that retained a European majority.[21] The *pied-noir* Henri Martinez, who was eighteen years old in 1960 and who ended up fighting for the Organisation Armée Secrète (OAS), described wartime Oran in a way that countered the impression created by these jazz festival organizers. Martinez wrote,

> Those who did not live this life cannot imagine the permanent tension that it contains. Existence continually threatened by the bomb that is hidden in a thousand different ways, in a basket, a carton of cigarettes, the cavity of a lamppost; the bullet shot from behind that pierces the neck, the trapped car that explodes, sweeping everything with its steel breath; the grenade that hits without any regard for age; all these risks induce suffocating anxiety when a child is late, mortal anguish for the husband who does not arrive.[22]

His remembrances of the city were linked to violence, bloodshed, and the constant threat of death. Obviously, the participants in the Semaine du Jazz and those who attended its performances were cognizant of this reality, but perpetuated an image of "Algerian" jazz undisturbed by war.

Those who went to the Semaine du Jazz were European residents whose presence augmented France's cultural and military vigor and denied the successes and claims of the Front de Libération Nationale (FLN) whose leaders were using any means at their disposal, including bombings and attacks on civilian populations, to rid Algeria of the French. In 1959, de Gaulle himself had used the word "self-determination" when speaking of Algeria's future, and in 1960, further alienated the settlers by referring to an "emancipated Algeria," an "Algerian Algeria," and an "Algerian Republic." By the time the Semaine du Jazz took place, a variety of indicators convincingly pointed to a changing reality, while the organizers of the event refused to see anything but the well-being of jazz and, by implication, the French colonial mission.

Members of the settler community often insisted that they felt an intrinsic and idealized belonging to Algeria, not to the French mainland. In 1961, the young historian Pierre Nora asked in his book *Les Français d'Algérie*, "What

French Algerian does not feel exiled in the metropole? It is not only the sun he misses, or his family but the familiar Arab with whom he feels more confident and has more in common with than the French of France; the one with whom very often he spent his 'salouetche' childhood."[23] Nora had been born in Paris, but lived from 1958 until 1960 in Algeria while he taught at the Lycée Lamorcière d'Oran. As a result, he came to his opinions about the settlers as an outsider, and was soon criticized for promoting a metropolitan French bias against the *colons*. He did witness the Algerian War firsthand from a highly Europeanized city, and observed Europeans on both the right and left of the political spectrum ignoring valid Arab and Berber claims to self-rule. Settlers often romanticized their connection to Algeria and overlooked the lived day-to-day realities of the Algerians who did not live on equal economic, political, or social terms with them. The *colons* continued to believe that they rightfully belonged in Algeria, even as events around them indicated their miscalculations. Because their connection to Algeria depended on French rule, as the decades after World War II unfolded, these settlers became members of a community that was all the time more entrenched as well as loyal to France, despite an often expressed preference for Algeria over the French mainland. As Muslim nationalism increased in intensity so did the settlers' self-conscious Gallicism.[24]

In late 1960, the United Nations recognized Algeria's right to self-determination, and in 1961, a referendum in both France and Algeria was held on this matter. In metropolitan France, 15 million voted in support of self-rule and 5 million voted against it, while in Algeria 1,749,969 voted yes and 767,566 voted no. This meant that 75 percent of voters in France approved of Algerian self-determination, while in Algeria the vast majority of settlers voted against the proposition.[25] The city of Algiers, "with its preponderance of pieds noirs had registered a resounding seventy-two per cent of 'nons.'"[26] The referendum ensured that self-rule would become a reality and that a clear divide would remain between what the French, settler, and indigenous Algerian populations wanted for this North African country.

In 1961, the *colon* paramilitary group the Organisation Armée Secrète embarked on a campaign of violence against French officials and citizens accused of going along with French governmental negotiations to end the war. Supporters clung to the idea of *l'Algérie française* and unsuccessfully attempted to assassinate de Gaulle on September 8, 1961. While members of both the FLN and the OAS planned and carried out escalating numbers of terrorist attacks, concert organizers held a Festival d'Alger that "reunited sixty jazz musicians, all of them Algerian." The musicians who participated in the Festival d'Alger—Christian Guérin, Jean-Christian Michel, Jacques Sany, Pierre Siste, and Olivier Despax—were themselves *colons* who claimed Algerian identity as their own. A *Jazz Hot* correspondent wrote that Sany had "represented Algeria in Juan-les-Pins in 1960," while he also labeled Despax "one of the best French guitarists," complicating the difference between being Algerian and French and giving voice to the colonial notion that the two identities were not irreconcilable but that they were in harmony with one another. In colonial Algeria, the term *Algerian* referred exclusively to settlers of European descent, not to the Arab-Berber population.[27] The organizer of the Festival d'Alger, Christian Guérin, had been leading his jazz orchestra in Algiers for a year and the musicians who belonged to his band included "the best Algerian musicians" as well as Frenchmen passing through the country like George Lalue.[28] Just like in the 1960 Semaine du Jazz, no musicians of Arab or Berber descent headlined the Festival d'Alger.

As both of these festivals made clear, national affiliations became murky signifiers in the hands of French jazz devotees in North Africa. While these men overlooked Arabs and Berbers, they used the label "Algerian" (as well as "Moroccan" in the newly-independent Morocco) for musicians born in these places but who were of European descent. As a result, a *jazzman français* did not have to be born in the metropole to be considered French but people rarely used this term to mean a nonwhite, non-European individual. White musicians and artists like Errol Parker (who had a Jewish background) monopolized membership in the category *jazzman français*. Members of the settler population also claimed the titles *jazzman algérien* and *jazzman du maroc* for themselves when they had either lived or been born in these countries. This, at a time when the word *algérien* held potent political meaning and signified widely-different ideas of belonging for the *colons*, different partisan factions within the metropole, and Algerian nationalists. The settlers maintained that they were Algerian, but their affiliation with their birthplace depended on French rule; without French authorities protecting their dominant societal position and property, the Arab and Berber populations outnumbered them by a ratio of eight to one. As the academic Ali Yedes has written, "The European-Algerians thrived on opposites and contradictions: they wanted to be Algerian but did not want to be associated with the indigenous Algerian character, nor did they accept the Metropolitan French conception of themselves as 'Pied-Noir;' on the other hand, they wished to be French, while insisting on their being different from the French of France."[29]

By the 1960s, different political groups within France supported a range of ideas regarding this nation in North Africa. These ideas extended from keeping Algeria French at all costs to endorsing Algerian independence. With the exception of a small minority, the Arabs and Berbers embraced an Algerian identity that excluded Europeans altogether. When *l'Algérie française* disappeared in 1962 and around some 650,000 people of European descent left Algeria for France, Algeria lost its conventional audience for jazz.[30] The Evian Agreements took away the ability of the Europeans in Algeria to claim allegiance to both France and Algeria. The agreement stipulated that after a transition period of three years, French citizens in Algeria could choose to be either Algerian or French nationals. If they became French citizens, they would become "foreigners" in Algeria. Dual nationality, something French negotiators had wanted at the outset, was no longer a possibility after Evian.[31] This meant that in theory, Europeans could have become "Algerians," but because of the reality of violence—famously represented by the ultimatum "the suitcase or the coffin"—they could not remain in Algeria after official independence in July of 1962. In the newly-sovereign Algeria, jazz had to mean something new, as it would no longer be defined and sustained by the European colonial population. For Algerians after 1962, appreciating jazz involved overcoming the false equation between it and European culture and dominance, and seeing jazz for the first time as a music originally of another oppressed and exploited people who had ethnic and cultural ties to Africa.

AN INDEPENDENT ALGERIA AND A PAN-AFRICAN IDENTITY

In the first year immediately following the war, the French jazz public largely stayed silent about the conflict and its impact, but when former FLN leaders established the weekly magazine *Révolution africaine* in Algiers, two notable French jazz supporters contributed to its pages. The French critic Philippe Koechlin wrote numerous articles about jazz in the first months of the magazine's publication; and, the radical French cartoonist Siné penned political cartoons, most notably through his series "La semaine politique de Siné." In the magazine's third issue, Koechlin wrote an article where he asked, "Where is jazz headed?" For his Algerian readers, he pointed out three important musical sources for jazz: the blues, gospel music, and Africa. For the rest of the decade, a focus on Africa would reshape and then come to define how people understood jazz in Algeria, especially as audiences began connecting the music to a larger political agenda that embraced anticolonialism and a shared African identity. Koechlin made this point clear when he quoted Art Blakey saying that "Africa is the beginning of all jazz," and when he pointed out how Max Roach condemned South African racial violence with his song entitled "Tears for Johannesburg." Koechlin noted that American jazz musicians used their fame for political ends and stressed the continued relevance of this music, asserting, "An art that is alive cannot disassociate itself from the social context from which the musician evolved, but can only reflect his soul and his most profound thoughts. Jazz is freedom in rhythmic ecstasy, aspirations translated into music from the deepest part of a person's being: jazz is more current than ever."[32] In Algeria, as understandings of the music progressed, French critics like Koechlin made an effort to guide Algerian audiences to better appreciate this music and to understand the historical realities behind it. Back in France, *Jazz Hot* let its readers know in a short article that *Révolution africaine* devoted space on its pages "to black African art and to jazz." French jazz periodicals rarely mentioned Algeria at this time and that *Jazz Hot* did so (however succinctly) showed that at least some members of its editorial board supported jazz in this newly independent nation.[33] It was no coincidence, of course, that *Jazz Hot* was the magazine that covered this news: Koechlin started working there in the 1950s and became its editor-in-chief in 1965, so that he became an early link between French professional critics and a nascent Algerian jazz community.

By 1964, French and American promoters resumed scheduling concerts in Algeria and remained hopeful, if at times unrealistically so, about the Algerian jazz audience and its relationship with France. In 1964, the Frenchman Georges Mark organized a jazz tour in Algeria that included artists like the French pianist Pierre Franzino, the American singer Shirley "Bunny" Foy, and the American drummer Ron Jefferson. Foy and Jefferson both lived in France at the time and Franzino and Foy eventually married. Foy and Jefferson's long-term residence in France highlighted the continued importance of American expatriates to the French jazz culture, whether at home or abroad. The musicians on this tour, who also included bassist J. M. Tombal, traveled to Bône (Annaba), Constantine, Mostaganem, Sétif, Philippeville, Bougie (Béjaïa), Algiers, and Blida. A writer for *Jazz Hot* claimed that a second tour with fifteen stops was going to take place in the near future "because jazz had found an enthusiastic public in Algeria." Radiodiffusion-Télévision Algérienne (RTA), which had taken over the new nation's airwaves and broadcast system after independence, aired a jazz radio program each night and a television show each week. Additionally, in June of 1964, the American Cultural Center organized a jazz festival with American musicians as part of the Foire Exposition in Algeria.[34]

The U.S. State Department sent the American Woody Herman to Algeria in 1966 as part of an international tour of Africa and Eastern Europe, and then sent Randy Weston a year later as he made a fourteen-nation tour of Africa. A U.S. Embassy official in Algiers thought that Algerians reacted positively to jazz and asserted that "jazz speaks in a special idiom to many Algerians." Members of the American government assumed that jazz could help bridge the divide between the West and Third World countries like Algeria. By the time of Weston's 1967 tour, another war—the Vietnam War—was causing tension around the world, and demonstrations against American involvement in Southeast Asia were taking place in Europe, Asia, and Africa. Not surprisingly, the conflict in Vietnam impacted Weston's reception in Algeria. The same U.S. official who claimed that jazz spoke to Algerians, wrote, "Weston was approached by two [Algerian] twenty-year-olds, who rather belligerently asked him how he, a Negro, could be playing when his country was committing atrocities in Vietnam."[35] This quote gives a rare, if secondhand, voice to Algerian nationals who found much at fault with the policies of European and American governments. Even if they admired jazzmen and appreciated their music, foreign audiences could also have a hard time separating French and American art forms from the imperial missions their nations represented. The two Algerians who questioned Weston articulated a belief that African-American musicians should have sympathy for the Vietnamese because of their shared history of abuse and exploitation, a history that Algerians also knew only too well. The sentiment that Vietnam and Algeria shared a common history of colonization was shared two years later by South Vietnamese writer Phan Tu when he said, "The profound links between Vietnam and Algeria make each Vietnamese feel at home in Algeria and each Algerian feel equally at home in Vietnam."[36]

During the Randy Weston tour, Algerian audiences made overt connections between themselves and African Americans. The Algerian newspaper *El Moudjahid* published an article entitled "Randy Weston in Algiers" in 1967. The paper had been the mouthpiece of the FLN from its founding in 1956 until the end of the war, and in 1967, *El Moudjahid* remained closely connected to the cause of Algerian nationalism.[37] In this article on Randy Weston, an Algerian writer stated, "For the first time since independence we can hear jazz, true jazz." The writer disparaged Woody Herman, who had performed in Algeria a year earlier, saying, "We cannot call Woody Herman's music jazz." Herman was a white musician, while Weston was black. The *El Moudjahid* correspondent indicated that a musician's authentic connection to jazz depended in some ways to his ancestral ties to Africa, and went on to declare that Weston's concert "is the proof that jazz is most popular in Africa, its cradle. . . . Without 'transplanted' Africans, jazz would never have existed."[38] Weston had made a public effort since 1960 to embrace a Pan-African vision. That year, he recorded *Uhuru Afrika*, a composition that celebrated the newly-independent nations of Africa, and whose name means "Freedom Africa" in Swahili.[39] Weston worked to make his African audiences realize the connection between jazz and Africa. In another Algerian paper, *An Nasr*, in 1967, Weston asserted that African music "gave birth to jazz," and went on to tell Algerian readers, "If there had not been any Africa there would not be any jazz."[40]

In 1969, from July 21 until August 1, individuals from Africa, the Americas, Eastern and Western Europe, and Asia met in Algiers to raise political and cultural awareness at the Pan-African Cultural Festival.[41] The Organization of African Unity (OAU) arranged the event with a preparatory committee whose eight members came from Algeria, Cameroon, Ethiopia, Guinea, Mali, Nigeria, Senegal, and Tanzania. A year earlier, the Algerian government had offered to host the festival, and secretary-general of the OAU Diallo Telli claimed, "This important decision gave the Algerian Government a large part of the responsibility for the enormous material, financial and technical burden for the preparation and running of the first Pan-African

Cultural Festival."[42] According to the program's manifesto, the festival's aim was to discuss the "realities of African culture;" the "role of African culture in the campaigns for national liberation and in the consolidation of African Unity;" and the "role of African culture in the economic and social development of Africa."[43]

The decade of the 1960s had brought independence not only to Algeria, but to a number of other African countries—including the Côte d'Ivoire, Mali, Kenya, Rwanda, Zimbabwe, Senegal, Congo, Togo, Dohomey, and Cameroon—so that there was a keen interest in discussing the continent's future. Black Panther Party members Eldridge and Kathleen Cleaver, Emory Douglas, and David Hilliard led the festival's American contingent. The Cleavers were living in exile in Algeria at the time and were interested in linking disparate African causes together. In a press conference during the festival, Eldridge Cleaver said, "The West has deformed African and Afro-American culture: all our ideas have been tarnished and disfigured. We must take our culture in hand and build it up again."[44] Cleaver and other Black Panther delegates discussed African liberation movements, in addition to the racial climate in the United States. Straddling the line between an American and French connection, Richard Wright's daughter Julia (who lived in Paris) as well as the poet Ted Joans (who spent significant periods of time residing in France) both attended. During the festival, an Afro-American Cultural Center was established with the hope of creating a permanent base for African-American art and expression in Algeria. Well-known African intellectuals and political activists were present at the Pan-African Cultural Festival, drawing the attention of global audiences and indicating a shared focus and optimism on the part of attendees about the continent's potential in a postcolonial age.

Among these individuals was Léopold Sédar Senghor, the Senegalese poet, politician, and early leader of the *négritude* movement.[45] The military ruler of Algeria, Houari Boumédiène, presided over the event, and the Algerian Ministry of Sport and Culture took part in organizing festival happenings.[46] The Algerian artist Houria Niati said the following about the festival from the vantage point of 2012, "It was absolutely amazing, explosive. People were embracing each other, there was total acceptance of what they were seeing. It was very pure, very untouched: raw Africa." She created an image of artists, politicians, and regular citizens coming together to share their cultures, fears, and ambitions. Local children attended performances, and people spoke in a diversity of languages: Arabic, Portuguese, French, English, Yoruba, and Swahili.[47]

In his inaugural speech at the Pan-African Festival, Houari Boumédiène told attendees that this event had "the task of holding the greatest artistic and literary reunion ever to embrace an entire continent." In addition, the festival was also "taking a further step forward in the continuing struggle against all forms of domination." He saw culture as playing a crucial role in fighting foreign power and control, as it was "the basic cement of all social groups, their prime means of inter-communication and of understanding the outside world, their reflection and transcendancy, their soul and their essence, their embodiment and their capacity for change."[48] At this gathering, participants understood culture to be closely connected to the goal of nourishing independent political and economic agency in Africa. In writing about the Pan-African Festival, the editor of the Algerian daily *Ach-Chaâb*, Mohamed Saidi, wrote about the need for these African nations to disentangle themselves from colonialist and neocolonialist cultures. For him, "the colonialist cultural presence in Africa is a part of the total colonial phenomenon," and needed to be extinguished. The desire to achieve complete freedom from European power included an interest in fostering culture away from colonial paradigms. Saidi asserted, "While it is clear that independent Africa cannot achieve progress without dealing heavy blows to all forms of colonialism, it is also clear that cultural liberation, as a means to total liberation, is one of the major tasks to be undertaken by Africa in her present-day struggle."[49] Echoing this sentiment and a desire to have organic and legitimately African cultural experiences, a lecturer at the Université d'Alger, M. D. Chabou, claimed, "We must first of all reclaim our authenticity and see to it that our culture is no longer endured but really lived and *assumed*."[50]

Jazz musicians performed at the Pan-African Cultural Festival, the most visible of whom were the Americans Oscar Peterson, Marion Williams, and Archie Shepp. In the words of the Algerian Ministry of Information and Culture, "In this month of July, 1969, the frontiers were obliterated in Algiers. Music had overthrown all barriers, making it possible for the various peoples who were present to understand one another without words. Everything was possible at Algiers at that moment."[51] American jazz musicians added to this enthusiasm for the cohesive powers of music, and in the late 1960s, they were also infusing their musical work with political goals and social advocacy. Because the American Leroi Jones (who later renamed himself Amiri Baraka) was unable to attend the festival, Shepp illustrated the writer's theories about "the rupture of free jazz and its return to African sources, creating a musical precedent full of promises for the future."[52] On stage, Shepp freestyled on his saxophone alongside Algerian and Touareg musicians playing drums, tambourines, and karkabous (metallic castagnettes). He told listeners, "We are still black, and we have come back. *Nous sommes revenues!* We have come back to our land of Africa, the music of Africa. Jazz is a black power! Jazz is a black power! Jazz is an African power! Jazz is an African music! Jazz is an African music! We have come back!"[53] Especially because of the deliberate political agenda of both the Black Panthers and free jazz, American artists made it clear to festivalgoers that jazz could be used and appreciated to reflect their own political causes, and that the music was not at its core linked to Europeans or to white Americans. Instead, jazz came to be framed as an anti-imperial music connected to the cause of human liberation, African identity, and black nationalism. The Algerian Ministry of Information and Culture proclaimed in the festival's wake, "In its turn jazz has become a weapon and proved that music cannot be dissociated from those who create it, and from the environment which gave it birth." Emphasizing the novelty of the event and its aesthetic relevance, this Algerian Ministry also went on to say that "from now on one can think and say that at Algiers on certain nights, a certain kind of Free-Jazz was born."[54] In a similar vein, French attendees were moved by the spirit of collaboration and hope for the future that seemed to define the event. In the words of a writer for *Jazz Magazine*, "Mother Africa had rediscovered her forgotten children who will leave again for places still more distant, to carry their message, proud of their négritude."[55]

During the Pan-African Cultural Festival, the reference point for jazz in Algeria was the United States and Africa, not France. Yet the French jazz community remained involved despite the unambiguous move away from colonial control that this event represented, seven years after Algerian independence. The mainstream French press covered the proceedings, and the French film critics and writers Jean-Louis Bory and Louis Marcorelles directly participated in the festival.[56] The French BYG/Actuel record label documented and released the festival's music sessions under the album title *Live At The Pan-African Festival*. After the event came to a close, BYG/Actuel's Jean Georgakarakos and Jean-Luc Young invited participating musicians to record their work at their Parisian studio. Some of the resulting albums were: Clifford Thornton's *Ketchaoua*, named after the district in Algiers where the musicians had performed; Sunny Murray's *Hommage to Africa*; Grachan Mocur III's *New Africa*; and Archie Shepp's two albums, *Yasmina, A Black Woman*, which had a North African picture for its sleeve art, and *Blasé*, whose last track was a song called "Touareg."[57] The Pan-African Cultural Festival exemplified a moment in time when international cooperation inspired artistic creation and a vision of the African and the African American working together across national boundaries. Even if direct French participation on the artistic and creative front was minimal in Algiers, politically-active members of the French jazz public moved to support its vision of global unity for members of the black diaspora.

Over the course of a decade, the meanings surrounding jazz in Algeria changed substantially, as did its audience there. In the early 1960s, the vast majority of fans and musicians were of European heritage: settlers and soldiers. Arabs and Berbers, on the other hand, were rarely mentioned by members of the French-Algerian jazz public who labeled *colons* as being both French *and* Algerian because these categories were not understood to be mutually exclusive, but complementary to one another. After Algerian independence in 1962, European jazz fans in Algeria disappeared and a new cadre of Algerian jazz aficionados slowly formed. In coming to appreciate the music, these Algerian nationals had to separate jazz from its correlation with colonial rule. As time went on, they began to value the music because of its aesthetic bond with Africa, and when African-American musicians brought jazz together with the causes of black nationalism and anti-imperialism, this gave Algerians a political reason to appreciate the music. Throughout the decade of the 1960s, jazz in Algeria was much more than a form of entertainment: it was affiliated with questions of national identity. As control of the nation transferred from French to Algerian hands, jazz appreciation underwent a metamorphosis that distanced it from Europe and connected it to Africa.

FRENCH NORTH AFRICA

Beyond Algeria, the French jazz public reached out to other North African locations linked to France through empire. Musicians and concert organizers expressed a desire to develop and to maintain jazz audiences in Morocco and Tunisia, and consequently arranged tours and festivals in these countries. During the colonial period, the European population in Morocco was considerably smaller than the one on Algeria. Across the country in the first half of the twentieth century, the French built new towns (*villes nouvelles*) for European settlers outside of the older Moroccan ones, and the city of Tangier came to have a reputation as an international trading center. French, Spanish, Italian, Greek, and Corsican immigrants went to Morocco to work as administrators, artisans, industrial workers, and farmers, so that by 1931, close to 162,000 Europeans lived in Morocco, 60 percent of them of French heritage.[58] Colonial urban planning allowed the French to more easily control the *casbahs* and *bidonvilles* (shantytowns) that were home to indigenous Moroccan residents and that were also chronically overcrowded. The construction of the *villes nouvelles* for the European population ensured that settlers remained separate from the Muslim and Jewish quarters, although the segregation was never complete as Europeans and Moroccans interacted at work, on farms, and in residential communities, sometimes even living in the same apartment complexes.[59] By the 1950s, "native" and "European" cities no longer existed side by side, but cities like Casablanca grew to become "a cacophonous mélange of native and foreigner, rich and poor, longtime residents and newcomers from the countryside, all muddled together in an explosive mix."[60] After independence, the vast majority of Europeans left Morocco, but some remained behind in urban centers and on French military bases, and these individuals played a crucial role in the Moroccan jazz community.

Jazz fans who lived in former colonial territories could have complex ties to their countries of origin and to France, ones that were impacted not only by a continued French economic and cultural presence, but also by France's military. After independence in 1956, 100,000 French troops remained in Morocco, and France pushed to keep alliances between the two nations in place. French leaders wanted an independent state that was united with France through permanent ties of interdependency, while Moroccan leaders wanted sovereignty for themselves. Soon after self-rule became a reality, a southern faction of the Moroccan Armée de Libération Nationale (ALN) attacked the Moroccan Forces Armées Royales (FAR) to protest French military regiments remaining in the region. This attack did not result in a French withdrawal, but instead illustrated the contentiousness of a continued French military presence on Moroccan soil, where some Moroccans identified the remaining French troops with a lack of complete national self-determination.[61]

Throughout the early 1960s, French residents in Morocco continued to promote jazz, and were much more visible on the jazz scene than members of the indigenous population. The Hot Club de Gharb and its leader Jacques Masson organized the first Festival de Jazz in Morocco in 1961 in the port city of Kénitra. Radiodiffusion-Télévision Marocaine (RTM) transmitted the proceedings to listeners and reportedly "more than a thousand spectators came from the four corners of Morocco: Rabat, Casablanca, Meknès, Fez, Tangier, Oujda, Marrakech." This jazz festival was not the first time jazz artists had made their way to Morocco and observers complimented the fans who attended for their long-term devotion to jazz. "The audience, quick to enthusiasm, was an audience of connoisseurs, since Morocco, don't forget, has already welcomed the 'Greats' of jazz: Louis Armstrong, Sidney Bechet and Mezz Mezzrow, Buck Clayton, Lionel Hampton, Dizzy Gillespie and Miles Davis." Less famous musicians took the stage at this 1961 festival though: the headliners were the trumpeter Conrad Matioscek, Panamanian vocalist Estin Mignott, and the German quintet the Wuff Combo.

In addition to these professional jazz musicians, local amateur jazz bands also performed and their membership reflected the strong American and European ties to jazz in Morocco. The musicians in both the Dixie Jazz Band of Rabat and the Moon Glows Quartet were Americans living on the U.S. Navy base in Kénitra. Even though these individuals did not have familial or cultural links to Morocco beyond the ones created by colonization and the American military, *Jazz Hot* proclaimed that the "jazzmen of Morocco came to experience their First Festival de Jazz" which was an "enormous success."[62] These "jazzmen of Morocco" were predominantly American and French, not citizens of the new Moroccan nation.

The U.S. government built five military bases in Morocco during the early Cold War. By the late 1950s, new long-range bombers made these bases obsolete so that the U.S military completely withdrew from Morocco by 1963. When the American soldiers departed, they took some of the most active members of the "Moroccan" jazz community with them, but the cultural impression they left behind lasted much longer. As the historian Susan Gilson Miller has illustrated, the U.S.–Morocco relationship was "built on the legacy of memories, mostly positive, of the American landings during World War II that brought chewing gum, be-bop, nylons and lipstick, and enhanced by the U.S. Food for Peace (PL 480) program during the Cold War."[63] In the end, whether Moroccan nationals continued to be interested in jazz depended as much on the image of the music cultivated by Americans as it did on the jazz community sustained by the French before and after the colonial period.

At a time when France's outlook in North Africa was far from certain and the war in Algeria entered its final violent stages, a writer for *Jazz Magazine* claimed that the success of the 1961 Festival de Jazz in Morocco "promises well for the future."[64] A year later, Martial Solal, Guy Pedersen, and Daniel Humair participated in the second Festival de Jazz in Morocco, which presented three concerts in Casablanca, one in Rabat, one in Kénitra, and one in Meknès.[65] Morocco had gained independence from France in 1956 in a much less contested situation than that which unfolded in Algeria, and had never been awarded the same department status during colonial rule. For some French observers, disheartened by the unfolding of events in Algeria, jazz concerts illustrated that France's cultural practices could persist in North Africa after independence, even if the festivals, concerts, and cabarets depended on Western audiences and not exclusively Moroccan ones.

In the early and mid-1960s, French jazz aficionados still played a noticeable leadership role in Moroccan jazz culture, as Moroccans were only starting to make the association between jazz and Africa. Some Europeans seemed hesitant to leave jazz in the hands of the local population, and as a result, the Frenchman Jacques Masson played an integral role in Moroccan jazz programming. Starting in the early 1960s, he hosted the weekly jazz program "Jazz d'aujourd'hui" on Radiodiffusion-Télévision Marocaine, and successfully lobbied to have the show increase its airtime from a half hour each Saturday to an hour, and to also include a Wednesday night broadcast. The jazz pianist Jean-Pierre Baty participated on the show as well, and the two hosts broadcast "news and interviews collected from Paris."[66] The audience for this show was allegedly "40% Moroccan," and Masson claimed, "Under our leadership, jazz clubs opened in Rabat, Tanger, Fez, and most recently, Casablanca."[67] According to *Jazz Magazine*, Masson did not host the show to enhance his own personal fame and so went by the assumed name of Jacques Nossam (which was Masson spelled backward).

However, in 1964, RTM made an effort to "Moroccanize" (*maroconiser*) its programs and therefore canceled the Wednesday show and reduced the

Saturday show back to a thirty-minute time slot. When Masson protested to RTM, he was told that jazz did not appeal to a "large public," but that if he and his supporters gathered letters of protest from listeners and presented them to the station in numerous enough numbers to prove that "this show is followed in Morocco as abroad," the program hours would be restored.[68] The show remained on air but Masson was never flooded with the letters of support that would have reinstated the lost time. A year later, *Jazz Hot* published a picture of "Nossam" and Baty with a caption explaining that these two men "can even bring to life on Radio[diffusion]-Télévision Marocaine popular jazz shows" that will earn "certain success." To demonstrate jazz's achievements in Morocco, the caption pointed out, "In Rabat, a restaurant grill room, le Blue Note, has recently opened, benefiting from an excellent discothèque."[69] These 1965 statements by *Jazz Hot* showed the French jazz public's continued optimism about the future of jazz in North Africa, even as Moroccans were rejecting French leadership in their cultural practices and politics. After independence, the effort to Moroccanize the culture meant limiting Moroccan audiences' exposure to French forms of art and entertainment, and in this upside-down framework inherited from the colonial era, jazz could be equated with European or French musical practices. In 1966, when the white American jazzman Woody Herman performed in Morocco, the American Associated Press reported that "he played before European audiences only,"[70] and in the late 1960s there were still branches of the Hot Club de France in cities like Meknès.[71] Even if jazz was understood to have a connection to African-American or general American musical traditions, it was not Moroccan, and was still part of a western and foreign aesthetic.

American artists actively worked to make the tie between jazz and North Africa stronger in the late 1960s. The Pan-African Cultural Festival was held in Algiers in 1969, and Randy Weston lived in Morocco for seven years starting in the late 1960s. After Weston performed at the Adgal Theater in Marrakech in the spring of 1967, listeners were said to have inundated the radio station with phone calls and letters asking for the session to be broadcast more than once. One person from Marrakech ostensibly threatened the DJ if he did not replay "this greatest moment in Moroccan jazz history" on the airwaves. The U.S. Foreign Service Office told Weston that it was "besieged" with Moroccan demands that Weston return to the country for the "1967 Festival de Jazz" at the American Embassy gardens in Rabat. The American organizers of the event speculated that "2,500 wildly enthusiastic fans" would attend Weston's show.[72] In 1968, the American Ambassador to Morocco Henry Tasca wrote to Weston to tell him,

> I have been particularly pleased with the enthusiastic reception which your compositions based upon Moroccan themes, such as the "Marrakech Blues,"

have had in Morocco. I am sure that the benefits which will be derived from your research work on African folk music will be of major significance. As you so well understand, Africans must be helped to rediscover their own music. They must learn to value their folk music, as you value it, realizing that the music of no other civilization can rival African music in the complexity and subtlety of its rhythms. At the same time, your research will help Americans to understand more fully the great debt that American jazz, blues, and spirituals owe to African music. Inevitably, the result of your work can only draw the African and American continents closer together.[73]

Weston's presence and popularity in Morocco indicated the growing connection between African-American artists and their North African audiences, a relationship that left little room for the French to claim an indispensible role in upholding the North African jazz culture. But this process took time and effort on the part of Moroccans and Algerians and men like Weston. In his autobiography, Weston noted that by the late 1960s, Moroccans "had limited exposure to African-American music." Young people "only got small doses of real black music through Voice of America broadcasts, but they were crazy for our music. James Brown was number one in all of Africa. But in Tangier and other parts of Morocco they only got weak imitations of our music through Europe, where cats would play an imitation of black music." In addition to this limited exposure to jazz, the general Moroccan population did not go listen to live jazz performances when they were available. In Weston's jazz club in Tangier, the African Rhythms Club, "the common folk" still did not attend his shows. The people who did come were the "local folks with money—businessmen, hoteliers, travel agents, military people, doctors—the professionals," as well as tourist groups, visiting diplomats, people who worked for the UN.[74] In the postcolonial world, jazz in Algeria and Morocco started to move away from the former metropole to become oriented to the people of Africa and to members of the African diaspora, but as it did so, it also remained an elite music.

In 1964, French pianist Armand Gordon took his orchestra to Tunisia, a nation that, like Morocco, had become independent from France in 1956. During the colonial era, Tunisia was home to over 100,000 European colonists, mostly of French and Italian descent, but the vast majority of them fled the country after the 1956 treaty recognizing Tunisian sovereignty was signed. There were numerous similarities in the socioeconomic and political situations in Algeria, Morocco, and Tunisia, as well as significant differences. Both Algeria and Morocco were home to large Arab and Berber populations, while Tunisia had less indigenous diversity and therefore a more homogenous Arab population. All three countries had large settlements of *colons*, in addition to local Jewish communities that predated the colonial period and lived predominantly in urban areas. The European settlers in these North African nations mostly resided in northern cities and on fertile farmland in rural areas.[75] After independence in 1956, a small French military presence remained in Tunisia for several years in strategic places like the Bizerte Naval Base, but the relationship between the two countries remained tense until the end of the Algerian War.[76] French influences endured in Morocco and Tunisia more so than they did in Algeria, so that the former colonizing power continued to have a hand in economic, strategic, political, and cultural interests beyond 1956. French authority was, of course, greatly reduced by independence but persisted nonetheless.[77]

In the context of the Cold War and decolonization, the United States government had a vested interest in cultivating diplomatic ties with newly-independent North African nations, and therefore made a concerted effort to build cultural links with Tunisians and Moroccans. To foster an American-Tunisian alliance, the U.S. State Department sent Wilbur de Paris to Tunisia as part of an eleven-nation African tour in 1957, and Herbie Mann went to both Tunisia and Morocco in 1959 as part of another international tour sponsored by the American State Department.[78] While in Tunisia, de Paris was interviewed by the United States Information Service in a show for Tunis radio. He also reportedly spent time with both French and Tunisian cultural groups, while the Tunisian press gave his music and performances positive reviews.[79] Because of U.S. cultural, political, and military initiatives in the newly-independent North African states, France was not the only western power with a presence or an interest in Morocco and Tunisia, and both American and French jazz artists were part of an effort to promote politically-subtle allegiances with local populations. When jazz artists went to Tunisia, their target audience was not the small remaining European population but the local Tunisian one.

After the French jazzman Armand Gordon returned from his visit to Tunisia in 1964, he stressed not only that the Tunisian youth were interested in jazz, but also that members of this small—but hopefully growing—jazz audience had been influenced by educational and musical experiences in France. He wrote to *Jazz Magazine*, saying, "In Tunisia, jazz is very alive and strongly valued by the young, especially among students." According to him, a number of these students had first learned about jazz in Paris and then, upon returning to their own country, sought to broaden the music's popularity there. The Tunisian government subsidized the Jazz Club de Tunisie, and the national radio system offered a weekly jazz program. In addition to these two public initiatives, "the Maison de la Culture opened a hall for the sake of jazz fans and the leaders of the club have already organized jam-sessions, record auditions, and film showings (*Jazz à Newport*, etc.)." Gordon noted that there were "very few jazz musicians in Tunisia," besides "the promising young alto saxophonist Ahmed Ben Miled," and he thought that more points of contact and communication between Tunisian musicians and "professional jazzmen" would benefit the former and lead to greater numbers of them. He was encouraged by the Conservatoire de Musique creating its own Jazz Club, which put together a jazz festival in Carthage where Maxim Saury, Stéphane Grappelli, and Kenny Clarke performed.[80] Gordon envisioned American and European professionals, teachers, and musicians guiding a growing Tunisian jazz community. When Frenchmen participated in such initiatives it helped to rebuild and reinforce a cultural link with France, especially before the music became more exclusively associated with African cultural identity in the late 1960s.

French companies at times used the image of French jazzmen in North Africa to appeal to French consumers and audiences back home. When these musicians experienced success abroad, they generated positive opinions about their artistic worth on a global jazz stage. By the late 1960s, as Africa became a desired location for its both real and imagined aesthetic connection to jazz, French artists made forays onto the continent and sometimes even into the local cultures. Whether these musicians performed for European crowds or North African ones, their presence in Africa was heralded. In 1968, the French band Les Barbecues performed in Tunisia. After they returned to France, the French company Selmer used a full-page picture of them in an advertisement appearing in *Jazz Magazine*. The image showed seven men standing on a Tunisian beach, three of them bare chested because of the obvious heat, and one of them on a camel. The company made instruments so three of the musicians were shown holding their Selmers: Christian de la Simone his clarinet, Erick Le Prince his trombone, and Didier Baston his trumpet (the other band members were Dominique Baston, Yves Guyon, Claude Gueroult de Flamesnil, and Jean-Claude Albert Weil).[81] The men exuded a confidence indicating that decolonization had impacted neither their artistic sensibility nor their projected sense of self-assurance. Their travels to Tunisia were meant to reflect their success as jazz artists, and the consequences of Tunisian independence and the growing disconnect between France and North Africa were absent from the image. Over the following decades, Les Barbecues would make international tours an important facet of their musical careers, playing in such places as Mozambique, Swaziland, Morocco, Turkey, Egypt, Côte d'Ivoire, Syria, the Antilles, and Haiti, ensuring their connections to a global jazz culture.[82]

An effort to blend jazz and North African music was apparent in the production of the 1969 film *Noon in Tunisia*. The movie was an international endeavor that included the participation of five jazz artists (American saxophonist and flutist Sahib Shihab, American trumpeter Don Cherry, French double bassist Henri Texier, Swiss drummer Daniel Humair, and Swiss pianist George Gruntz), and four Arab musicians from Tunisia (Jelloul Osman, Moktar Slama, Hattab Jouini, and Salah el Mahdi). The inspiration for the sixty-minute film came from the 1967 record *Noon in Tunisia* that was part of the *Jazz Meets the World* series produced by the German record label

Saba. In contrast to the jazzmen, the North African musicians played their own traditional instruments: the *zoukra*, the *mezoud*, the *nai*, the *bendire*, the *tabla*, and the *darbouka*. Despite the two groups' distinctive musical histories, the film showed "the interaction, the interpenetration of the rhythms of two musical cultures that immediately, by a knowing embrace, find each other in complete accordance." The 1967 record had included French violinist Jean-Luc Ponty and German bassist Eberhard Weber; for the film, Don Cherry and Henri Texier replaced them. Cherry claimed that the jazz artists and the Arab musicians had played together with "love" and that the two genres had much in common. As a visible sign of their collaboration, Sahib Shihab wore Arab clothes and some of the Arab musicians played in European dress. A European observer saw this as "a further sign of their fusion, of the interaction of jazz and Arab music achieved by *Noon in Tunisia*."[83] The record and the film both illustrated the global reach of the jazz community by the late 1960s, as their production depended on the musical visions of American, French, German, Swiss, and Tunisian artists. From the French perspective, the participation of Ponty on the record and Texier in the film showed the musical importance and relevance of French artists when it came to the international advocacy and future of jazz.

REPRESENTING FRANCE

After independence, governmental and cultural institutions used French musicians as links between France and its former sub-Saharan and Caribbean colonies. This idea was borrowed from the American State Department program of sending jazz artists like Louis Armstrong, Duke Ellington, Benny Goodman, Dave Brubeck, and Randy Weston to Africa, Asia, the Middle East, Latin America, the Soviet Union, and Eastern Europe. Begun in 1956, the U.S. State Department continued this program until 1978. That year, the United States Information Agency took over support for the trips and jazz became a smaller component of the U.S. government's foreign policy.[84] The State Department agenda, discussed more thoroughly in chapter 4, strove to capitalize on jazz's popularity and to use it as a means of improving people's opinions of the United States during the Cold War. This especially made sense in the 1960s, when people from a variety of African nations were increasingly aware of jazz. In 1969, an African writer asserted that in the former British colony of Ghana, "outside of soccer and boxing . . . jazz remains the national passion of a people who only believe in a choreographer god and whose funerals even dance."[85]

    Mirroring the American program, the French government supported a jazz tour in sub-Saharan Africa in 1963. But unlike their U.S. counterparts, French politicians and diplomats spent no further government money promoting jazz concerts abroad after this tour was over. Despite the paucity of French state funding, French jazzmen did tour in Africa and the Caribbean throughout much of the 1960s. The performances of these French artists in current and former colonies raised different questions than the American tours did, and each specific location had its own demographic realities. We have seen that in Algeria during the war, white French musicians played for white European settlers, and that in North Africa after independence the jazz culture moved incrementally away from French dominance into a realm informed and defined by a pan-African consciousness. In places like Guadeloupe, white French musicians played for primarily black audiences in what remained overseas departments, ensuring that the music carried different meanings to listeners there than in North Africa. In locations like Senegal or the Côte d'Ivoire where there was a small European population and where independence movements had found success by 1960, national groups looking to cement their own cultural identity could harness the potential of jazz.

Since before the war, jazz had occupied an important place in the lives of several well-known black intellectuals from across the French Empire. Leopold Sédar Senghor from Senegal and Léon-Gontran Damas from French Guiana had first come across jazz as students in Paris between the wars, and went on to use references to the music in their literary works. In studying philosophy at the Sorbonne in interwar Paris, the Antillean René Ménil's discovery of jazz had initiated his theoretical explorations into Antillean identity. These men's understandings of jazz allowed them to challenge cultural forms that had been imposed on French colonial subjects by the metropole and to connect as individuals with the cultures of the Black Atlantic.[86] The poetry and prose written by Damas, Senghor, and Ménil challenged the mindset and aims of the imperial agenda, and their uses of jazz were early precursors to the ways in which jazz was later manifested in events like the 1969 Pan-African Cultural Festival in Algiers. Jazz was harnessed as a means of disrupting the colonial narrative and establishing a common identity across the black diaspora.

Because, at its core, this music remained linked to African-American culture, people of African descent could claim it as part of their own aesthetic inheritance. When independence movements brought a new pride in indigenous forms of culture and a rejection of European standards, nationalists often accepted jazz once they divorced the music from the European colonial culture.[87] The history of jazz in France's former colonies was connected both to a history of colonization and to the international identity of the Black Atlantic, an identity that recognized and fostered a connectedness among black cultures in Africa, the Americas, and Europe during the twentieth century. In traveling beyond the metropole in the early postcolonial era, white French musicians made an effort to remain part of a world that was embracing the African and denying the centrality of the European.

In 1963, the French government sent Maxim Saury on a tour of West Africa as an "Ambassador of French jazz."[88] Under the patronage of the Ministère de la Coopération, Saury and his orchestra spent twenty-five days in Africa, performing in Senegal, the Congo, the Côte d'Ivoire, Togo, Dahomey, and Cameroon. All of these nations had become independent in 1960, and French leaders had political and economic incentives to maintain friendly relationships with the new governments and local populations.[89] It is important to point out that in terms of foreign policy after independence, the Ministère des Affaires Étrangères played only a tangential role in the relationship between France and French-speaking Africa. French political leaders instead used the Ministère de la Coopération to establish policy and sustain diplomatic links. Observers in both Paris and Africa came to see this governmental ministry as the one governing Franco-African affairs. Since its official establishment as a full ministry in 1961, the Ministère de la Coopération was responsible for military and civilian aid to newly-independent African countries.[90] Its support for the Saury tour reflected the agency's interest in cultural initiatives as well. In an interview, Saury himself acknowledged that his trip had been sponsored by the Ministère de la Coopération with "a goal of cultural propaganda" in mind.[91] Saury asserted that "the French over there do an enormous amount on all levels; they have simply realized that nothing positive has been done in the arts and more specifically in music."[92] Saury thought that exposing African audiences to jazz was a worthwhile effort because it sustained a French presence on the cultural front, not solely on military, economic, or humanitarian grounds. He promoted his interests as an individual musician by participating in this tour but also tacitly acknowledged the agenda of French politicians in de Gaulle's government who wanted to make sure Franco-African ties were not severed. In sanctioning the endeavor, the Ministère de la Coopération hoped that jazz would appeal to African listeners and bolster their ties to France.

The tour's supporters strove to employ jazz as a type of propaganda that would elevate France's stature in the eyes of African listeners. And, at a time and in an industry when French jazzmen were vying for recognition on an international stage that was dominated by Americans, French leaders were also trying to maintain a presence in Africa that did not depend on the United States or directly reflect support for American foreign policy. Saury claimed that African audiences preferred him to African-American musicians like Louis Armstrong because his whiteness made him unique in Africa. He told *Jazz Magazine*, that the tour was

> a success because, in all the towns where we went, we attracted many more spectators than Louis Armstrong or Cosy Cole had. That at least gave us affirmation. Louis Armstrong, so to speak, did not strike the Africans. I am sorry to say that because everyone knows that Armstrong is my idol. But, a

black who plays the trumpet, that does not surprise the black Africans. A black drummer, however great he is, and Cozy Cole is among the greatest, doesn't surprise them any more. But that whites know how to play rhythmic music—I say rhythmic because the word "jazz" signifies nothing to them—that appears an extraordinary thing to them.[93]

In general, Saury did not think that the Africans were enthusiastic about jazz. For most, the word meant absolutely nothing.

Saury's musicians played in front of a variety of audiences, both European and African, and the crowds could be rather large, ranging anywhere between 150 to 1,000 people. According to Saury, "There were official concerts with a public composed three quarters of Europeans, others reserved solely for black students, still others where the attendance was very mixed."[94] Not surprisingly, students were the most attentive audience for the music and Saury hoped that they, like French students since 1945, would embrace it. He and his orchestra played New Orleans jazz and perhaps this was one of the reasons the government selected him to represent French jazz abroad. Because Saury, like Louis Armstrong, specialized in the New Orleans style, he could attract more listeners than an avant-garde musician like Martial Solal. Saury himself asserted that the New Orleans style was ideal for promoting jazz, claiming, "It must be at all costs a music relatively simple and direct. Rhythm-and-blues would have also succeeded."[95] The French government must have at least partially agreed, because it chose him as *le ambassadeur* of French jazz.

In general, jazz critics and fans seemed to support this governmental effort to advance the cause of jazz in Africa. Before the Saury tour left, critic Jean-Louis Ginibre wrote, "We hope that this tour which follows that of Cozy Cole, organized by the American State Department, is successful so that others can be organized in the near future. At a time when, benefiting from the powerlessness of French unions and the Ministère du Travail, foreign musicians invade our country, it would be desirable for our jazzmen to have the chance to appear outside of our borders."[96] The critic Aris Destombes also felt that such a tour was overdue, asserting that a "long time after America—considering jazz as a peaceful means of propaganda—sent around the world its most representative jazzmen, France has its turn trying this adventure."[97] Because Saury's music was thought to have broad appeal, Destombes also optimistically claimed this tour was "condemned to succeed."[98]

Unfortunately for French jazzmen, the Ministère de la Coopération sponsored no further tours abroad. Saury, however, continued to perform in France's former colonies and overseas departments under the patronage of cultural centers, national radio broadcasting systems, and state-owned corporations. In April of 1965, he and his sextet went to Madagascar and Réunion under the sponsorship of the Centre Culturel Français and Radiodiffusion Nationale Malgache. Jean-Louis Ginibre declared the trip successful, writing, "Parades, processions, concerts in front of auditoriums sometimes grouping more that 2,500 people, jam-sessions with local musicians (Maxim Saury emphasized the value of certain Madagascan jazzmen, the Rabeson brothers especially) filled the eleven days of the tour, eleven days of popular enthusiasm."[99] The following year, Saury went to Tahiti, and then in 1969, he and his band went to Guadeloupe. On this latter tour, Claude Luter (another French New Orleans jazz musician) accompanied Saury as "guest artist." The government-owned airline Air France organized and sponsored the Guadeloupe trip and, because of this, Marcel Cazès, clarinetist and corporate delegate, also went along. Saury's group stopped in New York along the way but the musicians were much more encouraged by their reception in the Antilles. In an account written for *Jazz Magazine*, Saury wrote, "Adieu New York, vive la Guadeloupe!" as it was during the second leg of his journey that he met with an "excellent public, excellent welcome."[100] Saury himself championed these international concert tours, emphasizing after each one that important cultural contacts had been made between him, his musicians, and the local population. By the end of the 1960s, Saury was not among the most popular French jazz artists in France, undoubtedly due to some degree to his New Orleans style, the popularity of which had waned among forward-looking, young jazz fans, and because of the rising popularity of rock and roll. Yet he could still find audiences abroad to listen to his music. By connecting himself to the larger governmental and national initiative to keep France closely linked with its former colonies and overseas departments, Saury found an outlet for his music, a convivial audience, and a way to culturally represent jazz and France.

During the decade of the 1960s, musicians and cultural centers undertook other initiatives to promote jazz in Africa. In 1963, the French cultural counsel in Dakar, Senegal created a jazz club "where some local musicians are coming into being, playing in a modern spirit, in the style 'free jazz.'" According to Saury, "The goal of the [French] cultural council in Dakar is not however without interest: it would like that these Africans play jazz which, melodically, gets inspiration from Negro-American music, and which, rhythmically, be specifically African, that is to say based on the tam-tam. The creation of an orchestra is under way in Brazzaville as well."[101] Like the concert tours sponsored by the Ministère de la Coopération and cultural centers, the French cultural counsel in Dakar attempted to promote a music of its choice—jazz—with the local population, simultaneously seeking to Europeanize and Americanize music in Senegal, with the goal of making it more French-friendly and, therefore, potentially capable of improving France's own position in Senegalese society, culture, and maybe even politics. Jean-Loup Amselle has written that "Centres culturels francais" were "created in the former French colonies of Black Africa, starting with the center in Dakar, in 1959," with a twofold principle guiding them: "on the one hand, ensure the cultural influence of France, while on the other, encourage local cultural life."[102] The jazz club strove to accomplish these goals by introducing and promoting an American music.

By this time, jazz appreciation would not be reserved for Europeans or the French alone, as postcolonial leaders in West Africa began promoting the music on their own terms. Léopold Sédar Senghor became the first president of an independent Senegal in 1960, and in 1966, he expressed his continued admiration for this music by hosting the Festival of Negro Arts, to which he invited musicians and performers such as Louis Armstrong, Duke Ellington, Josephine Baker, and Marian Anderson. Through his actions, Senghor not only furthered his conception of *négritude* but he also helped to forge a transatlantic link between West Africa and the United States through jazz, a link that largely excluded the former colonizers. In this context, when French government entities and cultural centers worked to promote jazz, they were also trying to avoid their own obsolescence.

In another initiative to connect France with its former colonies and overseas departments, Jef Gilson's band (including bassist Gilbert Rovère and drummer Lionel Magal) went to Réunion and Madagascar in the spring of 1968 where the musicians delivered twelve concerts. The May upheavals in France prevented the band's return for well over a month, so the three musicians were able to observe jazz more closely in these places, especially in Madagascar. The *Courrier de Madagascar* interviewed Gilson during his stay, writing the following about him:

> Thanks to the Albert Camus Cultural Center, there was an unexpected event between our jazzmen and the Jef Gilson Trio. We knew very little Madagascan musicians who were attracted to traditional jazz. Each time that a "New Orleans" group came to Madagascar one felt the Jazz Club de Tananarive toeing the line a little. We didn't speak the same language. With Jef Gilson the effect was opposite. The connection was immediate, easy, disconcerting, unexpected. His music, like his sensibility, strangely corresponds to the temperament of Madagascan jazzmen. Like Jef Gilson, Gilbert Rovère and Lionel Magal, our jazzmen have always refused the easy concessions made to the idea "jazz for everybody."[103]

In his interview with the *Courrier de Madagascar*, Gilson expressed the same thought: that his trio and the Madagascan jazzmen shared a certain sensibility. He said, "Obviously, and this is very normal, we have slightly different temperaments, but in truth, at the bottom, we have the same way of 'feeling.'"[104] The positive connection between an avant-garde musician and the Madagascan population illustrated how governmental cultural initiatives (like the one that sent Saury) could not dictate or determine how the local population would receive the music. In the context of the government-sponsored 1963 tours, Saury and the Ministère de la Coopération assumed that New Orleans jazz would have the broadest appeal, but Gilson's 1968 trip to Madagascar illustrated an alleged attractiveness that free jazz had for some foreign audiences.

Gilson felt a certain ardor for the local music and culture and when he returned to France he expressed a desire to disseminate a variety of Madagascan music within the hexagon and throughout Europe. He maintained, "I intend, thanks to good recording equipment brought to Madagascar in my care (there is not a well-equipped studio there), to record the local jazz musicians, as well as these extraordinary choirs and folkloric musicians, in order to make all the forms of Madagascan music, so engaging, more widely known in Europe."[105] Gilson revisited Madagascar and Réunion a year later to fulfill his goal of increasing European recognition for these musicians. With cellist Jean-Carles Capon, he spent more than a month in Madagascar and a week in Réunion. In Tananarive, they organized an eighteen-day "jazz workshop" at the Albert Camus Cultural Center where they "gave courses, advice, and rehearsed with some of the best of the island's instrumentalists" as well as put together a band of nine musicians whose seven other members besides Gilson and Capon were Madagascan. According to *Jazz Magazine*, within this group, "some traditionally Madagascan instruments [like the *sodina*] mixed with saxophones and regular drums," mingling French and island culture.[106] On this second trip, Gilson also brought professional recording equipment with him—"123 kilograms of excess luggage"—to record Madagascan jazzmen and the island's folkloric musics. As part of the effort to promote these musics in Europe, Radiodiffusion-Télévision Française committed itself to broadcasting Gilson's recordings in France after his return. From April 9 to 17, Gilson and Capon organized a Semaine du Jazz in Tananarive, during which time there was an exhibit devoted to the posters of French artist Francis Paudras (who became well known among French jazz fans in the 1960s because of his close relationship with Bud Powell), numerous radio and television shows, and five concerts where Gilson's band received "a triumphant welcome" from Madagascan audiences.[107]

Gilson, the ever-vocal supporter of French jazz, also took up the cause of Madagascan jazz, commingling the future of both musics. Despite the steadfast backing he gave to Madagascans, Gilson also promoted French jazz by pushing his own music and educating the Madagascans about the French jazz scene and its lesser-known members like Paudras. Madagascans provided both a possible market and an audience for French jazz, and Gilson as a French jazzman certainly went there with more than benign cultural motives. His professional interests could not be separated from these two trips to Madagascar and Réunion, and despite his lack of direct affiliation with the French government, Gilson, like Saury before him, went to these places as a

French cultural ambassador, bolstering France's relationship with the government and people there. Like all French jazzmen traveling to France's overseas departments and former colonies, Gilson did represent France.

By the mid-1960s, French jazzmen had worked to forge a space for their music within postwar culture. Beyond the metropole, French jazzmen played in North Africa during the Algerian War and in Morocco and in Tunisia following independence, attempting to draw European audiences and eventually North African ones to their music. As the 1960s unfolded, jazz became increasingly identified with Africa so that it became more difficult for the French jazz public to inform either definitions of jazz or the music's political meanings for listeners in Africa, Asia, and the Caribbean, where populations had originally identified the music with the European colonizers. In the postcolonial era, jazz enthusiasts in what had formerly been French-controlled territories began to understand and to appreciate the music away from the Europeans who had been the first to bring the music to their countries, and to connect it with the aesthetic heritage and political identities of African Americans and Africans. Despite the growing obsolescence of French jazzmen in these locations abroad, these musicians persisted in going on tours and worked to cultivate links between themselves and these jazz communities beyond France, sometimes with the support of the French government and public cultural institutions. These artists acted as French citizens who lived out the optimistic vision of maintaining a permanent semblance of the Union Française as they traveled and played their music abroad. Back home, the French jazz community lauded these efforts to bring *jazz français* to a larger and more diverse audience of listeners, because for French jazz aficionados, when French musicians played their music on a global stage, they enhanced their nation's standing as an arbiter of international culture and made their artistic work relevant.

NOTES

1. Robin D. G. Kelley, *Africa Speaks, America Answers: Modern Jazz in Revolutionary Times* (Cambridge, MA: Harvard University Press, 2012), 85.

2. From the chapter "L'Algérie: La culture en question . . . " in *Alger 1969: 1er festival culturel panafricain*, ed. Omar Mokhtari (Algiers: Éditions Actualité Algérie, 1970), 32.

3. Jedediah Sklower, *Free Jazz, la catastrophe féconde: Une histoire du monde éclaté du jazz en France (1960–1982)* (Paris: L'Harmattan, 2006), 146.

4. Like Jeremy F. Lane, I have not been able to find specialized jazz critics from the colonized world (even though my study goes beyond the time period of his book). Lane has posited that "the absence of any specialist jazz critics from among France's indigenous colonial peoples reflected the much smaller overall size of the educated colonial elite at this time, itself the result of the more limited educational opportunities open to France's colonial subjects and citizens." Jeremy F. Lane, *Jazz and Machine-Age Imperialism: Music, "Race," and Intellectuals in France, 1918–1945* (Ann Arbor: University of Michigan Press, 2013), 31.

5. Frantz Fanon, *Toward the African Revolution: Political Essays*, trans. Haakon Chevalier (New York: Grove Press, 1967), 65–66. This book was published posthumously as Fanon died in 1961.

6. Jean-Dominique Brierre, *Le Jazz français de 1900 à aujourd'hui* (Paris: Éditions Hors Collection, 2000), 79.

7. Errol Parker, *A Flat Tire on My Ass* (Redwood, NY: Cadence Jazz Books, 1995), 1.

8. "Errol Parker, 72, Jazz Drummer and Pianist," *New York Times* (6 July 1998); "Errol Parker ne fait plus jazzer. Le pianist de "Lorre" est mort à New York à 72 ans," *Libération* (7 July 1998), http://www.liberation.fr/culture/0101252464–errol-parker-ne-fait-plus-jazzer-le-piantiste-de-lorre-est-mort-a-new-york-a-72–ans.

9. Parker, 3.

10. Charles Sowerwine, *France Since 1870: Culture Politics and Society* (New York: Palgrave, 2001), 309.

11. Martin Thomas, "Part Two: French Decolonization" in *Crises of Empire: Decolonization and Europe's Imperial States, 1918–1975*, eds. Martin Thomas, Bob Moore, and L. J. Butler (London: Hodder Education, 2008), 228–29.

12. Letter from Jean-Louis Gérard, "Q et R," *Jazz Magazine* 46 (March 1959), 7.

13. "Q et R par Frère Jazz" *Jazz Magazine* 50 (July 1959), 5.

14. "Cher Frère Jazz," *Jazz Magazine* 61 (July–August 1960), 7.

15. Susan Weiner, *Enfants Terribles: Youth and Femininity in the Mass Media in France, 1945–1968* (Baltimore: Johns Hopkins University Press, 2001), 144, 156. Also see Jean-Pierre Vittori, *Nous les appelés d'Algérie* (Paris: Messidor, 1983).

16. "Cher Frère Jazz," *Jazz Magazine* 75 (October 1961), 7.

17. Jean Crestet, "Un dur apprentissage," *Jazz Magazine* no. 83 (June 1962), 31.

18. Ibid.

19. "Cher Frère Jazz," *Jazz Magazine* 69 (April 1961), 5.

20. Pierre Voran, "Une Semaine du Jazz à Oran," *Bulletin du Hot Club de France* 102 (November 1960), 39.

21. Martin Thomas, "Part Two: French Decolonization" in *Crises of Empire: Decolonization and Europe's Imperial States, 1918–1975*, eds. Martin Thomas, Bob Moore, and L. J. Butler (London: Hodder Education, 2008), 236–37. The settler community was a thoroughly urban one, and Thomas writes, "[Algiers] had 296,041 registered non-Muslim residents; a further 63,588 lived in the districts of Maison-Blanche and Blida. Oran registered 204,393 non-Muslims, Bône 50,753, and the Constantine urban district 44,015."

22. Henri Martinez, *Et Qu'ils m'accueillent avec des cris de haine* (Paris: Éditions Robert Laffont, 1982), 29.

23. Pierre Nora, *Les Français d'Algérie* (Paris: Juillard, 1961), 177. A new edition of the book was released in 2012, Pierre Nora, *Les Français d'Algérie* (Paris: C. Bourgois, 2012). I have used the English translation from Ali Yedes, "Social Dynamics in Colonial Algeria: The Question of *Pieds-Noirs* Identity," *French Civilization and Its Discontents: Nationalism, Colonialism, Race* (Lanham, MD: Lexington Books, 2003), eds. Tyler Stovall and Georges Van Den Abbeele, 240.

24. Martin Thomas, *The French North African Crisis: Colonial Breakdown and Anglo-French Relations, 1945–62* (New York: St. Martin's Press, 2000), 13. For an early observation of this reality, see Douglas Johnson, "Algeria: Some Problems of Modern History," *Journal of African History*, vol. 5, no. 2 (1964).

25. Irwin M. Wall, *France, the United States, and the Algerian War* (Berkeley: University of California Press, 2001), 239; and Sowerwine, 312.

26. Alistair Horne, *A Savage War of Peace: Algeria 1954–1962* (New York: New York Review Books, 2006), 435. The referendum read, "Do you approve the Bill submitted to the French people by the President of the Republic concerning the self-determination of the Algerian population and the organization of the public powers in Algeria prior to self-determination?" See Horne, 434.

27. Jonathan K. Gosnell, *The Politics of Frenchness in Colonial Algeria, 1930–1954* (Rochester, NY: University of Rochester Press, 2002), 8.

28. "Festivals partout," *Jazz Hot* 167 (July–August 1961), 21.

29. Yedes, 244. For more on the conflicted identity of the *pieds-noirs*, see Pierre Bourdieu, *Sociologie de l'Algérie* (Paris: Presses Universitaires de France, 1961).

30. Martin Thomas, "Part Two: French Decolonization" in *Crises of Empire: Decolonization and Europe's Imperial States, 1918–1975*, eds. Martin Thomas, Bob Moore, and L. J. Butler (London: Hodder Education, 2008), 245. In addition to the settler population that left Algeria in 1962, around 130,000 Muslim *harkis* also departed from France. Also see Colette Zytnicki, "L'Administration face à l'arrivée des repatriés d'Algérie: L'exemple de la region Midi-Pyrenées (1962–1964)," *Annales du Midi* vol. 110, no. 224 (1998), 501–21.

31. Horne, 520.

32. Philippe Koechlin, "Renaissance ou déclin du Jazz?" *Révolution africaine* no. 3 (16 February 1963), 22.

33. *Jazz Hot* 185 (March 1963), 13.

34. "Jazz en Algérie," *Jazz Hot* 199 (June 1964), 11.

35. Penny M. Von Eschen, *Satchmo Blows Up the World: Jazz Ambassadors Play the Cold War* (Cambridge, MA: Harvard University Press, 2004), 171, 175–76. I have quoted Von Eschen's book here; the original quote can be found in an airgram to Department of State from American Embassy, Algiers, on "The Randy Weston Sextet in Algiers" (April 13, 1967), 2. Series 2, Box 31, Bureau Historical Collection.

36. Phan Tu, "The Struggle of South Vietnam Against Imperialist Cultural Domination," *African Culture: Algiers Symposium, July 21st–August 1st* (Algiers: Société Nationale d'Édition et de Diffusion, 1969), 264.

37. Monique Gadant, *Islam et nationalism en Algérie d'après "El Moudjahid," organe central du FLN de 1956 à 1962* (Paris, Éditions L'Harmattan, 1988); and Albert Fitte, *Spectroscopie d'une propaganda révolutionnaire: "El Moudjahid" des temps de guerre; juin 1956–mars 1962* (Montpellier: Université Paul Valéry, 1973).

38. "Randy Weston in Algiers," *El Moudjahid* (Algiers, April 4, 1967), original and English translation in Bureau Historical Collection. Also see Von Eschen, 172.

39. Ingrid Monson, *Freedom Sounds: Civil Rights Call Out to Jazz and Africa* (New York: Oxford University Press, 2007), 147–48.

40. "Return to Origins," *An Nasr* (Algiers, April 4, 1967), Bureau Historical Collection. To build Pan-African collaboration, Weston moved to Morocco after his 1967 tour and remained there for the next seven years. See Von Eschen, 172, 176–77.

41. The "List of Participants" only included Africans, but the "List of Guests and Observers" included individuals from Africa, the Americas, Eastern and Western Europe, and Asia. Out of these 155 "Guests and Observers," were 22 French men and women: Roger Barrié (professor), Jean Benoist-Mechin (writer), Jacqueline Delange (head of the Negro African Department at the Musée d'Homme in Paris), Roselène Dousset (anthropologist), Georges Feldhandler (program director of the Théâtre de Ville de Paris), Max-Pol Fouchet (writer), Pierre Fougeyrollas (director of the Institut Fondamental de l'Afrique Noire in Dakar), Robert Gessain (director of the Musée de l'Homme in Paris), Alain Gheerbrandt (writer), Francis Jeanson (writer), Julien Michel Leiris (director of research at the Centre National de la Recherche Scientifique), Jacques Maquet (research supervisor at the University of Paris), Pierre Meauze (curator at the Museum of African and Oceanic Arts in Paris), Albert Memmi (writer), Alfred Muller (specialist in ancient African arts), Jacques Nantet (writer), Renée Plasson-Stibbe (lawyer), Arlette Roth (research supervisor at the Centre National de la Recherche Scientifique), Jacques Roussillon (cultural field worker), Jean Suret-Canale (Africanist and deputy director of the Centre d'Etudes et de Recherches Marxistes in Paris), Marie-José Tubiana (research supervisor at the Centre National de la Recherche Scientifique), and Joseph Tubiana (professor). "List of Guests and Observers," *African Culture: Algiers Symposium, July 21st–August 1st* (Algiers: Société Nationale d'Édition et de Diffusion, 1969), 207–10.

42. "Address by Mr. Diallo Telli," *African Culture: Algiers Symposium, July 21st–August 1st* (Algiers: Société Nationale d'Édition et de Diffusion, 1969), 20. Telli was from Guinea.

43. "Pan-African Cultural Manifesto," *African Culture: Algiers Symposium, July 21st–August 1st* (Algiers: Société Nationale d'Édition et de Diffusion, 1969), 180. In 1963, the OAU was founded, and in 1964, the Commission of the OAU for Education and Culture was created. It met for the first time in Kinshasa, and then in 1966, gathered in Lagos and recom-

mended organizing "festivals of dramatic art and African handicraft, as well as art exhibitions." See *The Faces of Algeria: First Pan-African Cultural Festival* (Algiers: Ministry of Information and Culture/Wizarat al-Akhbar wa-al-Thaqafah, 1970), 36.

44. Quoted in *The Faces of Algeria: First Pan-African Cultural Festival* (Algiers: Ministry of Information and Culture/Wizarat al-Akhbar wa-al-Thaqafah, 1970), 24.

45. Pathé Diagne, *Léopold S. Senghor, ou, La négritude servant de la francophonie au Festival panafricain d'Alger: trente ans après* (Dakar: Éditions Sankoré, 2002).

46. In the "Pan-African Cultural Manifesto," he was named "President of the Revolutionary Council, President of the Council of Ministers of the Algerian People's Democratic Republic, and current Chairman of the Conference of Heads of State and Government of the Organization of African Unity."

47. Carinya Sharples, "Flashback: 21 July 1969. Pan-African Culture Festival Rocks Algiers," *ARISE* 18 (September 24, 2012), http://carinyasharplesjournalist.wordpress.com/2012/09/24/flashback-21-july-1969-pan-african-culture-festival-rocks-algiers/. In 2009, a second festival was organized by the Algerian government and the African Union in an attempt to recreate the collaborative atmosphere of the 1969 festival.

48. "Inaugural Speech by H. E. Houari Boumediene," *African Culture: Algiers Symposium, July 21st–August 1st* (Algiers: Société Nationale d'Édition et de Diffusion, 1969), 14–15.

49. Mohamed Saidi, "The Decolonization of African Culture," *African Culture: Algiers Symposium, July 21st–August 1st* (Algiers: Société Nationale d'Édition et de Diffusion, 1969), 230.

50. M. D. Chabou, "The Role of African Culture in Economic and Social Development," *African Culture: Algiers Symposium, July 21st–August 1st* (Algiers: Société Nationale d'Édition et de Diffusion, 1969), 297.

51. *The Faces of Algeria: First Pan-African Cultural Festival* (Algiers: Ministry of Information and Culture/Wizarat al-Akhbar wa-al-Thaqafah, 1970), 46.

52. Paul Alessandrini, "L'Amérique noir au festival d'Alger," *Jazz Magazine* 169–70 (September 1969), 16.

53. Archie Shepp, "We Have Come Back," *Live at the Pan-African Cultural Festival* (Paris: Actuel, 1969), sound recording. Also see the 1969 documentary, *Le Festival Panafricain d'Alger* by American filmmaker William Klein.

54. *The Faces of Algeria: First Pan-African Cultural Festival* (Algiers: Ministry of Information and Culture/Wizarat al-Akhbar wa-al-Thaqafah, 1970), 51, 54.

55. Alessandrini, 17. I have used the translation from *The Faces of Algeria: First Pan-African Cultural Festival* (Algiers: Ministry of Information and Culture/Wizarat al-Akhbar wa-al-Thaqafah, 1970), 26.

56. Two hundred ninety-three films were allegedly shown to more than 28,000 people. See *The Faces of Algeria: First Pan-African Cultural Festival* (Algiers: Ministry of Information and Culture/Wizarat al-Akhbar wa-al-Thaqafah, 1970), 65.

57. "Archie Shepp—Live at the Pan-African Festival," http://surrealdocuments.blogspot.com/2007/07/archie-shepp-live-at-pan-african.html.

58. William E. Watson, *Tricolor and Crescent: France and the Islamic World* (Westport, CT: Praeger Publishers, 2003), 99; and Susan Gilson Miller, *A History of Modern Morocco* (New York: Cambridge University Press, 2013), 111.

59. Martin Thomas, "Part Two: French Decolonization" in *Crises of Empire: Decolonization and Europe's Imperial States, 1918–1975*, eds. Martin Thomas, Bob Moore, and L. J. Butler (London: Hodder Education, 2008), 214, 216. Also see Zeynip Çelik, *Urban Forms and Colonial Confrontations: Algiers Under French Rule* (Berkeley: University of California Press, 1997); Paul Rabinow, *French Modern: Norms and Forms of the Social Environment* (Chicago: University of Chicago Press, 1989); and Janet Abu Lughod, *Rabat: Urban Apartheid in Morocco* (Princeton, NJ: Princeton University Press, 1980).

60. Miller, 115–6. Also see Jacques Berque, *French North Africa: The Maghrib between Two World Wars* (New York: Praeger, 1967).

61. Miller, 157, 159.

62. "Jazz à la carte," *Jazz Hot* 165 (May 1961), 42.

63. "In December 1959, Muhammad V negotiated an agreement with the United States to withdraw from its five military bases in Morocco acquired at the height of the Cold War as a part of America's Strategic Air Command (SAC) anti-Soviet early warning system. With the advent of a new generation of long-range bombers, the Moroccan bases were deemed no longer essential by the U.S. military and the withdrawal was completed by 1963. This amicable exchange over the shutdown of the bases became the cornerstone for the warm and increasingly close Moroccan-American friendship that developed over the course of Hassan [II]'s reign." See Miller, 165, 209; and I. W. Zartman, *Morocco: Problems of New Power* (New York: Atherton Press, 1964).

64. "Le premier festival de jazz au Maroc," *Jazz Magazine* 70 (May 1961), 18–19.
65. "Jazz à la carte," *Jazz Hot* 174 (March 1962), 31.
66. "Lettre du Maroc," *Jazz Magazine* 108 (July 1964), 5.
67. "Jazz au Maroc," *Jazz Hot* 199 (June 1964), 11; and "Lettre du Maroc," 7.
68. "Lettre du Maroc," 7.
69. "Jazz actualités," *Jazz Hot* 213 (October 1965), 10.
70. Von Eschen, 169. She quotes a memo to the Department of State from Charles M. Ellison on "AP Story on Woody Herman" (May 10, 1966), Series 2, Box 14, Folder 7, Bureau Historical Collection.
71. Randy Weston and Willard Jenkins, *African Rhythms: The Autobiography of Randy Weston* (Durham, NC: Duke University Press, 2010), 159. Weston played a gig for the branch of the Hot Club de France.
72. Letter to Randy Weston from the Foreign Service of the United States of America in Rabat, Morocco (May 11, 1967). A copy of the letter is printed in Weston and Jenkins, 155.
73. Letter to Randy Weston from Henry J. Tasca (July 18, 1968). A copy of the letter is printed in Weston and Jenkins, 157.
74. Weston and Jenkins, 186.
75. Thomas, 218.
76. Watson, 96, 98.
77. Thomas, 217.
78. Ingrid Monson, *Freedom Sounds: Civil Rights Call Out to Jazz and Africa* (Oxford: Oxford University Press, 2007), 127.
79. Lisa E. Davenport, *Jazz Diplomacy: Promoting America in the Cold War Era* (Jackson: University Press of Mississippi, 2009), 58.
80. Armand Gordon, "Nights of Tunisia," *Jazz Magazine* 105 (April 1964), 16.
81. "De retour de Tunisie" Selmer advertisement, *Jazz Magazine* 159 (October 1968), 52.
82. Les Barbecues: Jazz Nouvelle Orléans since 1960, accessed March 26, 2016, http://www.les-barbecues.fr/index.html.
83. Joachim Berendt, "Noon in Tunisia," *Jazz Magazine* 171 (October 1969), 19–20, 58.
84. But as late as 1992, Dizzy Gillespie went to Namibia with Secretary of State James Baker. Von Eschen, 250.
85. From the chapter "Le Ghana: Nous sommes descendus du ciel sur une chaîne d'or" in *Alger 1969: 1er festival culturel panafricain* (Algiers: Éditions Actualité Algérie), 124.
86. Jeremy Lane examines the work of each of these men in his *Jazz and Machine-Age Imperialism: Music "Race," and Intellectuals in France, 1918–1945*. In using the term *Black Atlantic*, I am referencing the pathbreaking work done by Paul Gilroy in his book *The Black Atlantic: Modernity and Double-Consciousness* (Cambridge, MA: Harvard University Press, 1993).
87. Little has been written on jazz in the former French colonies in this period, but Warren R. Pinckney Jr.'s article, "Jazz in Barbados," *American Music*, vol. 12, no. 1 (Spring 1994), 58–87, studies the link between jazz and a pan-African identity in Barbados.
88. Jean-Louis Ginibre, "Maxim, ambassaduer itinérant," *Jazz Magazine* 93 (April 1963), 19; and Jean-Louis Ginibre, "Une soirée chez Maxim," *Jazz Magazine* 96 (July 1963), 32. Ginibre made a pointed reference to American government spokesmen labeling musicians like Louis Armstrong and Dizzy Gillespie "ambassadors" as a result of their foreign tours (Ambassadeur du jazz français). The members of Saury's orchestra were: Jean-Claude Naude (trumpet), Michel Camicas (trombone), Pierre Escuras (banjo and guitar), Jean-Pierre Mulot (bass),

and Robert Péguet (drums). For this trip, Escuras had replaced the pianist Gérard Raingo-Pelouse who was normally a member of the group. The tour lasted from April 15 until May 7.

89. To reflect the changing power dynamic between France and her current and former colonial holdings, the Ministère des Colonies, in 1946, became the Ministère de la France d'Outre-mer. When former French colonies in Africa became independent, their relationship with France was then negotiated and governed through the Ministère de la Coopération. On these changing names of governmental ministries, see Guy de Luignan, *French-Speaking Africa Since Independence* (New York: Frederick A. Praeger, 1969), 33.

90. Francis Terry McNamara, *France in Black Africa* (Washington, DC: National Defense University Press, 1989), 183, 208.

91. Jean-Louis Ginibre, "Une soirée chez Maxim," *Jazz Magazine* 96 (July 1963), 32

92. Philippe Koechlin, "Le swing et l'afrique," *Jazz Hot* 189 (July–August 1963), 15.

93. Jean-Louis Ginibre, "Une soirée chez Maxim," *Jazz Magazine* 96 (July 1963), 32.

94. Ibid.

95. Ibid., 17.

96. Jean-Louis Ginibre, "Maxim, ambassadeur itinérant," *Jazz Magazine* 93 (April 1963), 19.

97. Aris Destombes, "Ambassador Saury," *Jazz Hip* 32 (Easter 1963), 46. This article was also published under the same title in *Jazz Hot* 186 (April 1963), 16.

98. Ibid.

99. Jean-Louis Ginibre, "Max l'explorateur," *Jazz Magazine* 119 (June 1965), 15.

100. Maxim Saury, "Maxim voyage," *Jazz Magazine* 167 (June 1969), 18–19.

101. Jean-Louis Ginibre, "Une soirée chez Maxim," *Jazz Magazine* 96 (July 1963), 32.

102. Jean-Loup Amselle, "Franco-African Artistic and Cultural Cooperation," *Empire Lost: France and Its Other Worlds*, ed. Elisabeth Mudimbe-Boyi (Lanham, MD: Lexington Books, 2009), 166.

103. Reprinted in Jeff Gilson, "Jazz à Madagascar," *Jazz Hot* 243 (October 1968), 18.

104. Ibid.

105. Ibid., 19.

106. "Jazz à Madagascar," *Jazz Magazine* 167 (June 1969), 15. The workshop lasted from March 12 to March 30.

107. Ibid., 16.

Conclusion

Improvising the Nation

In the 1950s and 1960s, the French were uneasy about preserving a distinct national identity in the face of weakened international authority, represented on one hand by an increasing American presence not only in Europe but throughout the world, and on the other hand by decolonization. What differentiated the postwar jazz scene from earlier years was that France's relationship with its colonies and with the United States had decisively altered. Overseas departments and territories were gaining independence from a much-weakened France, and the United States had attained dominance in the West when it came to military, economic, and cultural strength. In the 1950s and 1960s, jazz remained a well-established part of French entertainment, at a time when a heightened sense of cultural malaise and anti-Americanism indicated a fear about an impending French obsolescence. French nationals with predominantly European and Catholic backgrounds had begun to share their country with growing numbers of immigrants from the colonized world who did not share the same physical appearances or often the same religious practices. Postwar jazz culture revealed much about the values, concerns, and assumptions existent in French society during a time of change.

From the moment of jazz's arrival in France at the end of World War I, the music had held multiple meanings for audiences, variously representing freedom, the immoral, the primitive, the United States, the modern, the young, the male. I have attempted to illustrate how, depending on time and circumstances, these meanings reflected the concerns, ideals, and hopes of French listeners in the decades following World War II, often telling us much more about French society than about the music itself. To differing degrees, members of the French jazz public devoted their intellect, careers, money, and time to jazz, and in doing so revealed ongoing tensions in postwar France. In 1972, André Hodeir asked, "What are the meaning and exact role of jazz in our society?"[1] Hodeir thought that jazz had a place in France and hoped that the music portended "the tremendous wealth and variety of an expanding culture." For him, culture could not remain sclerotic and closed and continue to thrive. By embracing jazz, in its continual novelty and connection to the United States, French men and women participated in an art form that reached beyond national borders and linked them to American and African-American cultural practices. They inhabited a world defined by the pull between the global and the national, and had to negotiate these two competing forces. In jazz writings, there was a palpable sense of uncertainty about France's future. In a world defined by superpower authority, increasing European integration and the dissolution of empires, what position and what type of influence and control would France exert? What role would national borders play in the future? If passports and birthplaces grew obsolete, what would it mean to be French?

This divergence between the national and international was manifested in how French jazz critics, musicians, and fans addressed subjects surrounding the music and exposed regular inconsistencies in ideas about race and power. Members of the jazz public promoted antiracist platforms and politics while revealing deeply entrenched conceptions about black bodies and black musical acumen. They also remained silent about the wrongs of French colonization and about the atrocities of the Algerian War, even as they supported the initiatives and aims of the American civil rights movement. Some musicians and activists admired African-American musical leadership and prowess while trying to exclude these very same musicians from France because they were seen as economic competition. These inconsistencies exposed a culture and society in a state of flux and insecurity.

Many questions circulated around the writings, conversations, and concerns of French jazz enthusiasts. Despite the jazz public's rather small size in relation to the entire French population, this group of people—most of whom were well-educated, middle-class white men who participated in a rather exclusive subculture—addressed challenges and frustrations as they navigated postwar developments. In France, conflicting ideas persisted about jazz, revealing anxieties about not only sustaining this music in France but about the place of the nation in a new international order. What happened to art in a world that valued making money over artistic creativity? Could jazz maintain its audiences as the popularity of yé-yé and rock and roll grew? What would happen to French society if women were equal to men? How could *jazz français* exist if it had made no unique aesthetic contributions? Could "racial" difference be caused exclusively by culture? Could France maintain its presence in the former empire or compete with the international power of the United States? These questions had no direct answers and revealed a nation increasingly defined by ambiguity; long-lasting and intrinsic components of French society were permanently shifting and inaugurating an uncertain future. Postwar jazz appreciation reflected a worldview that expected white, male, European power and prestige and that was being destabilized by an evolving world.

Every theme-based chapter in this book has examined a societal component that was changing in the decades following World War II: youth culture and the place of women; the growth of minority populations in metropolitan France; the economic, military, and cultural strength of the United States; the weakening power and feared obsolescence of France; and the independence movements in the colonies. My aim has been to explore each of these subjects through the lens of jazz to show on a microcosmic level how sea changes in French society, culture, politics, economics, and foreign affairs were being addressed and negotiated. As women expanded their roles at citizens, some expanded their positions within youth culture and on the jazz scene. Jazzwomen and individuals like Juliet Gréco and Françoise Sagan challenged traditional notions of femininity and propriety through their connections to jazz culture and through their public personas; Mimi Perrin gained respect and a fan base though her musical talent and acumen. These women, as well as female jazz critics, were at the forefront during an era of representational change, yet male critics, musicians, and fans (much like the nation at large) were hesitant to open up spaces in which they could participate as equals.

The issues of race and cultural difference were arguably the most prescient ones the jazz public addressed, leading white Frenchmen to have telling discussions about the subjects of discrimination and antiracism. Of course, listening to jazz records and having an awareness of civil rights violations in the United States did not inevitably lead the French to have progressive attitudes towards racial minorities on their own soil. As experience showed, an increasingly visible "other" in the metropole resulted in proliferating acts of discrimination against extra-European immigrants and their descendants, and the popularity of musics like jazz did not indicate how individuals and groups would react to minority groups living and working in their midst. Jazz fans could be racist or antiracist, or claim to be the latter while also still holding insidious ideas about racial difference. There was no guaranteed correlation between musical tastes and the absence of prejudice. In the context of empire, the fact that jazz critics and fans supported one subaltern people (African Americans) did not lead to them supporting independence movements in Africa or Asia or objecting to French acts of violence and discrimination against people there. Despite these inconsistencies, the jazz public addressing the subject of civil rights and racial and cultural difference remained important. Through their written conversations and debates, French critics, musicians, and fans communicated their distinct conceptions over race and culture at a turning point in French history.

From the beginning, jazz's story in France was connected to African-American musicians. This meant that in the 1920s the music was intertwined with the negrophilia of the age and with racial concepts that required performers like Josephine Baker to represent the exotic, the African, and the American. These patterns of thinking faded but did not entirely disappear so that jazz appreciation after World War II still manifested racialized ways of understanding the music, even if the majority of commentators began to insist that culture not biology created the perceived black musical advantage. Blackness and jazz remained incontrovertibly linked to one another, creating a bifurcated vision: the black jazzman was emotional, virile, rhythmic, and active, while the white jazzman was more refined, polished, and cerebral. In white French minds, the white musician was often unable to play or to create jazz in the same authentic way, making him an inferior substitute for the black musician. Blackness guaranteed a type of legitimacy and vitality that was allegedly missing in white musicians. In discussions of black musicians, French commentators revealed an ongoing fascination with black male bodies. In this way, white Frenchmen admired a physical strength and endurance as well as a capacity for relaxation and flexibility. Critics disagreed over whether these traits had roots in biology or in the social experiences of African Americans, but most agreed on a fundamental musical dominance. White French jazzmen had reason to argue for the importance of "sociological constellations" because this conception of musical talent improved their own prospects as musicians.

Importantly, professional French critics attempted to move away from strongly racialized discourse in the 1960s by highlighting the power of culture to shape humankind and by recognizing the musical achievements of white musicians, both American and French. Not all of their contemporaries followed their lead, with some individuals continuing to insist on a physical and inherited black superiority. The debates and dividing lines over black and white musicians illuminated the ambiguities surrounding racism and cultural fundamentalism. Even if jazz enthusiasts used culture to characterize black musicians as aesthetically gifted, conceptions of blackness perpetuated long-lived racial categories. While the use of stereotypical language became less common and more covert, and influential jazz critics like Lucien Malson actively tried to upend them, perceived racial and cultural boundaries between black and white musicians persisted. The beliefs that had originally been based in biological difference endured even when racism was being consciously rejected.

The antiracism of professional critics, even if it did not lead jazz audiences down an active political path, pushed French observers to be cognizant about racial discrimination. Following a familiar juxtaposition, the United

States was often characterized as racist while France was portrayed as comparatively colorblind. Readers of *Jazz Hot* and *Jazz Magazine* were exposed to the instances of prejudices African-American musicians faced at home, and these readers were encouraged to endorse the goals of the American civil rights movement. This did not make members of the jazz public automatically antiracists, but it was not unusual for individuals to vocally champion the cause of civil rights in the United States. Left-leaning French supporters of jazz fixated on the wrongs black Americans faced and rallied to support them. With no similar cause to promote in the metropole—because the injustices of French racism were yet to be broadly recognized by the white French population—politically minded French jazz fans supported equality and justice for African Americans (at least in spirit as I have found no record of French jazz enthusiasts participating in actual protests in the United States or France).

French jazz fans, much like the general white population in France, were less often informed about instances of French discrimination, but professional critics in the 1960s tried to make these fans aware of racial prejudice in the hexagon. In the decades following World War II, France was becoming a multiracial and multicultural society, and jazz culture exhibited a cosmopolitan outlook by embracing African-American artistic expression. Supporting civil rights for French minorities and immigrant groups was a logical, if not automatic, extension of the self-professed antiracism of the majority of French jazz critics. Some jazz fans took up this cause, but less vocally than they did the cause of African-American civil rights. For decades, the French (not just jazz enthusiasts) avoided recognizing instances and patterns of French racial bias. Focusing on the United States was more common because this allowed French commentators and activists both to diminish American stature and to project French social norms as preferable to American ones. For the first decade and a half after the war, few among the French were willing to address the problem of racial discrimination in France. As the 1960s progressed, more members of the *franco-français* majority became aware of the French prejudices that were becoming easier to see because of the changing demographics of the country. Increasing numbers of sub-Saharan Africans, Asians, and North Africans were moving to France and well-entrenched beliefs about race as well as memories of colonial loss shaped white French reactions to immigrants, leading to discriminatory practices. Beginning in the 1960s, jazz critics were cognizant of specifically French forms of racism and urged listeners to recognize and to disrupt them.

At a time when French citizens were increasingly concerned about American political, economic, and cultural dominance, French jazz audiences used this music to criticize American consumerism, commercialism, and racism. Because jazz relied on improvisation, it was not easily standardized and therefore existed in opposition to two crucial aspects of consumer society: mass production and mass consumption. French commentators prized artistic creativity over profit-making, and censured American or Americanized companies when they placed commercial standards on artists. In the context of the Cold War, members of the French jazz public took advantage of American and Soviet policies to advance their own interests. They generally supported the American State Department's jazz tours abroad and any efforts Washington undertook to spread jazz appreciation globally, even if they disapproved of the American government's political motives. When Soviet leaders did not welcome American artists behind the Iron Curtain, French musicians traveled to Eastern Bloc countries. They brought jazz to the Soviet Union and to Soviet satellite nations, creating greater international leverage for themselves as jazz artists. Throughout these postwar decades, French jazz critics, musicians, and fans used an American music as a means of criticizing American racism and consumerism and showing conditional support for American foreign policy.

In a global framework defined by lessening French authority, French jazz enthusiasts worked to make a space for French jazz that would recognize national contributions to the music. French musicians sought to gain respect from their American counterparts as well as from their own fellow citizens. They had a hard time doing so because American, and especially African-American, artists were appreciated as the original creators and the continual innovators of the music. French jazzmen lobbied record companies, concert promoters, club owners, and even the government so that their music could have wider exposure. These musicians, along with other members of the jazz public, continued to advance the idea of French jazz, even if the music had no aesthetic definition but was simply played by French-speaking players or French citizens. The pull between the national and the global, the local and the universal, was apparent in discussions over French jazz. Even though French critics and musicians specifically lauded the universal nature of jazz because it appealed to people across national borders, they also wanted to ensure France's own specific place in this global culture. In an effort to improve the employment prospects of native jazz musicians, the Syndicat des Artistes Musiciens de Jazz pushed for limiting the number of foreign musicians hired in France. Because of job scarcity, these musicians lobbied the government to issue fewer work permits to nonnationals and wanted clubs, concerts, and *caves* to give preferential treatment to French artists. Some musicians and critics directly criticized this agenda, most visibly by creating two organizations in 1968: Action Musique and the Fédération des Musiciens de Jazz en France. These groups sought equality for all musicians: professional and amateur, French and foreign, and opposed the use any classifications based on passports or national belonging. That not all jazz musicians, critics, or organizations agreed on the subject of hiring French or foreign musicians illustrated again the ever-present tension between the national and the global in postwar France. Would French citizens have distinct rights or privileges in a world increasingly defined by international competition and cooperation? Should they?

Sidney Bechet and Django Reinhardt were both jazz celebrities in postwar France. Bechet was revered not only for his music but also for choosing to live in France during the last decade of his life, while Reinhardt was admired for making pioneering contributions to French jazz. But both men were understood as distinct from their white French contemporaries and their audiences put great weight on their ethnic and racial identities. Reinhardt and Bechet were idolized by the general public, lauded by professional critics, and lived privileged lives as a result of their professional successes, but the ways in which they were venerated shed light on postwar conceptions of difference. Bechet was not seen as a complete equal to his white French contemporaries because of the unbending influence of the colonial mindset, which linked blackness to colonial subjects and their assumed inferiority. This meant that even when professing admiration for Bechet, Charles Delaunay still referenced how the musician spoke in "petit nègre." When Delaunay did so, he revealed a conflation between the African American and the African that envisioned them both in a racialized and essentialized manner. Reinhardt was a member of the Roma ethnic group and had actually been born in Belgium. The fact that he did not get a French passport until he was twenty-four, did not prevent his fans from claiming him as the most inventive and important of French jazzman. Listeners embraced his Roma culture and argued that his musical genius would not have been possible without it. Bechet's and Reinhardt's admirers emphasized that both men lived outside of mainstream French society, one as an African-American expatriate and the other as a gypsy. This conferred musical and artistic advantages upon them, but also required them to remain different, "other." Despite being portrayed as musical virtuosos, neither man was represented as the equal of a white Frenchman.

In the context of empire, jazz reflected the changing status between France and its colonies. Until the end of the Algerian War, the music was connected to the white colonizers because the "Algerian" jazz community was composed of *colons* and soldiers of European descent. The labels "Algerian" and "French" were reserved for these individuals, not for the Arabs or Berbers who were fighting so desperately for independence, and there was no perceived inconsistency in interchangeably using these categories: a white jazzman born in Algeria could be both Algerian and French at the same time (but the same could not be said for members of the indigenous population whose identities were effaced). Until the end of the war, French jazz critics remained silent about the ongoing violence, projecting an optimistic view of "Algerian" jazz to readers back in the metropole. Despite *colons* being outnumbered eight to one in Algeria, French jazz enthusiasts infrequently acknowledged the existence of Arabs or Berbers. Until after independence, members of the indigenous Algerian population tended to connect jazz with the white colonizers and not with African-American origins. A similar situation existed in Morocco and Tunisia, where even after independence the jazz community was sustained by a European minority, American soldiers stationed in the region, and American musicians sent through the American State Department. Breaking the link between jazz and French colonization was made possible as African-American jazz musicians traveled to North Africa in greater numbers, with some of them even choosing to live there, and by a growing interest among the local populations in jazz. African-American artists worked to create bonds with African culture as part of their commitment to Pan-Africanism and anti-imperialism. As North African nations moved away from French control, jazz became distanced from Europe and connected to African and African-American cultural and political identities.

French jazzmen toured in former and current overseas departments and territories throughout much of the 1960s and the French government sent Maxim Saury to West Africa in 1963. When jazz artists like Saury or Jef Gilson played in Senegal, the Côte d'Ivoire, or Madagascar they encountered different circumstances and populations with varying degrees of receptiveness to them as Frenchmen. After independence, some nationalists were interested in claiming jazz as part of their own aesthetic inheritance because of its connection to African-American culture. With a new sense of pride in African culture and a desire to reject the European, these national groups became more open to appreciating jazz. Despite this shift in understanding jazz, French musicians continued to travel beyond the metropole to ensure the relevance of their music and to foster relationships with jazz communities outside of France as well as in overseas territories. When these artists brought their music to these various places across the globe, they were trying to build and sustain ties with the former members of the Union Française, because doing so not only provided them with wider audiences for their music, but also worked to ensure lasting French relevance in cultural, political and economic life.

Moving the conversation forward to twenty-first-century France, jazz demonstrates to those who today distrust cultural practices connected to the foreign, the immigrant, or the American, that such forms of cultural expression existed in France for much of the twentieth century and helped the French navigate subjects crucial to their national identity. Despite its complications, moral inconsistences, and failures, national identity remains an enduring fixture of the contemporary world and examining French conceptions of the nation provide crucial insights into values, concerns, and practices held by French individuals. Through jazz, postwar audiences addressed many of the most pressing issues of the day, including the loss of empire, the intensifying presence of racism on French soil, the global spread of American power, and the complicated task of maintaining a distinct French identity in the face of new realities that included a transatlantic youth culture and new expectations for women. Jazz's place in French society was framed by the traditional and the avant-garde, race and culture, black and white, male and female, French and foreign, racism and antiracism, national and global. There is no way to study jazz in postwar France and not see that this society was shifting in ways that challenged traditional cultural mores, illustrated by the friction between oppositional forces that would not allow France to subsist in an isolated or inert condition defined by native cultural practices. A hermetic and unchanging French culture did not exist. The continued integration of jazz into French society in the decades following World War II reinforced the reality of a heterogeneous French nation that, as part of its perpetual evolution, has integrated and included foreign elements for centuries.

NOTE

1. André Hodeir, *The Worlds of Jazz*, trans. Noël Burch (New York: Grove Press, 1972), 122–23.

Bibliography

Aldrich, Robert. *Greater France: A History of French Overseas Expansion.* London: Macmillan Press, 1996.
Allen, Ann Taylor. *Women in Twentieth-Century Europe.* New York: Palgrave Macmillan, 2008.
Amselle, Jean-Loup. "Franco-African Artistic and Cultural Cooperation," *Empire Lost: France and Its Other Worlds.* Edited by Elisabeth Mudimbe-Boyi. Lanham, MD: Lexington Books, 2009, 163–96.
Anderson, Benedict. *Imagined Communities: Reflections on the Origin and Spread of Nationalism.* London: Verso, 1983.
Anquetil, Pascal. "Géographie de jazz en France aujourd'hui." *Cahiers du jazz* 6 (January 1995), 29–34.
Archer-Shaw, Petrine. *Negrophilia: Avant-Gard Paris and Black Culture in the 1920s.* London: Thames & Hudson, 2000.
Armus, Seth D. *French Anti-Americanism (1930–1948): Critical Moments in a Complex History.* Lanham, MD: Lexington Books, 2010.
Auslander, Leora. *Cultural Revolutions: Everyday Life and Politics in Britain, North America, and France.* Berkeley: University of California Press, 2009.
"Avis." *Jazz [Hip]* no. 22 (rentrée 1960), 4.
Baker, Josephine, and Jo Bouillon. *Josephine.* Translated by Mariana Fitzpatrick. New York: Paragon House Publishers, 1988.
Balibar, Étienne, and Immanuel Wallerstein. *Race, Nation, Class: Ambiguous Identities.* London: Verso, 1991.
Balliet, Whitney. *American Musicians: Fifty-Six Portraits in Jazz.* New York: Oxford University Press, 1986.
———. "Pandemonium Pays Off." *Saturday Review*, 25 September 1954.
Balmer, Paul. *Stéphane Grappelli: With and Without Django.* London: Sanctuary, 2003.
Bantigny, Ludivine, and Ivan Jablonka, eds. *Jeunesse Oblige: Histoire des jeunes en France XIXe-XXIe siècle.* Paris: Presses Universitaires de France, 2009.
Baraka, Amiri (LeRoi Jones). *Blues People.* New York: William Morrow and Company, 1963.
Baro, Claude. "Le jazz et la société française." *Review internationale de musique française*, no. 8 (June 1982), 65–86.
Bass, Amy. *Not the Triumph but the Struggle: The 1968 Olympics and the Making of the Black Athlete.* Minneapolis: University of Minnesota Press, 2002.
Bechet, Sidney. *Treat it Gentle.* New York: Hill & Wang, 1960.
Begag, Azouz. *Ethnicity and Equality: France in the Balance.* Lincoln: University of Nebraska Press, 2007.

Benjamin, Walter. "The Work of Art in the Age of Mechanical Reproduction." *Illuminations*. Edited by Hannah Arendt. Translated by Harry Zohn. New York: Schocken Books, 1969, 217–51.
Berendt, Joachim. *The Jazz Book: From New Orleans to Rock and Free Jazz*. Translated by Dan Morgenstern and Helmut and Barbara Bredigkeit. New York: Lawrence Hill & Co., 1975.
Bergerot, Frank, and Arnaud Merlin. *The Story of Jazz: Bop and Beyond*. Translated by Marjolijn de Jager. New York: Harry N. Abrams, Inc., 1993.
Beriss, David. *Black Skins, French Voices: Caribbean Ethnicity and Activism in Urban France*. Boulder, CO: Westview Press, 2004.
Berliner, Brett A. *Ambivalent Desire: The Exotic Black Other in Jazz-Age France*. Amherst: University of Massachusetts Press, 2002.
Berque, Jacques. *French North Africa: The Maghrib between Two World Wars*. New York: Praeger, 1967.
Béthune, Christian. *Sidney Bechet*. Marseille: Éditions Parenthèses, 1997.
Blake, Jody. *Le Tumulte Noir: Modernist Art and Popular Entertainment in Jazz-Age Paris, 1900–1930*. University Park: Pennsylvania State University Press, 1999.
Bloom, Peter J. *French Colonial Documentary: Mythologies of Humanitarianism*. Minneapolis: University of Minnesota Press, 2008.
Boittin, Jennifer Anne. *Colonial Metropolis: The Urban Grounds of Anti-Imperialism and Feminism in Interwar Paris*. Lincoln: University of Nebraska Press, 2010.
Bourdieu, Pierre. *Sociologie de l'Algérie*. Paris: Presses Universitaires de France, 1961.
Bourdieu, Pierre, and Jean-Claude Passeron. *Les Héritiers: les étudiants et la culture*. Paris: Les Éditions de Minuit, 1964.
Bourdieu, Pierre, Jean-Claude Passeron, and Michel Eliard. *Les étudiants et leurs études*. Paris: Mouton, 1964.
Bourdieu, Pierre, and Loïc J. D. Wacquant. *An Invitation to Reflexive Sociology*. Chicago: University of Chicago Press, 1992.
Bredin, Jean-Denis. *The Affair: the Case of Alfred Dreyfus*. New York: George Braziller, 1986.
Brierre, Jean-Dominique. *Le jazz français de 1900 à aujourd'hui*. Paris: Éditions Hors Collection, 2000.
Briggs, Jonathyne. *Sounds French: Globalization, Cultural Communities, and Pop Music, 1958–1980*. New York: Oxford University Press, 2015.
Brocker, Xavier. *Le Roman vrai du jazz en Lorraine 1917–1991*. Jarville-La Malgrange: Éditions de l'Est, 1991.
Broschke, Ursula. *Paris without Regret: James Baldwin, Kenny Clarke, Chester Himes, and Donald Byrd*. Iowa City: University of Iowa Press, 1986.
Brown, Simone. *Dark Matter: On the Surveillance of Blackness*. Durham, NC: Duke University Press, 2015.
Brunet, Alain, Isabelle Leymarie, Jacques Bens, and Jacques B. Hess. "Le jazz, aujourd'hui." *Les Cahiers du jazz* 2 (November 1994), 29–33.
Burrin, Philippe. *France under the Germans: Collaboration and Compromise*. Translated by Janet Lloyd. New York: New Press, 1998.
———. *Living with Defeat: France under the German Occupation, 1940–1944*. Translated by Janet Lloyd. London: Arnold, 1996.
Campbell, James. *Exiled in Paris: Richard Wright, James Baldwin, Samuel Becket, and Others on the Left Bank*. Berkeley: University of California Press, 2003.
Camus, Albert. *Selected Essays and Notebooks*. Edited and translated by Philip Thody. Harmondsworth, UK: Penguin, 1979.
Cannon, Steve. "*Paname city rapping*: B-Boys in the *banlieus* and beyond." *Postcolonial Cultures in France*. Edited by Alec G. Hargreaves and Mark McKinney. New York: Routledge, 1997, 150–66.
———. "Globalization, Americanization and Hip Hop in France." *Popular Music in France from Chanson to Techno: Culture, Identity and Society*. Edited by Hugh Dauncey and Steve Cannon. Burlington, VT: Ashgate, 2003, 191–203.

Carles, Philippe, André Clergeat, and Jean-Louis Comolli. *Dictionnaire du jazz*. Paris: Robert Laffont, 1988.
Carles, Philippe, and Jean-Louis Comolli. *Free Jazz / Black Power*. Paris: Gallimard, 2000.
Carr, Graham. "Diplomatic Notes: American Musicians and Cold War Politics in the Near and Middle East, 1954–60." *Popular Music History* 1 (2004), 37–63.
Castigliola, Frank. *France and the United States: the Cold Alliance since World War II*. New York: Twayne, 1992.
Cazenave, François. *Les radios libres*. Paris: Presses Universitaires de France, 1984.
Çelik, Zeynip. *Urban Forms and Colonial Confrontations: Algiers Under French Rule*. Berkeley: University of California Press, 1997.
Chaperon, Sylvie. *Les années Beavoir, 1945–1970*. Paris: Fayard, 2000.
Chesnel, Jacques. *Le Jazz en quarantine (1940–1946)*. Cherbourg: Éditions Isoète, 1994.
Chilton, John. *Sidney Bechet: The Wizard of Jazz*. New York: Oxford University Press, 1987.
Citron, Marcia L. "Feminist Approaches to Musicology." *Cecelia Reclaimed: Feminist Perspectives on Gender and Music*. Edited by Susan C. Cook and Judy S. Tsou. Urbana: University of Illinois Press, 1994, 15–34.
Clark, Linda. *Schooling the Daughters of Marianne: Textbooks and the Socialization of Girls in Modern French Primary Schools*. Albany: State University of New York Press, 1984.
Claude, Jean. "Les maffias." *Le Monde libertaire* no. 103 (July 1964).
Cohen, Lizabeth. *A Consumer's Republic: The Politics of Mass Consumption in Postwar America*. New York: Alfred A. Knopf, 2003.
Collard, Susan. "French Cultural Policy: The Special Role of State." *Contemporary French Cultural Studies*. Edited by William Kidd and Siân Reynolds. London: Hodder Arnold, 2000, 38–50.
Cotro, Vincent. *Chants libres: Le free jazz en France, 1960–1975*. Paris: Éditions Outre Mesure, 1999.
Coulangeon, Philipp. *Les Musiciens de jazz en France*. Paris: L'Harmattan, 1999.
Creton, Laurent. *Histoire économique du cinéma français*. Paris: CNRS Éditions, 2004.
Crist, Stephen A. "Jazz as Democracy? Dave Brubeck and Cold War Politics." *The Journal of Musicology*, vol. 26, no. 2 (Spring 2009), 133–74.
Dahl, Linda. *Stormy Weather: The Music and Lives of a Century of Jazzwomen*. New York: Limelight Editions, 1989.
Dauncey, Hugh, and Steve Cannon, eds. *Popular Music in France from Chanson to Techno: Culture, Identity and Society*. Burlington, VT: Ashgate, 2003.
Davenport, Lisa E. *Jazz Diplomacy: Promoting America in the Cold War Era*. Jackson: University Press of Mississippi, 2009.
Davis, Angela Y. *Blues Legacies and Black Feminism: Gertrude "Ma" Rainey, Bessie Smith, and Billie Holiday*. New York: Pantheon Books, 1998.
de Grazia, Victoria. *Irresistable Empire: America's Advance through 20th-Century Europe*. Cambridge, MA: Belknap Press of Harvard University Press, 2005.
de Luignan, Guy. *French-Speaking Africa Since Independence*. New York: Frederick A. Praeger, 1969.
de Wenden, Catherine Wihtol. "From Migrants to Citizens: Muslims in France." *Politics and Religion in France and the United States*. Edited by Alec G. Hargreaves, John Kelsay, and Sumner B. Twiss . Lanham, MD: Lexington Books, 2007, 139–153.
Delaunay, Charles. *Delaunay's Dilemma: De la peinture au jazz*. Mâcon: Éditions W., 1985.
———. *Django Reinhardt*. Translated by Michael James. New York: Da Capo Press, 1982.
Derderian, Richard L. "Broadcasting from the Margins: Minority Ethnic Radio in Contemporary France." *Post-Colonial Cultures in France*. Edited by Alec G. Hargreaves and Mark McKinney. New York: Routledge, 1997, 99–114.
Destombes, Aris. "Un manifeste d'Aris." *Jazz Hot* no. 179 (September 1962), 10.
DeVeux, Scott. *The Birth of Be-Bop: A Social and Musical History*. Berkeley: University of California Press, 1997.
———. "The Emergence of the Jazz Concert, 1935–1945." *American Music* 7 (Spring 1989), 6–29.

Dewitte, Philippe. *Deux siècles d'immigration en France*. Paris: La Documentation Française, 2003.

———. *Les Mouvements nègre en France 1919–1939*. Paris: Éditions L'Harmattan, 1985.

Diagne, Pathé. *Léopold S. Senghor, ou, La négritude servant de la francophonie au Festival panafricain d'Alger: trente ans après*. Dakar: Éditions Sankoré, 2002.

Dorigné, Michel. *Jazz 1*. Paris: L'École SA, 1968.

———. *Jazz 2*. Paris: L'École des loisirs, 1970.

———. *Jazz, culture et société*. Paris: Éditions Ouvrières, 1967.

Dregni, Michael. *Django: The Life and Music of a Gypsy Legend*. Oxford: Oxford University Press, 2004.

———. *Django Reinhardt and the Illustrated History of Gypsy Jazz*. Denver, CO: Speck Press, 2006.

Dressel, David. "Hip-Hop Hybridity for a Globalized World: African and Muslim Diasporic Discourses in French Rap Music." *The Global Studies Journal*, vol. 2, no. 3 (2009), 121–43.

Drott, Eric. *Music and the Elusive Revolution: Cultural Politics and Political Culture in France, 1968–1981*. Berkeley: University of California Press, 2011.

Du Bois, W.E.B. *The Souls of Black Folk*. New York: Bantam, 1989.

Duchen, Claire. *Women's Rights and Women's Lives in France 1944–1968*. New York: Routledge, 1994.

Duhamel, Georges. *America the Menace: Scenes from the Life of the Future*. Translated by Charles Miner Thompson. Boston: Houghton Mifflin Co., 1931.

Dutilh, Alex. *Jazz de France: Jazz Musicians from France*. Paris: Centre national d'action musicale, 1989.

Edwards, Brent Hayes. *The Practice of Diaspora: Literature, Translation, and the Rise of Black Internationalism*. Cambridge, MA: Harvard University Press, 2003.

Englund, Stephen. "The Ghost of Nation Past." *The Journal of Modern History*, vol. 64, no. 2 (June 1992), 299–320.

Ezra, Elizabeth. *The Colonial Unconscious: Race and Culture in Interwar France*. Ithaca, NY: Cornell University Press, 2000.

Fabre, Michel. *From Harlem to Paris: Black American Writers in France, 1940–1980*. Urbana: University of Illinois Press, 1991.

Fanon, Frantz. "Racism and Culture." *Présence Africaine* 8–9–10 (June–November 1956), 122–31.

———. *Toward the African Revolution: Political Essays*. Translated by Haakon Chevalier. New York: Grove Press, 1967.

———. *The Wretched of the Earth*. Translated by Constance Farrington. New York: Grove Press, 1963.

Feldblum, Miriam. "Paradoxes of Ethnic Politics: the Case of Franco-Maghrebis in France." *Ethnic and Racial Studies*, vol. 16, no. 1 (January 1993): 52–74.

Fitte, Albert. *Spectroscopie d'une propaganda révolutionnaire: "El Moudjahid" des temps de guerre; juin 1956–mars 1962*. Montpellier: Université Paul Valéry, 1973.

Fogg, Shannon L. *The Politics of Everyday Life in Vichy France: Foreigners, Undesirables, and Strangers*. New York: Cambridge University Press, 2009.

Foley, Susan K. *Women in France Since 1789*. New York: Palgrave MacMillan, 2004.

Ford, Caroline. *Creating the Nation in Provincial France: Religion and Political Identity in Brittany*. Princeton, NJ: Princeton University Press, 1993.

Fordham, John. *Jazz*. New York: Dorling Kindersley, 1993.

Francis, André. *Jazz*. Translated by Martin Williams. New York: Grove Press, 1976.

Fry, Andy. *Paris Blues: African American Music and French Popular Culture, 1920–1960*. Chicago: University of Chicago Press, 2014.

Gabbard, Krin. *Jazz among the Discourses*. Durham, NC: Duke University Press, 1995.

———. *Jammin' at the Margins: Jazz and the American Cinema*. Chicago: University of Chicago Press, 1996.

Gadant, Monique. *Islam et nationalism en Algérie d'après "El Moudjahid," organe central du FLN de 1956 à 1962*. Paris, Éditions L'Harmattan, 1988.

Gaines, Kevin. "Duke Ellington, *Black, Brown and Beige*, and the Cultural Politics of Race." *Music and the Racial Imagination*. Edited by Ronald Radano and Philip V. Bohlman. Chicago: University of Chicago Press, 2000.
Gendron, Bernard. *Between Montmartre and the Mudd Club: Popular Music and the Avant-Garde*. Chicago: University of Chicago Press, 2002.
———. "Festishes and Motorcars: Negrophilia in French Modernism," *Cultural Studies*, vol. 4, no. 2 (May 1990), 141–55.
———. "Jamming at Le Boeuf: Jazz and the Paris Avant-Garde." *Discourse: Theoretical Studies in Media and Culture*, vol. 12, no. 1 (Fall–Winter 1989–1990), 3–27.
Gennari, John. *Blowin' Hot and Cool: Jazz and its Critics*. Chicago: University of Chicago Press, 2006.
Gérard-Vigneau, Francine, ed. *La musique dans la vie: jazz, rock, enseignement*. Paris: Les Éditions de l'illustration, 1985.
Gillet, Rachel Anne. "Jazz women, gender politics, and the Francophone Atlantic." *Atlantic Studies: Global Currents*, vol. 10, no. 1 (2013), 109–130.
Gilroy, Paul. *The Black Atlantic: Modernity and Double Consciousness*. Cambridge, MA: Harvard University Press, 1993.
Gioia, Ted. *The History of Jazz*, 2nd ed. New York: Oxford University Press, 2011.
Givan, Benjamin. *The Music of Django Reinhardt*. Ann Arbor, MI: University of Michigan Press, 2010.
Gosnell, Jonathan K. *The Politics of Frenchness in Colonial Algeria, 1930–1954*. Rochester: University of Rochester Press, 2002.
Gottlieb, Robert, ed. *Reading Jazz: A Gathering of Autobiography, Reportage, and Criticism from 1919 to Now*. New York: Pantheon Books, 1996.
Gourse, Leslie. *Madame Jazz: Contemporary Women Instrumentalists*. New York: Oxford University Press, 1996.
Grégoire, Ménie. *Le métier de femme*. Paris: Plon, 1965, 8.
Guérin, Daniel. *Décolonization du noir américain*. Paris: Les Éditions de Minuit, 1963.
———. *Où va le peuple américaine?* Paris: René Julliard, 1951.
Guilbaut, Serge. *How New York Stole the Idea of Modern Art: Abstract Expressionism, Freedom, and the Cold War*. Chicago: University of Chicago Press, 1983.
Haggerty, Michael. *A Flower for Kenny*. Unpublished manuscript, 1985.
Hall, Stuart. "What is this 'Black' in Black Popular Culture?" *Black Popular Culture*. Edited by Gint Dend. Seattle: Seattle Bay Press, 1992, 21–33.
Halsall, Albert W. *Victor Hugo and the Romantic Drama*. Toronto: University of Toronto Press, 1998.
Handy, Antoinette. *Black Women in American Bands and Orchestras*, Second Edition. Metuchen, NJ: Scarecrow Press, 1999.
———. *The International Sweethearts of Rhythm*. Metuchen, NJ: Scarecrow Press, 1983.
Hargreaves, Alec G. *Multi-Ethnic France: Immigration, Politics, Culture and Society*, 2nd ed. New York: Routledge, 2007.
Hargreaves, Alec G., and Mark McKinney, eds. *Postcolonial-Cultures in France*. New York: Routledge, 1997.
Hassinger, Jane. "Close Harmony: Early Jazz Styles in the Music of the New Orleans Boswell Sisters." *Women and Music in Cross-Cultural Perspective*. Edited by Ellen Koskoff. Westport, CT: Greenwood Press, 1987, 195–201.
"Le HCF communique." *Bulletin du Hot Club de France* no. 124 (January 1963), 40.
Helenon, Veronique. "Africa on their Mind: Rap, Blackness, and Citizenship in France." *The Vinyl Ain't Final: Hip Hop and the Globalization of Black Popular Culture*. Edited by Dipannita Basu and Sidney J. Lemelle. Ann Arbor, MI: Pluto Press, 2006, 151–66.
Hergé. *The Adventures of Tintin: Tintin in the Congo*. Copenhagen, Denmark: Egmont, 2005.
Hess, Jacques B. "Panassié: archéologue où vieillard?" *La Revue du jazz*, 2nd series, no. 1 (July 1952), 7.
Hobsbawm, Eric. *The Jazz Scene*. New York: Pantheon Books, 1993.
Hodeir, André. *Les Formes de la Musique*. *Que sais-je* series. Paris: Presses Universitaires de France, 1951.

———. "Improvisation and Composition." Translated by Frank Challis. *This is Jazz*. Edited by Ken Willimson. London: Newnes, 1960, 73–80.

———. "Jazz." *Panorama de l'art musical contemporain*. Edited by Claude Samuel. Paris: Éditions Gallimard, 1962, 120.

———. *Jazz: Its Evolution and Its Essence*. Translated by David Noakes. New York: Grove Press, 1956.

———. "Je n'appartiens pas 'troisième courant.'" *Jazz Hot* no. 162 (February 1961), 13.

———. *Since Debussy: A View of Contemporary Music*. Translated by Noël Burch. London: Secker & Warburg, 1961.

———. *Toward Jazz*. Translated by Noël Burch. New York: Grove Press, 1962.

———. *The Worlds of Jazz*. Translated by Noël Burch. New York: Grove Press, 1972.

Horne, Alistair. *A Savage War of Peace: Algeria 1954–1962*. New York: New York Review Books, 2006.

Horowitz, Donald L. "Immigration and Group Relations in France and America." *Immigrants in Two Democracies: French and American Experience*. Edited by Donald L. Horowitz and Gérard Norièl. New York: New York University Press, 1992.

Hubert-Lacombe, Patricia. *Le cinéma français dans la guerre froide, 1946–1956*. Paris: Harmattan, 1996.

———. "La guerre froide et le cinéma français, 1946–53." Thèse de 3e cycle, Institut d'études politiques, Paris, 1981.

Jackson, Jeffrey H. *Making Jazz French: Music and Modern Life in Interwar Paris*. Durham, NC: Duke University Press, 2003.

Jalard, Michel-Claude. "De Django et de divers." *Diaspason* no. 131 (December 1968), 56.

———. "Le Jazz." *Diaspason* no. 53 (November 1960), 27.

Jazz de France: Portraits-contracts. Paris: Centre national d'action musicale, 1989.

Janissier, Daniel. "Comment devenir critique de jazz." *Bulletin du Hot Club de France* no. 184 (January 1969), 8.

"Le Jazz." *Le Point* no. XL (January 1952).

"Le jazz en France." *L'Express* (21 May 1959), 36.

Jeancolas, Jean-Pierre. "L'arrangement Blum-Byrnes à l'épreuve des faits: les rélations (cinématographiques) franco-américaines de 1944 à 1948." *Bulletin de l'Association française de recherches sur l'histoire du cinéma* 13 (1992).

Jobs, Richard Ivans. *Riding the New Wave: Youth and the Rejuvenation of France After the Second World War*. Stanford, CA: Stanford University Press, 2007.

Johns, Robert L. "Josephine Baker." *Epic Lives: One Hundred Black Women Who Made a Difference*. Edited by Jessie Carney Smith. Detroit: Visible Ink Press, 1993, 15–21.

Johnson, Douglas. "Algeria: Some Problems of Modern History." *Journal of African History* vol. 5, no. 2 (1964).

Jordan, Matthew F. *Le Jazz: Jazz and French Cultural Identity*. Urbana: University of Illinois Press, 2010.

———. "The French Connection: Mythologies of *La Nouvelle Orléans* in French Discourse on Jazz." *European Journal of Cultural Studies* 14 (October 2011), 507–25.

Judt, Tony. *Past Imperfect: French Intellectuals, 1944–1956*. Berkeley: University of California Press, 1992.

Jules-Rosette, Bennetta. *Josephine Baker in Art and Life: The Icon and the Image*. Urbana: University of Illinois Press, 2007.

Kater, Michael H. *Different Drummers: Jazz in the Culture of Nazi Germany*. New York: Oxford University Press, 1992.

Keaton, Tricia. *Muslim Girls and the Other France: Race, Identity Politics, and Social Exclusion*. Bloomington: Indiana University Press, 2006.

Kelly, Michael, Tony Jones, and Jill Forbes. "Modernization and Avant-gardes (1945–1967)." *French Cultural Studies: An Introduction*. Edited by Jill Forbes and Michael Kelly. New York: Oxford University Press, 1995, 140–77.

Kelley, Robin D.G. *Africa Speaks, America Answers: Modern Jazz in Revolutionary Times*. Cambridge, MA: Harvard University Press, 2012.

———. *Race Rebels: Culture, Politics, and the Black Working Class*. New York: The Free Press, 1994.

———. "Forward." *The Vinyl Ain't Final: Hip Hop and the Globalization of Black Popular Culture*. Edited by Dipannita Basu and Sidney J. Lemelle. Ann Arbor, MI: Pluto Press, 2006, xi–xvii.

———. "'We Are Not What We Seem': Rethinking Black Working Class Opposition in the Jim Crow South." *Journal of American History*, vol. 80, no. 1, June 1993: 75–112.

Kenney, William H., III. "*Le hot*: the Assimilation of American Jazz in France." *American Studies* (1984), 5–24

Kenrick, Donald, and Grattan Puxon. *The Destiny of Europe's Gypsies*. New York: Basic Books, 1972.

Kernfeld, Barry. *What to Listen for in Jazz*. New Haven, CT: Yale University Press, 1995.

Kesteloot, Lilyan. *Black Writers in French: a Literary History of Negritude*. Translated by Ellen Conroy Kennedy. Philadelphia: Temple University Press, 1974.

Klein, Jean-Claude. "Borrowing, Syncretism, Hybridisation: The Parisian Revue of the 1920s." *Popular Music*, vol. 5. Cambridge, MA: Cambridge University Press, 1985.

Koechlin, Philippe. "Renaissance ou déclin du Jazz?" *Révolution africaine* no. 3 (16 February 1963), 22.

Kroes, Rob. "American Mass Culture and European Youth Culture." *Between Marx and Coca-Cola: Youth Cultures in Changing European Societies, 1960–1980*. Edited by Axel Schildt and Detlef Siegfried. New York: Berghahn Books, 2006, 82–105.

———. *If You've Seen One, You've Seen the Mall: Europeans and American Mass Culture*. Urbana: University of Illinois Press, 1996.

Kroes, Rob, R. W. Rydell, and D. F. J. Bosscher, eds. *Cultural Transmissions and Receptions: American Mass Culture in Europe*. Amsterdam: VU University Press, 1993.

Kuhn, Raymond. *The Media in France*. New York: Routledge, 1995.

Kuisel, Richard F. "The French Cinema and Hollywood: A Case Study of Americanization." *Transactions, Transgressions, Transformations: American Culture in Western Europe and Japan*. Edited by Heide Fehrenbach and Uta G. Poiger. New York: Berghahn Books, 2000, 208–23.

———. *The French Way: How France Embraced and Rejected American Values and Power*. Princeton, NJ: Princeton University Press, 2012.

———. *Seducing the French: the Dilemma of Americanization*. Berkeley: University of California Press, 1993.

Lacorne, Denis, Jacques Rupnik, and Marie-France Toinet, eds. *The Rise and Fall of Anti-Americanism: a Century of French Perceptions*. Translated by Gerry Turner. New York: St. Martin's Press, 1990.

Lahitte, Jacques. "Jazz-News: Situation de la presse spécialisée." *Arts* no. 502 (9–15 February 1955), 4.

Lamont, Michèle. "The Rhetoric of Racism and Anti-Racism in France and the United States." Manuscript, 1996.

Lane, Jeremy F. *Jazz and Machine-Age Imperialism: Music, "Race," and Intellectuals in France, 1918–1945*. Ann Arbor, MI: University of Michigan Press, 2013.

Lebovics, Herman. *Bringing the Empire Back Home: France in the Global Age*. Durham, NC: Duke University Press, 2004.

———. *Mona Lisa's Escort: André Malraux and the Reinvention of French Culture*. Ithaca, NY: Cornell University Press, 1999.

———. *True France: The Wars over Cultural Identity, 1900–1945*. Ithaca, NY: Cornell University Press, 1992.

Lebrun, Barbara. *Protest Music in France: Production, Identity and Audiences*. Burlington, VT: Ashgate, 2009.

Legrand, Anne. *Charles Delaunay et le jazz en France dans les années 30 et 40*. Paris: Éditions du Layeur, 2009.

Legrand, Gérard. *Puissances du jazz*. Paris: Arcances, 1953.

Lehman, Stephen. "I Love You With An Asterisk: African-American Experimental Music and the French Jazz Press, 1970–1980." *Critical Studies in Improvisation*, vol. 1, no. 2 (2005), 38–53.

Léon, Claude. "La critique (est aisée)." *Jazz Hot* no. 152 (March 1960), 27.

Lewis, George E. *A Power Stronger than Itself: The AACM and American Experimental Music.* Chicago: University of Chicago Press, 2008.

Loiseau, Jean-Claude. *Les Zazous*. Paris: Sagittaire, 1977.

Loosely, David L. *The Politics of Fun: Cultural Policy and Debate in Contemporary France*. Oxford: Berg Publishers, 1997.

Lott, Eric. *Love and Theft: Blackface Minstrelsy and the American Working Class*. New York: Oxford University Press, 1993.

Lughod, Janet Abu. *Rabat: Urban Apartheid in Morocco*. Princeton, NJ: Princeton University Press, 1980.

Lui no. 13 (January 1965)

Lui no. 23 (November 1965).

Maghraoui, Driss. "French Identity, Islam, and North Africans: Colonial Legacies, Postcolonial Realities." *French Civilization and Its Discontents: Nationalism, Colonialism, Race*. Edited by Tyler Stovall and Georges Van Den Abbeele. Lanham, MD: Lexington Books, 2003, 213–234.

Malson, Lucien. *Les enfants sauvage*. Paris: Bibliothèques 10–18, 2002.

———. *Les Maîtres du jazz: d'Oliver à Coltrane*. 10th edition. Paris: Presses Universitaires de France, 1993.

———. "Panassié méglomane." *La Revue du jazz*, 2nd series, no. 1 (July 1952), 5–6.

Margairaz, Michel. "Autour des accords Blum-Byrnes." *Histoire, économie, société* 3 (1982), 439–70.

Martinez, Henri. *Et Qu'ils m'accueillent avec des cris de haine*. Paris: Éditions Robert Laffont, 1982.

Mayer, Günter. "Popular Music in the GDR." *Journal of Popular Culture*, vol. 18:3 (Winter 1984), 145–58.

McCarren, Felicia. *French Moves: The Cultural Politics of* le Hip Hop. New York: Oxford University Press, 2013.

McClary, Susan. *Feminine Endings: Music, Gender, and Sexuality*. Minneapolis: University of Minnesota Press, 1991.

McKenzie, Brian Angus. *Remaking France: Americanization, Public Diplomacy, and the Marshall Plan*. New York: Berghahn Books, 2008.

McManus, Jill. "Women Jazz Composers and Arrangers." *The Musical Woman: An International Perspective*. Edited by Judith Lang Zaimont, Catherine Overhauser, and Jane Gottleib. Westport, CT: Greenwood Press, 1984, 197–208.

McMillan, James F. *Twentieth Century France: Politics and Society, 1889–1991*. London: Edward Arnold, 1992.

McMurray, David A. "La France arabe." *Postcolonial Cultures in France*. Edited by Alec G. Hargreaves and Mark McKinney. New York: Routledge, 1997, 26–39.

McNamara, Francis Terry. *France in Black Africa*. Washington, DC: National Defense University Press, 1989.

Meunier, Sophie. "Anti-Americanism in France." *French Politics, Culture and Society* 23 (2005), 126–41.

Michel, Andrée, and Geneviève Texier. *La Condition de la Française d'Aujourd'hui*. Paris: Éditions Gonthier, 1964.

Milhaud, Darius. "The Jazz Band and Negro Music." *Living Age* (18 October 1924), 172.

———. *Notes sans musique*. Paris: René Julliard, 1949.

Miller, Susan Gilson. *A History of Modern Morocco*. New York: Cambridge University Press, 2013.

Mokhtari, Omar, ed. *Alger 1969: 1er festival culturel panafricain*. Algiers: Éditions Actualité Algérie, 1970.

Monson, Ingrid. *Freedom Sounds: Civil Rigths Call Out to Jazz and Africa*. Oxford: Oxford University Press, 2007.

Moody, Bill. *The Jazz Exiles: American Musicians Abroad*. Reno: University of Nevada Press, 1993.
Mouly, Raymond. *Sidney Bechet, notre ami*. Paris: La Table Ronde, 1959.
Naylor, Philip C. *France and Algeria: A History of Decolonization and Transformation*. Gainesville: University of Florida Press, 2000.
Ndiaye, Pap. *La Condition noire: Essai sur une minorité française*. Paris: Calmann-Lévy, 2008.
Nettelbeck, Colin. *Dancing with DeBeauvoir: Jazz and the French*. Carlton, Victoria: Melbourne University Press, 2004.
Noiriel, Gerard. *Le Creuset français: histoire de l'immigration, XIXe–Xxe siècles*. Paris: Éditions du Seuil, 1988.
Noiriel, Gerard, and Donald L. Horowitz. *Immigrants in Two Democracies: French and American Experiences*. New York: New York University Press, 1992.
Nolan, Mary. *The Transatlantic Century: Europe and America, 1890–2010*. New York: Cambridge University Press, 2012.
Nora, Pierre. *Les Français d'Algérie*. Paris: Juillard, 1961.
———, ed. *Les Lieux de mémoire*. Paris: Gallimard, 1984.
Oliver, Paul. *Le Monde du blues*. Paris: Arthaud, 1962.
Ory, Pascal. "Notes sur l'acclimation du jazz en France." *Vibrations: revue d'études des musiques populaire* 1 (April 1985).
Panassié, Hugues. *La Bataille du jazz*. Paris: Éditions Albin Michel, 1965.
———. *Cinq mois à New-York*. Paris: Éditions Corrêa, 1947.
———. *Hot Jazz: the Guide to Swing Music*. Translated by Lyle and Eleanor Dowling. Westport, CT: Greenwood Press, 1970.
———. *Jazz Panorama*. Paris: Éditions Deux-Rives, 1950.
———. "Le Jazz symphonique: une trahison le Be-bop: un art en enfance." *Paris-Press* (22–23 February 1948), 2.
———. *Monsieur Jazz: Entretiens avec Pierre Casalta*. Paris: Stock, 1975.
———. *The Real Jazz*. Translated by Anne Sorelle Williams. New York: Smith & Durrell, 1943.
Panish, Jon. *The Color of Jazz: Race and Representation in Postwar American Culture*. Jackson: University Press of Mississippi, 1997.
Parker, Errol. *A Flat Tire on My Ass*. Redwood, NY: Cadence Jazz Books, 1995.
Pellegrinelli, Lara. "Separated at 'Birth': Singing and the History of Jazz." *Big Ears: Listening for Gender in Jazz Studies*. Edited by Nichole T. Rustin and Sherrie Tucker. Durham, NC: Duke University Press, 2008, 31–47.
Perchard, Tom. *After Django: Making Jazz in Postwar France*. Ann Arbor, MI: University of Michigan Press, 2015.
Perkins, William Eric, ed. *Droppin' Science: Critical Essays on Rap Music and Hip Hop Culture*. Philadelphia: Temple University Press, 1996.
Perrin, Michel. "Le jazz." *Les Nouvelles Litteraires* (1 April 1965), 12.
Pescheux, Jacques. "Un scandale." *Bulletin du Hot Club de France* no. 130 (September 1963), 25.
Petterson, James. "No More Song and Dance: French Radio Broadcast Quotas, *Chansons*, and Cultural Exceptions." *Transactions, Transgressions, Transformations: American Culture in Western Europe and Japan*. Edited by Heide Fehrenbach and Uta G. Poiger. New York: Berghahn Books, 2000, 109–23.
Pires, Mat. "The Popular Music Press." *Popular Music in France from Chanson to Techno: Culture, Identity and Society*. Edited by Hugh Dauncey and Steve Cannon. Burlington, VT: Ashgate, 2003, 77–96.
Pirsein, Robert William. *The Voice of America: A History of the International Broadcasting Activities of the United States Government, 1940–1962*. New York: Arno Press, 1979.
Placksin, Sally. *American Women in Jazz: 1900 to the Present, Their Words, Lives, and Music*. New York: Wideview, 1982.

Poiger, Uta G. "American Music, Cold War Liberalism, and German Identities," *Transactions, Transgressions, Transformations: American Culture in Western Europe and Japan*. Edited by Heide Fehrenbach and Uta G. Poiger. New York: Berghahn Books, 2000, 127–47.

———. "Fear and Fascination: American Popular Culture in a Divided Germany, 1945–1968." *Kazaaam! Splat! Ploof! The American Impact on European Popular Culture since 1945*. Edited by Sabrina P. Ramet and Gordana P. Crnković. Lanham, MD: Rowman & Littlefield Publisher Inc., 2003, 55–68.

———. *Jazz, Rock, and Rebels: Cold War Politics and American Culture in a Divided Germany*. Berkeley: University of California Press, 2000.

Poirrier, Philippe. "French Cultural Policy in Question, 1981–2003," *After the Deluge: New Perspectives on the Intellectual and Cultural History of Postwar France*. Edited by Julian Bourg. Lanham, MD: Lexington Books, 2004, 301–323.

Porter, Eric. *What Is This Thing Called Jazz? African American Musicians as Artists, Critics, and Activists*. Berkeley: University of California Press, 2002.

Portis, Larry. *French Frenzies: A Social History of Popular Music in France*. College Station, TX: Virtualbookworm.com Publishing, 2004.

Prevos, Andre J. M. "Postcolonial Popular Music in France: Rap Music and Hip Hop Culture in the 1980s and 1990s." *Global Noise: Rap and Hip Hop Outside the USA*. Edited by Tony Mitchell. Middletown, CT: Wesleyan University Press, 2001, 39–56.

———. "Two Decades of Rap in France: Emergence, Developments, Prospects." *Black, Blanc, Beur: Rap Music and Hip-Hop Culture in the Francophone World*. Edited by Alain-Philippe Durand. Lanham, MD: Scarecrow Press, 2002, 1–21.

Prévost, Xavier, "Le jazz, probablement . . . " *Les Cahiers du jazz* 6 (January 1996), 17–22.

"Le prix de l'humair lui." *Lui* no. 16 (April 1965), 23.

Pulju, Rebecca J. *Women and Mass Consumer Society in Postwar France*. New York: Cambridge University Press, 2011.

Queneau, Raymond. "Rendez-vous de juillet." *Bâtons, chiffres et lettres*. Paris: Gallimard, 1965, 152.

Rabinow, Paul. *French Modern: Norms and Forms of the Social Environment*. Chicago: University of Chicago Press, 1989.

Raeburn, Bruce Boyd. *New Orleans Style and the Writing of American Jazz History*. Ann Arbor, MI: University of Michigan Press, 2009.

Ranc, Yves. "Swing ou pas swing." *L'Oeuvre* (March 4, 1942), 4.

Rearick, Charles. *The French in Love and War: Popular Culture in the Era of the World Wars*. New Haven, CT: Yale University Press, 1997.

Régnier, Gérard. *Jazz et société sous l'Occupation*. Paris: L'Harmattan, 2009.

Rioux, Jean-Pierre. *The Fourth Republic, 1944–1958*. Translated by Godfrey Rogers. New York: Cambridge University Press, 1987.

Roberts, Sophie B. "A Case for Dissidence in Occupied Paris: The Zazous, Youth Dissidence, and the Yellow Star Campaign in Occupied Paris (1942)." *French History*, vol. 24, no. 1 (January 22, 2010), 82–103.

Roger, Philippe. *Rêves et cauchemare américains: les Etats-Unis au miroir de l'opinion publique française (1945–1953)*. Villeneuve d'Ascq: Presses Universitaires du Septentrion, 1996.

Rose, Phyllis. *Jazz Cleopatra: Josephine Baker in Her Time*. New York: Doubleday, 1989.

Rose, Tricia. *Black Noise: Rap Music and Black Culture in Contemporary America*. Middletown, CT: Wesleyan University Press, 1994.

Ross, Kristin. *Fast Cars, Clean Bodies: Decolonization and the Reordering of French Culture*. Cambridge, MA: MIT Press, 1995.

Rossinelli, Michel. *La Liberté de la radio-télévision en droit comparé*. Paris: Publisud, 1991.

Rousso, Henry. *The Vichy Syndrome: History and Memory in France*. Translated by Arthur Goldhammer. Cambridge, MA: Harvard University Press, 1994.

Ruppli, Michel. *The Clef/Verve Labels: A Discography (The Norman Granz Era, Volume 1)*. New York: Greenwood Press, 1986.

Sagan, Françoise. *Bonjour Tristesse*. Translated by Irene Ash. New York: Harper Perennial, 2001.

Sahlins, Peter. *Boundaries: the Making of France and Spain in the Pyrenees*. Berkeley: University of California Press, 1989.
Saidi, Mohamed. "The Decolonization of African Culture." *African Culture: Algiers Symposium, July 21st–August 1st*. Algiers: Société Nationale d'Édition et de Diffusion, 1969.
Samuel, Claude. *Panorama de l'art musical contemporain*. Paris: Éditions Gallimard, 1962.
Sartre, Jean-Paul. "Black Orpheus." *"What is Literature?" and Other Essays*. Translated by John MarCombie. Cambridge: 1988, 291–330.
———. "Présence noire." *Présence Africain* no. 1 (1947), 44–46.
Savage, Jon. *Teenage: The Creation of Youth Culture*. New York: Viking, 2007.
Schaeffner, André. "Notes sur la musique des Afro-Américaines." *Le Ménéstrel* no. 88 (August 6, 1926), 299.
Schaeffner, André, and André Coeuroy. *Le jazz*. Paris: Éditions Claude Aveline, 1926.
Schildt, Axel and Detlef Siegfried. "Introduction: Youth, Consumption, and Politics in the Age of Radical Change." *Between Marx and Coca-Cola: Youth Cultures in Changing European Societies, 1960–1980*. Edited by Axel Schildt and Detlef Siegfried. New York: Berghahn Books, 2006, 1–35.
Schiller, Willy. "La guerre des jazz gagne la France." *France Soir* (22–23 February 1948), 1.
Schlicht, Ursel. "'Better a Jazz Album than Lipstick' (*Lieber Jazzplatte als Lippenstift*): The 1956 *Jazz Podium* Series Reveals Images of Jazz in Gender in Postwar Germany." *Big Ears: Listening for Gender in Jazz Studies*. Edited by Nichole T. Rustin and Sherrie Tucker. Durham, NC: Duke University Press, 2008, 291–319.
Schröter, Harm G. *Americanization of the European Economy: A Compact Survey of American Economic Influence in Europe since the 1880s*. Dordrecht, the Netherlands: Springer, 2005.
Shipton, Alyn. "The New Orleans Revival in Britain and France." *Eurojazzland: Jazz and European Sources, Dynamic, and Contexts*. Edited by Luca Cerchiari, Laurent Cugny, and Franz Kerschbaumer. Boston: Northeastern University Press, 2012, 253–74.
Seck, Nago, and Sylvie Clerfeuille. *Les musiciens du beat africain*. Paris: Bordas, 1993.
Seigfried, André. *America at Mid-Century*. Translated by Margaret Ledésert. New York: Harcourt, Brace and Company, 1955.
Siclier, Sylvain. "Vingt ans de jazz en France: essai de chronologie." *Les Cahiers du jazz* 6 (January 1996), 23–28.
Silverman, Maxim. *Deconstructing the Nation: Immigration, Racism, and Citizenship in Modern France*. London: Routledge, 1992.
Singer, Barnett. *The Americanization of France: Searching for Happiness after the Algerian War*. Lanham, MD: Rowman & Littlefield Publishers, 2013.
Sirinelli, Jean-François. *Les baby-boomers: Une génération, 1945–1969*. Paris: Fayard, 2003.
Sklower, Jedediah. *Free Jazz, la catastrophe féconde: Une histoire du monde éclaté du jazz en France (1960–1982)*. Paris: L'Harmattan, 2006.
Sohn, Anne-Marie. *Âge Tendre et tête de bois: Histoire des jeunes des années 1960*. Paris: Hachette Littéraures, 2001.
Sowerwine, Charles. *France Since 1870: Culture, Society, and the Making of the Republic*. New York: Palgrave, 2001.
Starr, S. Frederick. *Red and Hot: The Fate of Jazz in the Soviet Union*. New York: Limelight Editions, 1985.
Stolke, Verena. "Talking Culture: New Boundaries, New Rhetorics of Exclusion in Europe." *Current Anthropology*, vol. 36, no. 1 (February 1995), 1–23.
Stovall, Tyler. *Paris Noire: African Americans in the City of Light*. New York: Houghton Mifflin Company, 1996.
———. "'No Green Pastures:' The African Americanization of France," *Empire Lost: France and Its Other Worlds*. Edited by Elisabeth Mudimbe-Boyi. Lanham, MD: Lexington Books, 2009, 67–86.
Taguieff, Pierre-André. *La force du préjugé: essai sur le racisme et ses doubles*. Paris: Gallimard, 1987.
Ténot, Frank. *Jazz*. Paris: Armand et Georges Israël, 1983.
———. "La Traversée éblouissante." *Sidney Bechet*. Edited by Fabrice Zammarchi. Paris: Éditions Filipacchi, 1989.

Ténot, Frank, and Philippe Carles, eds. *Le Jazz.* Paris: Librairie Larousse, 1977.
Thomas, Dominic. *Africa and France: Postcolonial Cultures, Migration, and Racism.* Bloomington: Indiana University Press, 2013.
———. *Black France: Colonialism, Immigration, and Transnationalism.* Bloomington: Indiana University Press, 2006.
Thomas, Martin. *The French North African Crisis: Colonial Breakdown and Anglo-French Relations, 1945–62.* New York: St. Martin's Press, 2000.
Thomas, Martin, Bob Moore, and L. J. Butler, eds. *Crises of Empire: Decolonization and Europe's Imperial States, 1918–1975.* London: Hodder Education, 2008.
Tournès, Ludovic. "Les hot clubs: des sociétés savantes au service de la diffusion du jazz." *Cahier du GRHIS* 6 (1997): 105–20.
———. *New Orleans sur Seine: Histoire du jazz en France.* Paris: Fayard, 1999.
———. "La réinterprétation du jazz: un phénomène de contre-américanisation dans la France d'après guerre (1945–1960)." *Play it Again Sim . . . : Hommages à Sim Copains.* Special edition of *Revue française d'études américaines* (December 2001), 72–83.
Trumpbour, John. *Selling Hollywood to the World: U.S. and European Struggles for Mastery of the Global Film Industry, 1920–1950.* Cambridge, MA: Cambridge University Press, 2002.
Tshimanga, Charles, Didier Gondola, and Peter J. Bloom, eds. *Frenchness and the African Diaspora.* Bloomington: Indiana University Press, 2009.
Tu, Phan. "The Struggle of South Vietnam Against Imperialist Cultural Domination." *African Culture: Algiers Symposium, July 21st–August 1st.* Algiers: Société Nationale d'Édition et de Diffusion, 1969.
Tucker, Sherrie. *Swing Shift: "All-Girl" Bands of the 1940s.* Durham, NC: Duke University Press, 2000.
Varolle, Marie. *La chanson raï.* Paris: Karthala, 1995.
Vian, Boris. "Hommage à Django Reinhardt." *Arts* (9–15 June 1954), 3.
———. *Jazz in Paris.* Edited by Gilbert Pestureau. Paris: Société nouvelle des éditions Jean-Jacques Pauvert, 1997.
———. *Le Manuel de Saint Germain-des-Près.* Edited by Noël Arnaud. Paris: Éditions du Chêne, 1974.
Vihlen, Elizabeth. "Jammin' on the Champs Elysées: Jazz, France, and the 1950s." *"Here, There and Everywhere": The Foreign Politics of American Popular Culture.* Edited by Reinhold Wagnleitner and Elaine Tyler May. Hanover, NH: University Press of New England, 2000, 149–62.
———. "Sounding French: Jazz in Postwar France." PhD dissertation, SUNY Stony Brook, 2000.
Vittori, Jean-Pierre. *Nous les appelés d'Algérie.* Paris: Messidor, 1983.
Von Eschen, Penny. *Race Against Empire: Black Americans and Anticolonialism 1937–1957.* Ithaca, NY: Cornell University Press, 1997.
———. *Satchmo Blows up the World: Jazz Ambassadors Play the Cold War.* Cambridge, MA: Harvard University Press, 2004.
von Zahn, Robert, ed. *Jazz in Nordrhein-Westfalen seit 1946.* Köln, Germany: Emmons, 1999.
Wagner, Jean. *Le Guide du jazz.* Paris: Syros, 1986.
Wagner, Jean, Frank Ténot, and Daniel Filipacchi. *Mais oui, vous comprennez le jazz.* Bruxelles: Éditions du jour, 1964.
Wagnleitner, Reinhold. *Coca-Colonization and the Cold War: the Cultural Mission of the United States in Austria after the Second World War.* Translated by Diana M. Wolf. Chapel Hill: University of North Carolina Press, 1994.
Wall, Irwin M. *France, the United States, and the Algerian War.* Berkeley: University of California Press, 2001.
———. *The United States and the Making of Postwar France, 1945–1954.* New York: Cambridge University Press, 2002.
Warne, Chris. "The Impact of World Music in France." *Post Colonial Cultures in France.* Edited by Alec G. Hargreaves and Mark McKinney. New York: Routledge, 1997, 134–49.
Watson, William E. *Tricolor and Crescent: France and the Islamic World.* Westport, CT: Praeger Publishers, 2003.

Weber, Eugen. *Peasants into Frenchmen: The Modernization of Rural France, 1870–1914.* Stanford, CA: Stanford University Press, 1976.
Weil, Patrick. *Qu'est-ce qu'un français? Histoire de la Nationalité française depuis la Révolution.* Paris: Éditions Grasset et Fasquelle, 2002.
Weiner, Susan. *Enfantes terribles: Youth and Femininity in the Mass Media in France, 1945–1968.* Baltimore: Johns Hopkins University Press, 2001.
Weston, Randy, and Willard Jenkins. *African Rhythms: The Autobiography of Randy Weston.* Durham, NC: Duke University Press, 2010.
Wiéner, Jean. *Allegro appassionato.* Paris: P. Belfond, 1978.
Williams, Patrick. *Django.* Marseille: Éditions Paranthèses, 1998.
Wilmer, Val. *Mama Said There'd Be Days Like This: My Life in the Jazz World.* London: Women's Press, 1980.
Wiser, William. *The Great Good Place: American Expatriate Women in Paris.* New York: W. W. Norton & Co., 1991.
"Working on France in American Universities: Interdisciplinary Perspectives." *French Historical Studies*, vol. 19, no. 2 (Fall 1995).
Yedes, Ali. "Social Dynamics in Colonial Algeria: The Question of *Pieds-Noirs* Identity." *French Civilization and Its Discontents: Nationalism, Colonialism, Race.* Edited by Tyler Stovall and Georges Van Den Abbeele. Lanham, MD: Lexington Books, 2003, 235–50.
Yonnet, Paul. *Jeux, modes et masses: La société française et le modern, 1945–1985.* Paris: Gallimard, 1985.
Yurchenco, Henrietta. "Mean Mama Blues: Bessie Smith and the Vaudeville Era." *Music, Gender, and Culture.* Edited by Marcia Herndon and Susanne Ziegler. Wilhelmshaven, Germany: Florian Noetzel Verlag, 1990, 241–51.
Zartman, I. W. *Morocco: Problems of New Power.* New York: Atherton Press, 1964.
Zwerin, Mike. *La Tristesse de Saint Louis: Jazz under the Nazis.* New York: Beach Tree Books, 1985.
Zytnicki, Colette. "L'Administration face à l'arrivée des repatriés d'Algérie: L'exemple de la region Midi-Pyrenées (1962–1964)." *Annales du Midi* vol. 110, no. 224 (1998), 501–21.

Index

AACM. *See* Association for the Advancement of Creative Musicians
Action Musique, 192–193, 240
Adler, Philippe, 17, 18, 24, 37n64, 68; on Sidney Bechet, 149, 171
ADJ. *See* Amis du Jazz
Africa, xiv, xv, 2, 23, 32, 33n3, 82–85, 96, 109, 114, 115, 116, 117n2, 119n33, 137, 139, 153, 165, 199, 201, 209, 210–215, 217, 218, 219, 221, 222, 223–227, 229, 234n89, 237, 242
African diaspora. *See* black diaspora
AFRS. *See* Armed Forces Radio Service
Afro-American Cultural Center (Algeria), 212
Albert-Weil, Jean-Claude, 20
Aldebert, Monique, 65–66
Algeria, xv, 109, 112, 114, 116, 123n157, 163, 195n7, 199, 217, 219, 220, 222, 241; under French control, 200–209; after independence, 209–215, 231n30
Algerian War, xv, 109, 112, 114, 116, 163, 177, 200–209, 217, 220, 229, 236, 241
Algerians, xv, 112–113, 206, 208, 209, 210, 215, 219
Americanization, xiii, xvii, 120n47, 133, 156n15, 160n137
Amis du Jazz (ADJ), 19, 37n76
André, Jacques, 15, 135, 148
anti-Americanism, xviii, 126, 133, 143, 235

Antibes Jazz Festival. *See* Festival d'Antibes
anti-imperialism, 106, 215, 242
Antilles, 119n29, 221, 222, 223, 226, 229
anti-racism, 80, 82, 105, 111, 114, 116, 117, 200, 205, 236, 237, 238, 239
anti-Semitism, 78, 109
Arabs : in Algeria, 200, 204, 207, 208, 214, 241; in France, 111, 112, 123n157; in North Africa, xv, 219, 221, 222
Armed Forces Radio Service (AFRS), 23
Armstrong, Louis, 4, 6, 10, 14, 28, 29, 31, 50, 53, 57, 58, 63, 91, 103–104, 110, 127, 129, 137, 138, 139, 140, 148, 162, 168, 170, 171, 175, 216, 222, 224, 225, 227, 233n88
Arvanitas, Georges, 69, 178, 191
Association for the Advancement of Creative Musicians (AACM), 107, 112
Association pour la Transculture, 20
Atlantic (record company), 41n146, 127
Attenoux, Michel, 146, 180, 205
Averty, Jean-Christophe, 18, 41n138, 102

Baker, Josephine, 63, 64, 83–85, 108, 110, 119n29, 145, 227, 238
Les Barbecues, 221
Basie, Count, 29, 53, 61, 68, 141, 175
Battle of Hernani, 10–12
Baty, Jean-Pierre, 217, 218
Beauvoir, Simone de, 32, 56

bebop, 1, 10, 12, 13, 19, 22, 25, 35n38, 46, 52, 53, 88, 99, 129, 146, 148, 188, 194
Bechet, Sidney, xix, 6, 14, 29, 30, 31, 49, 50, 109, 127, 144–152, 154, 159n90, 181, 216, 241
Begag, Azouz, 117n6, 123n157
Beiderbecke, Bix, 88, 94, 98
Belgrave, Barbara, 69, 70, 71
Berbers, xv, 200, 204, 208, 214, 219, 241
Berliner, Brett, 83, 123n137
the Bidule, 32
Black Atlantic, 119n33, 223
black diaspora, 82, 214, 219, 223
black nationalism, 107, 214, 215
Black Panther Party, 212, 213
Black Power, 106, 108, 213
Blakey, Art, 47, 93, 209
Blum-Byrnes agreement, 154n5
Bolling, Claude, 20, 172
Bourdieu, Pierre, xxn3, 52–53
Brubeck, Dave, 104, 133, 222
Bulletin du Hot Club de France, 13, 14, 15, 21; on French jazz, 187; on French racism, 112; on jazz in Algeria, 206; on race, 99
BYG/Actuel (record label), 214

Cahiers du Jazz, 13, 15, 17, 18
Calloway, Cab, 8, 106
Cameroon, 108, 211, 212, 224
Camus, Albert, 195n7, 227, 228
capitalism, xiv, 122n127, 125, 126, 128, 140
Capon, Jean-Carles, 228
Carles, Philippe, 16; in Algeria, 200; on French jazz, 164; on politics, 122n127; on women, 64
Carné, Marcel, 45, 46
Carter, Benny, 35n30, 168, 170
Caribbean, xv, 78, 85, 109, 115, 222, 229
Catholic Church, 3, 4, 57, 81, 120n47, 150, 235
Caveau de la Huchette, 32; and racism, 113, 114
caves, xiii, 1, 31–33, 43, 46, 48, 182, 187, 188, 202, 204, 240
Chambre Syndicale des Artistes Musiciens de Paris 182, 198n105
Chanson, Dominique, 189, 205

Charles, Ray, 29, 53, 63, 97, 133
Chevalier, Simone, 67–68
civil rights in France, 80, 114, 239
Clarke, Kenny, 10, 15, 32, 144, 163, 171, 181, 185, 190, 221
Cleaver, Eldridge and Kathleen, 212
Claude, Jean, 17, 18
Clergeat, André, 11, 18, 27, 63, 90
Club Saint-Germain-des-Près, 31–32, 42n156, 48
Coca-Cola, xiv, 126, 127
Cocteau, Jean, 2, 52, 82
Cold War, xiv, xv, xvi, 125, 132, 137–144, 153, 199, 216, 217, 220, 222, 240
Coleman, Bill, 144, 168, 190
colonization, xix, 78, 115, 122n127, 141, 199, 211, 216, 223, 236, 242
colons, xv, 163, 200, 202, 203, 207, 208, 214, 219, 230n21, 241
Coltrane, John, 24, 53, 61, 150, 175, 180
Combelle, Alix, 3, 14, 20, 31, 170, 172, 187, 188, 198n104
commercialism, xiii, 25, 107, 128, 131, 133, 135, 136, 147, 153, 239
communautarisme, 79, 81
communism, 125, 126, 127, 138, 140, 142, 153
Communist Party, 106, 139, 140, 143, 153
Comolli, Jean-Louis, 16, 61, 122n127, 164
Congo, 152, 212, 224
Conover, Willis, 23
consumerism, 125, 129–130, 134, 153, 154, 239, 240
Cook, Will Marion, 2, 82, 144
cool jazz 19, 194
Copans, Sim, 26, 27, 102
Côte d'Ivoire, 108, 212, 221, 223, 224, 242
Crestet, Jean, 204
cultural fundamentalism, xvi, 81, 100, 238

Damas, Léon-Gontran, 223
Davis, Miles, xvii, 12, 28, 46, 53, 103, 127, 133, 150, 175, 205, 216
decolonization, 79, 108, 115, 199, 220, 221, 235
Delage, Maurice, 86–87
Delaunay, Charles, 4, 5, 6, 7, 9, 14, 15, 21, 22, 26, 35n31, 136, 162; and Sidney Bechet, 145, 146, 151, 152, 241; and

Hugues Panassié, 10, 13; on race, 88–89, 93, 95; on Django Reinhardt, 166, 168; on the Roma, 167–168
Despax, Olivier, 93–94, 95, 207
Destombes, Aris, 14, 172, 185, 225
Dieval, Jack, 26
Dorigné, Michel, 14, 16
Double Six, 29, 67, 68–69, 191

Eisenhower, Dwight D., 103, 137, 138, 139
EJF. *See* Fédération Européenne de Jazz
Ekyan, André, 3, 172, 187, 196n52, 198n104
Ellington, Duke, 27, 28, 50, 53, 105–106, 129, 141, 168, 170, 205, 222, 227
Eudes, Dominique, 105, 106
Europe numéro 1 (radio station), 17, 24, 147
Evian Agreements, 208–209

Fanon, Frantz, 81, 99–100, 201
Feather, Leonard, 23, 88
Fédération des Musiciens de Jazz en France, 193, 240
Fédération Européenne de Jazz (EJF), 21–22
Festival d'Alger, 207–208
Festival d'Antibes, 29, 31, 149–150, 180
Festival de Jazz (Morocco), 216–217, 219
Festival of Negro Arts (Senegal), 227
Fifth Republic, 126, 154n1, 193, 206
Filipacchi, Daniel, 11, 13, 15, 17, 18, 24, 25, 37n70, 104, 129
Fitzgerald, Ella, 63, 64–66, 103, 133, 150
FLN. *See* Front de Libération Nationale
Fohrenbach, Jean-Claude, 174
Fontana (record company), 41n146, 185
Foy, Shirley "Bunny", 210
Francis, André, 26, 27, 28, 29, 61, 102
Franzino, Pierre, 210
free jazz, 16, 19, 22, 106–107, 108, 191, 194, 213, 214, 226, 228
Front de Libération Nationale (FLN), 114, 206, 207, 209, 211
Front National, xv, 117n5
Fry, Andy, xvi, xvii, 8, 9

Garner, Errol, 29, 133, 201

Gaulle, Charles de, 126, 154n1, 191, 193, 206, 207, 224
Gautier, Madeleine, 69, 71, 172
Gerber, Alain, 61, 63
German Democratic Republic, 11, 140
German occupation. *See* Occupied France
Gillespie, Dizzie, 10, 12, 21, 26, 31, 53, 61, 103, 127, 137, 138, 150, 175, 216
Gilson, Jef, 29, 191; on French jazz, 162, 168, 176, 179, 181; in Réunion and Madagascar, 227–229, 242
Ginibre, Jean-Louis, 18, 21, 26, 47, 225, 226
Goodman, Benny, 8, 88, 127, 137, 139, 141, 222
Goodwill Ambassador tours, xiv, xix, 137–139, 143, 157n55
Gordon, Armand, 219, 220, 221
GPM. *See* Groupement Professionnel des Musiciens du Hot Club de France
Granz, Norman, 31, 65, 103, 105, 134–136
Grappelli, Stéphane, 5, 87, 134, 166, 172, 173, 189, 196n52, 205, 221
Great Depression, xiii, 3, 6, 87, 186
Great War. *See* World War I
Gréco, Juliette, 32, 36n56, 46, 50, 54, 55, 56, 73n47, 237
Grégoire, Ménie, 56
Groupement Professionnel des Musiciens du Hot Club de France (GPM), 187–188
Guérin, Roger, 20, 178, 185, 189
Guinea, 108, 211, 231n42
gypsy. *See* Roma

Hallyday, Johnny, 147, 175
Hampton, Lionel, 57, 216
Harlem Hellfighters, 2, 82
Hausser, Michel, 20, 61, 178, 182; and the Syndicat des Artistes Musiciens de Jazz, 189, 190, 192, 194
Hawkins, Coleman, 32, 49, 168, 174
Herman, Woody, 210, 211, 218
Hess, Jacques, 12, 17, 18, 63; on race, 91–92, 93
Hilleret, Georges, 131, 188, 189
Hodeir, André, 12, 14, 15, 16, 18, 51, 52, 53, 56, 61, 70, 129, 132, 142, 143, 164, 185, 236; on the JATP, 135, 136; on

race, 89, 92, 93, 95; on women, 62, 64
Holiday, Billie, 63, 66, 68
Hollywood, xiv, 43, 63, 104, 126, 127
Hot Club de France, 3, 4–5, 9, 10, 11, 13, 15, 19, 21, 33, 164, 187, 218, 233n71
Humair, Daniel, 29, 47, 163, 173, 181, 185, 186, 191, 217, 221

IJC. See International Jazz Club
immigration, xv, xviii, 79, 81, 109, 113, 115, 116, 187, 239
independence movements (in the colonies), xv, xvi, 138, 199, 204, 212, 213, 220, 221, 223, 235, 237, 241
Indochina, 109, 116
Inter-Jazz, 20
International Jazz Club (IJC), 19, 20
interwar period, xii, xvi, 1, 2, 5–6, 17, 44, 53, 57, 82, 83, 85, 87, 95, 109, 116, 128, 182, 198n105, 223
Iron Curtain, xiv, 23, 142, 143, 144
Ivory Coast. See Côte d'Ivoire

Jackson, Jeffrey H., xvi, xvii, 86, 177
Jacquet, Illinois, 49, 103
Jalard, Michel-Claude, 15, 18; on Django Reinhardt, 168–169, 171
Janissier, Daniel, 16
JATP. See Jazz at the Philharmonic
Jazz. See Jazz Hip
Jazz à Juan. See Festival d'Antibes
Jazz at the Philharmonic (JATP), 27, 31, 65, 134–136, 147
Jazz Club de France, 19–20
Jazz Hip, 13, 14, 15, 26, 63, 65, 69; on French jazz, 162, 178
Jazz Hot, 4, 10, 12, 13, 14, 15, 17, 18, 19, 21, 22, 28, 69, 96, 130, 138, 139, 141, 172; on civil rights in the United States, 102, 103, 104, 105, 106, 239; on French jazz, 90, 180; on French racism, 113, 115–116; on jazz in Algeria, 207, 210; on jazz in Morocco, 216, 218; on the Syndicat des Artistes Musiciens de Jazz, 189, 191; on women, 57, 70
Jazz Magazine, 13, 14, 15, 17, 18, 19, 23, 26, 32, 49, 50, 69, 114, 130, 131, 132, 135, 143, 224, 226, 228; on Sidney Bechet, 146–147, 150; on civil rights in the United States, 102, 103, 104, 105, 106, 239; on French jazz, 175, 177–178, 180, 183, 185; on French racism, 114, 115; on the Goodwill Ambassador tours, 139, 143; on jazz in Algeria, 202–203, 204, 214; on jazz in Morocco, 217; on jazz in Tunisia, 220, 221; on race, 95–97; on Django Reinhardt, 172, 173; on women, 54, 56, 57, 58, 59, 61, 62, 63, 67
Jefferson, Ron, 210
Jews, 6, 7, 92, 114, 155n10, 186, 195n7, 195n8, 215, 219
Jordan, Matthew F., xvi, xvii, 85

Kenton, Stan, 21, 94, 142
Koechlin, Philippe, 17, 18, 37n64, 133, 209–210

Lafitte, Guy, 20, 29, 61, 127, 155n9, 178; and the Syndicat des Artistes Musiciens de Jazz, 189, 190, 194
Lambert-Hendricks-Ross Trio, 68–69
Lane, Jeremy F., xvi, xvii, 5, 8
Lebovics, Herman, 78, 117n2, 154n1
Legrand, Michel, 127, 141, 142, 150
Leiris, Michel, 86
Leloir, Arlette, 69, 70–71
Leloir, J.-P., 69–71
Longnon, Guy, 67, 146, 180
Luccioni, Roger, 179, 180, 181, 183
Luter Claude, 12, 20, 32, 42n157, 46, 127, 142, 145, 146, 226; and Sidney Bechet, 148, 149, 150

Madagascar, 225, 227–229, 242
Malson, Lucien, 11, 12, 14, 15, 16, 17, 18, 30, 32, 41n138, 61, 82, 111, 114, 140, 141, 143, 191; on fans, 47, 48, 52, 53; on French racism, 110, 111, 115–116; on race, 92–95, 97–99, 238; and the RTF Bureau du Jazz, 26, 27, 28, 29
Marxism, 140, 141
Masson, Jacques, 216, 217–218
McKendrick, Gilbert, 145
McRae, Carmen, 63, 66
Ménil, René, 223
Mezzrow, Milton (Mezz), 88, 92, 205, 216
Milhaud, Darius, 2, 82, 83–84, 85, 119n22

Ministère de la Cooperation, 224–225, 226, 228, 234n89
minority populations in France, xv, xviii, 80, 82, 109, 113, 115, 118n9, 169, 237
Modern Jazz Quartet, 26, 133, 180
Monk, Thelonius, xvii, 10, 53, 75n115, 162, 178
Morocco, 23, 201, 203, 208, 215–220, 221, 229, 231n40, 233n63, 242
El Moudjahid, 211
Mougin, Stéphane, 177
Mouly, Raymond, 149, 150, 151, 177
Mulligan, Gerry, 89, 97
multiculturalism, 79, 117n2
Muslims, xv, 207, 215, 231n30

Nardal sisters, 119n29
National Front. *See* Front National
négritude, 33n3, 100, 212, 214, 227
Nettelbeck, Colin, xvii
Netter, Michel, 17, 18, 24, 26, 40n125
New Orleans: jazz, 1, 4, 10, 12, 13, 14, 16, 19, 24, 32, 36n40, 36n57, 45, 48, 49, 50, 52, 53, 88, 99, 111, 146, 147, 148, 163, 191, 194, 225, 226, 228; revival in France, 10, 99
Noon in Tunisia, 221–222

OAS. *See* Organisation Armée Secrète
Occupied France, xiii, 6–10, 142, 166, 167, 195n8
Office de Radiodiffusion-Télévision Française (ORTF). *See* Radiodiffusion-Télévision Française
Organisation Armée Secrète (OAS), 206, 207

Pan-African Cultural Festival, 212–215, 218, 223, 232n47
Pan-Africanism, xv, 209, 211, 242
Panassié, Hugues, xii, 4, 6, 14, 15, 17, 21, 51, 61, 63, 69, 92, 102, 111, 112, 131, 146, 164, 188; on bebop, 10–11, 35n38; and French critics, 12–13; and the Hot Club de France, 3, 4–5, 19, 36n52; influence of, 13–14, 16; on race, 87, 99–100, 116, 128; on the radio, 26, 27, 28, 40n130, 102; on Django Reinhardt, 168, 170; on the United States, 128–129

Paris-Inter (radio station), 26–27, 29
Paris, Wilbur de, 220
Parker, Charlie, 10, 24, 32, 35n38, 91, 127, 162, 171, 201
Parker, Errol, 175, 201–202, 208
Passeron, Jean-Claude, 52–53
Pedersen, Guy, 163, 185, 186, 217
Pen, Jean-Marie Le, 117n2, 117n5
Perchard, Tom, xvii, 159n89, 165
Perrin, Mimi, 67, 68–69, 71, 237
Pescheux, Jacques, 12–13, 14
Peyrefitte, Alain, 28
Philips (record company), 133, 172
Polydor (record company), 133, 191
Ponty, Jean-Luc, 29, 164, 189, 191, 222
Poulain, André, 133, 191
Powell, Adam Clayton, Jr., 137
Powell, Bud, 35n38, 127, 144, 163, 181, 228
primitivism, 64, 78, 83, 84, 85, 86, 95, 96, 120n42, 128

Quintette du Hot Club de France, 5, 87, 88, 164, 166, 171, 173, 195n16

racism in France, xv, xvi, xvii, xix, 78, 79, 80, 81, 82, 97, 100, 108–117, 123n157, 238, 239, 243
Radiodiffusion-Télévision Française (RTF), 17, 18, 20, 22, 25–29, 30, 31, 187, 203, 228; Bureau du Jazz, 26, 27, 29
Radiodiffusion-Télévision Marocaine (RTM), 216, 217, 218
record sales, 30–31, 41n146, 127, 132–133, 181
Redd, Elvira, 62
Reinhardt, Django, xix, 5, 6, 7, 8, 9, 31, 50, 61, 87, 90, 97, 98, 144, 159n90, 161, 162, 164, 165–174, 176, 194, 201, 241
Reinhardt, Joseph, 166, 172, 196n52
Renaud, Henri, 11, 31, 48, 61, 133
Réunion, 225, 227–229
Revivalism. *See* New Orleans revival
Révolution africaine, 114, 209, 210
La Revue du jazz, 3, 13, 14, 129
Roach, Max, 32, 93, 209
rock and roll, xviii, 24–25, 30, 43, 44, 45, 47, 50, 56, 130, 132, 133, 140, 147,

181, 191, 203, 226, 236
Roma, 5, 161, 165, 166, 167–169, 171, 172, 173–174, 241
Ross, Annie, 68–69
Rostaing, Hubert, 31, 141, 166, 198n104
RTF. *See* Radiodiffusion-Télévision Française
RTM. *See* Radiodiffusion-Télévision Marocaine

SAMup. *See* Syndicat des Artistes Musiciens de Paris
Sagan, Françoise, 46, 54, 55, 56, 237
Sartre, Jean-Paul, 32
Saury, Maxim, 20, 32, 113, 146, 189; in Africa, 221, 224–226, 227, 228, 242; in Madagascar, Réunion, Tahiti and Guadeloupe, 225–226
Schécroun, Raphaël. *See* Parker, Errol
Selmer (instrument company), 127, 155n9, 221
Semaine du Jazz: in Oran, 205–206, 208; in Tananarive, 228
Senegal, 108, 152, 211, 212, 223, 224, 226, 227, 242
Senghor, Léopold Sédar, 212, 223, 227
settlers. *See* colons
Shepp, Archie, 213, 214
Siné, 15, 61, 106, 114, 132, 133, 134, 191, 209; on women, 58, 59, 66
Les Six, 83, 119n22
social class, xiii, 45, 50, 53, 55, 114, 115, 193
socialism, 125, 132
Solal, Martial, 20, 29, 161, 163, 164, 173, 178, 185, 186, 191, 195n8, 225; on French jazz, 176, 180; in North Africa Algeria, 201–202, 217
soldiers, 109; in Algeria, 200, 202–205, 241; in Morocco and Tunisia, 216, 217, 242; in Occupied France, 6, 8
Soviet Union, 125, 126, 137, 139, 140–143, 153, 222, 240
Stalin, Joseph, 140, 141
Sylvian, Patrice, 89–90
Syndicat des Artistes Musiciens de Jazz, 189–191, 193, 194, 240
Syndicat des Artistes Musiciens de Paris (SAMuP), 187, 188, 191–193

Tabou, 31, 32, 42n157
Ténot, Frank, 11, 12, 13, 15, 17, 18, 24, 37n64, 37n70, 135, 143, 145, 168; on commercialism, 131, 132; on French jazz, 175, 178, 184; on French racism, 110–111; and *Pour ceux qui aiment le jazz*, 24, 25; on race, 91, 92, 93
Third Republic, 4, 167
Tournès, Ludovic, xvi, 6, 164
trente glorieuses, xv, 78
Les Tricheurs, 45–46, 47
Tronchot, Jean, 68, 133
Tunisia, 215, 219–222, 229, 242

Union Française, 199, 229, 242
United Nations (UN), 165, 207, 219
United States, xii, xiii, xv, xvi, xvii, 3, 4, 6, 7, 9, 10, 13, 16, 17, 22, 24, 25, 30, 45, 57, 59, 68, 80, 83, 85, 87, 100, 125, 126, 127, 128, 129, 130, 134, 136, 142, 144, 151, 154, 161, 162, 174, 177, 182, 185, 186, 188, 193, 194, 200, 205, 214, 224, 227, 235–236, 237; civil rights in, xiv, xix, 77, 80, 101–108, 114, 121n96, 137, 138, 205, 236, 237, 239; gender in, 60–62, 63, 71; government of, xiv, 23, 140, 141, 143, 218, 220, 233n63; racism in, xiv, xix, 32, 77, 80, 81, 93, 99, 101–108, 109, 111, 112, 116, 125, 128, 138, 140, 153, 212, 237–240; State Department of, 137–139, 153, 210, 220, 222, 225, 240, 242
Urtreger, René, 61, 178, 189

Vaughan, Sarah, 49, 63, 66, 74n90, 91, 131, 150
Vian, Boris, 8, 11, 15, 31, 32, 42n156, 48, 102, 170
Vichy, 7, 8, 9, 167
Vietnam War, 210, 211
Vieux Colombier, 32, 145, 148, 150, 159n112
Villers, Michel de, 20, 141; on French jazz, 162, 171, 175, 177; on French racism, 113, 116; on the JATP, 135; on race, 90, 96
Vogue (record label), 30, 36n46, 147, 159n90
Voice of America (VOA), 23, 219

Vola, Louis, 166, 171, 196n52
Voran, Pierre, 206

Wagner, Jean, xi, 15, 16, 18, 68; on French jazz, 163, 173; on Django Reinhardt, 171, 173
Waller, Fats, 61, 63, 104
Weil, Jean-Claude Albert, 20, 38n84, 221
West Coast jazz, 22, 93, 163
Weston, Randy, 137, 210, 211, 218, 219, 222, 231n40
Whiteman, Paul, 4, 87, 119n35
World War I, xi, 2, 82, 109, 110, 139, 235

World War II, xii, xiv, xvi, xvii, xix, 1, 4, 6–10, 11, 45, 77, 87, 110, 126, 166, 186, 201, 217, 235

xenophobia, xv, 78

yé-yé, xviii, 17, 24–25, 30, 56, 181, 190, 236
youth culture, xiii, xvii, xviii, xix, 9, 22, 24–25, 43–50, 54, 56, 237, 243

Zazous, 6, 8–9, 35n25, 48, 49, 53
Zeppilli, Claude, 204–205

About the Author

Elizabeth Vihlen McGregor earned her BA from Boston College and her MA and PhD from Stony Brook University. She has taught history and the humanities at the United States Merchant Marine Academy, the State College of Florida, and Anna Maria College.